# The New Great Game

Studies of the Walter H. Shorenstein Asia-Pacific Research Center

Andrew G. Walder, General Editor

The Walter H. Shorenstein Asia-Pacific Research Center in the Freeman Spogli Institute for International Studies at Stanford University sponsors interdisciplinary research on the politics, economies, and societies of contemporary Asia. This monograph series features academic and policy-oriented research by Stanford faculty and other scholars associated with the Center.

ALSO PUBLISHED IN THE
SHORENSTEIN ASIA-PACIFIC RESEARCH CENTER SERIES

*Rebranding Islam: Piety, Prosperity, and a Self-Help Guru*
James Bourk Hoesterey (2015)

*Global Talent: Skilled Labor as Social Capital in Korea*
Gi-Wook Shin and Joon Nak Choi (2015)

*Failed Democratization in Prewar Japan: Breakdown of a Hybrid Regime*
Harukata Takenaka (2014)

*New Challenges for Maturing Democracies in Korea and Taiwan*
Edited by Larry Diamond and Gi-Wook Shin (2014)

*Spending Without Taxation: FILP and the Politics of Public Finance in Japan*
Gene Park (2011)

*The Institutional Imperative: The Politics of Equitable Development in Southeast Asia*
Erik Martinez Kuhonta (2011)

*One Alliance, Two Lenses: U.S.-Korea Relations in a New Era*
Gi-Wook Shin (2010)

*Collective Resistance in China: Why Popular Protests Succeed or Fail*
Yongshun Cai (2010)

*The Chinese Cultural Revolution as History*
Edited by Joseph W. Esherick, Paul G. Pickowicz, and
Andrew G. Walder (2006)

*Ethnic Nationalism in Korea: Genealogy, Politics, and Legacy*
Gi-Wook Shin (2006)

*Prospects for Peace in South Asia*
Edited by Rafiq Dossani and Henry S. Rowen (2005)

# The New Great Game

CHINA AND SOUTH AND CENTRAL ASIA
IN THE ERA OF REFORM

*Edited by Thomas Fingar*

Stanford University Press

Stanford, California

Stanford University Press
Stanford, California

© 2016 by the Board of Trustees of the Leland Stanford Junior University.
All rights reserved.

Printed in the United States of America on acid-free, archival-quality paper

Library of Congress Cataloging-in-Publication Data

The new great game : China and South and Central Asia in the era of reform / edited
by Thomas Fingar.
        pages cm — (Studies of the Walter H. Shorenstein Asia-Pacific Research Center)
        Includes bibliographical references and index.
        ISBN 978-0-8047-9604-0 (cloth : alk. paper) — ISBN 978-0-8047-9763-4 (pbk. : alk.
paper)
        1. South Asia—Foreign relations—China.  2. China—Foreign relations—South
Asia.  3. Asia, Central—Foreign relations—China.  4. China—Foreign
relations—Asia, Central.  5. China—Foreign relations—1976–  I. Fingar, Thomas,
editor.  II. Series: Studies of the Walter H. Shorenstein Asia-Pacific Research Center.
        DS341.3.C5N47 2016
        327.51054—dc23
                                                                    2015014221

ISBN 978-0-8047-9764-1 (electronic)

Typeset by Newgen in 11/14 Garamond

# Contents

| | | |
|---|---|---|
| *Figures, Map, and Tables* | | ix |
| *Acknowledgments* | | xiii |
| *Preface* | | xv |
| *Contributors* | | xvii |
| 1 | China and South and Central Asia in the Era of Reform and Opening<br>*Thomas Fingar* | 1 |
| 2 | China's Goals in South Asia<br>*Thomas Fingar* | 29 |
| 3 | India's Relationships with the United States and China: Thinking Through the Strategic Triangle<br>*S. Paul Kapur* | 53 |
| 4 | India's Rise and China's Response<br>*Hu Shisheng* | 69 |
| 5 | Perception and Strategic Reality in India-China Relations<br>*Srikanth Kondapalli* | 93 |
| 6 | Sino-Pakistan Ties: Trust, Cooperation, and Consolidation<br>*Syed Rifaat Hussain* | 116 |

7    Rebuilding Lifelines of Its Soft Underbelly: China Engages
     Its Southwest Frontiers                                          147
         *Swaran Singh*

8    Central Asia in Chinese Strategic Thinking                       171
         *Zhao Huasheng*

9    China as a Balancer in South Asia: An Economic Perspective
     with Special Reference to Sri Lanka                              190
         *Saman Kelegama*

10   China and Central Asia                                          216
         *Sebastien Peyrouse*

11   Managing Imperial Peripheries: Russia and China in Central Asia  240
         *Igor Torbakov*

12   China and South Asia: The Economic Dimension                    273
         *Vivek Arora, Hui Tong, and Cristina Constantinescu*

13   China's Engagement with South and Central Asia:
     Patterns, Trends, and Themes                                    305
         *Thomas Fingar*

     *Index*                                                         321

# Figures, Map, and Tables

FIGURES

| | | |
|---|---|---|
| 1.1 | China's perception of threats and contributions to development, 1979 | 7 |
| 1.2 | China's perception of threats and contributions to development from South and Central Asia, 1979 | 8 |
| 1.3 | China's perception of threats and contributions to development from South and Central Asia, 1992 | 9 |
| 1.4 | South and Central Asian perceptions of China's threat and ability to contribute to their development, 1992 | 10 |
| 1.5 | China's perception of threats and contributions to development from South and Central Asia, 2002 | 15 |
| 7.1 | China's bilateral trade with southwest neighbors, 2003–2012 | 155 |
| 9.1 | India's share of imports from small South Asian countries, 2005–2011 | 195 |
| 9.2 | China's share of imports from small South Asian countries, 2005–2011 | 195 |
| 9.3 | China's outward FDI flows to selected South Asian countries, 2004–2010 | 196 |
| 9.4 | Distribution of Chinese assistance in Sri Lanka, 2011 | 206 |
| 9.5 | Chinese FDI in Sri Lanka, 2005–2012 | 208 |

12.1    South Asia's trade with China as a percentage of each country's trade    277

12.2    South Asia's trade with China as a percentage of each country's GDP    278

12.3    China's trade with South Asia as a percentage of China's trade    280

12.4    Trade linkages for select economies: share of trade with largest regional economy    280

12.5    Trade linkages for select economies: trade with the region    281

12.6    The size of selected economies in South Asia and the value of their trade with China, 2012    282

12.7    Selected groups' and countries' economic size and trade with China, 2012    282

12.8    South Asia's direct investment into China    287

12.9    China's direct investment into Afghanistan, India, Sri Lanka, and Pakistan    287

12.10   China's direct investment into Nepal and Bangladesh    288

12.11   Tourists from China to South Asia    288

12.12   Tourists from South Asia to China    289

12.13   Incidence of preferential tariffs applied on imports to China from South Asia and ASEAN    291

12.14   China and India: high-technology exports, 1990–2011    294

12.15   China and India: medium-high-technology exports, 1990–2011    295

12.16   China and India: medium-low-technology exports, 1990–2011    295

12.17   China and India: low-technology exports, 1990–2011    296

12.18   China and India: electronic communications exports, 1990–2012    296

12.19   China and India: textiles and clothing exports, 1990–2012    297

12.20   China and India: bilateral trade in high-technology products, 1990–2012    297

12.21   China and India: bilateral trade in medium-high-technology products, 1990–2012    298

12.22  China and India: bilateral trade in medium-low-technology products, 1990–2012                                                      298

12.23  China and India: bilateral trade in low-technology products, 1990–2012                                                             299

12.24  Demographic outlook for China and South Asia: old-age dependency ratio                                                          300

MAP

China and its neighbors in South and Central Asia                 xxii

TABLES

7.1  Provincial ranks based on per capita GDP                     165

9.1  China's arms trade with South Asian countries, 1990–2012     200

12.1  China's and South Asia's shares in the world GDP            275

12.2  China and South Asia: GDP and regional shares, 2012         275

12.3  China's and South Asia's contributions to world GDP growth  276

12.4  China and South Asia: bilateral merchandise trade           277

12.5  China and India: five most important exports, as a percentage of total exports, 2011                                                279

12.6  Gravity model for trade of goods between China and the world  285

# Acknowledgments

This volume, like all successful endeavors, has many "parents." Each contributed in a unique way, but all contributions were essential. No individual scholar could have produced the insightful analyses of so many and so diverse dyadic and multiparty interactions, and any attempt to identify and explain spatial and temporal patterns, trends, and linkages would perforce be severely limited without high-quality case studies. This was a team effort, and I acknowledge, albeit inadequately, the important contributions of each member of the team.

The genesis of the project was an invitation from the Shorenstein Asia-Pacific Research Center's director, Gi-Wook Shin, to propose new ways to examine changing relationships in Asia and between Asian countries and other portions of the globe. His invitation spurred me to write down a number of observations about China's increasing engagement with other regions, sources, of dissatisfaction with existing explanations of what was happening and where it was headed, and an initial list of questions for empirical research. Over the next few months, Gi-Wook, Shorenstein APARC Associate Director for Research Dan Sneider, and APARC colleagues Mike Armacost, David Straub, Karl Eikenberry, Harry Rowen, and Don Emmerson critiqued and commented on successive drafts with the shared goal of developing a research strategy that, if successful, would significantly enhance our understanding of China's role and limitations in the global order. I am deeply grateful for their insights, suggestions, and frank and sincere criticism.

The project would have remained just an idea without the funding from APARC that made it possible to commission papers and convene meetings to talk through what we hoped to accomplish and to begin integrating the results of the research and synthesis undertaken by each of the contributors. Without funding, even the best research proposal is simply an interesting idea. Thanks to Gi-Wook, Dan, and Shorenstein APARC, this idea became a reality.

Dan Sneider and Rafiq Dossani (formerly at APARC and now with the Rand Corporation) were especially helpful in identifying potential contributors on and from the region and in explaining what we hoped to accomplish. The project continued to evolve through the process of explanation and responding to questions from potential and, later, actual contributors. Those who eventually authored chapters for this volume were, of course, indispensable for its success. Their backgrounds and affiliations are given at the beginning of the book, but I would be remiss not to list their names in this section as well. Thanks go to the contributors, without whom we could not have produced this book: Vivek Arora, Cristina Constantinescu, Hu Shisheng, Rifaat Hussain, Paul Kapur, Saman Kelegama, Srikanth Kondapalli, Sebastien Peyrouse, Swaran Singh, Hui Tong, Igor Torbakov, and Zhao Huasheng.

APARC colleagues Debbie Warren, Irene Bryant, and Wena Rosario were indispensible and indefatigable in managing correspondence and meeting arrangements, as was Tracy Hill, my incredible assistant based in the Center for International Security and Cooperation. Thank you all. APARC editor George Krompacky saved me repeatedly from computer errors that threatened to destroy large chunks of text and, more importantly, worked with the contributors to ensure that all graphics were in the correct format and file types. The final text is much better thanks to his efforts.

Shepherding the book through the editorial process required and benefitted from the efforts of APARC series editor Andy Walder, Stanford University Press editor Geoffrey Burn, and Stanford University Press editorial assistant James Holt. It was a pleasure working with them, and I appreciate their confidence in the project.

The contributions of all were essential, but I alone am responsible for the generalizations in Chapters 1 and 13. Others may, and I trust do, share many of the judgments expressed there, but they do not share responsibility for them and are not culpable for any errors that may remain. Finding and fixing them was my responsibility, and if any remain, I apologize.

Thomas Fingar
December 2015

# Preface

When everything comes together, the challenges of producing an edited volume are more than compensated by the increased understanding of complex problems that results from interaction among the contributors and insights that emerge from the juxtaposition of independently authored analyses. Most of the patterns and trends that become apparent when comparing and aggregating the interpretations in this volume were not anticipated when we began this project or predicted by any of the participants when we discussed alternative ways to explore and explain interactions among China and the countries of South and Central Asia. The decision to focus on specific dyads and multistate groupings without attempting to fit the analysis to a predetermined framework, model, or theory proved fruitful. We all learned new and important things about China's engagement and changes within and between the two subregions examined in this volume. I hope—and expect—that our readers will also discover new insights and deepen their understanding of China's perceptions, priorities, and policies and that they will gain similar insight into the ways in which regional states responded to perceived opportunities and risks resulting from China's rise and greater activism on the regional stage.

As director of the Shorenstein Asia-Pacific Research Center, I am pleased that the center was able to support the project and proud to include this volume in our series published by the Stanford University Press. It is the first of a planned series that will examine China's interactions with other regions of the world and, we hope, reveal additional trends and patterns transcending individual regions and strengthen confidence in our judgments about how and why those patterns exist. Neither this volume nor forthcoming ones attempt to predict the future, but the identification of trends, what drives them, and their implications for the countries involved provide a useful starting point for anticipating how events may unfold.

Tom Fingar's acknowledgment section properly cites the contributions of the many people who helped transform an interesting idea into a scholarly contribution to our understanding of China's objectives, how other countries perceive them, and how China's increased engagement with other parts of the world is changing both regional and global interactions. Many people contributed, but the genesis of the project was his observation, based on decades of experience as a State Department and intelligence community analyst, that all nations formulate foreign policy goals and strategies on the basis of their perception of perils and opportunities and that no nation ever achieves all that it hopes to achieve in the international arena.

What actually happens, he observed, almost always results from the interaction of multiple actors pursuing independent agendas with varying amounts of skill and resources. China's rise, he argued, makes it a more formidable player, but it does not and cannot have the ability to ignore the actions and aspirations of prospective partners and interested third parties. He translated this insight into a proposal and the proposal into a plan. His observation and argument made sense but remained to be subjected to rigorous empirical analysis. My Shorenstein APARC colleagues and I decided to fund the project because it appeared both possible and important to learn whether, or to what extent, his observations were correct and to discover the most important directions and drivers of China's global engagement. This book more than justifies the confidence we had in both Fingar and the project. More importantly, its publication makes the research of the contributors and the insights from the project available to students, scholars, and government officials seeking to understand and to influence developments in the global arena.

Gi-Wook Shin
Director
Walter H. Shorenstein Asia-Pacific Research Center

# Contributors

**Vivek Arora** is a deputy director in the International Monetary Fund's Strategy, Policy and Review Department, where he oversees the department's work on a range of emerging market issues, including capital flows and related policies, and has a range of country and policy review responsibilities. Arora was the fund's senior resident representative in China in 2006–2010 and in South Africa in 2004–2006. He joined the IMF in 1992 and has worked on a variety of country assignments, including the United States, Canada, Korea, and the Philippines. He has published research papers on economic growth and spillovers, emerging market finance, monetary and fiscal policy, exchange rate regimes, and the Chinese economy. Arora received a PhD in economics from Brown University and a BA (with honors) in economics from St. Stephen's College, Delhi University. He studied international finance at Harvard University under the Brown-Harvard Graduate Exchange Program.

**Cristina Constantinescu** is a research assistant in the International Monetary Fund's Strategy, Policy and Review Department. She worked previously in the Research Department of the World Bank. Her publications include a number of journal articles and book chapters on trade policy, trade in services, and international migration. She has a PhD in economics from the Catholic University of Louvain, Belgium; an MA in economics from Georgetown University; and BA degrees in accounting from the Academy of Economic Studies (Romania) and in international economics from the Romanian-American University.

**Thomas Fingar** is the inaugural Oksenberg-Rohlen Distinguished Fellow in the Freeman Spogli Institute for International Studies at Stanford University. From May 2005 through December 2008, he served as the first deputy director of national intelligence for analysis and, concurrently, as chairman of the National Intelligence Council. He served previously as assistant secretary of the State Department's Bureau of Intelligence and Research (2004–2005), principal deputy assistant secretary (2001–2003), deputy assistant secretary for analysis (1994–2000), director of the Office of Analysis for East Asia and the Pacific (1989–1994), and chief of the China Division (1986–1989). Fingar is a graduate of Cornell University (AB in government and history, 1968) and Stanford University (MA, 1969, and PhD, 1977, both in political science).

**Hu Shisheng** is a senior research fellow and the director of the Institute for South and Southeast Asian and Oceania Studies at the China Institutes of Contemporary International Relations (CICIR). Hu received his BA in Hindi language and literature and his MA in Sanskrit and Bali languages and literature in the Department of Oriental Studies at Peking University. He received his PhD in international politics and relations with a focus in ethnic and religious issues from CICIR in 2006. In 2004 he was a visiting scholar at Johns Hopkins University's School of Advanced International Studies. Hu's three research focuses include the political and security situations in India and Pakistan, ethnic and religious problems in South Asia, and Tibet. Hu published a book titled *Tibetans in Exile: The Construction of Group Identities and Its Embarrassment* (2008). His most recent research focuses on South Asia—particularly India, Pakistan, and Afghanistan security issues.

**Syed Rifaat Hussain** is a professor in the faculty of Social Sciences and Humanities (S3H) at the National University of Sciences and Technology (NUST) in Islamabad, Pakistan. Prior to his current position, he served as professor in the Department of Peace and Conflict Studies at the National Defense University in Islamabad, Pakistan. He has also served as professor and chairman of the Department of Defense and Strategic Studies at Quaid-i-Azam University in Islamabad, Pakistan, and as the executive director of the Regional Centre for Strategic Studies in Colombo, Sri Lanka. Hussain serves as a member of the editorial boards of many publications, including the *South Asia Journal, Strategic Studies,* and *Regional Studies.* He is the author of numerous books and publications, including *Afghanistan and 9/11: The Anatomy of a Conflict* (2002) and *From Dependence to Intervention: Soviet-Afghanistan Relations During the Brezhnev Era (1964–1982)* (1994). He received his MA and PhD in international studies from the University of Denver.

**S. Paul Kapur** is a professor in the Department of National Security Affairs at the Naval Postgraduate School. Previously, he was on the faculties of the Naval War College and Claremont McKenna College and was a visiting professor at Stanford University's Center for International Security and Cooperation. He also served as a postdoctoral fellow at the University of Chicago, where he received his PhD in political science. His research and teaching interests include nuclear weapons proliferation, deterrence, ethnoreligious violence, and the international security environment in South Asia. Kapur is author of *Dangerous Deterrent: Nuclear Weapons Proliferation and Conflict in South Asia* (2007) and, with Sumit Ganguly, *India, Pakistan, and the Bomb: Debating Nuclear Stability in South Asia* (2010). His work has also appeared in journals such as *International Security, Security Studies, Asian Survey, Nonproliferation Review, Washington Quarterly,* and *Asian Security,* as well as in numerous edited volumes.

**Saman Kelegama** is the executive director of the Institute of Policy Studies of Sri Lanka. He is a fellow of the National Academy of Sciences of Sri Lanka and was president of the Sri Lanka Economic Association from 1999 to 2003. He has published extensively on Sri Lankan and regional economic issues in both local and international journals. His latest books are *Foreign Aid in South Asia: The Emerging Scenario* (2012); *Trade Liberalization and Poverty in South Asia* (2011); *Migration, Remittances, and Development in South Asia* (2011); *Promoting Economic Cooperation in South Asia: Beyond SAFTA* (2010); and *Trade in Services in South Asia: Opportunities and Risks of Liberalization* (2009). He is the coeditor of the *South Asia Economic Journal* and serves as a referee for a number of international journals. He serves and has served on a number of government and private sector boards as an independent member. He received his PhD and MS in economics from the University of Oxford, and an MS in mathematics from the Indian Institute of Technology, Kanpur.

**Srikanth Kondapalli** is professor of Chinese studies at Jawaharlal Nehru University. He is educated in Chinese studies in India and China and holds a PhD in Chinese studies. He learned the Chinese language at Beijing Language and Culture University and was a postdoctoral visiting fellow at People's University, Beijing, from 1996 to 1998. He was a visiting professor at National Chengchi University, Taipei, in 2004; a visiting fellow at China Institutes of Contemporary International Relations, Beijing, in 2007; an honorary professor at Shandong University, Jinan, in 2009 and 2011; and a fellow at Salzburg Global Seminar in 2010. He has written two books and two monographs, coedited three volumes, and authored a number of articles in journals and edited volumes. He received the K. Subramanyam Award in 2010 for Excellence in Research in Strategic and Security Studies.

**Sebastien Peyrouse** is a research professor in the Central Asia Program at the Institute for European, Russian and Eurasian Studies at George Washington University. His main areas of expertise are political systems in Central Asia, Islam and religious minorities, and Central Asia's geopolitical positioning toward China, India, and South Asia. He has edited *Turkmenistan: Strategies of Power, Dilemmas of Development* (2011) and coedited *China and India in Central Asia: A New "Great Game"?* (2010); *The "Chinese Question" in Central Asia: Domestic Order, Social Changes, and the Chinese Factor* (2011); and *Globalizing Central Asia: Geopolitics and the Challenges of Economic Development* (2012). His articles have appeared in *Europe-Asia Studies, Nationalities Papers, China Perspectives, Religion, State and Society,* and the *Journal of Church and State.*

**Swaran Singh** is professor and chair at the Centre for International Politics, Organization and Disarmament at the School of International Studies, Jawaharlal Nehru University, New Delhi. He is president of the Association of Asia Scholars, general secretary of the Indian Association of Asian and Pacific Studies, and guest professor at Yunnan University of Economics and Finance in China. Singh has published over a dozen books and monographs and regularly contributes to journals and newspapers. He lectures at India's National Defense College, Defence Services Staff College, the Foreign Service Institute, and the Indian Institute for Public Administration. Singh is coeditor of *China by India: From Civilization to State* (2012), *Emerging China: Prospects for Partnership in Asia* (2012), and *Asia's Multilateralism* (2012); editor of *China-Pakistan Strategic Cooperation: Indian Perspectives* (2007); and coauthor of the Stockholm International Peace Research Institute policy paper "Regionalism in South Asian Diplomacy" (2007).

**Hui Tong** is an economist in the Research Department of the International Monetary Fund. His research focuses on international economics, corporate finance, and China's economy. He has published approximately twenty journal articles and book chapters, including in the *American Economic Review, Review of Financial Studies,* and the *Journal of International Economics.* His work has been featured in the *Wall Street Journal, Financial Times, VOX, China Daily,* and *People's Daily.* Tong received his PhD in economics from the University of California at Berkeley in 2004.

**Igor Torbakov** is a senior fellow at the Center for Russian and Eurasian Studies at Uppsala University, Sweden. A trained historian, he specializes in Russian and Eurasian history and politics. He was a research scholar at the Institute of Russian History, Russian Academy of Sciences in Moscow; a visiting scholar at the Kennan Institute, Woodrow Wilson International Center for Scholars in Washington, DC; a Fulbright scholar at Columbia University; a visiting fellow at Harvard University; a fellow at the Swedish Collegium for Advanced Study; a senior fellow at the Finnish Institute of International Affairs in Helsinki; and a visiting fellow at the German Council on Foreign Relations in Berlin. He holds an MA in history from Moscow State University and a PhD from the Ukrainian Academy of Sciences. His recent publications discuss the history of Russian nationalism, the links between Russia's domestic politics and foreign policy, and the politics of history and memory wars in Eastern Europe.

**Zhao Huasheng** is professor and director of the Center for Russia and Central Asia Studies, as well as director of the Center for Shanghai Cooperation Organization Studies at Fudan University in Shanghai, China. He has published analytical articles in Chinese, Russian, and English. His recent books include *Central Asia: Views from Washington, Moscow, and Beijing* (2007); coauthored with Eugene Rumer and Dmitry Trenin, *China's Central Asian Diplomacy* (2008); and *The Shanghai Cooperation Organization: Analysis and Outlook* (2012). Zhao earned an advanced degree in Chinese history from Nanjing University.

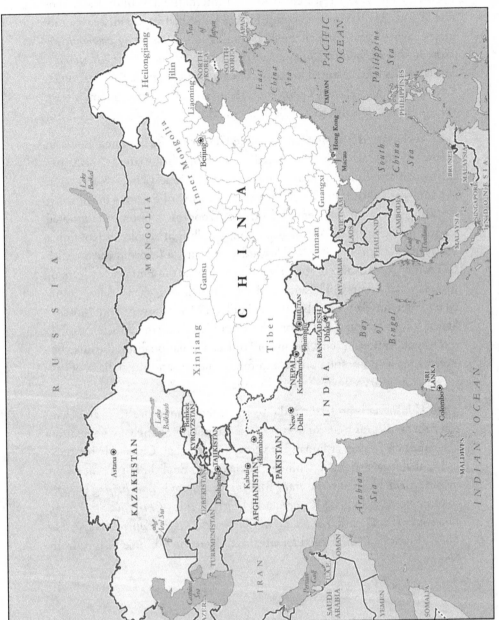

China and its neighbors in South and Central Asia

# ONE

# China and South and Central Asia in the Era of Reform and Opening

*Thomas Fingar*

China's rise and increasing activism in the world during the past two decades have produced admiration, anxiety, and an avalanche of academic and journalistic analysis and speculation about China's goals, actions, and intentions. Despite the large volume, amount of detail, and interesting insights produced by foreign and Chinese observers, the number of empirically based comparisons is small and the cases examined are often so diverse that it is difficult to determine what is being compared and how to interpret their findings. The net result is a collection of inconsistent judgments that call to mind the conclusions of the six blind men who touched different parts of the elephant.[1] For example, depending on the study consulted, one learns that China has a grand strategy and a rather detailed plan that guide its foreign interactions or that it addresses problems and opportunities in an ad hoc and pragmatic way.[2] Other studies reach different judgments on the extent to which China acts as a status quo power or is determined to change the international order,[3] has coherent and tightly coordinated policies or increasingly acts in ways reflecting the divergent interests of competing actors,[4] or manifests a new-type foreign policy to achieve win-win and mutually beneficial outcomes or ruthlessly pursues its own objectives with little regard for the interests of others.[5] Another dichotomy is that between analyses that emphasize historical continuities—the so-called Middle Kingdom Syndrome—and those that focus on China's communist authoritarianism and efforts to maintain party rule.[6]

Evidence can be found to support all these—and other—interpretations, but many of them are contradictory and not all of them can be correct.

More importantly, it is not obvious whether a particular course of action—for example, construction of infrastructure to facilitate trade with a neighboring country—was intended to preserve or change the status quo, or to restore China's preeminence or maintain communist rule. In short, the generalizations are not very helpful.

One reason for the disparate findings and generalizations about China's international behavior is that analysts approach the subject using different perspectives and expertise. The different perspectives can be summarized as those that deduce and explain the actions of China and other countries from the laws and lessons of international relations (IR) theory, China-centric interpretations that focus on China's goals and actions toward one or a few specific countries, and those that examine and interpret China's actions from the perspective of the target or partner country.

International relations-based analyses and predictions of China's goals and behavior focus on the nature and dynamics of regional and global systems. Most who write in this genre are IR specialists who do not claim to have deep knowledge of China or its policy-making processes. Their lack of deep knowledge about China is not regarded as a serious impediment because their system-dominant approach treats China as a generic rising power or, in more refined versions, a rising power "with Chinese characteristics."[7] In this approach, the modalities of decision making in China (and elsewhere) are much less important than the dynamics of the international or regional system in which it operates. Objectives and behaviors associated with rising states, such as a tendency to perceive the actions of others as intended to constrain or thwart the rising state's ascension to its "rightful" place in the regional or global order, are imputed to China, and Chinese actions are interpreted as evidence that it is behaving as a stereotypical rising power.[8]

The system-level analysis category can be further divided into "realist" and "liberal internationalist" subdivisions. Realists, like John Mearsheimer and Aaron Friedberg, generally interpret—and predict—China's behavior as intended to regain supremacy in Asia and, ultimately, to challenge the United States for global leadership.[9] Liberal internationalists like John Ikenberry, Bruce Jones, and Joseph Nye, in contrast, place greater emphasis on China's increasing integration into the US-led global order and growing dependence on that order for the attainment of its developmental and political objectives.[10]

IR theorists and others who focus on the international system tend to assess China's actions primarily in terms of its relationship with the United States and a small number of other major powers, and to interpret China's interactions with other countries as extensions or manifestations of Beijing's goals vis-à-vis the United States, India, or, in the first half of the period examined here, the United States and the Soviet Union.

A second genre of work on China's global engagement is more China-centric and tends to explain Chinese policy and behavior in terms of the country's history, culture, political system, domestic situation, and security calculus. Unsurprisingly, most who employ this approach are China specialists who build on their detailed understanding of the country.[11] In contrast to system-dominant analyses that emphasize universal factors, those by China specialists tend to focus on factors that are China-specific (although not necessarily unique to China), such as the nature of the political system, the importance of historical memory (and mythology) of China's past greatness and "century of humiliation," and increasing economic capabilities and requirements.[12]

China-centric analyses of China's actions on the world stage assign different importance to specific factors shaping Chinese perceptions and policies but generally focus on what China is attempting to do, and why it is attempting to do it, more than on the objectives and actions of the countries that are the target of China's attention. Implicitly, if not explicitly, China's aspirations and actions are treated as independent variables, and the reactions of other nations are assessed as dependent variables. The result is often an unbalanced assessment that gives inadequate attention to the goals, strategies, and second- and third-order consequences of a country's interaction with China.

The third and much smaller category of works on China's engagement with the world consists of those written from the perspective of other countries or regions.[13] From the perspective of a China specialist, most of these works provide unsatisfactory descriptions and explanations of China's objectives and policy calculus. However, and more important, they provide useful insights into the way the countries in question perceive China and its actions and what the other countries do to capitalize on opportunities resulting from China's rise and to mitigate adverse consequences for their own interests.[14]

The essays in this book attempt to redress this imbalance, in part, by demonstrating that the countries that interact with China do not simply respond to challenges and opportunities from the People's Republic. They have objectives of their own, sometimes leverage their relationship with China to entice or counterbalance third countries, and often seek to take advantage of spillover effects of engagement with China, such as the ability to use infrastructure financed or built by China in order to access specific markets or resources. Chapters 5, 6, 9, and 10 examine the perceptions and actions of countries in the region.

This volume builds on the insights of others who have examined foreign-policy dimensions of China's rise by employing empirical approaches to discover, describe, and explain China's interactions with the states of South and Central Asia during the period of "reform and opening" that began in 1979. All have eschewed single-issue focuses, diplomatic history, detailed chronologies, archival research, interview-based approaches, and other methodologies in favor of approaches that synthesize insights from their own and others' research to assess and explain what they regard as the most important drivers, characteristics, and trajectories of interactions between China and the nations of South and Central Asia. The contributors do not explicitly assess or apply the approaches and findings of others or develop broad generalizations, theoretical models, or detailed predictions of how events will unfold in the future. Instead they focus on three questions that, to the extent they can be answered, provide a basis for comparisons within and among regions, over time, and across issue areas. Those questions are

- What happened?
- Why did it happen that way?
- What impact have China's interactions with the countries studied had on China, the other countries, and the global system?

Taken together, the chapters in the volume provide the basis for addressing two additional questions—namely:

- What patterns, trends, and trajectories can be discerned when comparing the findings of the individual chapters?
- Do the findings of the book suggest or support predictions about future actions and interactions?

## Rationale for Focusing on a Single Region

The decision to focus on a single region was not the result of a Goldilocks-like judgment that attempting to cover the entire world would be too ambitious and focusing on a single country would preclude comparison and generalization, although both considerations are true. Nor did it result from a judgment that the countries in the region were especially important to China or that the evolution of China's engagement with South and Central Asia was particularly useful for understanding China's objectives and choice of policy instruments. The reason is less obvious and more subjective. During the decades that I have studied China's interaction with other countries, especially the fifteen years during which I supervised and edited assessments of developments in and interactions among all countries on all issues while a senior official in the US government, I thought that I observed patterns of behavior in China's relations with other countries that varied by region and over time.[15] The patterns appeared to result from changing Chinese assessments of the country's security situation and changing requirements of its quest for economic growth and rapid modernization. In addition to its other objectives, this book represents an attempt to refine and test preliminary judgments and hypotheses about China's priorities and calculus of decision.

The framework developed here is based on two key judgments about China's priorities. One is that national security always has highest priority even if it is not always identified as such. As used here, and in China, security is a compound and elastic concept that comprises the country's ability to deter or in other ways manage actual and imputed threats from abroad, threats to internal stability, and at least some of the time, threats to continued rule by the Chinese Communist Party.[16] Without security, in the analysis of Chinese officials, it is impossible to pursue other objectives. This implies that policy makers must do whatever is necessary to manage or mitigate military threats from abroad and internal or external threats to domestic stability and party rule. Chapters 2 and 4 address external threat concerns, and Chapters 7 and 8 examine the impact of concerns about internal stability.

The second highest priority is rapid and sustained development. Development, or modernization, has been a Chinese priority for more than a century, but its elevation to second position dates from the late 1970s. Modernization is seen as critical to the achievement of the prosperity and power necessary to ensure security, stability, and continued legitimacy of the regime. This implies that one of the principal considerations when Chinese leaders make foreign-policy decisions is whether a particular course of action or form of engagement with another country will assist or impede the quest for modernization. Chapters 4 and 7–11 illuminate different dimensions of this consideration.

This way of conceptualizing the Chinese calculus of decision posits that when thinking about whether, when, and how to engage with particular countries, two of the principal considerations are the nature and magnitude of the threat that they pose to China's security (or what they can do to mitigate the threat from others) and whether a country can provide what is most needed at a particular time to sustain a high rate of growth and acquisition of advanced technologies. This might be summarized as consideration of what they can do *to* China and what they can do *for* China.

Geopolitics is a strong determinant of both the nature of the threat to China and the potential to assist China's drive for development in specific ways. Thus, for example, countries located far from China generally pose less significant threats and have fewer historical issues than do countries located closer to China. The obvious and important exceptions are the United States and, particularly during the Soviet era, the USSR/ Russia. Similarly, the wealthiest and most advanced countries (in North America, Europe, and Northeast Asia) have the greatest ability to provide markets, capital, technology, and training. Nations in other regions have greater capacity to provide oil, timber, minerals, or other inputs to China's economy.

The sequence and way in which China engaged countries in different parts of the world after 1978 is consistent with what one would expect from an imputed regional grouping of countries in a matrix defined by relative threat to China and relative ability to meet China's developmental needs as they were defined at the beginning of the reform and opening era, and as security and developmental requirements changed after the Cold War and China's economy grew and became more sophisticated. The relative positions of different regions in 1979 are depicted in Figure 1.1.

At the beginning of reform and opening, South and Central Asia ranked relatively high on the security/threat dimension, mainly because the Central Asian states were part of the Soviet Union, Afghanistan was occupied by Soviet troops, and India was considered a de facto ally of the USSR. The region also ranked low on the contribution-to-development dimension because none of the states had the high-end inputs China needed at this stage of its drive for modernity. Given limited time and political capital, Chinese

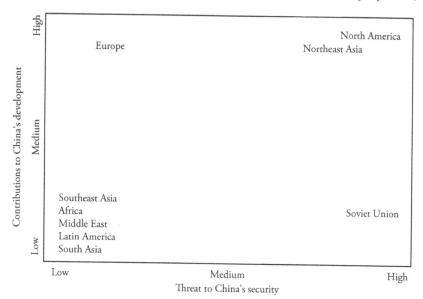

FIGURE 1.1 China's perception of threats and contributions to development, 1979

leaders focused on developing ties with other regions—namely, the United States, Western Europe, and Japan.

If one knows enough about China's security perceptions, strategy of development, and stage of development at any particular point in time, one need know only whether a particular country had and was willing to provide the specific items needed to sustain development in order to locate the country in this matrix. Doing so would provide a first-order indicator of whether and how China might engage with a particular country. Figure 1.2 depicts the relative positions of countries in South and Central Asia in the first phase of reform and opening. The positions suggest that none of the regional countries was a good candidate for engagement by China, and as history and Chapters 2, 4, 5, 7, 8, 12, and 13 demonstrate, none of these countries was a major target of China's engagement efforts in the 1980s.

Over time, with the collapse of the USSR, the adoption of economic reform in India, improved relations between the United States and India, and the cumulative success of China's economic strategy, Beijing's perception of threats and opportunities changed in ways that resulted in greater efforts to engage the countries of South and Central Asia. Figure 1.3 depicts the relative positions of regional countries in the early 1990s.

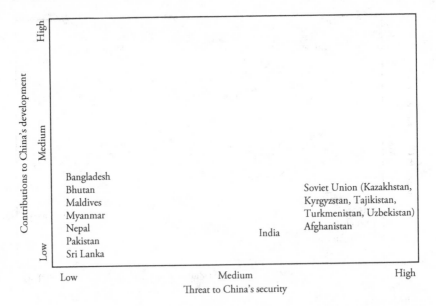

FIGURE I.2 China's perception of threats and contributions to development from South and Central Asia, 1979

Similar matrices for other regions of the world would show significantly different placement of countries. For example, the matrix for North America would rank all countries high on the capacity to contribute to China's development variable, but only the United States would be considered to pose a relatively high—albeit manageable—threat to China's security. European countries would be considered a low threat but have a high capacity to contribute to China's development, and Africa and Latin America would be low on both dimensions. The reason for mentioning, albeit very briefly, the assessed potential of other regions is to provide context for the judgment that the configuration depicted in Figure 1.1 suggests that China's policy toward South and Central Asia in the first decade of the reform era would accord higher priority to managing the security challenges in and from the region than to pursuing developmental objectives and that greater effort would be devoted to managing the security threat from the Soviet Union (e.g., by working the US–USSR–People's Republic of China (PRC) and PRC-India-Pakistan strategic triangles) than to security-related actions aimed directly at other states in the region.

The international situation and security dimension of China's relationship with the region changed dramatically in December 1991, when the

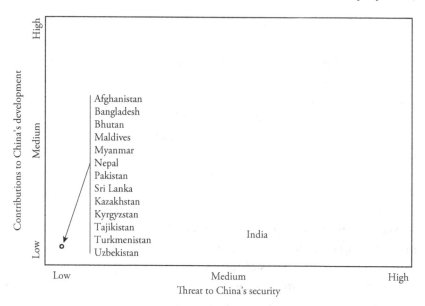

FIGURE 1.3 China's perception of threats and contributions to development from South and Central Asia, 1992

Soviet Union collapsed and the Cold War came to an end. Although it took time for the consequences and implications of these changes to be factored into Beijing's foreign-policy calculus, it soon became apparent that the military threat from the region had diminished and that China could think about its frontier regions differently than in previous decades. Other developments occurring at more or less the same time altered Beijing's perception of possibilities and potential problems in the region. One such development was the magnitude and accelerating pace of economic growth in China's eastern provinces. Sustained growth and rising expectations were increasing the demand for energy, metals, minerals, and other resources. Chinese firms and foreign investors began to look further afield for reliable supplies. They also began to take greater interest in the newly independent countries of Central Asia and hitherto neglected neighbors along the southwestern frontier.

A related but analytically distinct development was growing concern about the imbalance between development in the eastern and western provinces of China. This was seen as a multidimensional problem. One dimension involved concern that imbalances between east and west would eventually—and perhaps soon—slow growth at the national level. That was seen as a problem because the legitimacy of Communist Party rule rested heavily on its ability to meet escalating expectations by sustaining high rates of growth. It was also seen as a problem because the regions of the country that lagged most in terms of growth and modernization had the highest proportions of ethnic-minority inhabitants. The congruence of changed security circumstances and increased recognition that more had to be done to increase rates of growth in the frontier regions enabled and required Beijing to reformulate its approach to South and Central Asia. Swaran Singh, in Chapter 7, accurately characterizes the resultant change as a paradigm shift in the way Beijing thought about and engaged countries in the region.

The ways in which other countries perceived China also had changed by the mid-1990s, primarily because of its sustained economic growth and increasing engagement with other parts of the developing world, principally Southeast Asia. As China began to evince greater interest in engaging the states on its southern and western periphery, countries in the region were more receptive than they would have been in the 1980s. A rough approximation of their relative receptivity to engagement with China is depicted in Figure 1.4.

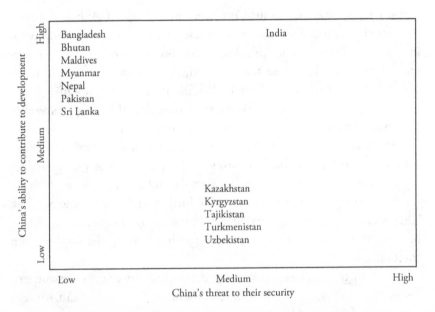

FIGURE 1.4 South and Central Asian perceptions of China's threat and ability to contribute to their development, 1992

## Framework for Understanding China's Foreign Policy

After Mao Zedong died and the Gang of Four was removed in 1976, surviving Communist Party leaders inherited a country that was almost as poor, technologically backward, and vulnerable as it was when the PRC was established almost three decades earlier. A critical exception to this generalization was that China had acquired sufficient nuclear weapons to deter attack by stronger nations, including nuclear powers like the United States and the Union of Soviet Socialist Republics. However, thirty years of frequent and drastic policy changes, disruptive political movements, and unsuccessful attempts to devise a uniquely Chinese road to modernity had caused the country to fall even further behind the major powers and many of China's East Asian neighbors.[17] Recognizing the perils the situation entailed for China and for the Communist Party, Deng Xiaoping and other senior leaders decided to adopt an approach that had enabled others to modernize quickly. That approach became known as "reform and opening."[18]

Security and development are the two most important objectives of the new strategy and the twin pillars undergirding the priorities and policies that China has pursued since 1978. As used here, each of these terms subsumes a number of goals with profound implications for China's foreign policies. Thus, for example, "security" refers to the ability of the country to deter or defeat a military aggressor as well as judgments about the likelihood of attack by specific adversaries. Despite China's nuclear deterrent, Mao had judged that war with the United States, the Soviet Union, or some combination of "imperialist powers" was both inevitable and imminent. This judgment had shaped China's foreign policies and its economic priorities for decades.[19] To justify changes to policies derived from that assessment, Deng and his colleagues had to alter Mao's judgment on the imminence of military conflict. They did so by proclaiming that although war was still inevitable, it was no longer imminent.[20] That reassessment opened a window of opportunity and underscored the urgency of acting before the window was closed by rival states.

We will probably never know the extent to which the new judgment was the result of an objective assessment undertaken to determine whether changes in the international situation made changes in Chinese policy necessary or possible or whether it was contrived to rationalize a previously made decision to adopt the approach that had proven successful for Japan and other East Asian nations. I suspect that it was a bit of both and involved an iterative process that moved between focusing on what China's leaders wanted to do and what was required to be able to pursue the desired course. Be that as it may, the reassessment both changed the possibility space and strongly influenced, even mandated, key aspects of China's foreign policy.

Examples of the ways in which the new assessment expanded the range of policy options available to Beijing (i.e., the possibility space) include providing a rationale to shift from a strategy that maximized autarky to one that accepted greater dependence on other countries, lowering the priority of military preparedness to permit reallocation of investment to production of light industrial products and consumer goods, and capitalizing on the comparative advantages of China's coastal provinces despite their greater vulnerability to attack. These and similar changes were—and are—critical to the success of Deng's strategy of development. Chinese leaders repeatedly affirm the importance of this relationship when they declare that a peaceful international environment is essential for the success of China's quest for rapid and sustained development.[21]

The declared importance of the international environment to the success of the post-Mao strategy for transforming China from a vulnerable and victimized (in Chinese eyes) nation into a prosperous, secure, and influential player on the world stage influences China's foreign policy in several ways. To begin with the most obvious, China's foreign policy must strive to protect and enhance national security. Among other requirements, this entails using diplomacy to prolong the window of opportunity by persuading other nations that China's rise is beneficial for them as well as for China, defusing situations with the possibility to escalate into conflict or other actions with the potential to derail Chinese plans, and maintaining basically good relations with the United States.[22] As China has become more deeply engaged around the world, it has become more vulnerable to localized unrest that could endanger its access to energy and other resources or the safety of Chinese citizens and investments. In contrast to its behavior in the 1960s and 1970s, when Beijing encouraged or supported insurgencies and local rivalries in many parts of the world, China now has a growing stake in stability abroad as well as at home.[23]

Domestic stability is also an important component of China's national security calculus. History, ideology, and Beijing's own past actions toward other countries have taught China's leaders to be wary of foreign attempts to weaken the country by fostering unrest and secessionist tendencies. This concern is particularly salient in China's dealings with the nations of South and Central Asia because China's vast western and southwestern regions are home to minority peoples who have many reasons to be dissatisfied with their treatment by Beijing and China's Han majority and have numerous ties to fellow ethnics living on the other side of China's borders.[24] As Chapters 7 and 8 demonstrate, difficulties and dilemmas associated with China's frontier regions have complicated China's domestic and regional foreign policies for a very long time.

Given the importance of security, it is natural, even inevitable, that one of the most important criteria employed by Beijing when deciding whether, when, and how to engage with other countries is the effect that engagement would have on China's own security and internal stability. Once, this was a fairly straightforward calculation of relative power and the relative danger that each country posed to China's interests. Mao decided to lean to the Soviet Union in 1949 because he judged that the United States posed the greater immediate danger and that Stalin would provide more assistance to China's self-strengthening effort.[25] Two decades later, he began to lean toward the United States to counter the perceived greater threat from Moscow.[26] China's alignment with Pakistan began in response to concerns about the direct threat from India and, more importantly, the danger to China posed by New Delhi's relationship with Moscow.[27] An additional reason for Beijing to cultivate a special relationship with Pakistan was to encourage Islamabad to pursue precisely the kind of relationship with Washington that Chapter 6 describes, because doing so limited the efficacy of US efforts in the 1950s and 1960s to contain communism through a series of multilateral alliances.

The calculation has become more complicated, in part because the countries that are perceived to pose the greatest long-term threat to China (the United States and its allies) are also the countries that can do the most to assist or impede China's modernization strategy. Prudence dictates that Beijing pursue hedging behaviors to deter or in other ways constrain potential adversaries. But hedging risks alienating countries whose cooperation is essential to the success of developmental policies. In South and Central Asia, China's principal security concerns relate more to the relationships that India and Kazakhstan have with third countries of greater security concern to China (like the United States and Russia) than to direct military threats from regional states themselves. Hostile military action and overt aggression are not the only, or always the primary, security concerns of Beijing, however. Beijing now appears more concerned about the dangers of terrorism, subversion, and external support to restive minorities in China's frontier regions. Among the dilemmas this poses for Beijing is that of finding the right balance between facilitating cross-border engagement to promote economic growth and local prosperity and limiting opportunities for contacts and activities that threaten internal stability and Beijing's ability to control its frontiers.

Development is the second pillar and objective of China's domestic and foreign policies, and one can often explain and predict China's approach to and engagement with particular countries by examining what the other countries can do to assist or impede China's quest for sustained economic growth and modernization. Some countries can provide capital, technology, training, and markets for goods produced in China. Others can provide resources (e.g., oil, metals, minerals, timber), transport routes, and markets for Chinese products. Some can provide items from both lists, and some can provide little or nothing that China wants without resolution of political issues, construction of infrastructure, or other measures to satisfy requisite conditions for engagement.

In the early 1980s, China assessed the threat from Afghanistan and India to be moderately high because of their relationship to the Soviet Union. India constituted an independent threat, but Beijing was more concerned about India's role in the imputed Soviet effort to surround and constrain China than it was about the threat of an independent Indian attack. The Soviet Union had greater capacity to assist China's quest for development than indicated by its placement in Figure 1.1, but the constituent republics located in Central Asia were among the least developed in the USSR, and Beijing doubtless assessed that Moscow was unlikely to provide the kinds of assistance required by the reform and opening strategy even if China had wanted it to, which it did not.

Figure 1.5, a security and development matrix depicting China's view of South and Central Asia in the twenty-first century, reflects the increasing importance of the region as a provider of inputs needed to sustain growth at the national level and as an economic partner playing a key role in the development of minority areas on the Chinese side of the border. China's security concerns about the region would remain at more or less the same level, but the nature of concern gradually shifted away from military and geostrategic threats toward threats to stability and internal security from Islamic terrorists and cross-border support to separatists and disgruntled minorities in Xinjiang and other border provinces.

The analytic framework outlined here is a starting point, not an infallible predictor of how China perceives particular countries at a specific point in time. Historical interactions, cultural similarities and differences, the concerns and objectives of partner countries, and the actions of third parties enter into the mix as well. What actually happens is a vector formed by forces pushing events toward somewhat—or very—different goal sets. The chapters that follow illustrate the relative importance of security and developmental goals in the perceptions and policies of China and its neighbors in South and Central Asia. But they also illustrate the importance of changes in the global system and the policies of particular dyads, triads, and larger groups of countries.

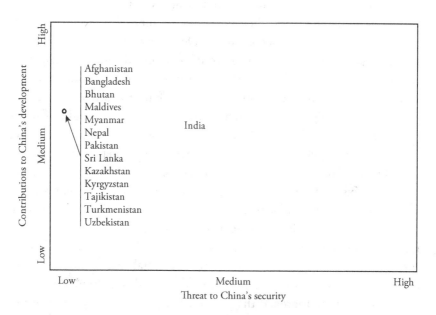

FIGURE 1.5 China's perception of threats and contributions to development from South and Central Asia, 2002

*Focus and Principal Findings of Individual Chapters*

Security concerns and efforts to address them are examined by all contributors to this volume, but they are a particular focus of Chapters 2 and 3. In Chapter 2, Thomas Fingar traces the evolution of China's security-related perceptions and policies affecting South and Central Asia from 1978 until the present. He argues that, for more than a decade after China adopted its reform and opening strategy in 1978, Beijing perceived South Asia primarily as a security problem to be managed and saw little potential for the region to contribute to China's quest for development. He also argues that Beijing was more concerned about the potential threat inherent in New Delhi's relationship with Moscow than it was about India's own capabilities and intentions. To address this perceived threat, China (1) maintained its special relationship with Pakistan in order to complicate New Delhi's defense planning and thereby reduce further the direct threat from India and (2) strengthened its relationship with the United States to counterbalance the Soviet Union and its Indian partner. During this phase, which lasted until the early 1990s, Beijing did not consider the region important to the success of its drive for sustained development (except to the extent that security-related developments there could affect China's drive to modernize).

Dissolution of the Soviet Union in December 1991 changed Beijing's security calculus by weakening the country it considered its principal security threat and reducing the importance of security considerations in China's perception of South and Central Asia. Fingar examines how China interpreted and adjusted to the new situation as it evolved and as China's economic success and policy changes in India and other regional countries opened new possibilities for China to benefit from closer ties with the region. He describes the period from roughly 1992 to 2001 as one of transition and adjustment in which the region loomed smaller in China's security and developmental calculus than in the preceding and subsequent periods. After 2001, he argues, Beijing's security concerns in the region centered on improving ties between Washington and New Delhi and imputed US desire to use bases and other relationships in Central Asia to surround and contain China. To counter what it assessed to be Washington's intentions, China adopted an approach that included expanding economic ties and improving its relationships with regional countries. The new approach was intended to check US influence, reduce the threat of cross-border terrorism, and capitalize on new opportunities to acquire resources and expand markets for Chinese goods.

In Chapter 3, Paul Kapur focuses on the third period examined by Fingar and looks more closely at Indian perceptions and management of the India-China-US strategic triangle. According to Kapur, India considers the threat from China to be its most serious security challenge and devotes more attention to countering that threat than to deterring or dealing with Pakistan. The asymmetry between the way China perceives the threat from India and the way India views the threat from China is also apparent when juxtaposing Chapters 4 and 5.

Although Kapur notes that New Delhi does not have a fully formulated strategy for managing the India-China-US strategic triangle, he describes elements that, taken together, constitute a multifaceted approach to countering the perceived threat from China. Those elements include investments to enhance India's conventional military capabilities, particularly those of its naval forces; efforts to expand and strengthen India's relations with the United States and to ensure that the United States maintains a robust interest and presence in the region; and efforts to improve relations with China by cooperating in the international arena when and where it can. Kapur argues that Indian strategists believe they must steer a course that hedges against potential dangers from China without appearing to be "anti-China" while encouraging the United States to remain actively engaged in the region without subordinating India's interests to those of the United States.

Geostrategic considerations also figure prominently in Chapter 4, by Hu Shisheng, and Chapter 5, by Srikanth Kondapalli, but both of these authors seek to provide a broader picture of Sino-Indian relations and how that relationship affects their dealings with other countries in and outside the region. Hu's chapter summarizes Chinese perceptions of India's rise and its implications for China. His analysis identifies strengths and weaknesses in India's political, social, and economic systems and concludes that India will continue to become more modern, more prosperous, and more powerful but will not be able to overtake China and thus will not become a serious threat to Chinese security or the attainment of China's other objectives. These judgments allow China to be rather relaxed about Indian efforts to hedge against uncertainty about China by increasing its military power and strengthening ties with the United States and other Asian-Pacific countries.

According to Hu, China recognizes that India's hedging behavior is undertaken for defensive reasons and is confident that India will not become part of a "counter-China coalition."

Hu argues that Beijing and New Delhi recognize that they have more to gain through cooperation than from attempts to constrain one another and that both are willing to live with issues and disputes (e.g., territorial conflicts, the structural trade imbalance, and relations with third countries, such as China's special relationship with Pakistan) that cannot be resolved at the present time. He also argues that they have a common interest in reforming the international system in ways that give greater weight to emerging powers and developing states and that each has become more accepting of the other's growing presence in its own traditional spheres of influence. Hu's concise explanation for the attitudes and developments he describes is that the requirements of sustained development now trump the security concerns of both nations. This judgment may well prove to be premature.

Kondapalli's chapter examines Sino-Indian relations from an Indian perspective and presents a somewhat less optimistic assessment than does Hu's chapter. Kondapalli characterizes the contemporary relationship as one marked by a mix of common purpose, mutual suspicion, and intractable problems. This leads each side to support and exploit the rise of the other when it is possible to do so but also to impede or constrain the other when doing so is deemed necessary to protect its own interests. Kondapalli describes legacy issues and intractable problems as real constraints on what the countries can or want to do together and, like Kapur, emphasizes the extent to which India perceives China to be its most important security challenge.

In contrast to Hu, who characterizes India's rise as not threatening to China's interests and aspirations in the eyes of the Chinese, Kondapalli argues that Indians see China as actively trying to constrain their own rise. He agrees that both sides attempt to play down elements of rivalry in the relationship but provides examples illustrating that it is not always possible to sidestep intractable problems (e.g., limitations on border trade because border disputes remain unresolved). Hu's chapter provides greater detail on what China regards as strengths and weaknesses in the Indian system than Kondapalli's explication of Sino-Indian relations does when describing China's rise and objectives. But both contributors identify essentially the same factors as most important in shaping perceptions of and policies toward one another. Hu's treatment of developments generally depicts them as moving in ways that favor cooperation and China's interests; Kondapalli's analysis places greater emphasis on impediments to cooperation and on Indian efforts to protect Indian interests from the consequences of China's policies toward the region.

China and Pakistan have long characterized their relationship as "higher than the Himalayas, deeper than the Indian Ocean, and sweeter than honey."[28] In Chapter 6, Syed Rifaat Hussain examines the origins of this unique relationship and why it endures despite changes in the international system and China's relationship with India. He argues that the relationship has always been more than just an alliance of convenience to counterbalance a common enemy, India, and that it will endure because of mutual trust and China's sensitivity to Pakistan's security dilemma. In making this argument, Hussain contrasts China's reliability to sometimes perfidious and demanding behavior by Pakistan's other ally, the United States, and illustrates the depth and uniqueness of the relationship by citing China's assistance to Pakistan's effort to acquire nuclear weapons. His chapter illustrates the extent to which Pakistan now depends on China for military and economic assistance but does not address the question of whether China's improving relationship with India has diminished Pakistan's value as a security partner. He does, however, note that Pakistan has become increasingly important as a transit route for energy and other resources destined for China and that China's investments in infrastructure projects will help integrate China and the region.

Although Hussain does not say so explicitly, his analysis suggests that Pakistan's value to China may be shifting from one that is overwhelmingly security-based to one that is increasingly based on the contribution that Pakistan can make to China's quest for development. His chapter also suggests that Pakistan's role in China's security calculus may be shifting away from concern about military security toward greater concern about internal stability and discusses how activities based in Pakistan contribute to terrorism and minority unrest in China's southwest frontier region. What impact this shift will have on the bilateral relationship is difficult to predict because it will require that Pakistan do more things responsive to Beijing's wishes than merely remaining hostile to India and refraining from close alignment with the United States.

Pakistan is the only country in the region with a long history of close relations with China. Natural barriers, Indian dominance of the subcontinent, and mutual disinterest in engagement severely limited interaction between China and the smaller states of South Asia until the late 1990s. Relations entered a new and far more dynamic stage in the twenty-first century. Several factors account for this change, including China's rapid growth and growing demand for resources and markets. Chapter 9, by Saman Kelegama, examines this and other reasons for the dramatic increase in China's relationships with its smaller neighbors to the southwest.

The primacy of security concerns that dominated China's perception of and policies toward its neighbors to the west and southwest during the first decades of reform and opening—as indeed they had for thousands of years—began to change in the 1990s. Many developments contributed to the change, including the end of the Cold War, the cumulative effects of China's economic success that increased demand for energy and other resources and the funds and knowledge necessary to expand cross-border engagement, and increasing restiveness among China's minority peoples. Security concerns did not disappear, but they became less focused on the danger of military attack, encirclement, and the ability of major powers to exploit relations with China's neighbors to contain and constrain China's rise and more focused on cross-border threats to internal stability.

Chapter 7, by Swaran Singh, and Chapter 8, by Zhao Huasheng, describe and analyze how these changes led to a paradigm shift in the way China perceived its frontier areas and the approach it now employs to foster growth in its border provinces and deeper engagement with the countries of South and Central Asia. Singh's chapter focuses on the domestic drivers of change in China's approach and the transition from long-standing policies of neglect, disparagement, and distrust to promotion of engagement in order to ensure peace and development along China's southwestern frontier. He argues that transport and other infrastructure improvements undertaken by Beijing to facilitate growth and maintain control in the southwest created opportunities for influence and economic benefit when extended across the borders to neighboring states. In other words, foreign-policy benefits from cross-border engagement were a spillover gain rather than a primary reason for the decision to lower barriers and build bridges across the frontier.

Zhao's chapter describes the evolution of China's strategic thinking since 1991, when dissolution of the Soviet Union produced newly independent states in Central Asia. China's first priority was to protect its own security by resolving border disputes and establishing relationships with peoples and political units that had been under Russian/Soviet dominion for more than a century. After this was accomplished, China's next steps were guided by the priority Beijing attached to modernization and sustained economic growth and to alleviating the threat to internal security posed by the new upsurge in terrorism and separatist activities in Xinjiang. Zhao examines the reasons for and evolution of Chinese policies centered on security, energy, transportation, and other forms of economic engagement and policies related to geostrategic concerns about the country's "rear area." Like Singh's analysis of China's engagement with the smaller states of South Asia, Zhao's discussion argues that Beijing's primary motivations related to concern about unrest and uneven development in its own frontier regions.

Saman Kelegama, in Chapter 9, argues that most of the smaller regional states (the exceptions are Afghanistan and Bhutan) welcome China's greater interest and involvement for both economic and political reasons. China's quest for resources and markets, ability and willingness to invest in infrastructure projects necessary to facilitate trade, and record of exceptionally rapid growth during the past two decades make it a desirable economic partner and a counterbalance to India's economic dominance and political arrogance. Chinese investments are designed to bring benefits to China, but they also provide income, jobs, and multifunctional infrastructure beneficial to the receiving countries. Moreover, China's initiatives and responsiveness are in stark contrast to India's history of benign neglect and, Kelegama argues, have prompted India to take a more active interest in the development of its long-neglected neighbors.

Like Kelegama, Sebastien Peyrouse, in Chapter 10, looks at China's engagement with neighboring countries from the perspective of the non-Chinese parties. In contrast to Kelegama's generally favorable characterization of the consequences of China's engagement with the smaller states of South Asia, Peyrouse's chapter, on China and Central Asia, provides a more downbeat assessment. The chapter suggests that the newly independent states were even more eager than China to resolve border disputes, but even so, it took years to reach agreement, and none of the agreements has been published, fueling suspicion and concern that leaders of the new states may have conceded too much to their more powerful neighbor. Indeed, discomfort with the power differential and the way Beijing is perceived to exploit it is a recurring theme in this chapter, which also looks at energy development, water management, and the consequences of opening borders.

Although China's Central Asian neighbors benefit economically from Chinese investments, purchases, and exported goods, Peyrouse describes unhappiness about the extent to which leaders appear to have yielded to Chinese demands, discontent about Chinese business practices and tendency to use Han Chinese workers rather than hire locals, and uncertainty about China's ultimate intentions.

The demise of the Soviet Union transformed China's security situation in ways that shaped its perceptions, possibilities, and policies around the globe, but nowhere more than in Central Asia. As Igor Torbakov argues in Chapter 11, the dramatic reversal of Russian and Chinese fortunes at the end of the twentieth century triggered a new round in the long-running competition for imperial primacy in Central Asia. His analysis of current Russian thinking with respect to its place in the world and the role of Central Asia in regaining international influence underscores the fact that Kazakhstan, Kyrgyzstan, Tajikistan, Turkmenistan, and Uzbekistan could find a receptive ear should they seek assistance from Moscow to counter perceived attempts at domination by Beijing and that this both empowers the Central Asian states and, to some extent, constrains China's options in the region.

Torbakov's chapter also illuminates the flip side of Zhao's discussion of "Xiyu" (western lands) as extending from the eastern border of Xinjiang across the vast expanse of Central Asia. History and cultural ties facilitate engagement with Central Asia and enable Beijing to use Xinjiang as a bridgehead to extend its economic and political power into Central Asia, but they also entail inherent vulnerabilities for Beijing as it attempts to alleviate discontent among the minorities that inhabit its far western frontier. Torbakov, like Peyrouse, indicates that it remains to be seen whether—or the extent to which—China will continue to interact with regional states as independent countries or will attempt to restore a form of imperial control.

In Chapter 12, Vivek Arora, Hui Tong, and Cristina Constantinescu focus on the economic dimension of China's engagement with South Asia to clarify the magnitude of trade and financial integration that has resulted and to determine the extent of competition and complementarities. Their analysis indicates that trade and financial engagement between China and South Asia are increasing rapidly but still constitute a very small percentage of all countries' totals, that the percentage is higher for the South Asian partners than it is for China, and that the magnitude and degree of integration are still much lower than predicted by the gravity model and similar predictive methodologies.

Topography, size of the economies, transport costs, and the fact that Pakistan is the only South Asian country that has a Free Trade Agreement with China help explain why the degree of integration is much lower than it is, for example, between China and Southeast Asia. Another factor may be that South Asia in general and India, which accounts for the largest percentage by far of all economic activity in the region in particular, are not well integrated into global production and supply chains. Arora, Tong, and Constantinescu's study shows that regional and cross-border integration are increasing, that China's engagement is a major factor driving the process, and that there are far more complementarities than examples of direct competition between China and South Asian countries.

Taken together, the chapters in this volume develop findings that are consistent with the security and contribution-to-development framework described earlier because they indicate that what Beijing judged to be possible and desirable in terms of engagement to advance China's modernization agenda was contingent on prior judgments about the security situation. They also demonstrate the importance of exogenous developments in the international system, the first and foremost of which was the demise of the Soviet Union, and an evolution in China's security calculus reflecting decreased concern about external aggression and increased concern about external and internal threats to domestic tranquility. Additional trends are discussed in Chapter 13.

Relationships among countries, cultures, and peoples in the vast swath of territory examined in this book have changed dramatically in the last two decades, and the consequences of changes still unfolding seem certain to drive events and relationships in new directions at an accelerating pace. China has been a major driver and beneficiary of increased economic engagement, but its initiatives and responses have been—and will continue to be—shaped by developments largely beyond its control. The short list of such developments includes the demise of the Soviet Union, India's adoption of transformative economic reforms, and the rise of Islamic extremists in Pakistan. "Smaller" regional states, a category that includes all but China, India, and Russia, are benefitting in certain ways from China's efforts and ambitions in the region, but all are uncertain about ultimate intentions and where events are headed, and all are hedging against uncertainty in ways that could affect the course of events.

The Great Game has changed, but it has not ended. Interdependencies and integration are changing the calculus and possibility space of actors large and small, and any attempt to capture what is happening must acknowledge that the best one can hope for is a snapshot in time with somewhat greater ability to explain how and why developments occurred as they did than to predict where they are headed. This book provides a temporal snapshot of China's engagement with South and Central Asia during the first thirty-five years of Beijing's latest quest for modernization, wealth, and power. It focuses on China's objectives and actions in this diverse region but both assumes and demonstrates that what actually happens is also shaped by the perceptions and policies of other actors and that outcomes often differ from what any had intended and pave the way for new initiatives and responses.

China's objectives and actions are not the only or at all times most important determinants of what happens in bilateral and regional relationships. Each of the other countries in the region has goals and priorities of its own and views China's actions and perceived ambitions through lenses colored by experience, expectations, and relationships with third countries. None is simply a passive target of initiatives from China. When the national objectives of these countries align with or are compatible with those of China, relationships evolve quite differently than they do when the goals are perceived to be in conflict. Each seeks not only to protect itself from unwanted dependence on and interference from China but also to use China to protect and advance its own security, economy, and other interests. What actually happens is a function of how well or badly each party manages the interplay of compatible and competing objectives. No party ever achieves all that it wants, but the benefits for each must outweigh the costs if the relationship or mode of engagement is to endure.[29]

Although the primary focus of this book is on what China is doing and seeks to achieve from its engagement with the countries of South and Central Asia, the chapters demonstrate that what China is able to achieve—and the cost it must pay to achieve it—are shaped by global and regional developments and by the preferences of participants inside and outside the region. Initiatives trigger responses, and responses create new challenges and opportunities. The game involves multiple players, many moves, and continuous learning. The process could lead to increased tensions and clashes of interest, subdivision of the players into two or more contending blocs, or attempts to align with or against China. But that has not yet happened, and it many never occur because the net effect of China's interactions with the countries in South and Central Asia has been steadily increasing interdependence and modestly greater integration.

As this book goes to press, in mid-2015, Chinese statements about and policies toward South and Central Asia are evolving in ways that suggest that decision makers in Beijing have noted, interpreted, and responded to patterns and developments revealed through the juxtaposition of insights from the book's case studies summarized in Chapter 13. This is particularly the case with respect to lessons about the economic, social, and political benefits of infrastructure projects that facilitate the movement of goods, people, and ideas; increase prosperity both locally and in more distant places; and deepen ties among companies, communities, and countries.

Xi Jinping obviously had not read this book when he announced initiatives in late 2013 to build a "new Silk Road" with Central Asia or a "maritime silk road" with states in South and Southeast Asia, but the logic and rationale for these initiatives, and for the subsequently announced new Asian Infrastructure Investment Bank, are consistent with the lessons and implications of the findings presented here.[30] So, too, are the reactions of other state and nonstate actors in and outside the region and the ways in which Xi's proposals have been modified to accommodate the concerns and objectives of other countries. Beijing's initiatives to further integrate the region in ways that enhance China's prestige and influence and improve the lot of people on both sides of borders are logical extrapolations of lessons inherent in the findings and insights presented here. How they will be implemented and how they will affect perceptions, performance, and future policies of China and the other regional players remain to be seen.

*Notes*

1. See "Elephant and the Blind Men," *Jainworld.com*, http://www.jainworld .com/education/stories25.asp (accessed May 4, 2015).

2. See, for example, Robert Sutter, *Chinese Foreign Relations: Power and Policy Since the Cold War*, 3rd ed. (Lanham, MD: Rowman and Littlefield, 2012), chap. 1; Avery Goldstein, *Rising to the Challenge: China's Grand Strategy and International Security* (Stanford, CA: Stanford University Press, 2005); Thomas Christensen,

"China," in *Strategic Asia, 2001–2002*, ed. Richard Ellings and Aaron Friedberg (Seattle, WA: National Bureau of Asian Research, 2001), 27–70; and Wang Jisi, "China's Search for a Grand Strategy," *Foreign Affairs* 90, no. 2 (2011): 68–79.

3. See the analysis and citations in Alastair Iain Johnston, "Is China a Status Quo Power," *International Security* 27, no. 4 (2003): 5–56; and Feng Huiyun, "Is China a Revisionist Power?" *Chinese Journal of International Politics* 2 (2009): 313–334.

4. See, for example, Marc Lanteigne, *Chinese Foreign Policy: An Introduction* (New York: Routledge, 2009); and Linda Jakobson and Dean Knox, *New Foreign Policy Actors in China* (Stockholm: Stockholm International Peace Research Institute, 2010).

5. See, for example, Su Hao, "Harmonious World: The Conceived International Order in Framework of China's Foreign Affairs," in *China's Shift: Global Strategy of the Rising Power*, ed. Masafumi Iida (Tokyo: National Institute for Defense Studies, 2009), 29–55; David Haroz, "China in Africa: Symbiosis or Exploitation?" *Fletcher Forum of World Affairs* 35, no. 2 (2011): 65–88, http://www.fletcherforum.org/wp-content/uploads/2013/12/Haroz_FA.pdf; and "Relations with Myanmar: Less Thunder out of China," *The Economist*, October 6, 2011, http://www.economist.com/node/21564279.

6. See, for example, David Shambaugh, *China Goes Global: The Partial Power* (Oxford: Oxford University Press, 2013); and Roderick MacFarquhar, "How Serious Is Xi Jinping About Tackling Corruption in China?" *The Atlantic*, June 28, 2013, http://www.theatlantic.com/china/archive/2013/06/how-serious-is-xi-jinping-about-tackling-corruption-in-china/277345/.

7. See, for example, Aaron L. Friedberg, "Hegemony with Chinese Characteristics," *National Interest*, July–August 2011, pp. 18–27, http://web.clas.ufl.edu/users/zselden/coursereading2011/Friedberg.pdf.

8. Ibid.; Stephen M. Walt, "How Long Will China Tolerate America's Role in Asia?" *Foreign Policy*, December 2, 2013, http://www.foreignpolicy.com/posts/2013/12/02/whats_the_big_question_answer_the_us_and_china.

9. See, for example, John J. Mearsheimer, "The Gathering Storm: China's Challenge to US Power in Asia," *Chinese Journal of International Politics* 3, no. 4 (2010): 381–396; and Aaron L. Friedberg, *A Contest for Supremacy: China, America, and the Struggle for Mastery in Asia* (New York: W. W. Norton, 2011).

10. See, for example, G. John Ikenberry, *Liberal Leviathan: The Origins, Crisis, and Transformation of the American World Order* (Princeton, NJ: Princeton University Press, 2011); and Bruce Jones, *Still Ours to Lead: America, Rising Powers, and the Tension Between Rivalry and Restraint* (Washington, DC: Brookings Institution, 2014).

11. Examples include David Shambaugh, ed., *Tangled Titans: The United States and China* (Lanham, MD: Rowman and Littlefield, 2013); Robert Ross and Zhu

Feng, eds., *China's Ascent: Power, Security, and the Future of International Politics* (Ithaca, NY: Cornell University Press, 2008); and Susan L. Shirk, *China: Fragile Superpower* (Oxford: Oxford University Press, 2008).

12. See, for example, Sisheng Zhao, ed., *Chinese Foreign Policy: Pragmatic and Strategic Behavior* (Armonk, NY: M. E. Sharpe, 2004).

13. Examples include Riordan Roett and Guadalupe Paz, eds., *China's Expansion into the Western Hemisphere* (Washington, DC: Brookings Institution, 2008); Robert I. Rotberg, ed., *China into Africa: Trade, Aid, and Influence* (Washington, DC: Brookings Institution, 2008); Ian Storey, *Southeast Asia and the Rise of China: The Search for Security* (New York: Routledge, 2013); and Srikanth Kondapalli and Emi Mifune, eds., *China and Its Neighbors* (New Delhi: Pentagon Press, 2010).

14. This essay does not intend or pretend to provide a comprehensive summary of this vast literature. An overview of what has been written and the approaches adopted can be found in Sutter, *Chinese Foreign Relations*.

15. Beginning in early 1994, when I became Deputy Secretary of State for Analysis in the Bureau of Intelligence and Research, my official job description included responsibility for analysis of all countries and issues. This remained a part of my job description when I became Assistant Secretary for Intelligence and Research, chairman of the National Intelligence Council, and deputy director of National Intelligence for Analysis. During this time I reviewed, edited, and approved more than 13,000 analytic pieces covering a total of more than 190 countries.

16. See, for example, "Xi Jinping Expounds Security Commission Role," *Xinhuanet*, November 15, 2013, http://news.xinhuanet.com/english/china/2013-11/15/c_132892155.htm.

17. See, for example, A. Doak Barnett, *China's Economy in Global Perspective* (Washington, DC: Brookings Institution, 1981).

18. See, for example, Ezra F. Vogel, *Deng Xiaoping and the Transformation of China* (Cambridge, MA: Belknap Press, 2011); and Li Lanqing, *Breaking Through: The Birth of China's Opening-Up Policy* (Oxford: Oxford University Press, 2009).

19. See Barry Naughton, "The Third Front: Defense Industrialization in the Chinese Interior," *China Quarterly* 115 (1988): 351–386.

20. Deng Xiaoping made this point many times. See, for example, "Peace and Development Are the Two Outstanding Issues in the World Today," March 4, 1985, and "Speech at an Enlarged Meeting of the Military Commission of the Central Committee of the Communist Party of China," June 4, 1985, in *Selected Works of Deng Xiaoping*, vol. 3, http://archive.org/stream/SelectedWorksOfDeng XiaopingVol.3/Deng03_djvu.txt.

21. See, for example, Wang Yi, "Peaceful Development and the Chinese Dream of National Rejuvenation," China Institute of International Studies, March 11, 2014, http://www.ciis.org.cn/english/2014-03/11/content_6733151.htm; and Sujian

Guo, ed., *China's "Peaceful Rise" in the 21st Century: Domestic and International Conditions* (Aldershot, UK: Ashgate, 2006).

22. See, for example, Bonnie S. Glaser and Evan S. Medeiros, "The Changing Ecology of Foreign Policy-Making in China: The Ascension and Demise of the Theory of 'Peaceful Rise,'" *China Quarterly* 190 (2007): 291–310.

23. See, for example, William R. Heaton, "China and Southeast Asian Communist Movements: The Decline of Dual Track Diplomacy," *Asian Survey* 22, no. 8 (1982): 779–800; and Michael R. Chambers, "The Evolving Relationship Between China and Southeast Asia: The Legacy of Policy Changes," in *Legacy of Engagement in Southeast Asia*, ed. Ann Marie Murphy and Bridget Walsh (Singapore: Institute of Southeast Asian Studies, 2008), 281–310.

24. See, for example, Morris Rosabi, ed., *Governing China's Multiethnic Frontiers* (Seattle: University of Washington Press, 2004).

25. See, for example, Dieter Heinzig, *The Soviet Union and Communist China, 1945–1950: The Arduous Road to the Alliance* (Armonk, NY: M. E. Sharpe, 2004).

26. See, for example, Vogel, *Deng Xiaoping*, 311–348; and Henry Kissinger, *On China* (New York: Penguin, 2011), 202–339.

27. John W. Garver, *Protracted Contest: Sino-Indian Rivalry in the Twentieth Century* (Seattle: University of Washington Press, 2001).

28. Hu Jintao, "Address at Islamabad Convention Center: 'Carry on Traditional Friendship and Deepen All-Round Cooperation,'" cited in Michael Beckley, "China and Pakistan: Fair-Weather Friends," *Yale Journal of International Affairs*, March 2012, p. 9, http://yalejournal.org/wp-content/uploads/2012/04/Article-Michael-Beckley.pdf.

29. See, for example, Kenneth N. Waltz, *Theory of International Politics* (New York: McGraw Hill, 1979); and Stephen M. Walt, *The Origins of Alliances* (Ithaca, NY: Cornell University Press, 1987).

30. See, for example, Wu Jiao and Zhang Yunbi, "Xi Proposes a 'New Silk Road' with Central Asia," *China Daily*, September 8, 2013, http://usa.chinadaily.com.cn/china/2013-09/08/content_16952304.htm; Wu Jiao and Zhang Yunbi, "Xi in Call for Building of New 'Maritime Silk Road,'" *China Daily*, October 4, 2013, http://usa.chinadaily.com.cn/china/2013-10/04/content_17008940.htm; "Chronology of China's 'Belt and Road' Initiatives," *Xinhuanet*, February 5, 2015, http://news.xinhuanet.com/english/china/2015-02/05/c_133972101.htm; and Jane Perlez, "Xi Hosts 56 Nations at Founding of Asian Infrastructure Bank," *New York Times*, June 29, 2015, http://www.nytimes.com/2015/06/30/world/asia/xi-jinping-of-china-hosts-nations-at-asian-infrastructure-investment-bank-founding.html.

TWO

# China's Goals in South Asia

*Thomas Fingar*

China's goals in South Asia are shaped by geography, geopolitics, history, factor endowments, and national priorities. Geography is relatively immutable; the Himalayas will always be an impediment to movements across land borders. But political systems and alignments change, history can be reinterpreted, and development and technology can change the value of factor endowments. Conditions and changes shape perceptions of what is necessary and what is possible, and perceptions shape national priorities and the means—policies—used to achieve them.[1] This chapter examines the evolution of China's perceptions and policies with respect to South Asia during the three and a half decades since Deng Xiaoping announced the policy of reform and opening.[2]

South Asia did not figure prominently in the calculus of Deng and the other Chinese leaders who decided in the late 1970s to abandon Mao Zedong's quest for a uniquely Chinese path to security, prosperity, and international influence. Instead, they determined to follow the path that had enabled Japan and the other "Asian tigers" to achieve rapid and sustained economic growth and, through growth, to enhance China's security and domestic stability. The key to the success of the Japanese model and the strategy they were developing for China was to gain access to markets, capital, technology, and training available in the US-led free world. That, in turn, required a cooperative relationship with the United States. It was not coincidental that Beijing announced the establishment of formal diplomatic relations with the United States at the same plenum that announced the shift from isolation and autarky to reform and greater participation in the international system.[3] What China needed most to ensure the success of the new strategy was not available in the developing world. South Asia did not have what China needed—with one important exception.

The exception was the potential to derail Deng's strategy by threatening China's security. According highest priority to economic growth, which the new policies did, required abandoning or redefining the worldview that had provided the context for China's foreign and developmental policies during the preceding three decades. Mao, and apparently most other Chinese leaders, accepted the proposition that war (between the "socialist world" and the "capitalist world" or simply between China and its enemies) was inevitable.[4] This perception shaped budget allocations, decisions on where to locate factories, and policies that minimized foreign trade and dependence on foreign partners. Deng paved the way for reform and opening by redefining the international situation and declaring that although war was still inevitable, it was not imminent.[5]

This created a window of opportunity for China to pursue self-strengthening through internal reform and exploitation of opportunities available through participation in the free-world system. Better relations with the United States were assumed to reduce the threat to China from the United States and its allies while counterbalancing—and reducing—the threat from the Soviet Union.[6] In South Asia, only India had the potential and possible incentive to pose a military threat to China. Of greater concern to Beijing was the danger that Moscow would use its relationship with New Delhi to contain or threaten China. Preventing that from happening, or from crossing a threshold that could reopen debate in China about the feasibility of the new strategy according higher priority to development than to immediate security requirements, became the number one goal of China's South Asia policy.

### Setting the Stage

South Asia did not figure prominently in China's new security and developmental strategy, but relationships, perceptions, and goals from the past continued to exist and to shape interactions. Legacy factors, such as the degree of enmity and suspicion between China and India and Beijing's "special" relationship with Islamabad continued to shape perceptions and decisions affecting relationships between China and all countries in the region.[7] That being the case, it is useful to review the state of play that existed in the late 1970s.

Although it is often noted that for long periods China and India were the largest, richest, and most powerful empires in the world, their relationship was always more distant than one might expect from their proximity. Separated by the world's highest mountains and having limited interactions because neither empire was a significant naval power, they did not trade, did not fight, and had only limited cultural contacts. Neither has a large diaspora population from the other. One consequence of this limited interaction is that China has much less historical baggage vis-à-vis South Asia than it does with the states of Northeast and Southeast Asia. Indeed, most of the legacy issues that affect South Asian relations with China arose after the British Raj ended (1947) and the Communists declared victory in China's civil war (1949).

During the first decade of India's independence and the existence of the People's Republic of China (PRC), both emphasized their shared victimization at the hands of Western colonialists/imperialists.[8] Actual and imagined similarities and shared determination to forge a more just international system seemed to be more important than the fact that they had adopted very different political systems and become the world's largest democracy and most populous socialist country. This period of bonhomie lasted for little more than a decade. The relationship deteriorated after India granted safe haven to the Dalai Lama in 1959 and border disputes led to a short but symbolically significant war in 1962. The war led to enduring Chinese hostility and disdain for India, and deep Indian fear and resentment of China.[9]

In the years after the 1962 war, China moved away from the Soviet Union and deepened its relationship with Pakistan. Mao broke with Moscow primarily for ideological reasons but also because he chafed at China's little-brother status in the relationship. Ideology was neither an inducement nor an impediment to China's tilt toward Pakistan. Beijing's motivation was almost entirely geopolitical. At the time, Pakistan was still a member of two explicitly anticommunist alliances (CENTO and SEATO), but that clearly was less important to Beijing than Islamabad's location and antipathy toward India.[10] Indeed, Chinese calculations and objectives during the period up to the late 1970s were primarily of the "enemy of my enemy is my friend" variety. Finding ways to annoy India and complicate its security calculations was more important than pursuit of better relations or expanded economic ties.

Beijing's moves away from the Soviet Union and toward Pakistan were matched by Indian moves away from the United States and toward Moscow. Ideology played little role in this realignment. Despite the fact that both India and the United States were democracies, the United States was discomforted by India's socialist economy and preference for nonalignment.[11] When the United States curtailed arms deliveries to India during the 1965 war with Pakistan and reaffirmed the ban during the 1971 war, India turned to Moscow for weapons and other forms of support to counter China's assistance to Pakistan.[12]

Obviously China's relationships with the countries of South Asia were more complex than described in this brief summary of the situation in the late 1970s. Much more could be—and has been—written about intraregional dynamics and China's relationships with each of the countries in the region, but for the purposes of establishing a baseline for the changes described here, it is sufficient to highlight the following points:

- China's relationships with the states of South Asia as of the late 1970s were shaped primarily by geostrategic considerations; history, culture, ideology, trade, and other factors were much less important.
- China's relationship with India was the most important determinant of its relationships with other countries in the region. When Sino-Indian relations deteriorated after 1959, China deepened its relationship with Pakistan to complicate India's security calculus.
- Other countries in the region were more worried about India than they were about China. This created opportunities for China to develop cooperative relations with India's neighbors.
- The nations of South Asia had never been subjected to Chinese imperial or cultural dominance and were less worried about Chinese actions and ambitions than were the former vassal states of Northeast and Southeast Asia.

## Shift from Autarky and Experimentation to Acquiescence and Imitation

Three decades of Maoist excess and experimentation had left China poorer and weaker than its rivals. Gains from the peace dividend after decades of conflict and generous aid from the Soviet Union had been squandered by politically driven experiments during the Great Leap Forward (1958–1962) and the decade-long excesses of the Cultural Revolution (1966–1976).[13] Militarily, economically, and technologically, China was falling further behind the Soviet Union, the United States, Japan, and many other countries. Even India was doing better in the race to modernize; by the late-1970s, India's GDP per capita exceeded China's by roughly 25 percent.[14]

By the time of Mao's death in 1976, China had been experimenting with "Chinese" strategies of development for more than a century. All had failed. Whether failure was caused by deficiencies in the strategies, the fact that they were constantly disrupted or discarded because of conflict or political whim, or both is less relevant than the fact that they left China weak and impoverished. Mao's successors decided to discard experimentation in favor of following the path that had enabled Japan, Taiwan, and the Republic of Korea to achieve sustained high levels of economic growth. The incentives to find and implement a strategy that would produce results included desire to improve the lot of the Chinese people, recognition that continued privation imperiled the legitimacy of Communist Party rule, and fear that stronger nations would again seek to take advantage of a poor and weak China (despite its nuclear weapons).[15] The last of the incentives listed here was probably the most important. The ultimate goal of reform and opening was (and is) to make China more secure by making it more modern, more prosperous, and more stable.

Beijing's decision to follow the path pioneered by Japan was a necessary but insufficient condition for actually doing so. The other essential element was US willingness to allow China to participate in the free-world system without abandoning its Communist Party–led political system.[16] China's relationship with the United States had improved marginally since Richard Nixon's visit in 1972, but it was by no means certain that Washington would permit a nonally with a Communist government to join the free-world club. By mid-1978, however, the Carter administration had decided and signaled to Beijing that it was prepared to enable and assist China's quest for wealth and power.[17]

Deng seized the opportunity. Chinese statements from the time indicate that advocates of the new strategy argued that it was imperative to act quickly, before the temporary window of opportunity closed, and that participation in the US-led system was a tactical expedient that would ultimately increase China's freedom of action on the world stage by making it stronger and more influential. Many in Washington had different expectations. Like

Deng, they were eager to lock in the new arrangement before Deng or other key Chinese leaders died or lost their nerve. They were also eager to get started because one of the principal reasons for engaging China in this way was to make it a stronger and more confident partner in what was still expected to be a protracted standoff with the Soviet Union. Another reason, albeit one not shared by everyone in the administration, was confidence that modernization via participation in the liberal international order would transform China in ways beneficial to the United States.[18]

Chinese and American aspirations and expectations differed, but they had many points in common. One is that both were motivated by security considerations. The primary objective of both was to strengthen their individual and collective ability to deter and defeat the military, ideological, and economic threats posed by the Soviet Union and its allies. Another is that both sought to maintain a peaceful international environment conducive to trade and other transactions now subsumed under the rubric of globalization. If the world became more dangerous and less stable, China would have to direct more resources to short-term security needs.

The considerations just summarized entailed significant consequences for Chinese foreign policy. One was that it had to be attentive to US interests and concerns. Beijing and Washington both understood that China would not be an ordinary participant in the free-world system and was likely to use means and pursue objectives not always welcome by the United States and/or its allies. Beijing understood that obtaining the security benefits of its new relationship with the United States required that the Soviet Union and other "third countries" remain convinced that American and Chinese interests were sufficiently in synch that Washington would stand with its new security partner.[19]

A second consequence for Chinese foreign policy was that it could no longer promote or applaud unrest in other parts of the globe because unrest anywhere could jeopardize the peaceful international environment needed to ensure rapid development. It took some years before China was able to reorient its foreign policy from promoting revolution to promoting peace and stability. But as it did so, China began to modify its policies and its actions. The changes in China's foreign policy began to show up first in its positions on United Nations–sponsored peacekeeping operations.[20] Later it became more apparent in its policies toward governments and insurgent groups in Southeast Asia and, still later, in South Asia.[21]

Pursuit of China's reform and opening strategy followed a template that accorded different weights and priorities to all regions and countries. Highest priority went to the United States because it played a critical role in assuring China's security; access to its own markets, capital, technology, and training facilities; and indirect access to the resources and capabilities of its free-world allies. The United States also played a critical role in maintaining international peace and the smooth operation of the free-world system. The template accorded second highest priority to maintaining good relations and cooperation with other members of the free world, especially Japan and the Western European nations with the biggest markets and greatest ability to invest in China's development.

China hoped—and expected—to be able to use its relationships with other developed democracies to balance and limit its dependence on the United States by applying the so-called three-worlds theory of international relations that posited America's allies would welcome partnership with China to offset US power.[22] Application of such classic balance of power arrangements was intended to limit China's vulnerability to the demands of the United States and other OECD nations and make it possible for China to take advantage of capitalist eagerness for a piece of the China market to play firms and nations against one another for China's benefit. Things did not work out exactly as China had hoped, but concentrating on the most developed countries in the US-led system did bring substantial and early benefits to China.[23]

In the first stage of China's reform and opening policy, it neither needed nor sought oil, metals, minerals, or other natural resources from abroad, and it did not seek developing world markets for its manufactured goods. This enabled, and to some extent required, paying little attention to countries that did not have the potential to provide what China most needed to jumpstart economic growth. All China required from most countries and regions was that they remain relatively peaceful and refrain from doing anything that could endanger China's own security and/or strategy of development. In 1979, South Asia ranked quite low on China's list of immediate priorities. That situation proved to be short lived.

## *1979–1992: South Asia as Security Problem, Not an Economic Partner*

China's newly adopted strategy of development was predicated on the judgment that near-term threats to the nation's security could be managed by using its tacit partnership with the United States to counterbalance the Soviet Union and reduce the likelihood of attack by the United States and/or its allies. The strategy was also predicated on avoidance or management of conflicts elsewhere in the world that could jeopardize the will and ability of highly developed free-world nations to assist China's quest for rapid and sustained economic growth. During the initial decade of China's opening to the outside world, South Asia was unable, and probably unwilling, to contribute in positive ways. But developments in and involving the region did command China's attention because they were perceived to threaten the requisite conditions of security and stability.

In the late 1970s, the Soviet Union was still regarded as posing the greatest threat to China's security.[24] Beijing calculated that it could manage the short-term dimensions of the threat through its relationship with the United States, but it was less confident of its ability to manage the longer-term threat from Moscow. One reason for uncertainty about the longer term was the assumption, even conviction, that the willingness of the United States and its allies to assist China's modernization would be short lived. If—when—the West pulled back or turned against China, Beijing would have to manage the Soviet threat on its own. Viewed through that lens, specific developments involving South Asia were troubling to Beijing and evoked significant policy responses.

In an age of intercontinental missiles and other long-range systems, Chinese geostrategic thinkers continue to talk, and presumably think, in terms reminiscent of an earlier era. This is most clearly the case when they assert or express concern about imputed intentions of a country, in this case the Soviet Union, to "surround" China through conquest, alliances, and partnerships.[25] Moscow's relationship with India both fed and confirmed this suspicion. Stated another way, although China was not overly concerned about an independent threat from India, it did worry about the perceived threat inherent in the Soviet-Indian partnership.[26]

We can gain insight about China's thinking at this time from what it said and did after Vietnam overthrew the Khmer Rouge regime in Cambodia in December 1978. China was an early and ardent supporter of Pol Pot and his murderous regime during the Maoist era, and support continued after Mao's death.[27] In December 1978, just days after Deng announced the policy of reform and opening, Vietnam—with Soviet support—sent troops into Cambodia and quickly overthrew China's closest ally in Southeast Asia.

Deng visited the United States in January, creating the impression that Washington had endorsed China's attack on Vietnam later that month.[28] The express purpose of the attack was to teach Vietnam that it was imprudent to disregard China's security concerns by aligning with the Soviet Union. That may have been China's intent, but the attack, despite China's poor showing on the battlefield, seems to have conveyed a different lesson to China's neighbors—namely, that it would be prudent to seek external support to counterbalance an obviously more assertive China and that such support might not be forthcoming from the United States. This made the Soviet Union a more attractive partner.

Vietnam's alliance with Moscow and Moscow's support for the ouster of China's Khmer Rouge ally strengthened Chinese convictions regarding Soviet intentions to surround China by forging strategic partnerships with nations that already had strained relationships with the PRC. Moscow's designs, active involvement in Afghanistan, and India's apparent receptivity raised security concerns about South Asia. Those concerns were elevated to an even higher level in December 1979 when Soviet troops invaded Afghanistan. Beijing interpreted these events as a serious and immediate threat to its own security.[29]

Beijing adopted a three-pronged strategy to deal with the security challenge in and from South Asia. One prong was to strengthen its relationships with India's neighbors, especially Pakistan. It did so by providing diplomatic support and increasingly sophisticated weapons.[30] The second prong was to increase the cost to the Soviet Union by providing military and other forms of assistance to the resistance in Afghanistan.[31] The third prong was to cooperate with the United States and Pakistan to aid the Afghan resistance.[32] This three-way cooperation not only raised the cost of the Soviet occupation; it also enabled China to bolster its new relationship with the United States. From Beijing's perspective, this cooperation with the United States underscored the importance of the united front against Soviet hegemony and reinforced the US-China strategic partnership to contain the Soviet Union. Cooperating with the United States might also have been designed, in part, to prolong the period in which Washington and its allies would be willing to assist China's modernization. Some in Beijing might have calculated or expected that cooperation would increase American tolerance for China's efforts to bolster Pakistan's ability to annoy and distract India.[33]

Regardless of exactly what Beijing expected to ensue from its cooperation with the United States in Afghanistan, it fit well with the objectives
and methods of the Ronald Reagan administration that took office in 1981.
Reagan's campaign rhetoric and the switch from a liberal Democrat to a
conservative Republican administration raised questions about the durability of US willingness to assist China's modernization.[34] Cooperation in
Afghanistan helped keep open the window of opportunity during the period in which engagement had yet to produce a critical mass of commercial
and other ties.

The first phase of China's engagement with South Asia during the era of
reform and opening witnessed increasingly numerous official visits and diplomatic interchange, but trade remained minimal.[35] China's interests and
goals in the region were limited almost entirely to the security arena. Moreover, South Asia was primarily a venue for Chinese activity focused on its
principal adversary, the Soviet Union, and its principal strategic partner, the
United States. This situation changed during the next phase of interaction.

### 1992–2001: External Conditions Change, and So Do China's Priorities

The end of the Cold War enabled and required China to adjust its policies
toward many regions, including South Asia. The Soviet withdrawal from
Afghanistan in 1989 removed one link in the chain of states perceived as dangerous by Beijing because they were allied with a strong adversary and located
on China's periphery. The demise of the Soviet Union itself in December
1991 ended the danger of Soviet encirclement. It also changed Beijing's view
of India because India without the Soviet Union was perceived as much less
dangerous to China and its interests. This, in turn, changed Chinese views
on the strategic utility of its relationship with Pakistan.[36]

The end of the Cold War also changed Chinese perceptions of and concerns regarding the United States. Concerns about Soviet intentions and
capabilities triggered and undergirded rapprochement between Washington and Beijing and provided the principal rationale for enabling China to
become stronger through access to opportunities available only in the free
world. That being the case, Beijing naturally worried—expected—that the
United States would lose enthusiasm for China's efforts to become more
powerful, and that the anticipated closing of the window of opportunity

could occur at any time. China, like all other countries that had looked to Washington during the Cold War, was less dependent on the United States for security. Indeed, many in China and elsewhere began to regard the danger of pressure from the United States as even more worrisome than the dangers of a bipolar world.[37] With the Soviet Union out of the equation, China needed a way to protect its security by developing a new arrangement to counterbalance and constrain the United States.

Though China was more worried about Washington, it still needed American cooperation and assistance to achieve its developmental goals. The reform and opening strategy was working. It had taken several years for China to make necessary internal reforms, adopt (or acquiesce to) rules and norms of the free-world system, attract foreign direct investment, build facilities, and begin to realize the benefits of export-led growth, and China's sunk costs were relatively high. Big payoffs were still over the horizon, and China still had a long way to go to become a middle-income country. It still needed the cooperation of United States and access to the US-led system. In other words, China's long-term security depended on its ability to prolong access to opportunities available only in what had been known as the free world.

In addition to uncertainty about whether or for how long the United States would facilitate China's rise, Chinese officials had to be concerned that the end of the Cold War would open the way for many other countries to gain access to the opportunities that had been available only to China and formal allies of the United States. With the demise of the Soviet Union, the term *free world* became instantly anachronistic, and the liberal international order that had been off-limits to Soviet allies or unacceptable to nonaligned nations became the only game in town.[38] For the first time since adoption of the new strategy, China faced the prospect of serious competition from other developing countries, many of which had considerably less authoritarian governments than did China.

Three additional factors remain to be introduced into Beijing's calculus with respect to South Asia. All warrant more extensive treatment than they receive here. One involved changes in US perceptions, priorities, and policies with respect to Pakistan. The Soviet invasion of Afghanistan in 1979 had rekindled US interest in Pakistan and paved the way for the resumption of military sales and foreign aid and a relatively greater willingness to overlook Pakistani developments of concern to the United States.[39] This interest was reduced or abandoned shortly after the last Soviet soldier withdrew from

Afghanistan. In 1990, Washington again curtailed military assistance.[40] The stated and decisive reason was that the cutoff was triggered by Pakistan's nuclear weapons program, but the broader reason is that Washington's interest and stake in Pakistan declined substantially when the Soviet Union left Afghanistan and even more when the Soviet Union ceased to exist. Additional sanctions were imposed after Pakistan's 1998 nuclear tests.[41]

The second factor was that, by the early 1990s, India had begun to adopt more open economic policies.[42] This changed the calculus of both China and the United States. China faced the possibility that India would become a serious competitor for foreign direct investment, loans from the World Bank and other international financial institutions, and low-skill/ low-wage opportunities in increasingly global production chains. China had a thirteen-year head start, but the fact that India was a democracy was thought to give it a competitive advantage. Reforms to India's economic system substantially increased US interest in broadening and deepening its relationship with India. Beijing noted this and worried that US interest in India could reduce US willingness to assist China's modernization.[43]

A third factor in the new equation was growing US concern about the spread of nuclear and missile technologies and the roles played by Pakistan and China. The dynamic here was complicated and only imperfectly understood, but some of the key elements were that China was providing assistance to Pakistan's nuclear and missile programs, and that Pakistan (and/or Pakistani agents) were providing nuclear assistance to North Korea, Iran, and Libya. China was also providing direct assistance to Iran's nuclear and missile programs.[44] India was also developing several new missiles and building nuclear warheads; Pakistan sought to match what India was doing, ratcheting up the level of sophistication and the danger of both an out-of-control arms race and the potential for escalation. The United States was putting increasing pressure on China to halt the sale of both missiles and nuclear technologies, including sales to Pakistan.[45]

Before describing what China did with respect to South Asia during this period, it will be useful to examine how the factors just summarized shaped China's perceptions of and priorities toward the region. Security remained China's number-one concern, but Beijing's security calculus changed. With the Soviet Union gone, Beijing no longer had to worry about Moscow-led efforts to surround China with pliable clients of the USSR. This meant that Beijing no longer had to view India through the lens of concern about Moscow. India by itself was not considered to pose a very serious security threat to the PRC. That, in turn, reduced the need for and value of a relationship with Pakistan designed primarily to complicate India's security calculations and to raise the costs to Moscow of its South Asian ambitions.

Elimination of the Soviet threat raised two kinds of security concerns with respect to the United States. One set centered on the possibility that the United States would use its probably temporary unipolar status to spread American ideology (e.g., liberal democracy, human rights, competitive markets, and free trade) and effect regime change in countries that did not acquiesce immediately to US demands for change. This concern led China to champion early establishment of a multipolar world in which the United States might be primus inter pares but would be incapable of acting unilaterally.[46] The second set of concerns centered on China's need to prolong its privileged access to the benefits of participation in the US-led system. Participation in that system was helping China to grow rapidly and add technical and, increasingly, military capabilities judged essential to ensure security over the long term.

Changes in the international system prompted changes in Chinese foreign policy toward many countries and regions, but we focus here on what it did with respect to South Asia. Perhaps the most important changes in perception and policy were those centered on judgments about India's danger as a rival and potential value as a partner and associated judgments about the costs and benefits of the special relationship with Pakistan. India was seen to pose less of a threat because it was no longer aligned with the Soviet Union.[47] India was still an ideological and nascent economic rival, but it also offered new potential for economic cooperation. Pakistan, on the other hand, began to appear less necessary to annoy and confound India and more significant as an impediment to prolonging China's access to the US-led liberal order.

Probably the biggest source of friction in US-China relations during this period was Beijing's sales of nuclear and missile technologies. The friction was greatest with respect to Iran, where China had done more and been caught in a lie more often, but it also extended to Pakistan. By the mid-1990s (before the 1998 nuclear tests), China terminated most of the proliferation activities that the United States found objectionable, including those involving Pakistan. Prolonging access to the US-led system that facilitated China's rise seemingly trumped China's determination to remain an all-weather friend to Pakistan.[48]

It would be both easy and an error to overstate the magnitude of China's tilt away from Pakistan and toward India, but that such a tilt was occurring was increasingly apparent. For example, after years of inaction, China and India resumed talks to defuse their border disputes and exchanged a number of high-level visits. The talks and visits did not score any major breakthroughs, but there was marked improvement in the tone of the relationship.[49] Avoiding instability inimical to the developmental plans of both nations was surely a part of the calculation of each side, as was the potential for mutually advantageous economic ties. An additional, and probably stronger, motivation was to explore ways to cooperate with each other and with other countries to check the unipolar power of the United States and, for China, to limit the potential for improving relations between the United States and India to become an "anti-China" coalition of democracies with the express goals of pressing for regime change in China and containing China's rise.[50]

### 2001–Present: Increasing Rivalry and Cooperation

China's security concerns with respect to South Asia continued to evolve in the late 1990s and early years of the twenty-first century. Picking 2001 as a breakpoint captures an important subset of the changes—namely, those associated with the US-led war on terrorism and renewed military operations in Afghanistan, but China's goals and policies were also shaped by other dynamics. One of the dynamics was China's sustained economic growth and increasing demand for energy, minerals, and other resources needed by its growing economy and increasingly prosperous middle class. The search for additional sources of supply led to greater Chinese interest and involvement in parts of the world that had been much less important to the success of the reform and open policy during its first two decades. This search, encapsulated by Beijing's 1999 admonition to go abroad, caused China to look at South Asia as more than the locus of potential security problems.[51]

Changes occurring in South Asia also influenced Chinese perceptions and priorities. In Pakistan, the interplay of increasing political and religious extremism, poor economic performance, and the seeming inability of government agencies and the political system to manage the nation's increasingly serious problems made it a potentially less reliable and more costly partner. The situation in India seemed to be moving in a more positive direction. Economic reform was producing higher rates of growth and greater engagement in the global economy, including steady increases in trade with China. The picture was not uniformly positive from Beijing's perspective, however. India continued to expand and improve its military capabilities, especially its nuclear, naval, and missile forces—that is, capabilities with the potential to threaten or challenge China.[52] It also continued to expand and strengthen its relationships with the United States and nations on China's periphery.[53]

Changes of the kinds summarized earlier acquired greater importance in Chinese thinking about the region, but they paled in comparison to the impact of events triggered by the terrorist attacks on September 11, 2001. Beijing approved of and supported US retaliation against the Taliban regime in Afghanistan because the regime had provided support and safe haven to al Qaeda, but China later became concerned about the scale and purpose of US and US-led military operations.[54] The Taliban regime was quickly overthrown and a new government, headed by Hamid Karzi, was established in December 2001. But the United States did not leave Afghanistan. Instead, it rebuilt relations with Pakistan, secured base access in Uzbekistan and Kyrgyzstan, and appeared to be settling in for an extended stay.

Chinese commentators, doubtless reflecting the thinking of at least some officials, began to express concern that these activities were part of a new US plan to surround China on the west, just as had been imputed to the Soviet Union in the 1980s.[55] These concerns were reinforced by Chinese perceptions and worries about the improving state of US-Indian relations, symbolized by the agreement (in 2005) to conclude the US-India Civil Nuclear Agreement and US efforts to sell advanced military equipment to New Delhi.[56] They were further reinforced—confirmed, in the view of some Chinese—by US efforts to revitalize its relationships with allies in East Asia and what it interpreted as US support for the Association of Southeast Asia Nations (ASEAN) countries that have territorial disputes with China.[57] Beijing saw India as attempting to strengthen its own relationships with many of the same countries and interpreted these moves as inherently anti-China.[58] Another strand in the string of Chinese concerns centered on discussion, by 2008 Republican presidential candidate John McCain and others, of a possible "league of democracies."[59] In Beijing, such discussions, together with US measures to bolster its alliance relationships and improving US-Indian relations, were interpreted as intended to check China's rise. Those harboring fears about such a possibility could also point to US support for the return to democracy in Pakistan.

A second dimension of China's changing security concerns in the region centered on proven and potential links between terrorist training and coordination in Pakistan-controlled Kashmir, in Pakistan proper, and along the Pakistan-Afghanistan border, as well as among Uighur separatist groups in western China. Chinese concerns about unrest and separatism in Xinjiang province and other areas with large Muslim populations antedates the events of September 11, but these concerns intensified after Beijing confirmed that an unknown number of Chinese Uighurs had received training in camps located in Pakistan before returning to Xinjiang to conduct acts of terrorism.[60]

China's fears may be exaggerated—the number involved appears to be small—but the number of terrorist incidents in China is growing, as is the number of demonstrations by Uighur groups and clashes between Uighurs and Chinese police.[61] Before September 11, some Chinese accused the United States of fomenting and abetting Muslim unrest in China. Such accusations have largely disappeared; they have been replaced by statements that describe the threat to China from Islamic extremists in terms reminiscent of the way George W. Bush administration officials described the terrorist threat to the United States.[62]

China has adjusted its policies toward South Asia in ways designed to alleviate threats to its security implied or inherent in all the changes summarized here. To address its concerns about the US presence, imputed plans to surround China, and concerns about Islamic extremists, it has sought to reinforce other methods by working through the Shanghai Cooperation Organization (SCO). China took the lead in establishing this group in 1996, when it was known as the Shanghai Five and consisted of China, Russia, Kazakhstan, Kyrgyzstan, and Tajikistan, primarily to limit Russia's ability to reassert influence in Central Asia. It also took the lead in expanding and redefining the organization in 2001, when Uzbekistan joined and the counterterrorism mission was given much greater importance.[63] Afghanistan, Pakistan, and India (as well as Iran and Mongolia) have observer status. Beijing has blocked US efforts to become an official observer.

The SCO has few accomplishments, but it is the first multilateral organization formed and catalyzed by China. When depicted on a map treating observer nations as part of the group, it covers a huge expanse of territory and contains almost half the people in the world, but to date its potential exceeds its performance. Nevertheless, as a sign of Chinese concern about the region, and the specific problems addressed by the SCO, it warrants attention as a possible harbinger of Chinese approaches elsewhere and for its significance in future Chinese policy toward South and Central Asia.

The third facet of China's revised policies toward the region is focused on its need for resources to sustain the high growth rates that undergird the legitimacy of party rule. Apparently preferring, when possible, to rely on internal supply lines that do not require transit on the high seas or through vulnerable choke points, Beijing has evinced considerable interest in developing production and transport facilities in South (and Central) Asia.[64] Afghanistan's rich deposits of key metals and minerals are largely undeveloped. China appears prepared to invest the large sums required and to accept the risks of operating in a country that is likely to remain unstable for a considerable time.[65]

China did not contribute to the International Security Assistance Force for Afghanistan, but it has contributed modestly (approximately $250 million) to reconstruction funding. Beijing may calculate that avoiding the stigma of participation of what is widely seen as an occupation force and avoiding friction with the Afghan government, of the kinds experienced by nations seeking to reduce corruption, enhance democracy, and increase capacity, will make it easier for Chinese entities to operate in Afghanistan after most of the troops and aid workers have departed. Beijing's calculus might be right. But this approach risks underscoring China's reputation for free riding on the efforts of others and having to intervene unilaterally to protect its investments and its people.

The quest for resources and more secure lines of communication—as well as political and humanitarian reasons—has led China to significantly increase aid to and investment in Pakistan. China does not want Pakistan to be unstable or become a failed state, and it will do what it can, and what it thinks will work, to prevent that from happening. This could become an increasingly costly burden because it seems unlikely that the United States will continue to pump large amounts of money into the country after most of its troops have been withdrawn from Afghanistan in 2016.

China's largest project in Pakistan is the port of Gwadar that is currently under construction and will be operated by the Chinese.[66] China is also building a major port in Sri Lanka and investing heavily in the Hambantota Development Zone.[67] The ports will be important hubs for China's seaborne commerce and, potentially, could be used by China's navy when it is able to patrol more extensively to defend its commercial ships and sea-lanes.

China's stake in the region continues to shift from narrowly defined security concerns centered on India, especially its earlier relationship with the Soviet Union and evolving ties to the United States, to broader concerns about stability and economic security. Trade between China and all countries in the region is greater than is the trade between any two countries in South Asia. Trade and investment fosters interdependence and increases the stake that all countries have in the stability and capacities of all other countries on which they depend for markets, manufactured products, commodities, and transit routes. This makes it a safe prediction that China's stake in the region will increase, and all regional countries, including India, will become increasingly dependent on China.

## Net Assessment

China's relationship with South Asia has long centered on Beijing's security concerns. A clear, but unannounced, objective of China's policy is to ensure that no nation outside the region is able to use alliances, partnerships, or other relationships to surround, contain, or constrain China. During the Cold War, the Soviet Union was regarded as the country most likely to exploit relations with India and Afghanistan to China's detriment. This made Pakistan a natural partner in a classic "enemy of my enemy is my friend" arrangement. China responded to the end of the Cold War by forming the Shanghai Five (later the SCO) to constrain Russia from dominating the Central Asian states that had been part of the USSR, and to make it more difficult for the United States to replace the USSR as a major player in the Great Game.

India was and is the strongest nation in the region and the one that hedges most strongly against the possibility of Chinese assertiveness. It does so by building its own military capabilities and by informal cooperation and alignment with the United States and countries in Southeast Asia. China counters this by maintaining its own constructive relationship with the United States and by taking advantage of the desire of India's neighbors to enlist China's assistance to counterbalance the strongest country in the region.

China's most pressing concern with respect to the region comes not from major powers but from terrorists and the danger of instability in Pakistan. Pakistan regards China as an all-weather friend—in contrast to the fair-weather friendship with the United States—and will become more dependent on China as the United States draws down in Afghanistan and curtails the massive payments it has provided for more than a decade.

Other states in the region fear China less than they worry about India. They welcome Chinese investment, arms, and diplomatic attention. There is little ideological appeal and no cultural affinity, but there are also no significant historical obstacles to "normal" state-to-state and economic relations. The desire of these states to have relationships with China that enable them to counterbalance India gives China marginal additional leverage in its dealings with India, but long-standing security concerns and animosities are giving way to mutual economic interests and a shared stake in preserving stability in the region so that all can pursue their developmental objectives and preventing the sale or loss of nuclear weapons to nonstate actors.

Prospects for gradual expansion and deepening of relations between all countries in the region and China exceed those for deepening of relationships among regional states. They also exceed those for military conflict between China and India. That said, South Asia is likely to remain much less important to China's developmental and security policies than many other regions of the world.

*Notes*

1. See, for example, Yaacov Y. I. Vertzberger, *The World in Their Minds: Information Processing, Cognition, and Perception in Foreign Policy Decisionmaking* (Stanford, CA: Stanford University Press, 1990); and Robert Jervis, *Perception and Misperception in International Politics* (Princeton, NJ: Princeton University Press, 1976).

2. For additional information on Deng's policy of reform and opening, see Ezra F. Vogel, *Deng Xiaoping and the Transformation of China* (Cambridge, MA: Belknap Press, 2011), especially chaps. 7–12.

3. See "Communiqué of the Third Plenary Session of the 11th CPC Central Committee," December 22, 1978, *Beijing Review*, October 10, 2008, http://www .bjreview.com.cn/special/third_plenum_17thcpc/txt/2008-10/10/content_156226.htm.

4. For several examples of Mao's thinking about the inevitability of war, see Xiaobing Li and Hongshan Li, *China and the United States: A New Cold War History* (Lanham, MD: University Press of America, 1998).

5. See, for example, Carol Lee Hamrin, *China and the Challenge of the Future* (Boulder, CO: Westview Press, 1990), especially chap. 5.

6. See, for example, Robert S. Ross, *Chinese Security Policy: Structure, Power and Politics* (New York: Routledge, 2009), especially chap. 2.

7. See, for example, Aparna Pande, *Explaining Pakistan's Foreign Policy: Escaping India* (New York: Routledge, 2011), chap. 5.

8. See, for example, John W. Garver, *Protracted Contest: Sino-Indian Rivalry in the Twentieth Century* (Seattle: University of Washington Press, 2001), chap. 4.

9. See, for example, J. Mohan Malik, "South Asia in China's Foreign Relations," *Pacifica Review* 13, no. 1 (2001): 73–90.

10. For more on Pakistan's membership in these two anticommunist alliances, see Mohammed Ayub Khan, "The Pakistan-American Alliance," *Foreign Affairs* 42, no. 2 (1964): 195–209; and Chapter 6.

11. See Dennis Kux, *India and the United States: Estranged Democracies, 1941–1991* (Washington, DC: National Defense University Press, 1992).

12. Garver, *Protracted Contest.*

13. See, for example, Harry Harding, *China's Second Revolution: Reform After Mao* (Washington, DC: Brookings Institution Press, 1987), chap. 2.

14. World Bank, *World Development Indicators* database, http://databank .worldbank.org/data/reports.aspx?source=world-development-indicators#.

15. See Vogel, *Deng Xiaoping*; and Thomas Fingar, "China's Vision of World Order," in *Strategic Asia 2012–13: China's Military Challenge*, ed. Ashley Tellis and Travis Tanner (Seattle, WA: National Bureau of Asian Research, 2012), 343–373.

16. Fingar, "China's Vision."

17. Vogel, *Deng Xiaoping*, chap. 11 and the works cited on pp. 789–795.

18. Ibid.; Fingar, "China's Vision."

19. See, for example, Ross, *Chinese Security Policy*, chap. 8.

20. See Stefan Stahle, "China's Shifting Attitude Towards United Nations Peacekeeping Operations," *China Quarterly* 195 (2008): 631–655.

21. See, for example, Bronson Percival, *The Dragon Looks South: China and Southeast Asia in the New Century* (Westport, CT: Praeger, 2007); and John W. Garver, *The China-India-U.S. Triangle: Strategic Relations in the Post–Cold War Era* (Seattle, WA: National Bureau of Asian Research, 2002).

22. Deng Xiaoping, "Speech by Chairman of the Delegation of the People's Republic of China, Deng Xiaoping, at the Special Session of he U.N. General Assembly," April 10, 1974, http://www.marxists.org/reference/archive/deng-xiaoping/1974/04/10.htm.

23. See Barry Naughton, *Growing Out of the Plan: Chinese Economic Reform, 1978–1993* (Cambridge: Cambridge University Press, 1996).

24. See, for example, Thomas Robinson, "China Confronts the Soviet Union: Warfare and Diplomacy on China's Inner Asian Frontiers," in *The Cambridge History of China*, vol. 15, *The People's Republic, Part 2: Revolutions Within the Chinese Revolution, 1966–1982*, ed. Roderick MacFarquhar and John K. Fairbank (Cambridge: Cambridge University Press, 1991), 218–300.

25. See, for example, John W. Garver and Fei-Ling Wang, "China's Anti-encirclement Struggle," *Asian Security* 6, no. 3 (2010): 238–261.

26. See, for example, John W. Garver, "The Indian Factor in Recent Sino-Soviet Relations," *China Quarterly* 125 (1991): 55–85.

27. See, for example, Nayan Chanda, *Brother Enemy: The War After the War* (New York: Harcourt Brace, Jovanovich, 1986); and David P. Chandler, *The Tragedy of Cambodian History: Politics, War, and Revolution Since 1945* (New Haven, CT: Yale University Press, 1993).

28. Vogel, *Deng Xiaoping*, chap. 11.

29. Garver, *Protracted Contest*, chap. 8.

30. Ibid.; Daniel Byman and Roger Cliff, *China's Arms Sales: Motivations and Implications* (Santa Monica, CA: RAND, 1999), chap. 3.

31. See, for example, Steve Coll, *Ghost Wars: The Secret History of the CIA, Afghanistan, and Bin Laden, from the Soviet Invasion to September 10, 2001* (New York: Penguin, 2004).

32. Coll, *Ghost Wars*; S. Mahmud Ali, *US-China Cold War Collaboration, 1971–1989* (New York: Routledge, 2005), chap. 7.

33. See, for example, "Declassified Documents Show That, for over Fifteen Years, Beijing Rebuffed U.S. Queries on Chinese Aid to Pakistani Nuclear Program," *National Security Archive*, March 5, 2004, http://www.gwu.edu/~nsarchiv/NSAEBB/NSAEBB114/press.htm.

34. See, for example, Henry Kissinger, *On China* (New York: Penguin, 2011), chap. 14.

35. See Garver, *Protracted Contest*, chap. 8.

36. See, for example, Garver, *The China-India-U.S. Triangle*; and Waheguru Pal Singh Sidhu and Jingdong Yuan, *China and India: Cooperation or Conflict* (Boulder, CO: Lynne Rienner, 2003), chap. 1.

37. See, for example, Kissinger, *On China*, chap. 17; and Yuan-kang Wang, "China's Response to the Unipolar World: The Strategic Logic of Peaceful Development," *Journal of Asian and African Studies* 45, no. 5 (2010): 554–567.

38. See, for example, Charles A. Kupchan, *No One's World: The West, The Rising Rest, and the Coming Global Turn* (New York: Oxford University Press, 2012); and Robert Kagan, *The World America Made* (New York: Alfred A. Knopf, 2012).

39. See, for example, "A. Q. Khan's Nuclear Network: US Sanctions Against Pakistan over Nuclear Weapons," *History Commons*, http://www.historycommons

.org/timeline.jsp?aq_khan_nuclear_network_tmln_us_intelligence_on_pakistani_
nukes=aq_khan_nuclear_network_tmln_us_sanctions&timeline=aq_khan_nuclear
_network_tmln (accessed May 4, 2015).

40. Ibid.; Paul K. Kerr and Mary Beth Nikitin, *Pakistan's Nuclear Weapons:
Proliferation and Security Issues* (Washington, DC: Congressional Research Service,
March 19, 2013), http://www.fas.org/sgp/crs/nuke/RL34248.pdf.

41. Kerr and Nikitin, *Pakistan's Nuclear Weapons.*

42. See, for example, Jalal Alamgir, *India's Open-Economy Policy: Globalism,
Rivalry, Continuity* (New York: Routledge, 2009).

43. See, for example, David M. Lampton, *Same Bed, Different Dreams: Managing US-China Relations, 1989–2000* (Berkeley: University of California Press, 2001),
chap. 7.

44. See Evan S. Medeiros, *Reluctant Restraint: The Evolution of China's Nonproliferation Policies and Practices, 1980–2004* (Stanford, CA: Stanford University Press,
2007), chaps. 2–3.

45. Ibid.; Bates Gill, *Rising Star: China's New Security Diplomacy*, rev. ed.
(Washington, DC: Brookings Institution Press, 2010), chap. 3.

46. See, for example, Yang Deng, "Hegemon on the Offensive: Chinese Perspective on the US Global Strategy," *Political Science Quarterly* 116, no. 3 (2001):
343–365.

47. Garver, *Protracted Contest,* chap. 8; Garver, *The China-India-U.S. Triangle.*

48. Chapter 6 anticipates that China will continue to accord special status to
its relationship with Pakistan, but I do not share that judgment. I view China's
attitude toward Pakistan (and other countries) as shaped more by instrumental
considerations than by loyalty or appreciation for past contributions, and by expectations that Islamabad is unlikely to be less calculating and perfidious in its
future dealings with China than in its past relations with the United States.

49. Jonathan Holslag, *China and India: Prospects for Peace* (New York: Columbia University Press, 2010), chap. 2.

50. See, for example, Garver, *The China-India-U.S. Triangle;* and Jia Qingguo,
"Learning to Live with the Hegemon: Evolution of China's Policy Toward the US
Since the End of the Cold War," *Journal of Contemporary China* 14, no. 44 (2005):
395–407.

51. See "Freeman Briefing, May 27, 2008: Issue in Focus: China's 'Going Out'
Investment Policy," Center for Strategic and International Studies, http://csis.org/
files/publication/080527_freeman_briefing.pdf. Chapter 4 presents a more san-
guine assessment of India's military buildup.

52. See Gurmeet Kanwal, "India's Military Modernization: Plans and Strategic
Underpinnings," National Bureau of Asian Research, September 24, 2012, http://
www.nbr.org/research/activity.aspx?id=275#.UcDUweD88so; and Hash V. Pant,

"India Comes to Terms with a Rising China," in *Strategic Asia 2011–12: Asia Responds to Its Rising Powers—China and India*, ed. Ashley J. Tellis, Travis Tanner, and Jessica Keough (Seattle, WA: National Bureau of Asian Research, 2011), 101–128.

53. See Mohan Malik, "India Balances China," *Asian Politics and Policy* 4, no. 3 (2012): 345–376.

54. See David Finkelstein, "China and Central Asia: Enduring Interests and Contemporary Concerns," CNA, September 2010, http://www.cna.org/sites/default/files/research/D0023642.A1.pdf.

55. See, for example, Andrew J. Nathan and Andrew Scobell, "How China Sees America: The Sum of Beijing's Fears," *Foreign Affairs* 91, no. 5 (2012): 32–47; and Kenneth Lieberthal and Wang Jisi, *Addressing U.S.-China Strategic Distrust* (Washington, DC: Brookings Institution, 2012), http://www.brookings.edu/~/media/research/files/papers/2012/3/30%20us%20china%20lieberthal/0330_china_lieberthal.

56. See, for example, Siddharth Varadarajan, "People's Daily Commentary on the Indian Nuclear Deal," *Reality, One Bite at a Time* blog, September 1, 2008, http://svaradarajan.blogspot.com/2008/09/peoples-daily-commentary-on-indian.html; and D. S. Rajan, "China Worried over US-India Military Cooperation," *Rediff*, September 24, 2009, http://news.rediff.com/column/2009/sep/24/china-worried-over-us-india-military-cooperation.htm.

57. See, for example, Robert Sutter and Chin-Hao Huang, "China–Southeast Asia Relations: US Interventions Complicate China's Advances," *Comparative Connections*, October 2010, http://csis.org/files/publication/1003qchina_seasia.pdf.

58. See, for example, Li Hongmei, "India's 'Look East Policy' Means 'Look to Encircle China'?" *People's Daily*, October 27, 2010, http://en.people.cn/90002/96417/7179404.html.

59. See, for example, Robert Kagan, "The Case for a League of Democracies," *Financial Times*, May 13, 2008, http://carnegieendowment.org/2008/05/13/case-for-league-of-democracies/28lb.

60. See, for example, Michael Wines, "China Blames Foreign-Trained Separatists for Attacks in Xinjiang," *New York Times*, August 1, 2011, http://www.nytimes.com/2011/08/02/world/asia/02china.html.

61. The largest recent clashes occurred in July 2009. See, for example, Edward Wong, "Riots in Western China amid Ethnic Tension," *New York Times*, July 5, 2009, http://www.nytimes.com/2009/07/06/world/asia/06china.html?ref=global-home.

62. See, for example, Davide Giglio, "Separatism and the War on Terror in China's Xinjiang Uighur Autonomous Region," United Nations Peace Operations Training Institute, http://cdn.peaceopstraining.org/theses/giglio.pdf (accessed May 4, 2015).

63. Chien-peng Chung, "The Shanghai Co-operation Organization: China's Changing Influence in Central Asia," *China Quarterly* 180 (2004): 989–1009.

64. See, for example, Erica Downs, "China Buys into Afghanistan," *SAIS Review* 32, no. 2 (2012): 65–83; and Alexandros Petersen, "A Hungry China Sets Its Sights on Central Asia," *The Atlantic*, March 5, 2013, http://www.theatlantic.com/china/archive/2013/03/a-hungry-china-sets-its-sights-on-central-asia/273746/.

65. Downs, "China Buys into Afghanistan."

66. See, for example, Ghulam Ali, "China's Strategic Interest in Pakistan's Port at Gwadar," *East Asia Forum*, March 24, 2013, http://www.eastasiaforum.org/2013/03/24/chinas-strategic-interests-in-pakistans-port-at-gwadar/.

67. Sudha Ramachandran, "China Moves into India's Back Yard," *Asia Times*, March 13, 2007, http://www.atimes.com/atimes/South_Asia/IC13Df01.html.

# THREE

# India's Relationships with the United States and China
## Thinking Through the Strategic Triangle

*S. Paul Kapur*

India's triangular relationship with China and the United States is an extremely important one, not just for Indian interests but also for the future of the Indian and Pacific Ocean regions. India's relations with China and the United States have varied widely in the past and have included periods of outright war, cold peace, and close strategic cooperation. How are Indian security elites likely to manage these relationships in the future?

Before addressing this question, one might ask whether Indian security managers actually possess a vision for the India–United States–China strategic triangle. Critics have argued that, on a number of the most pressing security issues, Indian strategic thinking has been lacking. For example, critics maintain, the Indians often buy conventional weapons systems without articulating a clear plan for them, take seemingly contradictory positions regarding the size and diversity of the nuclear force that they need to generate an acceptable level of deterrence, threaten robust retaliation against state sponsors of terrorism and then remain quiescent in the face of highly provocative terrorist acts, and seek to assume an international leadership role but seem hesitant to shoulder collective global burdens on issues ranging from the prevention of nuclear weapons proliferation to the protection of human rights.[1] Do the Indians have a more coherent approach to managing their relationships with China and the United States? Or is Indian thinking on this issue similarly underdeveloped?

Admittedly, the Indians do not have a fully formulated strategy for managing the India–United States–China triangle. Indeed, their statements and positions on this issue can be difficult to decipher and at times appear to be in tension with one another. Nonetheless, it is possible to discern broad themes in the Indian approach to dealing with the United States and China. As I explain later, the most important of these themes, which affects all others, is Indian concern about growing Chinese power. This concern not only drives Indian policy toward China; it also fundamentally affects Indian strategic calculations regarding the United States. India's policies toward the United States and China are thus interconnected, and it is impossible to understand the Indian position on one without considering its position on the other.

## China as Number One

Indian security elites view China as their number-one strategic challenge. They have no desire for conflict with China and believe that they can realize significant joint economic gains with the Chinese; indeed, China is India's largest trading partner. Nonetheless, the Indians are convinced that China poses the greatest of India's long-term strategic dangers.[2]

Analysts and commentators tend to focus the majority of their attention on the security competition between India and Pakistan. Of course, the Indo-Pakistani rivalry is extremely serious. The two countries have fought four conventional wars against each other. They continue to battle one another at the nonstate level, with the Pakistanis supporting an anti-Indian insurgency in the disputed territory of Jammu and Kashmir. This has generated spin-off terrorist violence in India proper, such as the 2008 attacks on Mumbai. Finally, the two countries have sizable nuclear arsenals trained on one another.[3]

Despite all these problems, however, Pakistan does not pose a significant, long-term strategic threat to India. Pakistan suffers from a number of severe handicaps, including economic stagnation, sectarian and ethnic strife, relatively limited territorial and human resources, and a government that struggles to provide its citizens with basic public goods. The Fund for Peace ranked it thirteenth out of the world's 125 most fragile states, between Guinea and Nigeria.[4]

In the military sphere, Pakistan does possess capable conventional and nuclear forces. These forces, however, are primarily defensive; they seek mainly to prevent India from using its superior conventional military capabilities to attack Pakistan, potentially resulting in a catastrophic Pakistani defeat similar to that of the 1971 Bangladesh war.[5] Pakistani nuclear forces are becoming more dangerous as Pakistan develops a battlefield nuclear capacity, which will feature small, short-range weapons stationed close to the Indo-Pakistani border in an effort to compensate for growing Indian conventional military capabilities. This will increase the likelihood of any Indo-Pakistani conventional confrontation escalating to the nuclear level. Such escalatory danger may give India pause if it contemplates aggressive military action against Pakistan in the future.[6] But there is little chance that it will enable Pakistan to launch any type of military offensive designed to capture large portions of Indian territory, to threaten India's nuclear second-strike capability, or to gain significant coercive leverage over India.

The Indians' main concern with Pakistan is its use of Islamist militants to fuel discontent and launch attacks in Indian Kashmir, as well as to strike targets within India proper. This strategic use of militancy can attrite Indian resources, inflict significant damage on India's population and territory, and potentially trigger an Indo-Pakistani conventional military conflict.[7] But these dangers, though significant, do not approach the magnitude of the challenge from China. Even major terrorist incidents, such as the 2008 attacks on Mumbai or possible Indo-Pakistani military confrontations, do not threaten to leave India economically and militarily outpaced by a regional competitor. China, if it continues on its current growth trajectory, could do that.[8]

Therefore, the main future challenge for Indian security managers is not Pakistan but China. China presents India with a twofold problem: material and ideational. At the material level, China possesses a more powerful military than does India. China's defense budget is roughly 2.5 times India's and the Chinese active-duty military is approximately 1.7 times larger. China also outmatches India in a range of conventional military capabilities, possessing roughly twice as many combat aircraft as India, four times as many submarines, and five times as many main battle tanks.[9] China's prowess is likely to grow further as it devotes more resources to defense in the coming years. Indeed, China appears likely not only to outspend India but also to become the world's largest military spender in the next two decades.[10] Higher Chinese defense spending will be facilitated by the relative robustness of its economy. With a gross domestic product of approximately $9 trillion, which is growing at about 8 percent per year, the Chinese economy is bigger and expanding more rapidly than India's $2 trillion economy, which is growing at only about 5 percent per year.[11]

At the ideational level, China's authoritarian political system reduces the transparency of its decision-making processes. This increases the difficulty of discerning Chinese intentions and heightens the incentives for Indian strategists to make worst-case assumptions regarding likely Chinese plans and preferences.[12] Exacerbating this problem are outstanding Sino-Indian border disputes. These disputes have led to past military confrontations, including a bloody 1962 war in which India was badly beaten, losing fourteen thousand square miles of territory to the Chinese. These disputes continue to fuel periodic diplomatic and military flare-ups. The problem is also worsened by China's assertive regional behavior, which recently has triggered confrontations over territorial disagreements with Vietnam, the Philippines, and Japan. This is leading many Indian strategists to conclude that China does not seek an egalitarian international commons in the Asia-Pacific region but rather prefers some form of Chinese-led hierarchy or hegemony.[13] Although it is theoretically possible, the real threat in such a scenario is not an outright Chinese invasion of India or a catastrophic Sino-Indian war. The danger, rather, is that through years of superior economic growth China could amass an overwhelming preponderance of power. This could leave India nominally free but unable in practice to resist Chinese coercive pressure.[14]

### Possible Indian Strategies

How can India ameliorate this danger? One possible response would be to adopt internal balancing strategies in order to increase India's military power. The Indians are, in fact, improving their military capabilities at both the conventional and the nuclear levels. In the conventional realm, India has become a major arms importer. Indeed, India was the world's largest arms purchaser between 2008 and 2012.[15] Specific Indian defense projects include raising a new mountain corps better to protect India's borders with China, updating fleets of ageing combat aircraft, and expanding the reach and sophistication of the navy by acquiring ships ranging from submarines to aircraft carriers. Overall, Indian leaders plan to spend $80 billion on further modernization programs by 2015.[16]

The Indians are also working to improve their nuclear weapons capabilities. Prime Minister A. B. Vajpayee originally justified India's 1998 nuclear tests with explicit reference to the threat from China.[17] Although nuclear weapons will not be useful to the Indians in every area of Sino-Indian security relations, they can provide India with a final line of defense, preventing China from threatening India's sovereignty or survival. Given China's significant conventional military superiority, this offers the Indians important reassurance.

As a result, the Indians are seeking both qualitative and quantitative improvements to their arsenal. For example, the Indians continue to produce fissile material and are increasing their production capacity. They are also significantly improving their delivery capabilities with platforms like the Agni V and the supersonic BrahMos cruise missile and diversifying their range of delivery platforms, working to develop the land-, air-, and sea-based capabilities needed to field a full nuclear triad.[18] Recently, following the test flight of its intermediate-range Agni V ballistic missile, Indian officials publicly stressed that Indian nuclear forces could now reach into all parts of Chinese territory. This point was not lost on the Chinese, who warned Indian leaders not to think that the missile test had bought them too much leverage against China.[19]

Internal balancing is not the only strategy that the Indians can employ to insulate themselves against the potential dangers of growing Chinese power; external balancing can be useful as well. Indian strategists envision that their external balancing efforts may, to varying degrees, involve United States support. India shares interests with the United States on a wide spectrum of strategic issues. Many of them, ranging from the promotion of free trade to countering Islamist terrorism, are unrelated to China. In addition to these issues, however, both countries share an interest in hedging against the uncertainties associated with China's rise.[20]

In the view of Indian security elites, United States support for Indian hedging strategies would not necessarily require the two countries to enter into any explicit partnership to constrain China or to engage in other formal cooperation. At the lower end of the spectrum, they believe that they could benefit simply from continued active US regional engagement, which would enhance security in the Indian and Pacific Ocean regions. An active presence enables the United States to use its diplomatic leverage and military power to provide regional public goods, such as secure sea-lines of communication, freedom of navigation, and more broadly, what it calls a "rules-based international order."[21] The provision of these goods generates a type of informal deterrence in the region, discouraging destabilizing behavior that would threaten to undermine them. Indian strategists value such informal deterrence. For although it involves relatively little explicit coordination with the United States, it can significantly enhance Indian security, leveraging US power to discourage possible disruptions associated with growing Chinese military and economic might.[22]

At the higher end of the spectrum, Indian external balancing efforts could involve more active cooperation with the United States to generate security in the Indian and Pacific Ocean regions. The nature of this cooperation could range widely. Some Indian strategists and officials, though favorably disposed toward closer US-India coordination, would be wary of departing too far from India's traditional nonaligned stance and working closely with the United States. They would prefer Indo-US cooperation to focus on measures, such as the transfer of military and other dual-use technology, that allow India better to protect itself but limit the United States' ability to interfere in Indian foreign and defense policy. By striking such a balance between cooperation and autonomy, they believe that India might also reduce the danger of appearing to be a pawn in US plans to contain China. If overly close US-India cooperation creates such an impression, it could threaten or anger China, making it more confrontational than it otherwise would be. Too-close cooperation could also create domestic political problems, given the Indian public's longstanding suspicion of American power.[23]

Other Indian strategists would support even closer cooperation between the United States and India, deliberately designed to contain the dangers of a rising China. This group views the Chinese challenge as particularly serious and believes that Indian and US interests on this issue are closely aligned. Neither country, the stategists believe, wants to see the domination of the Indo-Pacific Ocean region by a single hegemon; both want an egalitarian, open maritime commons, and both seek to create institutions promoting transparency and rule of law. These strategists would, therefore, support tight strategic coordination between India and the United States, potentially including steps toward military interoperability.[24]

At present, it is unclear where on this spectrum of cooperation Indian policy will ultimately fall. Any decisions will occur only after vigorous internal debates. It is important to note, however, that even if India moves toward relatively robust cooperation with the United States, it will continue to view its relationship with China as being extremely important. China is India's top trading partner. It wields considerably more military power than India, and unlike the United States, it is located in India's immediate geographic neighborhood. The maintenance of amicable Sino-Indian relations is thus essential to India, helping it continue expanding its economy while avoiding destructive military competition or confrontation. Thus, regardless of the nature of their relationship with the United States, the Indians will work hard to avoid confrontation with the Chinese and to cooperate with them wherever possible.[25]

We should also note that, although Indian and United States strategic interests overlap in many areas, they are by no means perfectly aligned. Numerous irritants and disagreements exist in the relationship, ranging from recriminations over India's recent failure to purchase US fighter jets to US frustration with India's nuclear liability law and Indian resentment at US attempts to pressure India into ostracizing Iran. Many of these problems, like US disappointment regarding some recent Indian military purchases, are relatively minor and are probably surmountable. Others, however, like pressure regarding Iran, engage delicate Indian strategic and domestic political sensitivities, and may not be amenable to compromise.[26]

It is also worth noting that, despite their considerable respect for Chinese power, Indian security elites are not all equally concerned about China. Indeed, some strategists believe that the dangers of China's rise may have been exaggerated. In this view, recent economic stumbles, demographic challenges, internal regional fissures, and poor relations with neighboring countries may impede the growth of Chinese power. Thus, even if China's rise is a foregone conclusion, the speed and extent of that rise could be in doubt. And this, in turn, could reduce the near-term likelihood of China's emergence as a hegemon able to force its will on India and other regional states. This uncertainty may increase the confidence of some members of the Indian strategic community as they contemplate their future relationship with the Chinese.[27]

Despite these complicating factors—internal debates over the optimal level of Indo-US cooperation; disagreements with the United States on a range of strategic and political irritants; the Indians' belief in the importance of good Sino-Indian relations; and a sense, in some circles, that China will pose less of an immediate threat than many have feared—the incentives will remain strong for India to cooperate more closely with the United States over the long term. China, regardless of its precise growth trajectory, will emerge as an important regional force in the years ahead, able to play a significant role in shaping the Indian Ocean and Asia-Pacific security environments. India will have no choice but to develop strategies to hedge against the potential dangers of Chinese power. Closer US-India strategic cooperation will be central to any hedging strategies, regardless of specific irritants in the relationship. India simply will not possess the economic, diplomatic, or military resources to go it alone.[28] As one senior Indian strategist put it, "At some point India will have to choose whom it wants to deal with—China or the United States. There is no doubt in anyone's mind as to the answer to that question."[29]

## The Problem of Trust

Despite the emergence of these strong cooperative incentives, an important obstacle to tight Indo-US security coordination remains from decades past: the issue of trust. This problem will pose perhaps the most significant impediment to close cooperation between the two countries in the future. Indians have long believed that the United States, which has historically supported Pakistan with large amounts of financial and military aid, which blocked Indian access to nuclear materials and technologies following India's 1974 "peaceful" nuclear explosion, and which levied economic sanctions against India in the wake of its 1998 nuclear tests, could not be relied on for critical military or diplomatic support.[30] Although this problem receded in recent years as India-US relations warmed, it has returned as a potentially significant difficulty. Indeed, many Indian security elites worry that the United States will prove to be a particularly unreliable partner in the years ahead.

The specific source of the current trust problem is the perception that the United States lacks the ability or the desire to remain actively engaged in the Indian Ocean/Asia-Pacific region. The drivers of this perception include general US fiscal disarray, looming cuts to the defense budget, impending withdrawal from Afghanistan, and US movement toward a significantly smaller nuclear arsenal. Indians fear that these could be signs of impending US global retrenchment. Such retrenchment would make the United States a poor choice for a regional security partner. Indeed, the establishment of close security relations with a retreating United States could hold significant dangers for India; the Indians would risk antagonizing China by partnering with the United States, only to be abandoned by the United States and eventually forced to face the Chinese alone.[31]

The logical solution to this problem would be a credible United States commitment to remain actively engaged in the Asia-Pacific region. The United States policy of rebalancing to Asia could serve just such a purpose. Although the policy is still in its early stages, United States leaders discussing the rebalance have sought to make clear the high geopolitical stakes that they see in Asia, have committed to shifting 60 percent of US naval forces to the Asia-Pacific region, and have identified India as a critical partner in the rebalance policy. Moreover, the manner in which US officials discuss the policy tends to be realist in nature, using language such as "global presence," "strengthening alliances and partnerships across all regions," "effectively operating . . . across all domains," and "defeating aggression by our adversaries, including those who seek to deny our power projection." Such language suggests assertive engagement and competition rather than retreat or retrenchment.[32] Considered in this light, it would appear that the rebalance could address the credibility concerns that the Indians are now voicing, signaling the United States' ongoing resolve to remain an active power in the Indian Ocean/Asia-Pacific region.

Indian strategists state that if the rebalance is, in fact, to address their concerns, the United States will have to explain more precisely the meaning of the policy. The United States has been an Asian power since the days of Commodore Perry. Given this long history of regional involvement, what about the rebalance policy will be new? What capabilities and commitments will it bring to bear that are not already part of the United States' strategic posture in Asia? What will it require of India and other regional countries? More important, regardless of its precise contours, will the rebalance policy help India to maintain and enhance norms and structures of law, commerce, and military power that ensure egalitarian, open access to the Indian Ocean/Asia-Pacific maritime domain, particularly in the face of a rising China that may have different preferences? For Indian strategists concerned about US commitment to the region, this is a crucial test that the rebalance policy needs to meet. To the extent that it can do so, the rebalance may help to assuage concerns about US global retreat and the desirability of the United States as a strategic partner. If the policy fails to do so, Indian concerns are likely to remain unabated.[33]

The more effectively the United States, through the rebalance and other policies, is able to reassure India of its resolve to remain globally engaged, the less likely India is to find regional strategic challenges such as those posed by China to be deeply threatening. This, in turn, will reduce the incentives for India to engage in potentially disruptive balancing behaviors, such as conventional and nuclear arms racing. The more India fears US retreat from the Indian and Pacific Ocean regions, by contrast, the greater the likelihood that it will engage in such balancing. This behavior might well threaten China, which could respond with increased competitive behavior of its own.[34] Thus, the manner in which India manages relations with China, its primary strategic competitor, will be determined to a significant degree by future US policy toward the Asia-Pacific region. This is an indication of how close US-India relations have grown in recent years and of the level of potential danger that the Indians perceive in rising Chinese power. And it reminds us that Indian relations with China and the United States must not be understood separately but rather in the context of one another. How India deals with China will be affected by its relationship with the United States. And the nature of its relationship with the United States will be determined, to a significant degree, by its concerns about China.

## Notes

S. Paul Kapur is a professor in the Department of National Security Affairs at the US Naval Postgraduate School and an affiliate at Stanford University's Center for International Security and Cooperation. The views that he expresses here are his own and do not necessarily reflect those of the Department of Defense or any other government agency. He thanks Ryan Jacobs for able research assistance.

1. See "India as a Great Power: Know Your Own Strength," *The Economist*, March 30, 2013, http://www.economist.com/news/briefing/21574458-india-poised-become-one-four-largest-military-powers-world-end; Stephen P. Cohen and Sunil Dasgupta, *Arming Without Aiming* (Washington, DC: Brookings Institution, 2010); George K. Tanham, *Indian Strategic Thought: An Interpretive Essay* (Santa Monica, CA: RAND, 1992); Vipin Narang, "Five Myths About India's Nuclear Posture," *Washington Quarterly* 36, no. 3 (2013): 143–157; Indrani Bagchi, "Strike by Even a Midget Nuke Will Invite Massive Response, India Warns Pak," *Times of India*, April 30, 2013, http://timesofindia.indiatimes.com/india/Strike-by-even-a

-midget-nuke-will-invite-massive-response-India-warns-Pak/articleshow/19793847 .cms; Somini Sengupta and Robert F. Worth, "India Vows No Retaliation," *New York Times*, December 11, 2008, http://www.nytimes.com/2008/12/12/world/ asia/12mumbai.html; Raj Chengappa and Shishir Gupta, "The Mood to Hit Back," *India Today*, May 27, 2002, pp. 27–30; and Ian Hall, "Tilting at Windmills? The Indian Debate over Responsibility to Protect After UNSC 1973," *Global Responsibility to Protect* 9, no. 1 (2013): 84–108.

2. See C. Raja Mohan, "China's Rise, America's Pivot, and India's Asian Ambiguity," *Seminar India* 641 (January 2013), http://carnegieendowment .org/2013/01/31/china-s-rise-america-s-pivot-and-india-s-asian-ambiguity; "China, Not Pakistan, Is India's Main Threat," NDTV, June 28, 2011, http://www.ndtv .com/article/india/china-not-pakistan-is-india-s-main-threat-115257; "China Poses Bigger Threat than Pakistan: Arun Shourie," *New Indian Express*, October 19, 2013, http://www.newindianexpress.com/states/tamil_nadu/China-poses-bigger -threat-than-Pakistan-Arun-Shourie/2013/10/19/article1843428.ece; and Rajat Pandit, "Two-Front War Remote, but Threat from China Real," *Times of India*, October 12, 2012, http://timesofindia.indiatimes.com/india/Two-front-war-remote -but-threat-from-China-real/articleshow/16775896.cms.

3. See generally Sumit Ganguly, *Conflict Unending: India-Pakistan Tensions Since 1947* (New York: Columbia University Press, 2002); Syed Shoaib Hasan, "Why Pakistan Is 'Boosting Kashmir Militants,'" *BBC News*, March 3, 2010, http://news.bbc.co.uk/1/hi/world/south_asia/4416771.stm; Hans M. Kristensen and Robert S. Norris, "Indian Nuclear Forces 2012," *Bulletin of the Atomic Scientists* 68, no. 4 (2012): 96–101; and Hans M. Kristensen and Robert S. Norris, "Pakistani Nuclear Forces 2011," *Bulletin of the Atomic Scientists* 67, no. 4 (2011): 91–99.

4. Fund for Peace, "Failed States Index 2012," 2012, p. 4, http://www.fundfor peace.org/global/library/cfsir1210-failedstatesindex2012-06p.pdf; see also Anatol Lieven, *Pakistan: A Hard Country* (New York: Perseus Books, 2011), 3–40; and Jayshree Bajoria, "Pakistan's Fragile Foundations," Council on Foreign Relations, March 12, 2009, http://www.cfr.org/pakistan/pakistans-fragile-foundations/ p18749.

5. See S. Paul Kapur and Sumit Ganguly, "The Jihad Paradox: Pakistan and Islamic Militancy in South Asia," *International Security* 37, no. 1 (2012): 114. Note that nuclear weapons have helped Pakistan aggressively challenge the status quo, but only when employed in combination with other types of capabilities, such as Pakistan-supported Islamist militants. Pakistani nuclear weapons alone have played a defensive role, deterring any potential Indian retaliatory attack against Pakistan. See generally S. Paul Kapur, *Dangerous Deterrent: Nuclear Proliferation and Instability in South Asia* (Stanford, CA: Stanford University Press, 2007).

6. See Feroz Hasan Khan, "Pakistan as a Nuclear State," in *Pakistan: Beyond the "Crisis State,"* ed. Maleeha Lodhi (Karachi, Pakistan: Oxford University Press, 2011), 279; and Rajesh Basrur, "South Asia: Tactical Nuclear Weapons and Strategic Risk," *RSIS Commentaries*, no. 65/2011 (April 2011), http://www.rsis.edu.sg/wp-content/uploads/2014/07/CO11065.pdf.

7. See Kapur and Ganguly, "The Jihad Paradox," 111–141.

8. See Sunil Khilnani, Rajiv Kumar, Pratap Bhanu Mehta, Prakash Menon, Nandan Nilekani, Srinath Raghavan, Shyam Saran, and Siddharth Varadarajan, *Non-Alignment 2.0: A Foreign and Strategic Policy for India in the 21st Century* (New Delhi: Center for Policy Research, 2012), 13; C. Raja Mohan, "Sino-U.S. Power Play in Asia: India's Imperatives," *Asia Blog*, April 10, 2013, http://asiasociety .org/blog/asia/sino-us-power-play-asia-indias-imperatives; and Kanti Bajpai, "Stumbling Tiger, Leaping Dragon?" *Times of India*, February 6, 2010, http:// timesofindia.indiatimes.com/edit-page/Stumbling-Tiger-Leaping-Dragon/article show/5539962.cms.

9. "Military Capabilities (China and India)," IHS Jane's database, 2013, http:// janes.ihs.com.

10. John Chipman, "Military Balance 2013 Press Statement," International Institute for Strategic Studies, March 14, 2013, http://www.iiss.org/en/about%20us/ press%20room/press%20releases/press%20releases/archive/2013-61eb/march-c5a4/ military-balance-2013-press-statement-61a2.

11. See Niranjan Rajadhyaksha, "How Far Ahead of India Is China?" *Livemint*, February 5, 2013, http://www.livemint.com/Opinion/9b5DO3aWhYDONSGd GV5lwI/How-far-ahead-is-China.html; and Steven Rattner, "India Is Losing the Race," *New York Times*, January 19, 2013, http://opinionator.blogs.nytimes .com/2013/01/19/india-is-losing-the-race/.

12. See Deepak Kapoor, "India's China Concern," *Strategic Analysis* 36, no. 4 (2012): 663, 665; Hash V. Pant, "Ambitious Neighbours Need Good Fences," *Telegraph*, November 22, 2012, http://www.telegraphindia.com/1121122/jsp/opinion/ story_16223462.jsp#.Va6pnIvZr8E; and Gurmeet Kanwal, "Defence Cooperation for Strategic Outreach," *Tribune*, July 17, 2012, http://www.tribuneindia.com/2012/ 20120717/edit.htm#6.

13. See Bharat Karnad, "Playing Hardball with China," *Security Wise*, December 16, 2011, http://bharatkarnad.com/2011/12/16/playing-hardball-with-china/; Sudhanshu Tripathi, "India's Concerns About China: The Escalating Military Threat," *World Affairs: The Journal of International Issues* 17, no. 3 (2013): 28–39; Monika Chansoria, "The US-China Contest: Is It All About the 'Pivot'?" Center for Land Warfare Studies, October 14, 2013, http://www.claws.in/1091/the-us -china-contest-is-it-all-about-the-%E2%80%9Cpivot%E2%80%9D-dr-monika

-chansoria.html; and Brahma Chellaney, "China's Hydro-Hegemony," *New York Times*, February 7, 2013, http://www.nytimes.com/2013/02/08/opinion/global/chinas-hydro-hegemony.html.

14. Author interviews with senior Indian Ministry of Foreign Affairs officials and members of Parliament, 2010–2012, New Delhi; Mohan, "China's Rise, America's Pivot, and India's Asian Ambiguity."

15. See "China Replaces UK as World's Fifth Largest Arms Exporter, Says SIPRI," Stockholm International Peace Research Institute, March 18, 2013, http://www.sipri.org/media/pressreleases/2013/ATlaunch.

16. See Mark Magnier, "India on Military Buying Spree," *Seattle Times*, April 1, 2012, http://www.seattletimes.com/nation-world/india-on-military-buying-spree/; Nicholas R. Lombardo, "India's Defense Spending and Military Modernization," *Current Issues*, no. 24 (2011), http://csis.org/files/publication/110329_DIIG_Current_Issues_24_Indian_Defense_Spending.pdf; and Gurmeet Kanwal, "Strike Corps for the Mountains," *India Strategic* 8, no. 8 (2013): 26–29.

17. See "Nuclear Anxiety: Indian's Letter to Clinton on the Nuclear Testing," *New York Times*, May 13, 1998, http://www.nytimes.com/1998/05/13/world/nuclear-anxiety-indian-s-letter-to-clinton-on-the-nuclear-testing.html. See also Toby Dalton and Jaclyn Tandler, "Understanding the Arms 'Race' in South Asia" Carnegie Endowment for International Peace, September 13, 2012, http://carnegieendowment.org/2012/09/13/understanding-arms-race-in-south-asia/dtjo.

18. See Ajey Lele and Parveen Bhardwaj, "India's Nuclear Triad: A Net Assessment," Institute for Defence Studies and Analyses, Occasional Paper No. 31, April 2013; and Shannon N. Kile and Hans M. Kristensen, "World Nuclear Forces: Indian Nuclear Forces," in *SIPRI Yearbook 2013: Armaments, Disarmament and International Security* (London: Oxford University Press, 2013), chap. 6.6.

19. As an editorial in the state-run *Global Times* put it, "India should not overestimate its strength. Even if it has missiles that could reach most parts of China that does not mean it will gain anything from being arrogant during disputes with China. India should be clear that China's nuclear power is stronger and more reliable. For the foreseeable future, India would stand no chance in an overall arms race with China." "India Being Swept Up by Missile Delusion," *Global Times*, April 19, 2012, http://www.globaltimes.cn/content/705627.shtml.

20. See Ashley J. Tellis, "Nonalignment Redux: The Perils of Old Wine in New Skins," Carnegie Endowment for International Peace, July 10, 2012, http://carnegieendowment.org/2012/07/10/nonalignment-redux-perils-of-old-wine-in-new-skins.

21. White House, "National Security Strategy," February 2015, p. 1, https://www.whitehouse.gov/sites/default/files/docs/2015_national_security_strategy.pdf.

22. S. Paul Kapur, "The Effects on South Asia of Deep US Nuclear Reductions," *Nonproliferation Review* 20, no. 2 (2013): 279–288.

23. See Rory Medcalf, "India Poll 2013," Lowy Institute, May 20, 2013, p. 15; Deepa M. Ollapally and Rajesh Rajagopalan, "India: Foreign Policy Perspectives of an Ambiguous Power," in *Worldviews of Aspiring Powers: Domestic Foreign Policy Debates in China, India, Iran, Japan and Russia,* ed. Henry R. Nau and Deepa M. Ollapally (Oxford: Oxford University Press, 2012), 101–105; C. Raja Mohan, "India: Between 'Strategic Autonomy' and 'Geopolitical Opportunity,'" *Asia Policy* 15 (2013): 21–25; "India Has to Be Wary of U.S. Influence," *The Hindu,* December 7, 2012, http://www.thehindu.com/todays-paper/tp-national/tp-newdelhi/india-has -to-be-wary-of-us-influence/article4172878.ece; Pratnashree Basu, Swagat Saha, and Mihir Bhonsale, "US Needs to Treat India as an Exception," Observer Research Foundation, July 16, 2013, http://www.observerindia.com/cms/sites/orfonline/ modules/report/ReportDetail.html?cmaid=54597&mmacmaid=54598; Saurav Jha, "U.S.-India Relations: Case-by-Case Basis, with No Guarantees," *World Politics Review,* February 9, 2012, http://www.worldpoliticsreview.com/articles/11428/u-s -india-relations-case-by-case-basis-with-no-guarantees; Arvind Gupta, "Prospects for Indo-US Relations After President Obama's Visit," Institute for Defence Studies and Analyses, December 6, 2010, http://www.idsa.in/idsacomments/ ProspectsforIndo-USrelationsafterPresidentObamasvisit_ArvindGupta_061210; and "US Attempts to Rope in India to Contain China: Report," *Economic Times,* February 20, 2012, http://articles.economictimes.indiatimes.com/2012-02-20/ news/31079740_1_china-india-relations-sino-indian-ties-china-and-india.

24. See "The China Challenge: Present and Former NSAs Debate India's Options," Indo Asian News Service, February 28, 2012, https://en-maktoob.news .yahoo.com/china-challenge-present-former-nsas-debate-indias-options-161927712 .html; Kanwal, "Defence Cooperation for Strategic Outreach"; Arun Kumar Singh, "Post-script to Ladakh," *Asian Age,* June 7, 2013, http://archive.asianage.com/ columnists/post-script-ladakh-563; C. Raja Mohan, "India, the United States and the Global Commons" (working paper, Center for a New American Security, U.S.- India Initiative Series, October 2010), 12–14; C. Raja Mohan, "Let's Get Real," *Indian Express,* June 6, 2012, http://archive.indianexpress.com/news/let-s-get-real/ 958268/; Ajaya Kumar Das, "India-U.S. Maritime Partnership: Time to Move Forward," *RSIS Policy Brief,* August 2012, pp. 4–5; Brahma Chellaney, "Asia's New Tripartite Entente," *Project Syndicate,* January 10, 2012, http://www.project -syndicate.org/commentary/asia-s-new-tripartite-entente; and S. Paul Kapur, "2010 U.S.-India Strategic Engagement," Defense Threat Reduction Agency, Conference Report No. ASCO 2010-037, September 2010, p. 5.

25. See "There Is No Mutually Agreed Border Between India, China: Alka Acharya," *IBN Live,* May 20, 2013, http://ibnlive.in.com/news/there-is-no

-mutually-agreed-border-between-india-china-alka-acharya/392879-3.html; M. K. Bhadrakumar, "Engaging China as a Friendly Neighbour," *The Hindu*, April 10, 2008, http://www.thehindu.com/todays-paper/tp-opinion/article1236391.ece; M. K. Bhadrakumar, "Strategic Realism," *Deccan Herald*, April 1, 2013, http://www.deccanherald.com/content/323186/strategic-realism.html; Alka Acharya, "The Strategic Stasis in the India-China Relationship," *Economic and Political Weekly* 48, no. 26–27 (2013): 25–29; and Ananth Krishnan, "Climate Cooperation Changing India-China Ties, Says Jairam Ramesh," *The Hindu*, April 9, 2010, http://www.thehindu.com/news/international/climate-cooperation-changing-indiachina-ties-says-jairam-ramesh/article392921.ece.

26. See Nitin Gokhale, "Behind India's US Fighter Snub," *The Diplomat*, May 27, 2011, http://thediplomat.com/2011/05/27/behind-india%E2%80%99s-us-fighter-snub/2/; "Nuclear Liability Law Poses Challenge to Indo-US N-Deal," *Economic Times*, September 13, 2013, http://articles.economictimes.indiatimes.com/2013-09-13/news/42041663_1_liability-law-nisha-desai-biswal-civil-nuclear-cooperation; Seema Sirohi and Samir Saran, "Looking Beyond the Honeymoon," *The Hindu*, September 29, 2012, http://www.thehindu.com/opinion/op-ed/looking-beyond-the-honeymoon/article3946259.ece; Alok Bansal, "Iran: Its Strategic Importance," *Strategic Analysis* 36, no. 6 (2012): 856–857; and Mohammed Wajihuddin, "India's 3.5 Crore Tehran Lobby," *Economic Times*, February 19, 2012, http://articles.economictimes.indiatimes.com/2012-02-19/news/31077171_1_iran-islamic-revolution-tehran.

27. See generally Subramanian Swamy, "Chinese Economy: A Ticking Time Bomb!" *Indian Defence Review*, November 17, 2012, http://www.indiandefencereview.com/news/chinese-economy-a-ticking-time-bomb/; "India Must Work Towards Better Ties with China, Says JNU Don," *Pioneer*, September 26, 2010; Subhash Kapila, "China Strategically Cornered Globally: India's Strategic Window of Opportunity," South Asia Analysis Group, Paper No. 5525, July 9, 2013; and S. C. Tyagi, "Can China Avoid the Economic Downturn," United Service Institution of India, August 30, 2012, http://www.usiofindia.org/Article/?pub=Strategic%20Perspective&pubno=33&ano=923.

28. See Tellis, "Nonalignment Redux."

29. Senior Indian strategic analyst, interview by the author, September 2012, New Delhi.

30. See Kanwal Sibal, "The Arc of the India-US Partnership," *Indian Defence Review* 27, no. 2 (2012), http://www.indiandefencereview.com/news/the-arc-of-the-india-us-partnership; Dennis Kux, *India and the United States: Estranged Democracies, 1941–1991* (Washington, DC: National Defense University Press, 1992), 279–344; Snehlata Panda, "India and the United States: Perceptions and Policy," *Strategic Analysis* 23, no. 1 (1999): 111–120; and S. Paul Kapur and Sumit Ganguly,

"The Transformation of US-India Relations: An Explanation for the Rapprochement and Prospects for the Future," *Asian Survey* 47, no. 4 (2007): 643–666.

31. See "Cut from the Same Cloth," *Hindustan Times*, February 3, 2013, http://www.hindustantimes.com/edits/cut-from-the-same-cloth/article1-1005896.aspx; Monika Chansoria, "Can US Back Its Asian Pivot?" *Sunday Guardian*, February 9, 2013, http://www.sunday-guardian.com/analysis/can-us-back-its-asian-pivot; Deepa M. Ollapally and Yogesh Joshi, "Indian Debates on America's Rebalance to Asia," Sigur Center for Asian Studies, Policy Brief July 2013, pp. 3–5; Arun Sahgal, "India and US Rebalancing Strategy for Asia-Pacific," Institute for Defence Studies and Analyses, July 9, 2012, http://www.idsa.in/idsacomments/IndiaandUS RebalancingStrategyforAsiaPacific_asahgal_090712; Ravi Shankar, "An Empire in Decline," *New Indian Express*, September 8, 2013, http://www.newindianexpress .com/magazine/An-empire-in-decline/2013/09/08/article1770839.ece; Sibal, "The Arc of the India-US Partnership"; and Mohan, "India: Between 'Strategic Autonomy' and 'Geopolitical Opportunity,'" 25.

32. See Leon E. Panetta, "Shangri-La Security Dialogue," speech given at the International Institute for Strategic Studies Shangri-La Dialogue, June 2, 2012, Singapore, http://www.defense.gov/speeches/speech.aspx?speechid=1681; and Leon E. Panetta, "Sustaining U.S. Global Leadership: Priorities for 21st Century Defense," Department of Defense, January 2012, http://www.defense.gov/news/ Defense_Strategic_Guidance.pdf.

33. Author interviews with senior Indian strategic analysts, members of Parliament, and Ministry of Foreign Affairs officials, September and December 2012, New Delhi, India; Manoj Joshi, "US, India and the New Lack of Strategic Trust," *Mid-day*, June 25, 2013, http://www.mid-day.com/columnists/2013/jun/250613-us -india-and-the-new-lack-of-strategic-trust.htm; Mohan, "India: Between 'Strategic Autonomy' and 'Geopolitical Opportunity,'" 25; "Cut from the Same Cloth."

34. Kapur, "The Effects on South Asia," 284. In the absence of a credible US commitment to the region, India would also be likely to engage in more active external balancing with regional states such as Australia, the Philippines, Vietnam, and Japan. It is difficult to know, however, how threatening China would perceive such behavior to be relative to closer Indian relations with the United States. By contrast, China would almost certainly view relatively greater Indian military capabilities to be more threatening than weaker Indian military capabilities. Robust Indian internal balancing efforts resulting from a lack of confidence in the United States would thus stand a good chance of increasing Sino-Indian tensions over what they would otherwise be.

# FOUR

# India's Rise and China's Response

*Hu Shisheng*

The growing strength and influence of China and India are changing the way they perceive and respond to one another and the way they are viewed by other nations. They have much in common (e.g., vast territories, enormous populations, rich cultures, and deep dissatisfaction with key aspects of the global order), but their fraught history, different political systems, and seemingly incompatible aspirations for regional dominance constrain cooperation and foster competition. How—and how effectively—they manage their bilateral relationship will shape the power shift in Asia and their ability to reform the international system. What they do and how they attempt to do it will be shaped by their priorities, perceptions of one another, and the actions of third parties. This chapter focuses primarily on Chinese perceptions and responses to India's rise.[1]

By and large, Chinese scholars and government officials have viewed the rise of India as a positive development, not a major source of concern. They anticipate—or hope—that a rising India will become China's strategic partner in a joint effort to reform the existing global economic order by increasing their voting rights in international institutions, safeguarding their prerogatives as developing countries, and working for the benefit of all emerging powers. Toward this end, China has endeavored to enhance strategic coordination and cooperation with India in international institutions, including the United Nations, the World Bank, the International Monetary Fund, the G-20, and the BRICS Summit. China has also sought to work with India on global developmental issues, such as climate change, Doha round trade negotiations, labor standards, intellectual property rights, and human rights, on which Beijing and New Delhi have similar goals and policies.[2] China's willingness to work with India and relatively benign view of India's rise are reinforced by conviction that structural factors and inherent contradictions in India's political system will prevent India from overtaking China in terms of comprehensive national strength. This conviction, which is based on Chinese perceptions and assessments of Indian capabilities, undergirds Beijing's judgment that India does not and will not pose a serious threat to China's interests. This perception—conviction—has been reinforced by China's consistently better economic performance, as measured by the widening gaps in both total gross domestic product (GDP) and GDP per capita.[3]

## India's Prospects for Achieving Great Power Status

Indian leaders aspired to great power status even before the country achieved independence from British colonial rule.[4] Their aspirations were largely unrealized until the end of the Cold War transformed the international arena and reforms alleviated contradictions between India's multiparty democratic political system and its rigid, state-controlled socialist economy.[5] Indeed, strong democratic institutions and beliefs and the deregulation of economic activities in the early 1990s have been critical to India's emergence as a rising power with tremendous potential to become an even more formidable and influential nation.

India's rise to great-power status has been and will continue to be facilitated by its favorable geostrategic conditions, large and youthful population, and rich cultural legacy. Indian culture and civilization have been dominant on the Asian subcontinent for a very long time, but they also exert strong influence in Southeast Asia and countries arrayed along the rim of the Indian Ocean.[6] The influence of Indian culture is apparent even in Tibet and more distant parts of East Asia.

India is a nation of superlatives in other ways as well. Its national territory exceeds that of all but six countries, and it ranks second in the world in terms of both population and arable land. India also benefits from favorable geographic and demographic factors. Its central location on the subcontinent relegates its South Asian neighbors to the periphery of the land mass and gives India unparalleled advantages to control the Indian Ocean and maritime chokepoints. It is also able to exercise influence through members of the Indian diaspora willing to serve as cultural envoys, diplomatic bridges, or political lobbyists for their country of origin. Thus, for example, the Indian Caucus in the US Congress played an important role in facilitating the conclusion of the 2008 US-India Civil Nuclear Agreement.[7]

India has already become an important global player. Its economy has grown by about 7 percent annually since it dismantled the "license Raj" (a convoluted system of licenses, permits, and quotas that had long stifled economic activity) in the early 1990s.[8] Among the big economies, only China has achieved a higher rate of growth. India's economy is now the ninth largest in the world, with a GDP of approximately $2 trillion.[9] Growth of the Indian economy slowed significantly as a result of the 2007–2008 global financial crisis and concomitant economic recession, especially in the United States and the European Union, which have been the major export markets and sources of foreign direct investment (FDI) for India. But the slowdown forced New Delhi to undertake reforms that included relaxing restrictions on foreign investment in retail, insurance, civil aviation, infrastructure, manufacturing, and other sectors. Moreover, reducing the budget deficit by cutting financial subsidies should facilitate a second wave of rapid growth, if the reforms are actually implemented.[10]

Other factors contributing to India's favorable prospects for sustained rapid development include abundant manpower, a vigorous internal market, an impressive information technology-enabled service industry, highly developed legal and financial systems, vigorous protection of intellectual property, and very competitive private firms. Competition among India's state governments (e.g., those of Gujarat and Maharashtra) to foster growth and attract investment adds additional impetus to the process of development.[11]

India has also been taking steps to modernize its military capabilities with the goal of making the transition from a big military country to a powerful military country. With the third largest army, fifth-ranked navy, and one of the most powerful air forces in the world, India is well on the way to achieving this goal. Further modernization is to be achieved through a tripartite approach that combines indigenous research and development (R&D), joint R&D, and purchases of military equipment and technology from abroad. Indigenous R&D enabled India to become the fourth country with the capability to deliver nuclear weapons via intercontinental ballistic missiles, the fifth country to have self-made medium and heavy aircraft carriers, and the sixth country to have nuclear-powered submarines. The Stockholm International Peace Research Institute calculates that India was the largest importer of weapons from 2007 to 2011.[12] This three-part approach has enabled India to make impressive progress in its effort to build a nuclear triad of bombers, ballistic missiles, and submarine launched missiles and to maintain three carriers in the Indian Ocean.

Diplomatically, India has been both visible and vocal on the world stage, particularly in the Indo-Pacific region. New Delhi has developed good relations with all the major powers and country-groups in the region and beyond. India's democratic dividend (as the world's largest democratic country) has proven to be an important asset in its effort to do so. Only some of the nations in the region worry about the threat posed by India, and all things considered, the external environment is favorable for India to become a globally influential power.

In addition to the conditions just noted, India benefits from the existence of a number of societal shock absorbers and safety valves. Its principal religious faiths and the Hindu caste system contribute to strongly fatalistic attitudes among the ordinary people, with the majority being content with their lot in this life. The multiparty voting system has enabled all classes and groups to vent their frustration and dissatisfaction in ways that usually prevent eruption of the social and political volcano. The long tradition of a professional public service underpins a strong and stable system of governance, despite changes of government. The leftist movement and one-man–one-vote system of voting have forced successive governments to maintain rigid labor laws to safeguard the rights of employees and a system of representation designed to protect minorities.[13] These and other systems and regimes constitute an architecture that contributes to the maintenance of social stability and prevent destructive distortion of national development like what happened in China during 1960s and 1970s.

The conditions outlined here have enabled India to achieve rapid development since the 1990s and to become a significant emerging power in the international arena. India's rise is irreversible, but a number of internal and external factors are likely to constrain the pace.

One constraint is the fragmented character of the political system, which has reduced government efficiency and capacity to make and implement policy decisions. There are too many parties to achieve electoral or policy outcomes with coherent programs or approaches to address national problems.

There were 192 registered parties in India's first general election (in 1951–1952). The number had risen to 369 in the 2009 election. Fragmented politics leads to coalition governments and requires lengthy political bargaining to achieve compromise solutions that satisfy no one and often are internally inconsistent. Coalition politics are the norm at both the national and local government levels, and even the largest parties are susceptible to blackmail by smaller partners. Policy making at the national level is often hostage to local issues and parochial politics, making it difficult to develop or pursue a long-term strategy. Excessive democracy, or at least the multiplicity of competing parties, has slowed India's rise. One consequence is that the gap between China and India, measured in term of comprehensive strength and even in GDP per capita, could continue to widen.

Excessive and nonproductive subsidies constitute a second constraint because they limit the financial resources and capacity of governments at all levels to foster economic and social development. The system of voting only for a single candidate in elections involving hundreds of political parties has forced many parties to become more sectarian and narrowly focused, emphasizing the parochial interests and even irrational aspirations of their own voting blocks. This fuels an ethos of competitive populism and equalitarianism in India's economic and social policy-making institutions. Political parties scrambling for votes have championed and enacted many kinds of subsidy polices (e.g., those for cooking fuel, electricity, food, and rural employment.[14]

The subsidies on diesel oil and cooking fuel alone could total $15 billion annually, an amount equal to 1 percent of GDP.[15] In 2011, the cost of all governmental subsidies equaled 2.5 percent of GDP, far outstripping the 1.5 percent target set by the fiscal budget for that year.[16] The Rural Employment Guarantee Project has cost $6–7 billion each year, which equals annual expenditures of the Interior Ministry. Subsidies are a major contributor to India's severe budget deficit, which has equaled 5–6 percent of GDP in recent years. Budget deficits have forced the government to limit expenditures on electric power, transportation, and other infrastructure needed for sustained development and on public goods like basic education and health. For many years, India has invested only about 3.5 percent of GDP to improve infrastructure, far short of the estimated ideal sum of 8 percent of GDP.[17] As a result, India's economy has been caught in a vicious cycle characterized by high deficits leading to low infrastructural investment leading to low growth rates that lead to high deficits.

Another constraint is that basic productive elements lack fluidity. The movement of labor, land (acquisition), goods, and capital in India is quite limited. The high degree of employee protection mandated by Indian labor laws and regulations has discouraged the establishment of new businesses and the expansion of existing facilities.[18] Currently, 87 percent of workers in organized manufacturing sectors are employed in small factories employing fewer than ten people. Rigid labor laws not only restrict labor flows by limiting job opportunities; they also obstruct capital flows because weak enforcement of bankruptcy laws slows the exit of firms and makes it difficult to redeploy capital. The caste system and rural jobs programs have also exacerbated the situation by discouraging unemployed or underemployed workers in the countryside from seeking jobs elsewhere in the country.

Inadequate infrastructure not only impedes the movement of goods and productive materials; it also increases the cost and reduces the competitiveness of India's manufactured products. For example, more than a third of Indian food rots between the farm gate and consumers.[19] It has been estimated that the inadequacy of India's infrastructure reduces GDP growth by about two percentage points each year.[20]

India's rise is also constrained by a number of societal problems, including class struggle, ethnic conflicts, and terrorist threats. The problems are not new; successive governments have faced at least four kinds of internal security threats ever since India gained independence from British colonial rule. One such threat comes from separatist groups, of which five or six have sought ethnic independence in Northeast India since before India's independence. Islamic militants still seek separation in India-administered Kashmir, and conflict between Muslims and Hindus still flares up from time to time, as happened in Gujarat in 2002.[21]

The Naxal or Naxalite movement (sometimes described as "Maoist") dates from the early 1960s. Former prime minister Manmohan Singh repeatedly described Naxalism as the "biggest internal security threat" to India's long-term stability.[22] Naxal-related conflicts result in approximately one thousand deaths each year, but since 2010 the government has killed or captured nearly 60 percent of those classified as key leaders of the Naxal militants. The Naxal movement has suffered a severe setback, but leftist extremists are still active in about 200 of India's 630 districts. The Naxalists are composed mainly of marginal and backward people from the so-called Scheduled Tribes, lower castes (Scheduled Castes), other backward classes, and religious minorities.[23] Leftist militants active in mountainous areas with rich mineral resources have hindered the exploration and exploitation of coal, iron ore, and other minerals, impeding energy production and economic growth.[24]

## The Two Faces of India's China Policy

Chinese analysts who study India generally agree that India will continue to grow at a relatively fast pace but consider it unlikely that India will be able to narrow the gap between its own comprehensive national strength and that of China. Indeed, we judge it likely that the comprehensive strength gap will widen in the foreseeable future. This prospect has already increased India's strategic anxiety and determination to develop a hedging strategy focused on China. To balance China's potential strategic challenges, India would like to increase its security and strategic interactions with the United States and its allies and strategic partners. At the same time, however, the fact that China and India are at different stages of development creates opportunities for cooperation that capitalize on their respective strengths. Moreover, and most important, the need to address common strategic challenges have forced India and China to coordinate and cooperate in a number of areas as if they were natural strategic partners.[25]

Some of the issues on which India and China have conflicting views and interests are long-standing and, in some respects, irresolvable. These include a number of issues beginning with the letter T (territorial disputes, Tibet, trade balances, transborder water issue, and third-party relationships).[26]

Under present conditions, and for the foreseeable future, it seems highly unlikely that Beijing and New Delhi can find a mutually acceptable settlement for their territorial disputes. Tibet-related issues appear equally intractable because India's democratic and fractured political system makes it hard for any Indian government to disband the Tibetan Government in Exile or to adopt a more restrictive policy toward the Dalai Lama, who enjoys great popular support in the democratic international community. The trade imbalance is largely a function of India's internal impediments to growth; India cannot balance its trade with China unless and until it significantly reduces the obstacles to the movement of labor, capital, and goods. This would take years to achieve. Transborder water issues are also largely structural in nature because China's management of upriver water flows inevitably affects India as a downriver country. Third-party relationships are difficult because India has always been sensitive and uneasy about China's close relationship with its neighbors, especially Pakistan.[27] The increasingly visible presence of China in the Indian Ocean and surrounding areas, and the growing number of overlapping interests in peripheral regions, exacerbate this dimension of the problem.

The combination of the concerns just summarized has caused India to regard China as the source of its major security challenge and principal strategic rival. The "China threat" commands a great deal of attention in India and is said to have many specific manifestations. One is the threat that China would invade India and solve border disputes by force.[28] Another posits that China would use river water as a weapon against India.[29] Still other variants argue that China is encircling India by partnering with India's neighbors, that China would launch a nuclear attack against India, and that China would attempt to foster the disintegration of India.[30]

The dominant strand in discussions and debates among Indian strategic thinkers and academic specialists in conjunction with the sixtieth anniversary of the 1962 Sino-Indian border conflict argued that Indian policy should hedge against the possibility of more aggressive Chinese behavior. In particular, their arguments called for more rapid modernization, preparations to resist Chinese military attacks, and increasing India's capacity to counterbalance China by strengthening India's relationships with China's neighbors in East Asia. Other suggestions called for enhancing India's ability to exercise dominance in the Indian Ocean, the Arabian Sea, the Bay of Bengal, and the strategic chokepoints along the Indian Ocean rim. The reason for doing this was to gain greater capabilities to disrupt China's major energy and trade routes, if necessary.[31] At present, the essence of India's hedging policy toward China can be summarized as maintaining absolute control of the South Asian landmass, enhancing India's dominance in the Indian Ocean, pursuing deep engagement with the Asia-Pacific powers, and modernizing both spear and shield.

Based on their assessment that border issues cannot be solved in the near future, officials and analysts call for strengthening and modernizing India's military deployment in the frontier regions. The goal is to achieve localized military advantage to prevent China from changing the status quo along the border (which is favorable to India) by military means. Efforts to strengthen India's defenses along its northern border with China made by successive

Indian governments include constructing and upgrading the frontier military infrastructure and increasing military manpower in the frontier region.[32] These efforts seem to have intensified in the years since 2008. New Delhi has enhanced its rapid-response capacity along the disputed border by expanding road networks (plans call for construction of seventy-three strategic roads in Arunachal Pradesh, the Indian state on territory claimed by China). Other measures include stationing Su-30MKI aircraft at Tezpur (as many as three squadrons by the year 2015), adding two divisions (about fifty thousand to sixty thousand troops) and two batteries of BrahMos missiles in the Northeast, and upgrading advanced landing grounds (ALGs) in the frontier regions. "Nonalignment 2.0: A Foreign and Strategic Policy for India in the Twenty First Century," published in February 2012 with strong support from the government, suggests that India should have a three pronged "asymmetric strategy" to "convince the Chinese to back down" from any "major offensive" in the frontier region. The suggested strategy includes being able to trigger an immediately effective insurgency in the areas occupied by Chinese forces, integrating the frontier regions and their people by speeding up and improving communication links to the heartland, and enhancing Indian naval capacities for the sake of balancing against China in the event of a crisis.[33]

India has evinced concern about the increased presence of the Chinese Navy in the Indian Ocean since China's Navy began to participate in the UN-mandated antipiracy mission around the Gulf of Aden in December 2008, but India is also building its maritime power. The goal of building a "Blue Water Navy," declared in 2003, envisions becoming a major maritime power equipped with three carrier fleets with a total of 130 warships.[34] To speed its own naval modernization, India purchased the carrier *Gorshkov*, which it renamed the INS *Vikramaditya*. The indigenously built *Vikrant* is to be commissioned by 2018, and a second Indian-built carrier is anticipated. In addition to leasing and purchasing Russia-built nuclear powered submarines, India is building its own nuclear submarines, the first of which, the advanced technology vessel (ATV) *Arihant*, was launched in 2009. India is also modernizing its naval bases. Taken together, these efforts have given India the capacity to disrupt China's energy and trade route through the Indian Ocean. India's advantage over China on the sea has partially offset its relatively inferior position on land.

The third element of India's strategy is to increase its security interactions with the Asia-Pacific powers by taking advantage of neighboring states' unease about China's strategic intentions. The goal is to secure a more favorable position in the future regional security architecture. The Barack Obama administration's "Asia Rebalance" strategy, the disputes over maritime sovereignty in the Western Pacific, and strategic competition in the Asia-Pacific region create opportunities for India to expand its engagement with the United States and other Asia-Pacific countries. India has used these opportunities to gradually upgrade its "Look East" policy to a "Move East" policy and is now making efforts to transform it into an "Indo-Pacific Strategy."[35]

During the process, India has become very active in its security diplomacy in this region. Examples include the enhancement of bilateral defense and security interactions with Japan, including the establishment of 2+2 (foreign ministers plus defense ministers) dialogues; participation in the pan-Pacific naval exercises, which included all Asia-Pacific countries except China and North Korea; intervention in South China Sea territorial disputes by declaring free navigation in the South China Sea to be to India's national interest; the proclamation that the Indian Navy is preparing for the contingency of being called on to protect Indian economic interests in the disputed South China Sea; support of the Association of Southeast Asia Nations' (ASEAN's) efforts to negotiate a Code of Conduct with China; and military cooperation with Vietnam.[36] The common element in all the preceding security interactions between India and Asia-Pacific powers is that they do not include China.

India's hedging strategies generally evoke little concern on the part of Chinese security analysts because they tend to believe that India has adopted these hedging policies mainly for defensive reasons. The assessed goal of the strategies is to guard against uncertainties about the future of Sino-India relations and China's future behavior. This assessment is supported by the fact that India has treated China as both a potential threat and an important strategic partner with whom it maintains frequent strategic interactions.

There appears to be a consensus in India's ruling elite that it is necessary—and possible—to stabilize the bilateral relationship with China. Over the past ten years, top leaders of both countries have met nearly thirty times, economic relations have expanded by leaps and bounds, and scores of bilateral mechanisms have been established to enhance mutual understanding, coordination, and crisis management. India and China also have cooperated in a variety of bilateral, multilateral, and global forums. Prompt and successful settlement of the 2013 face-off incident demonstrated the utility of the elite consensus regarding the possibility for stable relations.[37] The existence of that consensus made it easier for top leaders to calm angry publics and reduce media hyping of the story. The incident also demonstrated the value of the various border-related mechanisms in crisis management.

India and China have been natural strategic partners on issues of global development. Both champion the rights of developing countries, as when they call for reform of international economic institutions (such as the International Monetary Fund and the World Bank); coordinate positions in negotiations on climate change and World Trade Organization Doha Round proposals; and cooperate to uphold the global trading system, safeguard food supplies, and enhance energy security. They have also found common ground on other issues, agree that neither poses a threat to the other, and view each other as partners, not rivals or competitors.

Of course, rhetorical statements about common ground and abundant room for both to develop without impinging on the other do not, by themselves, reduce strategic mistrust, but they could lead to significant cooperation. For example, during the past ten years, every state visit and summit meeting between these two countries has produced specific forms of constructive and even strategic cooperation. Indeed, repetition of common-ground rhetoric seems to have played a role in persuading the two governments of the need for concrete actions to convince domestic and international audiences that they mean what they have said.

China considers it unlikely that India would join the counter-China coalition. India has regarded its strategic engagement with Asia-Pacific powers as a useful path to recognition as a global power. But it has been careful to avoid being drawn into arrangements that could limit its freedom of action. For example, although the United States, Japan, Vietnam, and other nations that view China with deep strategic mistrust have encouraged and expected India to play a "linchpin" role in checking China's rise, India has maintained its "equal distance" policy to avoid friction with China and to ensure that its own interests will not be harmed by conflict or better relations between China and its neighbors. This approach is the reason India made no official comment when former US secretary of defense Leon Panetta declared that India was a "linchpin" in America's strategy of "rebalance to the Asia-Pacific region" during his June 2012 visit to India.[38] It is also the reason India decided to pull out of planned trilateral naval exercises with Japan and the United States in November 2013.[39]

China has confidence in India's efforts to maintain its strategic independence. More important, both sides believe they have the resources and capacity to disrupt or derail the rise of the other. For example, each country could take advantage of the other's internal difficulties or uneasy relations with its immediate neighbors to stir up trouble, as was done during the Cold War. Moreover, both countries have the military means to inflict heavy damage to the other's economic and social infrastructures. Furthermore, both countries expect their bilateral interactions to facilitate rather than impede their own rise to developed economy status.

A third factor shaping the relationship is that India has become less hostile toward China's increasingly visible presence in India's traditional sphere of influence, and China has similarly become more accepting of India's expanded presence. For example, India's external affairs minister, Salman Khurshid, stated that India must accept "the new reality" of China's presence in areas India once considered its exclusive sphere of influence.[40] Mutual acceptance of the expanding roles of the other is also reflected in the Joint Statement signed during Chinese Prime Minister Li Keqiang's visit to India in May 2013. The statement says, "The two sides support multilateral cooperation mechanisms in Asia, take a positive view of each other's participation in regional and sub-regional cooperation processes, and support each other in enhancing friendly relations with their common neighbors for mutual benefit, and win-win results."[41]

China and India have reaffirmed the importance of bilateral maritime cooperation and one should anticipate increased cooperation between China and India in South Asia, ASEAN forums, East Asia, and along the Indian Ocean Rim—all arenas in which such cooperation has been scarce. Were China to be admitted to the South Asian Association for Regional Cooperation (SAARC) and India to the Shanghai Cooperation Organization (SCO) (both currently have observer status), it would be an even more vivid indication of the mutual acceptance of the other's larger regional footprint.

Another indication of the character of the bilateral relationship is that Indian local governments anticipate more and deeper economic relations and culture-cum-people interaction with China. India's coastal and economically developed states in particular have been paying increasing attention to their economic relations with China's provinces. Then chief minister of Gujarat Narendra Modi, whose state has enjoyed the fastest growth during the past ten years, has referred to Gujarat as "India's Guangdong." Chinese local leaders are eager to visit Kerala, a state regarded by Chinese elites as a model for building a harmonious society.[42]

In recent years, the CEOs of large Chinese companies have begun a serious dialogue with Indian state governments like Gujarat and Maharashtra. These states have a much better infrastructure, including electric power and business-friendly policies. Another example of new attitudes and forms of cooperation is shown in the relationship between India's northeastern states and China's southwestern provinces. For many years, the northeastern states have called for more subregional cooperation, including cooperation with China, to shed their image as India's backwater. New Delhi had long worried that such openness could benefit local separatists by making it easier for them to obtain external assistance. This was the primary reason that the Kunming Initiative to facilitate subregional cooperation among Bangladesh, Myanmar, India, and China had achieved nothing more significant than sponsorship of two-car rallies in fourteen years. But now, thanks to greater self-confidence in New Delhi and significantly greater mutual trust among the four countries, the Bangladesh-China-India-Myanmar (BCIM) Economic Corridor could have greater success. Indeed, provincial interactions could become a powerful force driving improvement of Indo-China relations.

A fifth dimension and shaping factor is that Indian syndicates and giant business groups expect to deepen and widen cooperation with Chinese counterparts. In the past, these Indian Groups have focused primarily on the US and European markets. However, the huge emerging market in China and the recession's impact on the US and European markets have prompted Indian businesses to pursue opportunities resulting from the development of China's economy and society. Indian firms want to develop strategic cooperation with Chinese counterparts to take advantage of not only the huge potential of their own and each other's markets but also the opportunities available in third-country markets.

Indian companies with a competitive edge, notably those producing pharmaceuticals and providing IT services, have already established operations in China. Examples include Dr. Reddy's Laboratories, Aurobindo Pharma, Wipro, NIIT, Infosys, Tata Consultancy Services (TCS), and Aptech, among others. Seven large Chinese banks, including the Bank of China and Huaxin Bank, are serviced by TCS, and the Shanghai Foreign Exchange Center uses a newly developed trading system built by TCS. Building IT architecture and applications platforms for newly developed "intelligent" cities in China is also a new growth engine for Indian IT giants.[43]

These examples make clear that India is still somewhat ambivalent about how to treat China strategically. However, Chinese geostrategic thinkers and leaders believe it possible for China to alleviate India's concerns and ambivalence by strengthening and expanding strategic cooperation and by acknowledging India's own security concerns. Chinese governments have been doing precisely that for the last three decades.

## New Type of Major Power Relations Between India and China

Despite disagreements on specific issues, Sino-Indian relations have been quite stable during the past decade. They have also manifested a number of unique features that, taken together, suggest a model for a new type of relationship between major powers. Key features of the new type of relationship can be grouped into four categories.

### THE ABILITY TO MAINTAIN STABLE RELATIONS DESPITE CLEAR DIFFERENCES AND DISAGREEMENTS

India and China have competing models of development, territorial disputes, ideological differences, and a number of legacy problems but have nevertheless managed to maintain a high degree of stability in their relationship since relations were normalized in the late 1980s. During the past ten years, there have been no dramatic changes in their bilateral relationship. Indeed, the past ten years have been the most stable decade since the establishment of formal diplomatic relations in 1950.

Top leaders of both countries recognized that, although some disputes could not be resolved, expanding cooperation would reduce the weight or relative importance of inherent and intractable disagreements. They also calculated that increased cooperation would make it easier to find areas of agreement and to resolve their differences in a mutually acceptable way. At the very least, it could create a more favorable environment for the management of future problems and crises. This is the reason the Chinese government has vigorously encouraged India to build and strengthen regional economic arrangements, and to cooperate with China in third countries and regional groupings (e.g., in Nepal, around the Indian Ocean, and in international mechanisms like the G20 and BRIC Summit). The latest Chinese initiative is the effort to foster development in the BCIM Economic Corridor.[44]

THE EQUAL IMPORTANCE OF POLITICAL AND ECONOMIC DRIVERS

China's relationships with other countries are dominated by either political interactions or economic transactions. Its relationship with India is unique because political and economic interactions are equally important. Politically, top leaders of both countries have met with unusual frequency. During the last ten years, China's former president Hu Jintao and former prime minster Wen Jiabao met one-on-one with India's Prime Minister Manmohan Singh twenty-six times. The prime ministers established a hotline to facilitate direct communication whenever needed. It is no exaggeration to say that the countries' most senior leaders have guided Sino-India relations.

An economic pillar also undergirds the relationship. China has been India's number-one trade partner several times since 2007. In 2002, bilateral trade was only about $4.9 billion. By 2011, it had soared to $73.9 billion. Bilateral trade declined to $65 billion in 2012 because of the global recession, but the complementarities of their economies ensure that economic interactions will remain at a very high level. The high tempo of leadership interactions and the dynamic economic relationship will continue to counteract the negative impact of enduring disputes and the hostility found in surveys of public opinion.[45]

THE REQUIREMENTS OF SUSTAINED DEVELOPMENT
TRUMP CONCERNS ABOUT SECURITY

The highest priority of both India and China is to achieve rapid development and sustained economic growth. As a result, doing what is necessary to achieve that priority objective is more important than attempting to achieve absolute security or to counter every possible threat to security. Stated another way, for both countries, bilateral relations have been shaped mainly by the requisites of common development and only secondarily by concerns about the security threat posed by the other country.

Leaders and governments in both countries are focusing on what they regard as their historic mission to lead the transition from developing to developed country status.[46] To achieve their developmental goals, both governments need development-friendly environments at home and abroad.

Maintaining such an environment requires peace and stability. This, in turn, puts a premium on tamping passions fueled by concerns about threats to security. The logic of this prioritization is a strong determinant of the current character of Sino-India relations.

THE ESTABLISHMENT OF MECHANISMS TO MANAGE AND RESOLVE PROBLEMS

China and India have established numerous mechanisms to manage, defuse, and ultimately resolve disputes. One set of mechanisms was created to address their border disputes.[47] Specialized components of the mechanism include the Joint Working Group, the Joint Expert Group, the Special Envoy regime, the Boundary Consultation and Coordination Mechanism, Flag Meetings between frontier forces, and the hotline between the army units on opposite sides of the border. These mechanisms are designed to manage and seek mutually acceptable solutions to contingencies that arise along the border. Using these mechanisms, the two countries have established guiding principles for resolving the border dispute and successfully managed various kinds of border crises. One indicator of their efficacy is that not a single shot has been fired across the disputed border since 1967. When Li Keqiang visited India in 2013, he and Prime Minister Singh agreed to begin a Sino-Indian Maritime Security Dialogue.[48] The two countries have also agreed to hold bilateral talks on Tibet issues in the future.

*Future Trajectory of Sino-India Relations*

In the years since China and India began to normalize their relations in 1988, especially in the past ten years, China's South Asia policy has gradually accorded greater importance to India and Sino-India relations. Indeed, this increased emphasis can be found in China's Asia and global policies as well. For example, ever since the 1999 Kargil clashes between Pakistan and India, China has adopted a more neutral position on the Kashmir issue. Thanks to the unremitting efforts of Chinese officials, Beijing and New Delhi established the Sino-Indian Strategic Cooperative Partnership in 2005.[49] Moreover, greater sensitivity to India's security concerns persuaded the Chinese government to reduce China's unconventional military cooperation with Pakistan, and to invite India to participate in China's economic activities in Nepal, Sri Lanka, and Myanmar.

China did this, in part, to elicit reciprocal steps by India that would enable Beijing to realize Chinese objectives. For example, the success of the Chinese-initiated BCIM Economic Corridor depends on cooperation between China and India, and such cooperation was constrained by China's security concerns. Cooperation between India and China is important in other arenas as well. For example, the success of collaborative undertakings by the BRICS depends largely on the extent and efficacy of joint efforts by China and India.

Based on what has occurred during the previous ten years and the logic underpinning their new relationship, it is likely that Sino-Indian relations will continue to expand and deepen in the decade ahead, and that their cooperation will contribute to power-shifting changes in the international system. If, or when, this happens, some may regard it as a return to the past because, in the 1950s, China and India worked together and contributed much to the global and regional strategic rearrangement that occurred in the post–World War II and post-decolonization era. This was a time when India and China were especially vocal advocates of the "Five Principles of Peaceful Co-existence" first set forth in 1954.[50]

The concatenation of many recent developments (e.g., the simultaneous rise of China and India and the global financial crisis and concomitant recession) has made the Asia-Pacific region the focus of world attention. Increased attention is warranted because of the scale and dynamism of regional economies and changes in regional security dynamics. One clear reflection of this is the priority accorded Asia in the Obama administration's strategy to "rebalance" American forces, diplomacy, and economic activity. India and China play central roles in the transformation that is taking place.

These developments make it possible and imperative for India and China to work together to build a more peaceful and prosperous future. They cannot afford to wait for chance developments or a third country to create conditions conducive to their continued return to positions of greater influence and responsibility on the regional and world stage. For India and China, the age of the free ride and free lunch is over. They must play a more active and constructive role, individually and together, than they have for a very long time. One reason they must do so is that the more they rise, the more other powers will attempt to restrict their growth and strategic influence. China and India have the resources and capacity to make more constructive contributions to the establishment of a more inclusive, open, balanced, diversified, win-win, mutually dependant security and economic architecture in the Asia-Pacific region.

As the developing countries with the largest populations, China and India must overcome numerous internal difficulties as they negotiate the transition from developing to developed country status. Both must find a new and less disruptive path to global leadership because our increasingly fragile planet cannot afford attempts by these two giant countries to follow the path to greater power and influence pioneered by the nations that rose to preeminence in past centuries. To develop a better model of ascent, India and China must draw on the wisdom and philosophies of their long histories and rich civilizations, and must follow a more sustainable route to wealth and power. In doing so they have much to learn from and much to contribute to each other. Each will be more successful if it learns to cooperate with the other.

The top leaders of both countries have often stated that the region and the world are large enough to accommodate their simultaneous rise to developed country status—in other words, neither need fear a zero-sum outcome. But they have also warned that unless China and India find ways to cooperate, the development of each will be constrained by perceptions that they are in inevitable competition with one another. The less they are able to cooperate, the more intense, even vicious their competition will appear. Stated another way, the only way to ensure adequate space for both to reach developed country status is through cooperation.

Moreover, expanding cooperation and identifying more common ground and shared interests will reduce the number and severity of disputes in the bilateral relationship. Even if differences remain intractable for another decade or more, their weight and urgency will be diminished if viewed in the context of a larger and expanding set of cooperative undertakings. Ultimately, expanded and deeper cooperation and identification of more common interests could create an atmosphere more conducive to settling their most difficult disputes.

The fact that Xi Jinping visited Russia on his first foreign trip as president of China and that Li Keqiang's first trip as prime minister was to India attests to the high priority that the new generation of China's leaders ascribes to relations with China's neighbors. It can be said—and seen—that the new team of Chinese leaders regard relations with China's neighbors as being just as important for the success of their nation's development strategy as are those with the United States. Building a cooperative and harmonious neighborhood is imperative if China is to be accepted as a rising global power. China's dream cannot be realized if its neighbors are sleepless with worry about China's intentions. The reverse is also true; they cannot realize their own aspirations if their actions make China uneasy. Therefore, China's new leaders must take the initiative to improve relations *between* China and its neighbors and *among* its neighbors. One such step would be to provide clear support for India's desire to have a permanent seat on the UN Security Council.

China and India each have their own dreams and aspirations, but both share the dream of joining the club of top global powers. Realizing that dream will require the unremitting efforts of both nations for several generations.

*Notes*

1. For other analyses of Sino-Indian relations see, for example, Ashley J. Tellis, Travis Tanner, and Jessica Keough, eds., *Strategic Asia 2011–12: Asia Responds to Its Rising Powers—China and India* (Seattle, WA: National Bureau of Asian Research, 2011), especially the chapters by M. Taylor Fravel and Harsh V. Pant; Jonathan Holslag, *China and India: Prospects for Peace* (New York: Columbia University Press, 2011); and Amardeep Athwal, *China-India Relations: Contemporary Dynamics* (New York: Routledge, 2008).

2. Chen Deming, "China and India Work Together for a Brighter Future," Ministry of Commerce, People's Republic of China, January 20, 2010, http://english.mofcom.gov.cn/article/zt_ciecf/lanmub/201001/20100106760141.shtml.

3. For data on GDP and GDP per capita for India and China, see the World Bank's *World Development Indicators*, available at http://data.worldbank.org/data -catalog/world-development-indicators.

4. See, for example Jawaharal Nehru, *The Discovery of India* (Calcutta: Signet Press, 1946).

5. India's emergence as an increasingly important regional and global power is described in Waheguru Pal Singh Sidhu, Pratap Bhanu Mehta, and Bruce Jones, eds., *Shaping the Emerging World: India and the Multilateral Order* (Washington, DC: Brookings Institution Press, 2013); and Tellis, Tanner, and Keough, *Strategic Asia 2011–12*.

6. See, for example, Robert D. Kaplan, *The Revenge of Geography* (New York: Random House, 2012), especially chap. 12.

7. For more on the Indian Caucus, see Shazia Aziz Wulbers, *The Paradox of EU-India Relations: Missed Opportunities in Politics, Economics, Development Co-operation and Culture* (Plymouth, UK: Lexington, 2011), 31–33; and Gerald Felix Warburg, "Nonproliferation Policy Crossroads: Lessons Learned from the US -India Nuclear Cooperation Agreement," *Nonproliferation Review* 19, no. 3 (2012): 451–471.

8. M. Emran Shahe, M. Imam Alam, and Forhad Shilpi, "After the 'License Raj': Economic Liberalization and Aggregate Private Investment in India," Social Science Research Network, August 2003, http://papers.ssrn.com/sol3/papers.cfm?abstract_id=411080.

9. World Bank, *World Development Indicatiors*.

10. Tu Jin Tan, "Twenty Years On: A Second Wave of Reforms," *Project Firefly*, February 6, 2013, http://www.project-firefly.com/node/15200.

11. Krishna Chaitanya Vadlamannati, "A Race to Compete for Investment Among Indian States? An Empirical Investigation," http://www.uni-heidelberg.de/md/awi/professuren/intwipol/regional.pdf (accessed May 14, 2015).

12. Paul Holtom, Mark Bromley, Pieter D. Wezeman, and Siemon T. Wezeman, "Trends in International Arms Transfers, 2011," *SIPRI Fact Sheet*, March 2012, http://books.sipri.org/product_info?c_product_id=443#.

13. For more on the leftist movements and socialist traditions of India, see E. M. S. Namboodiripad, "The Left in India's Freedom Movement and in Free India," *Social Scientist* 14, nos. 8–9 (1986): 3–17.

14. Rajesh Kumar Singh, "Indian Political Parties Vie over Largesse Before Elections," *Reuters*, February 3, 2014, http://www.reuters.com/article/2014/02/03/us-india-politics-idUSBREA120TL20140203.

15. Rakesh Sharma and Mukesh Jagota, "India Lifts Diesel Prices to Trim Deficit," *Wall Street Journal*, September 14–16, 2012, p. 4.

16. See "Feeding India's Beast," *Wall Street Journal*, March 19, 2012, p. 17.

17. "India's RBI Says More Infrastructure Spend, Farm Output Needed to Sustain Growth," *Forbes*, August 30, 2007; "IMF Seeks Reforms to Boost India Infrastructure Spending," *Business Today*, October 12, 2013, http://businesstoday.intoday.in/story/imf-seeks-reforms-to-boost-india-infrastructure-spending/1/199535.html.

18. A company in India with one hundred or more employees must seek permission and approval from the local government when it decides to sack employees for any reason, even if it is on the verge of bankruptcy. A factory in extreme difficulties cannot declare or apply for bankruptcy without the approval of local governments.

19. See Anant Vijay Kala, "Pressure to Cut Rates Rises as India Inflation Slows," *Wall Street Journal*, August 15, 2012, p. 4.

20. See Santanu Choudhury, Romit Guha, and Saurabh Chaturvedi, "Blackout Tarnishes India's Reputation," *Wall Street Journal*, August 2, 2012, p. 3.

21. "Deadly Violence Erupts Again in India's Hindu-Muslim Conflict," *New York Times*, May 9, 2002, http://www.nytimes.com/2002/05/09/world/deadly -violence-erupts-again-in-india-s-hindu-muslim-conflict.html.

22. "Naxalism Biggest Threat to Internal Security: Manmohan," *The Hindu*, May 24, 2010, http://www.thehindu.com/news/national/naxalism-biggest-threat -to-internal-security-manmohan/article436781.ece.

23. United Nations in India, "Scheduled Castes and Scheduled Tribes," http:// in.one.un.org/task-teams/scheduled-castes-and-scheduled-tribes (accessed May 14, 2015).

24. "Anti-Naxal Operations to Free Mineral Zones," *Rediff News*, October 30, 2009, http://news.rediff.com/report/2009/oct/30/anti-naxal-ops-to-free-mineral -zones.htm.

25. Such as how to deal with or change the existing order and rules of the game dominated by incumbent powers, how to sustain benefits from the global trade, how to ensure sustainable development at home, and how to jointly stabilize their overlapping regions.

26. India's worries about China's management of shared waters include concerns that China would use water as strategic leverage against India and link it to the solution of border issues, that China would construct dams to divert water and cause drought and damage in India, and that China's water projects and economic activities would cause pollution of India's rivers. Proposals to divert Tibetan waters to northern China put forward by some Chinese scholars in the 1990s are particularly worrisome to many Indians. Chinese governments have repeatedly assured Indian officials that China would not divert shared rivers for any purpose. Water projects in the upper reaches are mainly for irrigation and electricity, which will not affect the general flow of rivers. In 2006, the two countries established a Joint Expert Level Mechanism to discuss interaction and cooperation on provision of flood assistance, hydrological data, emergency management, and other issues regarding transborder rivers. Most such data are to be provided by the Chinese side.

27. Sino-Pakistan relations had once replaced the border dispute as the biggest obstacle to normalizing Sino-India relations. But in the past ten years, with Pakistan being marginalized and distracted by antiterror civil war, natural disasters, and political chaos, India's concerns about Pakistan have shifted from how Pakistan treats India to how Pakistan manages its internal problems. Indian leaders and scholars have repeatedly emphasized the importance of cooperation between India and China to manage the spillover effect of a failed or Talibanized Pakistan.

28. Sunil Khilnani, Rajiv Kumar, Pratap Bhanu Mehta, Prakash Menon, Nandan Nilekani, Srinath Raghavan, Shyam Saran, and Siddharth Varadarajan,

"Nonalignment 2.0: A Foreign and Strategic Policy for India in the Twenty First Century," 2012 http://www.cprindia.org/sites/default/files/working_papers/Non Alignment%202.0_1.pdf.

29. See, for example, "Indian Scholars Worry About Water Interception by China," *Sinonet*, August 14, 2009, http://www.sinonet.org/news/world/2009-08-14/ 36354.html; Brahma Chellaney, "China's Dam Frenzy a Threat to Water Security," *South China Morning Post*, March 11, 2013, http://www.scmp.com/comment/ insight-opinion/article/1187716/chinas-dam-frenzy-threat-water-security; and Brahma Chellaney, *Water: Asia's New Battleground* (Washington, DC: Georgetown University Press, 2011).

30. See, for example, D. S. Rajan, "China Should Break Up the Indian Union, Suggests a Chinese Strategist," Chennai Centre for China Studies, C3S Paper No. 325, August 9, 2009, http://www.c3sindia.org/india/719; and "China's India Policy: Murder with Borrowed Knives," *Economic Times*, August 12, 2009, http://articles .economictimes.indiatimes.com/2009-08-12/news/28387859_1_india-china -relations-china-s-india-state-councilor-dai-bingguo.

31. See, for example, Naomi McMillen, "Fiftieth Anniversary of the 1962 Sino-Indian Border War: An Interview with Arun Sahgal," National Bureau of Asian Research, October 30, 2012, http://www.nbr.org/research/activity.aspx?id=290.

32. According to the report by the *Times of India* on June 1, 2013, India's Cabinet Committee on Security was expected to approve a proposal by the army to deploy over forty thousand additional troops, including a mountain strike corps, two independent infantry brigades, and two independent armored brigades, to "plug its operational gaps along the entire line of actual control (LAC) with China, as well as to acquire offensive capabilities." The cost could be $14.3 billion, which would be spread across India's 12th Five Year Plan (2012–2017) and could even stretch into the 13th Five Year Plan (2017–2022). Between 2009 and 2010, India beefed up its LAC presence by raising two new infantry divisions consisting of thirty-five thousand troops. Indian officials maintain that their decision to beef up forces along the LAC is a response to what they perceive as China's military modernization in the Tibetan Autonomous Region. The plan to deploy additional mountain strike forces along the LAC has been under consideration for some time, but now it was triggered by the three-week standoff along the LAC that began in April. "Govt Set to Clear 40,000-Strong Force Along China Border," *Times of India*, June 1, 2013, http://timesofindia.indiatimes.com/india/Govt-set-to-clear -40000-strong-force-along-China-border/articleshow/20374185.cms.

33. Khilnani et al., "Nonalignment 2.0," 41–42

34. N. Janardhan, *Boom amid Gloom: The Spirit of Possibility in the 21st Century Gulf* (Reading, UK: Ithaca Press, 2011), 172.

35. India's foreign secretary, Ranjan Mathai, proclaimed the success of this strategy at the tenth meeting of the Bangladesh-China-India-Myanmar (BCIM) Forum for Regional Cooperation in Kolkata in April 2012 when he said that the "Look East" policy had led to India's robust reengagement with its eastern neighbors and emergence as "a significant player in the strategic dynamics" of the region. See Shastri Ramachandaran, "Why India Must Go Beyond Merely Looking East," *DNA*, March 26, 2012, http://www.dnaindia.com/analysis/1667415/column-why -india-must-go-beyond-merely-looking-east.

36. Manu Pubby, "Ready to Protect Indian Interests in South China Sea: Navy Chief," *Indian Express*, December 4, 2012, http://www.indianexpress.com/news/ ready-to-protect-indian-interests-in-south-china-sea-navy-chief/1040119/; David Brewster, "India's Strategic Partnership with Vietnam: The Search for a Diamond on the South China Sea?" *Asian Security* 5, no.1 (2009): 24–44.

37. Rajat Pandit, "India-China Border Pact Outlines Steps to Defuse Face-Offs Between Rival Troops," *Times of India*, October 23, 2013, http://timesofindia .indiatimes.com/india/India-China-border-pact-outlines-steps-to-defuse-face-offs -between-rival-troops/articleshow/24615961.cms.

38. Leon E. Panetta, "The U.S. and India: Partners in the 21st Century," June 6, 2012, http://www.defense.gov/speeches/speech.aspx?speechid=1682.

39. Shishir Gupta and Pramit Pal Chaudhuri, "Fearing China, India Pulls Out of War Games," *Hindustan Times*, May 13, 2013, http://www.hindustantimes.com/ india-news/newdelhi/fearing-china-india-pulls-out-of-war-games/article1-1059257 .aspx.

40. Harsh V. Pant, "Harsh V Pant: Salman Khurshid's China Challenge," *Business Standard*, December 23, 2012, http://www.business-standard.com/article/ opinion/harsh-v-pant-salman-khurshid-s-china-challenge-112122300041_1.html.

41. Ministry of External Affairs, Government of India, "Joint Statement on the State Visit of Chinese Premier Li Keqiang to India," May 20, 2013, http://www .mea.gov.in/bilateral-documents.htm?dtl/21723/Joint+Statement+on+the+State+ Visit+of+Chinese++Li+Keqiang+to+India.

42. Kerala Pradesh is very unique in India in that Christians and Hindus are living peacefully, over 90 percent of Keralan women are literate, hundreds of thousands of Kerala families have members working overseas, and this state has been ruled by Communists for decades. "A New Boss at Tata: From Pupil to Master," *The Economist*, December 1, 2012, http://www.economist.com/news/21567390 -ratan-tatas-successor-cyrus-mistry-has-some-dirty-work-do-pupil-master.

43. See Anil K. Gupta and Haiyan Wang, "China and India: Greater Economic Integration," *China Business Review*, September 1, 2009, http://www .chinabusinessreview.com/china-and-india-greater-economic-integration/; and the

list of Indian companies in China prepared by the Indian embassy in Beijing at http://www.indianembassy.org.cn/indian_companies_in_china.htm.

44. Li Keqiang, "Seize the New Opportunities in China-India Strategic Cooperation," speech given at the Indian Council of World Affairs, May 21, 2013, New Delhi, http://in.china-embassy.org/eng/zt/likeqiang2013/t1042474.htm.

45. See, for example, "New Poll Reveals Indian 'Hopes and Fears,'" *ABC,* May 20, 2013, http://www.abc.net.au/news/2013-05-20/an-indian-opinion-poll-by -lowy-institute/4701082. This poll, prepared by the Lowy Institute and the Australia India Institute, reveals that the majority of Indians consider Pakistan and China to be the biggest foreign threats to their nation. Up to 94 percent of Indians see Pakistan as a security threat; 83 percent regard China as a security threat.

46. See, for example, Li Keqiang, "A Handshake Across the Himalayas," *The Hindu,* May 20, 2013, http://www.thehindu.com/opinion/lead/a-handshake -across-the-himalayas/article4730374.ece. This article was published during Li's visit to India.

47. The border disputes cannot be solved in the foreseeable future mainly for two reasons. First, two countries' preferred settlements are too different from each other. China wants meaningful readjustment of the disputed border, which is quite against India's demand to maintain the status quo. Second, the two central governments lack the political will and even the political capacity to think out of the box how to solve this ticklish issue. The two countries are undergoing dramatic social and economic transformations. For India, the coalition government, which often clubbed with scores of political parties, will collapse at any time when it makes visible readjustment about the border with China. However, for the Chinese government, any acceptance of the status quo arrangement would mean a rising China would accept a border that the weakest central governments in modern history of China since 1914 had rejected. This could be very deadly for the Communist Party of China's (CPC's) ruling in China, since all kinds of dissident and dissatisfied forces supported by rising nationalism could make full use of this development to launch nationwide anti-CPC and antigovernment mass demonstrations.

48. Ministry of External Affairs, Government of India, "Joint Statement."

49. "China, India to Build Strategic Partnership," *Xinhua,* April 12, 2005, http://www.china.org.cn/english/2005/Apr/125627.htm.

50. See "The Five Principals of Peaceful Co-existence," *Peoples Daily Online,* June 28, 2004, http://english.peopledaily.com.cn/200406/28/eng20040628_147763 .html.

# FIVE

# Perception and Strategic Reality in India-China Relations

*Srikanth Kondapalli*

The two sides welcome each other's peaceful development and regard it as a mutually reinforcing process. There is enough space in the world for the development of India and China. . . . Both countries view each other as partners for mutual benefit and not as rivals or competitors.

> —*"Joint Statement on the State Visit of Chinese Premier Li Keqiang to India," May 20, 2013*[1]

We want the world to prepare for the peaceful rise of China as a major power. So, engagement is the right strategy both for India as well as for the United States. We ourselves have tried very hard to engage China in the last five years. Today China is one of our major trading partners. We have also to recognise that we have a longstanding border problem with China. We are trying to resolve it through dialogue. In the meanwhile, both our countries have agreed that pending the resolution of the border problem, peace and tranquillity should be maintained on the borderline. Having said that, I would like to say that I have received these assurances from the Chinese leadership at the highest level. But there is a certain amount of assertiveness on the part of the Chinese, I do not fully understand the reasons for it, that has to be taken note of.

> —*Prime Minister Manmohan Singh, November 23, 2009*[2]

Relations between India and China continue to be characterized by declarations of bonhomie, shared experience, and common purpose diluted and constrained by mutual suspicion and intractable problems. Rivalry impedes cooperation, and rhetoric proclaiming that the region is big enough to accommodate the simultaneous rise of both huge and ambitious nations is belied by competitive and hedging behavior. As young nation-states descended from ancient empires, India and China recognize the advantages of cooperation but find it difficult to compromise and impossible to change what each regards as immutable strategic reality.[3] This chapter provides a brief but broad overview of Indian interests, objectives, perceptions of China, and actions to take advantage of and/or defend against China's rise.

Indian perceptions of China during the past decade or so have been shaped by what the leaders of both countries refer to as their simultaneous "rise." Indeed, the simultaneous rise of India and China is arguably the most important development in Asia in many years because of its profound implications for both the region and the international system. Thanks to reforms that began in China in 1978 and have been implemented in India since 1991, both countries have achieved substantial increases in the size and sophistication of their economies. Measured in terms of purchasing power parity, China's $18 trillion gross domestic product (GDP) was the world's largest in 2014, and India's economy held the number-three position with a GDP of $7.3 trillion, according to the World Bank.[4] Despite slower growth rates in 2012 (about 7.9 percent for China and 5.5 percent for India), estimates by PricewaterhouseCoopers, Citibank, and others predict that both countries will grow at higher rates over the medium term.[5]

Another indicator of how much and how fast India and China are rising is the size of their military budgets. In 2013, China's military budget made it the largest defense spender in Asia and second largest in the world with allocations of $119 billion. India, with defense expenditures of $46 billion, was ranked eighth in the world.[6] Other estimates indicate that China could become the world's largest defense spender in the medium term.[7] As the preceding figures indicate, both India and China are rising powers able to play increasingly important roles in the international system. But they face different challenges and opportunities, and each of them pursues policies tailored to its respective circumstances.

Although the ways in which India and China are rising reflect the parameters and priorities of their domestic reform agendas and the unique features of each political system, how each pursues its objectives and what each is able to achieve is also shaped by external factors. One such external factor is the conduct and success of the other rising power and the extent to which each of the two seeks to exploit, encourage, support, impede, or constrain the other's rise. At a minimum, each seeks to shape and utilize the external environment to facilitate its own rise. Toward that end, both seek to downplay and diminish external security threats in order to focus on internal rejuvenation.

More than a decade ago, India attempted to shape perceptions by declaring, "There is enough space and opportunity in the region for both India and China to prosper."[8] The slogan is intended to convince citizens of both countries that the rise of one would not lead inevitably to clashes with the other and that each could explore opportunities in its respective areas of influence in Asia. This formulation has been repeated by both Indian and Chinese leaders and has been incorporated into their joint statements.[9] This also indicates that both India and China have played down any explicit rivalry or inveterate hostility between them and attests to the imperatives of their domestic developmental agendas.

Despite affirming in many joint statements that the success of each country could contribute to the rise of the other, the reality is more complicated. China's rise has been facilitated not only by its own resources and the efforts, talent, and management abilities of its people but also by access to the markets, capital, and technologies of the United States, the European Union, Japan, South Korea, Taiwan, Singapore, and overseas Chinese. India played almost no role during the important early phases of China's rise. However, most Chinese visitors—presidents, premiers, and others— regularly made stops in Mumbai and Bangalore (India's commercial and software hubs) part of their itineraries. As a result, several Indian companies entered China's market and have made significant contributions to the latest phase of China's development. Desire to assist China's rise was not their primary reason for investing there. Rather, it was to profit from China's increasingly lucrative internal market.

India began its liberalization program more than a decade later than China but has grown at an average rate of 8 percent per year during the last decade. Like China, India has benefited from globalization and, as in the case of China, the major contributors to the rise of India have been companies from the United States, the European Union, Japan, South Korea, Singapore, and Taiwan. Mirroring the pattern just described, several Chinese companies now operate in India, including Huawei, ZTE, and Harbin Power Company. As a result of these Chinese investments, nearly 10 percent of India's electricity is now generated by Chinese-supplied power equipment, and Chinese mobile handsets worth $3–4 billion are sold in the

Indian market each year. Nevertheless, Indians remain suspicious of China, and participation by Chinese firms in projects judged important for national security continue to experience visa problems and other delays. The suspicion and delays indicate that allowing China to play a role in India's rise remains controversial.

One can gain further insight into Indian and Chinese judgments about the risks and opportunities resulting from the rise of the other country by examining how they interact in specific policy arenas. The areas examined here are economic and trade relations, activities affecting "core interests" (Tibet and Kashmir), security relations, regional order (in South Asia and the South China Sea), and international order (relations with the United States and interactions in multilateral institutions). Looking at a number of different types of interaction also facilitates judgments about the extent and ways in which India and China contribute to and constrain one another's rise.

## Economic and Trade Relations

Economic interchange between India and China is increasing because both sides find it to be mutually beneficial. But the magnitude of trade and investment is smaller than many think it should be.[10] Impediments include disagreements involving discriminatory policies, the magnitude of the trade imbalance, and lack of investment. Leaders acknowledge the problems and have initiated mechanisms to address them. In 2003, during the visit of Prime Minister Vajpayee to China, the two sides agreed to start a dialogue process on macroeconomic relations. Three strategic economic dialogues had been held by 2014. Related meetings include the first financial dialogue (on learning from each other about sustainable development processes), which took place between the two finance ministers in April 2006, and the first CEO forum, which was held during Premier Li Keqiang's visit to New Delhi in May 2013.[11]

In just two decades, bilateral trade between India and China increased substantially. Indeed, China is now India's largest trading partner. Bilateral trade, which was only a negligible $264 million in 1991, increased to $65 billion in 2013.[12] Leaders of both countries have made reaching $100 billion in bilateral trade by 2015 an agreed target. In the last decade, the value of Chinese exports to India increased more rapidly than did the value of Indian products exported to China, creating a huge imbalance in favor of

China. Between 2007 and 2013, India's estimated trade deficit with China totaled $164 billion. The trade deficit has become a contentious issue between the two countries. India has demanded market economy status in China because Indian products, specifically pharmaceuticals and software, are discriminated against in the China market. China has not yet acceded to this demand, a fact that could lead to bilateral trade wars.

The disjuncture in trade arises, in part, from the fact that India's trade is conducted mainly by private companies, whereas China's trade has a heavy state imprint. Although maritime trade between the two countries increased by leaps and bounds, border trade has remained negligible, primarily because the border dispute remains unresolved. Currently, border trade is limited to just three locations—namely, Shipki La and Kauril (both in the middle sector) and Nathu La (in the Sikkim sector). Moves to expand trade from Arunachal Pradesh and Ladakh were resisted by China. An estimated $100 million worth of trade passes through these three border posts each year. It consists primarily of foodstuffs, salt, herbal medicines, and other local products. Border trade is unlikely to increase significantly unless there is a breakthrough on the border dispute.

The respective rise of China and India is attributable, in part, to the amount of investment each has received for infrastructure development projects and establishment of special economic zones. In aggregate, China received more than $1 trillion in foreign direct investment (FDI) at the rate of nearly $50 billion every year since Deng Xiaoping's "southern tour" in 1992. In 2014, according to United Nations Conference on Trade and Development (UNCTAD) estimates released in January 2015, China became the largest recipient of FDI, with $128 billion.[13] This has expanded China's infrastructure facilities. In contrast, FDI into India totals only $253 billion.[14] These numbers suggest that China has invested little in the Indian market despite India's desire for more investment from abroad. China's cumulative investment in India up to late 2012 amounted to about $657 million. For comparison, Indian investment in China totaled about $470 million.[15] Judged on the basis of this dimension, China's role in the rise of India has been limited. However, more than two hundred Indian companies—producing automobiles, iron and steel, and so on—have set up shop in China and are exploring lucrative markets. A bilateral investment-promotion and investment-protection agreement was signed in November 2006 and is to remain in force for ten years.[16] Overall, India has invested more in

China than China has in India. Unable to attract sufficient investment from China, India has invited Japan, South Korea, Singapore, Taiwan, and others to invest in its infrastructure projects.

The disparity between Indian investment in China and Chinese investment in India has produced two very different camps or views in India. One holds that trade with China has benefited the commercial and industrial sectors and maintains that engagement with China should be strengthened. The other view, espoused by a subset of the chambers of commerce, argues that India should stand its ground in insisting on compliance with provisions of the World Trade Organization mandating nondiscrimination in trade practices and complying with the requirements of market economy status.

## Tibet and Territorial Disputes

A second arena providing insight into whether and how India and China contribute to or constrain the other's rise is that involving "core" security interests. China has declared Tibet to be one of its core interests (others include Taiwan and, more recently, the South China Sea). China's military deployments in Tibet, including ballistic missiles, have transformed Tibet from its traditional role as a buffer zone between India and China into the locus of a direct threat on India's border. India recognized Tibet as a part of China in 1954, with revisions made in 1988 and 2003.[17] However, Indians have been reluctant to accept China's contention that Tibet is an "inalienable" or "historical" or "integral" part of China.[18]

China had indicated that the 1962 border clashes were mainly a result of India providing refuge to the fleeing Dalai Lama in 1959. Today more than 160,000 Tibetan refugees have resettled in different parts of Nepal, Bhutan, and India. Under pressure from China, India had agreed that the Tibetans living in India would not be allowed to play any anti-China political role from Indian soil. However, bilateral relations between India and China were strained by the Lhasa protests in 1988 (following conferral of the Nobel Peace Prize on the Dalai Lama), in March 2008 (when disturbances spread to traditional parts of Tibet in Amdo and Kham), and in 2012–2013, when over one hundred self-immolation cases were reported. The maximal position of China appears to be that the Tibetans living in India must be returned to China. This is not acceptable to India because, among other reasons, civil society supports the Dalai Lama and the nonviolent religious approach of the Tibetans.

The territorial dispute between India and China, which was cited by Chinese leaders as one of the factors that led to the border clashes in 1962, is distinct from but related to disagreements regarding Tibet. Talks have been held at various levels for at least three decades, but in 1988 both sides decided that failure to resolve border issues should not preclude exploration of ways to deepen relations in other fields. Border issues essentially festered in the background until the 2013 Depsang Plains incursion by Chinese troops in the western sector returned this dispute to a central position in the relationship.[19] Three decades of discussions between officials of both countries have failed even to clarify the line of actual control between the two sides.

Developments over time, including failure to resolve the border dispute, innumerable border transgressions, and repeated Chinese references to Arunachal Pradesh as "southern Tibet" since 2005 have created a "China threat" camp in India. Those holding such views also point to rising Chinese nationalism, and PRC efforts to achieve strategic domination through military modernization, logistical improvements, and deployments along the border. Both sides have tried to assuage feelings by suggesting that the borders remain largely peaceful and tranquil, but the Depsang Plains incident and others prompted India to establish a strike corps in 2013 and to revamp forward landing grounds, air bases, and the like. Differing positions on Tibet-related issues, in conjunction with the unresolved border dispute, cause the two largest countries in Asia to spend vast amounts of money to counter each other. This situation could continue for decades to come.

## Pakistan

China's engagement with nations bordering India is, naturally, a matter of considerable interest and sensitivity. True in a broad sense, this is especially the case with regard to China's relationship with Pakistan and the military assistance that Beijing provides to Pakistan, Nepal, Bangladesh, and Sri Lanka. Many of the joint statements issued by India and China have referred to this concern as "mutual sensitivities."[20] Bilateral relations between Indian and China have improved significantly, but such sensitivities persist. Beginning soon after the 1962 border clashes with India, China developed close relations with Pakistan to balance against India's rise.

Today, China and Pakistan have what they characterize as an "all-weather" relationship in which China provides conventional and strategic military assistance to Islamabad with the intent and effect of constraining India's rise. China's objective was made very clear by its call for a "common" fight with Pakistan against "expansionism and hegemonism" in South Asia.[21] Military equipment that China provided to Pakistan was used against India during conflict situations. China is also investing in multibillion-dollar road, railway, and hydroelectricity projects in Pakistan-occupied Kashmir. According to Selig Harrison, China reportedly deployed seven thousand to eleven thousand troops in this area.[22] Earlier China had stated that this is a disputed area. India is critical of these Chinese actions because they affect its core interest. Another development of concern to India is China's control of the Gwadar port, at the invitation of the Pakistan defense ministry.[23]

A feature that could create trouble between Pakistan and China is the spread of terrorism. Today, China has accused elements in Pakistan of creating trouble in Xinjiang.[24] China wants Pakistan to do more to curb connections between militant groups and the Uighurs. Although China has stated that it condemns all forms of terrorism and is also engaged in a dialogue process with India on this subject, it has not been very forthcoming. Both India and China have declared that terrorism is their main national security challenge but there is still no concrete or effective cooperation between the two. The impediment seems to be Beijing's close political ties to Islamabad.

Another issue complicated by Beijing's relationship with Islamabad is preparation for the post–International Security Assistance Force (ISAF) situation in Afghanistan. The withdrawal of ISAF troops has important implications for regional states like India, China, Russia, Tajikistan, and Iran. India and China have been discussing this matter for the last three years, and even elevated the discussion to a regional dialogue process, but the talks have not been fruitful, probably because of the Pakistan factor in China's calculations. Nevertheless, the May 2013 joint statement between the premiers of India and China referred to support to an "Afghan-led, Afghan-owned" reconciliation process.[25]

China's transfers of conventional weapons to Nepal in 1987 and 2001 (in violation of the Indo-Nepal Treaty of 1950), institutionalization of defense contacts with Dhaka, and arms supplies to Colombo to combat the Liberation Tigers of Tamil Elam insurgency also fuel concern in India. But they are not as disturbing to New Delhi as is the provision of nuclear and ballistic missile components and technologies to Pakistan. This dimension of China-Pakistan relations constrains India's rise.

China's conventional and strategic weapons and technology transfers to Pakistan, and to a lesser extent to other South Asian countries, and its recent role in the Indian Ocean have strengthened the "China threat" camp in India. Although Indian leaders do not mention this issue any longer—not since then defense minister George Fernandes opined that China constituted "potential enemy number one" in 1998—concern has not diminished.[26] That is why India has used joint statements, including the latest in May 2015, to remind China of the importance of "respect and sensitivity to each other's concerns, interests and aspirations."[27]

India-China relations have become more extensive and diverse, but China's relationship with Pakistan remains the most important barometer for measuring the health of the India's relationship with China.

## South China Sea

China closely watches Indian moves toward the East and South China Seas, particularly India's "Look East" policy that began in 1992 with economic and technological aspects as the focus but later acquired strategic and security dimensions. This can be illustrated by the case of Indian oil companies' involvement in areas controlled by Vietnam.

Sustained high rates of growth have caused India's consumption of energy resources to skyrocket. Indian public- and private-sector energy companies alike are making major strides in exploration, drilling, and distribution of hydrocarbons both at home and in many parts of the world. As two of the largest consumers of hydrocarbon resources, India and China have strong incentives to cooperate in the energy sector and have, in fact, developed a number of cooperative mechanisms. An example of such mechanisms is the 2005 Memorandum of Understanding, which endorses joint projects in third countries.[28]

In Sudan, for example, Indian and Chinese companies shared drilling and distribution tasks.[29] But all is not harmonious; Indian and Chinese companies compete in several countries, such as Myanmar, where Chinese companies were able to displace Indian allocations in Rakhine state. In Kazakhstan, China's superior contacts with the political establishment proved detrimental to the Indian companies participating in the bidding process. In the case of the South China Sea, China and India appear to have embarked on a collision course. Two Indian companies, the public-sector company OVL and the private company Essar, have been allocated oil blocks by Vietnam. The blocks awarded to OVL in June 2006 are said by China to be in the disputed territories, but Essar had been drilling in faraway places in the South China Sea. The OVL's 127 block proved to be unpropitious because it hit hard rock. The 128 block became controversial when what had been a commercial venture was ensnared in the territorial dispute between Vietnam and China.[30]

China reportedly applied coercive diplomacy to prevent an Indian naval vessel, the INS *Airawat*, from entering the region in July 2011. The next development was that China's Foreign Ministry spokesman in Beijing called for the withdrawal of all foreign companies conducting drilling operations in the region. Tension increased further when the Chinese navy cut cables of drilling platforms in the region. Eventually, in May 2012, the Indian government announced temporary withdrawal from this 128 block.[31] However, by September that decision had been reversed and the company restarted operations at the request of the Vietnamese.[32] India's official position at the Association of Southeast Asian Nations (ASEAN) Regional Forum meetings was not well received by China. India stated at this forum that, although it does not side with any party to the territorial dispute, United Nations law should be respected and freedom of navigation should be observed.[33] This was an important statement because nearly 55 percent of Indian trade passes through the South China Sea. Tension between India and China increased and China began to articulate suspicions about collusion among India, Vietnam, and the United States.[34]

## Defense Ties

What the defense establishments of India and China are doing is another source of insight into how they view the rise of one another. The defense ministries of India and China have been at loggerheads since the 1962 border clashes. The stalemate continues despite recent agreements covering military exchanges (May 2006), confidence building measures (in 1993, 1996, and 2005) and joint operations between their respective defense forces (such as in hand-in-hand operations). After China enhanced its military presence and modernized its forces in Tibet, the Indian side initiated efforts to strengthen its conventional and strategic-deterrence capabilities. Similarly, after news spread about China's construction of highways (which now connect 80 percent of the counties), railway lines, five airfields nearer to the border, and robust fiber optic networks—China now can easily mobilize more than twenty-five divisions in Tibet—India decided to build twelve strategic roads in the trans-Himalayan border region. It also established a new strike corps, constructed three new air bases in Arunachal Pradesh, and upgraded many forward landing grounds. India also established an integrated ballistic missile program and undertook to build a ballistic missile defense system. The April 15–May 5, 2013, Chinese incursion in eastern Ladakh indicated to India that its deterrence capabilities needed to be strengthened further. Nevertheless, despite mutual distrust, action-reaction military buildups, and other signs of a classic security dilemma, the probability of an all-out conflict between these two nuclear states is extremely low.

## Relations with the United States

Each country's relationship with the United States is another useful indicator because of the latter's preeminent position in the international system. The role of and relations with the United States have been central to Chinese policy since the reform and opening policies were announced in 1978. Simply stated, maintaining reasonably good relations with the United States is critical to the success of reform and China's rise. Despite disagreement on many contentious issues—illustrated by the Taiwan Strait crisis of 1995–1996; the EP-3 surveillance plane incident in 2001; differences involving human rights and governance, currency manipulation, and proliferation-related actions; and other issues—China has managed to maintain sufficiently stable relations with the United States to avoid derailment of its drive for sustained growth. Both countries have developed mutually beneficial relations in trade, investment, and technology transfers, and as President Obama has stated, the United States welcomes the rise of China.[35] In June 2013, at the Sunnylands, California, meeting between Presidents Obama and Xi, the latter suggested a new type of major country relations with "no conflict and confrontation."[36]

India's relations with the United States began to improve in the 1990s and reached a new high in 2005–2008 with the signing of a ten-year defense cooperation agreement and a civil nuclear technology agreement.[37] One of the barometers for gauging the response of business communities to political visits in the era of globalization is the reaction of the stock exchanges. During President Bush's visit to New Delhi in 2006—a landmark visit that strengthened US-India relations—the Mumbai stock exchange increased by several thousand points. In contrast, stocks remained essentially unchanged during visits to India by top leaders from China and visits to China by Indian prime ministers.

The United States is now the most important external partner for both India and China. Both have diversified relations to include other major powers such as Russia, the European Union, and Japan. The relationship of India, China, and the United States can now be described as a strategic triangle in which each seeks to keep the other two closer to itself than those two are to each other. Thus, for example, India and China both watch carefully the ways that the United States interacts with each of them in an attempt to gauge whether either is gaining or losing influence. For example, India took note of and resents the US-China joint sponsorship of United Nations Security Council resolution 1172, which calls on India (and Pakistan) to "roll back, cap, and eliminate" their nuclear weapons programs. Another case that evoked Indian concern was the inclusion of South Asia in the US-China ambit in the November 2009 joint statement of the presidents of the United States and China in what had the appearance of being a "G-2."

China is equally attentive to the US-India relationship and has expressed misgivings about the US-India Civil Nuclear Agreement, the ultimately aborted US-India-Japan-Australia quadrilateral security dialogue, and the US rebalancing strategy in the Asia-Pacific.[38] During his visit to Beijing in October 2013, Indian Prime Minister Manmohan Singh offered "strategic reassurance" to China by stating that "as large neighbours following independent foreign policies, the relationships pursued by India and China with other countries must not become a source of concern for each other."[39] This was not the first such effort by India to reassure China. In March 2012, speaking to President Hu Jintao, Singh said, "India has no intention of and will not participate in any strategy aimed at containing China."[40] However, it is not clear whether China made any explicit reciprocal "strategic reassurance" to India. Providing such reassurance would be important because China's revisionist positions in the international system, strategic uncertainty about the goals and consequence of China's rise, the global and regional power transition debate, and other developments involving China are unnerving for New Delhi, Washington, and many others.

## Role in Multilateral Institutions

A fifth arena in which to assess Indian and Chinese behavior relative to one another's rise is the multilateral one. The indicator is whether or the extent to which New Delhi and Beijing seem to be modulating their differences or exacerbating areas of conflict. China and India are members or observers of different international and regional institutions like the United Nations, the G-20, the World Trade Organization, the East Asian Summit, the Brazil-Russia-India-China-South Africa (BRICS) forum, the Shanghai Cooperation Organization, the South Asian Association for Regional Cooperation, and others. The pattern of behavior in these organizations is a mixed one.

India supported the People's Republic of China's entry into the United Nations from 1950 until it was admitted in 1971. A widely circulated story holds that India was offered a permanent seat on the Security Council in 1955 but declined in favor of offering that seat to Beijing. Prime Minister Jawaharlal Nehru denied this story at the time, but the fact that it still circulates attests to the strength of belief that relations between India and China were once very close and that they could and should be similarly close in the future.[41] Today, India and China coordinate their activities in the UN mainly in terms of opposing any weakening of the UN Charter, specifically provisions on intervention and protecting developing countries' interests. Nevertheless, whereas other members of the Permanent Five have supported Indian candidature for a permanent seat on any enlarged version of the Security Council, China's position has been ambiguous. Since 2009, however, China has supported a "greater role" for India in international institutions, "including in the UN." This position was reiterated in the May 2013 joint statement between the premiers of India and China.[42]

India and China are both members of the eighteen-member East Asian Summit (EAS) group. At the first meeting of this group, in Kuala Lumpur in 2005, China was initially reluctant to support India's candidature, suggesting instead that the EAS should be a ten-plus-three grouping (including the ten ASEAN members and China, Japan, and South Korea). However, India still managed to secure membership with the support of Singapore and Japan.[43] In the seven meetings of the EAS held through 2012, India and

China did not clash directly on any major issue and, in fact, supported the overall thrust of discussions on trade, integration, and countering nontraditional security challenges. One area of disagreement with China was that India expressed support for a pan-Asian free trade area rather than multiple bilateral free trade areas.

A third major multilateral institution in which both India and China have been active participants is the BRICS forum. Five meetings of this forum had been held by 2013, with agendas that included overcoming infrastructure funding problems, countering trade protectionism, proposing solutions to problems of climate change, resolving regional security challenges (such as North Korea, Iran, Libya, and Syria), and so forth. Both India and China also argue for reform of the International Monetary Fund (IMF) and the World Bank, specifically to address quota and governance issues. Although IMF governance mechanisms were reformed in 2010, the BRICS have only 13 percent of the voting rights in this forum, despite producing nearly a quarter of global economic growth in 2013.[44] Currently, China's percentage of the quota stands at 4 percent, and voting rights total 3.81 percent. For India, the comparable figures are 2.44 percent and 2.34 percent, respectively.[45]

Another relevant multilateral institution, albeit one in which there is limited contact between India and China, is the Shanghai Cooperation Organization (SCO). China is one of the founding members; India joined as an observer in 2005. For India, the SCO is useful because of its focus on countering terrorism and countering drug trafficking and small-arms smuggling, border management, energy security, and expanding economic and trade relations. China had helped form the SCO as a buffer against NATO expansion, as a counterbalance to Russia, and to promote mutually beneficial relations in energy, trade, and so forth. Nevertheless, although Russia is said to have agreed to India's candidature for full membership, China had not so far indicated its position.

The membership in the SCO issue indicates significant differences between the attitude and approaches of India and China. Based on the June 2002 and April 2004 regulations adopted by the SCO member states, aspirant states for SCO membership should show "respect for the sovereignty, territorial integrity, and equal rights of the member states."[46] The relevant provisions specify positive and negative demands on the aspirant states and organizations, implying that potential entrants should have a clean record with the United Nations system (no sanctions, violations, etc.). They also specify that candidates for membership should not have any territorial disputes with the SCO states and that they should not have any conflicting interests with those of the SCO states.[47] Although these criteria may or may not be enforced by the SCO in admitting new members, the restrictions do suggest that a great deal of diplomatic bargaining may be required, especially because consensus of the SCO members is required. In 2010, Regulations on Accepting New Members were formally signed. Although no progress was achieved in the debate on admitting new members, in June and October 2002 and again in February 2003, India had indicated that it subscribed to the principles of the SCO and that it intended to apply for membership. In April 2004, India applied for membership in the SCO. The membership issue was raised, with energy as a crucial component in Indian calculations, during the visit of the Indian foreign minister to the SCO summit in 2005.[48]

In June 2006, India again signaled its intention to join the SCO.[49] India had attended SCO meetings since 2005 but was represented only at the level of the foreign minister, petroleum minister, or commerce minister. Participation at this level indicated India's interest in this organization, but it was not until the Yekaterinburg Summit meeting in 2009 that representation was raised to the level of the prime minister, though India was still not a full member of the organization. Prime Minister Manmohan Singh is reported to have said that the representative of a billion people would not be sitting in the corridor sipping coffee when the SCO members were deliberating policy issues. Singh's attendance was facilitated by the fact that Russia, the host of the 2009 SCO Summit, convened that meet almost simultaneously with the BRIC Summit on June 16, 2009. Singh visited the SCO gathering against the backdrop of the global financial crisis.[50] His participation was also facilitated by newly adopted changes to the format of SCO meetings that enabled representatives from observer countries to participate in restricted and plenary meetings with the SCO heads of state for the first time. But India still has not been granted full membership in the SCO.

The situation with respect to membership in the South Asian Association for Regional Cooperation (SAARC) is similar. India is a dominant state within this grouping because of its geography, population, resources, growth rates, and overall strength. China became an observer of the SAARC process at the fourteenth summit meeting in New Delhi in 2007. Others, including

Japan, the European Union, South Korea, and the United States were also admitted in this category at that meeting. China's admission was strongly supported by Pakistan, Nepal, and Bangladesh. China has expressed its desire to become a full member of the SAARC, but that has not happened. Moreover, at the seventeenth SAARC Summit, which was held in Maldives in 2011, members called for a "comprehensive review of all matters relating to SAARC's engagement with Observers." The summit also suggested "strengthen[ing] SAARC mechanisms."[51] These decisions may have been motivated, in part, by the desire of some members to delay or block China's membership.

These examples illustrate that India and China take somewhat different positions in multilateral institutions on issues such as inclusivity, agenda, and the global commons.[52] Thus far, however, their respective positions have not become contentious issues between them. As important, they hold increasingly similar positions on many other principles of multilateralism, including reciprocity, nondiscrimination, nonexclusivity, nonspecificity of enemy, confidence-building measures, and so forth. On these issues, India-China interaction in multilateral institutions has been growing and is likely to continue because several of these principles have not been realized. One significant difference is that China seems to view multilateral institutions as useful to counter the United States and to assist its own rise in the global system. India does not share these objectives.

## Conclusion

India and China are rising in the international economic and military power matrix, and both are trying to reshape the regional and global architecture in ways conducive to their own rise, but their bilateral relationship evinces signs of both cooperation and dissonance. Review of their interactions does not indicate significant efforts either to facilitate the simultaneous rise of both or likely to result in mutual decline. What it does indicate is that the two countries are rising independently, and that the mode and pace of their rise is shaped primarily by their domestic conditions and policies.

China is making concerted efforts to sustain its own rise and is cognizant of what is happening in India. Chinese analysts seem to hold different views on whether India's rise could be conducive for China's. Those who argue that it can point to the possibility for cooperation in the software industries and in multilateral institutions, specifically on issues relating to the protection of state sovereignty, developmental interests, and the like. However, others in China argue that the Indian "dream of becoming a great power" (*daguo xintai*) needs to be watched carefully because of its implications for China and China's influence in the South Asian region. They also underscore the importance of closely monitoring the state of India's relationship with the United States.

To counter India's imputed "great power" ambitions, China had developed policies to constrain India by providing inducements and alternatives to some South Asian states. These efforts are complemented by China's development of economic and military bases in the Indian Ocean Region. To counter these moves by China, India has been strengthening its conventional and strategic deterrence capabilities, working to build an inclusive security architecture at the regional and international levels by inviting participation by several powers and deepening and expanding its relationships with the United States, Japan, the European Union, Russia, Australia, and others. For example, India has sought to negotiate a regional maritime arrangement with Sri Lanka and Maldives, and cooperates with the Asian regional navies to counter piracy in the Indian Ocean.

Indian debates about China's rise hinge on the extent to which they view China through the lens of business opportunities or the lens of challenges to India's security. However, owing to the lack of any concrete initiative to push economic cooperation between the two rising giants to higher and mutually beneficial outcomes, the security perspective is gaining ground in India. Given the asymmetries in power relations between the two, China looms larger in the Indian security calculus than vice versa. But as Indian capabilities grow in the coming decades, the weight of security concerns could gradually diminish.

As both countries perceive each other through the prism of national interests, interactions between India and China have elements of cooperation, competition, and security challenge. They sometimes act as partners, as they do in multilateral processes that influence the regional and international order. For the foreseeable future, the relationship is likely to continue to be marked by suspicion, ambivalence, and hedging rather than to tip decisively in the direction of amity or antagonism.

*Notes*

1. The full statement can be found at http://www.mea.gov.in/bilateral-docu ments.htm?dtl/21723/joint+statement+on+the+state+visit+of+Chinese+Premier+Li +Keqiang+to+India.

2. See "PM at the Council on Foreign Relations (Q & A Session)," November 23, 2009, http://archivepmo.nic.in/drmanmohansingh/press-details.php? nodeid=1029. A year later, Singh suggested to an Indian editorial team that China is striving for a low level equilibrium in South Asia. See "China Wants India in State of Low-Level Equilibrium: PM," *Times of India*, September 7, 2010, http:// articles.timesofindia.indiatimes.com/2010-09-07/india/28215059_1_india-and -pakistan-bilateral-ties-outstanding-issues.

3. For background information on India-China relations, see John W. Garver, *Protracted Contest: Sino-Indian Rivalry in the Twentieth Century* (Seattle: University of Washington Press, 2001); and Mohan Malik, *China and India: Great Power Rivals* (Boulder, CO: First Forum Press, 2011).

4. World Bank, "Gross Domestic Product 2014, PPP," *World Development Indicators*, July 1, 2015, http://databank.worldbank.org/data/download/GDP_PPP.pdf. The United States held the number-two position, at $17.4 trillion.

5. PricewaterhouseCoopers, "World in 2050: The BRICs and Beyond; Prospects, Challenges and Opportunities," January 2013, http://www.slideshare.net/ PWC/world-in-2050-the-brics-and-beyond-prospects-challenges-and-opportuni ties. According to a Citibank report, Indian GDP based on purchasing power parity is expected to reach $85.97 trillion by 2050, whereas China's will reach $80.02 trillion and the United States' will reach $39.07 trillion by that year. See "With $85 Trillion, How India Can Become World's Largest Economy," *Economic Times*, November 12, 2011, http://articles.economictimes.indiatimes.com/2011-11 -12/news/30391268_1_largest-economy-demographic-dividend-indian-economy.

6. "Military Expenditure by Country, in Constant (2011) US$ M., 1988–2013," SIPRI Military Expenditure Database, http://milexdata.sipri.org/files/?file=SIPRI +military+expenditure+database+1988-2013.xlsx.

7. According to a RAND Corporation study, China is expected to post at least a 5 percent increase in its defense allocations by 2025. See Keith Crane, Roger Cliff, Evan Medeiros, James Mulvenon, and William Overholt, *Modernizing China's Military: Opportunities and Constraints* (Santa Monica, CA: RAND, 2005), 226, http://www.rand.org/content/dam/rand/pubs/monographs/2005/RAND_ MG260-1.pdf. See also Anthony H. Cordesman, Ashley Hess, and Nicholas S. Yarosh, *Chinese Military Modernization and Force Development: A Western Perspective* (Washington, DC: Center for Strategic and International Studies, 2013), chap. 5, https://csis.org/files/publication/130725_chinesemilmodern.pdf. Another

study projecting until 2050 by the London-based International Institute for Strategic Studies suggested that China could spend as much as the United States is spending by as early as 2025. See Giri Rajendran, "Chinese-US Defence Spending Projections" March 19, 2013, http://www.iiss.org/en/iiss%20voices/blogsections/iiss-voices-2013-1e35/march-2013-6eb6/china-us-defence-spending-6119.

8. See, for example, Natwar Singh, "Inaugural Address at 7th Asian Security Conference," January 27, 2005, http://www.idsa.in/node/1553.

9. See, for example, Ministry of External Affairs, Government of India, "Joint Communiqué of the Republic of India and the People's Republic of China," December 16, 2010, http://mea.gov.in/bilateral-documents.htm?dtl/5158/Joint+Communiqu+of+the+Republic+of+India+and+the+Peoples+Republic+of+China; and "Joint Statement on the State Visit of Chinese Premier Li Keqiang to India."

10. See, for example, "India and China: Friend, Enemy, Rival, Investor," *The Economist*, June 30, 2012, http://www.economist.com/node/21557764; and S. K. Mohanty, "India-China Bilateral Trade Relationship," July 2014, http://rbidocs.rbi.org.in/rdocs/Publications/PDFs/PRSICBT130613.pdf.

11. For additional details, see Teshu Singh, "Sino-Indian Strategic Economic Dialogue: An Analysis," *IPCS Issue Brief*, no. 184 (March 2012), http://www.ipcs.org/pdf_file/issue/IB184-Teshu-IndiaChina.pdf.

12. "China Emerges as India's Top Trading Partner: Study," *Times of India*, March 2, 2014, http://timesofindia.indiatimes.com/business/india-business/China-emerges-as-Indias-top-trading-partner-Study/articleshow/31268526.cms.

13. UNCTAD, "Global FDI Flows Declined in 2014; China Becomes the World's Top FDI Recipient," *Global Investment Trends Monitor*, January 29, 2015, http://unctad.org/en/PublicationsLibrary/webdiaeia2015d1_en.pdf.

14. Government of India, "Fact Sheet on Foreign Direct Investment (FDI), from April, 2000 to March, 2012," March 2012, http://dipp.nic.in/English/Publications/FDI_Statistics/2012/india_FDI_March2012.pdf. For a comparative account on FDI flows, see World Bank, "Foreign Direct Investment, Net Inflows (BoP, Current US$)," 2014, http://data.worldbank.org/indicator/BX.KLT.DINV.CD.WD.

15. Embassy of India, Beijing, "India-China Bilateral Relations: Trade and Commercial Relations," http://www.indianembassy.org.cn/DynamicContent.aspx?MenuId=3&SubMenuId=0 (accessed May 15, 2015).

16. "India, China Set for Closer Economic Ties," *The Hindu*, November 22, 2006, http://www.thehindu.com/todays-paper/tp-business/india-china-set-for-closer-economic-ties/article3051023.ece.

17. Although in 1954, India recognized Tibet as a part of China obliquely, the 1988 joint statement between the two countries suggested that Tibet is an "autonomous region of China"—with emphasis on the autonomy aspect of Tibet. The

June 2003 joint statement between the two countries was more explicit in stating, "The Tibet Autonomous Region is a part of the territory of the People's Republic of China." See "Trade Agreement Between the Republic of India and the People's Republic of China," October 14, 1954, http://www.liiofindia.org/cgi-bin/disp.pl/in/other/treaties/INTSer/1954/14.html?query=1954; "Sino-Indian Joint Press Communique," December 23, 1988, http://in.china-embassy.org/eng/zygxc/wx/t762866.htm; and "Declaration on Principles for Relations and Comprehensive Cooperation Between the People's Republic of China and the Republic of India," June 25, 2003, http://in.china-embassy.org/eng/zygxc/wx/t22852.htm.

18. See, for example, Elliot Sperling, *The Tibet-China Conflict: History and Polemics* (Washington, DC: East-West Center Washington, 2004), ix–x. These three descriptors provide absolute powers to the PRC over other countries vis-à-vis Tibet. However, in the backdrop of the talks between India and China on the territorial dispute (which includes territories once claimed by Tibetans historically) and the presence of the Tibetan émigré in India, India was reluctant to include any of these three words in the joint statements.

19. See Manoj Joshi, "Making Sense of the Depsang Incursion," *The Hindu*, May 7, 2013, http://www.thehindu.com/opinion/op-ed/making-sense-of-the-depsang-incursion/article4689838.ece.

20. See, for example, "Joint Statement on the State Visit of Chinese Premier Li Keqiang to India."

21. Wang Taiping, writing for the Ministry of Foreign Affairs during the 1970s, termed the Sino-Pak objective as "common struggle" [*gongtong douzheng*] with Pakistan against "expansionism [*kuozhang zhuyi*] and hegemonism [*baquan zhuyi*]" in southern Asia. See Wang Taiping, ed., *Zhonghua renmin gongheguo wiajiaoshi, 1970–1978* [PRC's diplomatic history, 1970–1978] (Beijing: World Knowledge, 1999), 110.

22. Selig S. Harrison, "China's Discreet Hold on Pakistan's Northern Borderlands," *New York Times*, August 26, 2010, http://www.nytimes.com/2010/08/27/opinion/27iht-edharrison.html.

23. See "Pakistan Rejects Indian Concerns over Gwdar Port," *Express Tribune*, February 15, 2013, http://tribune.com.pk/story/507549/pakistan-rejects-indian-concerns-over-gwadar-port/.

24. See "Xinjiang Unrest: China Blames Unrest on Pakistan-Trained Terrorists," *Express Tribune*, August 2, 2011, http://tribune.com.pk/story/221828/china-blames-xinjiang-unrest-on-terrorists/.

25. "Joint Statement on the State Visit of Chinese Premier Li Keqiang to India."

26. Peter Martin, "Beyond 1962: How to Upgrade the Sino-Indian Relationship," *Foreign Affairs*, April 15, 2015, https://www.foreignaffairs.com/articles/china/2015-04-15/beyond-1962.

27. Government of India, "Joint Statement Between the India and China During Prime Minister's Visit to China," May 15, 2015, http://pib.nic.in/newsite/PrintRelease.aspx?relid=121755.

28. Ministry of External Affairs, Government of India, "Joint Statement of the Republic of India and the People's Republic of China," April 11, 2005, http://www.mea.gov.in/bilateral-documents.htm?dtl/6577/Joint+Statement+of+the+Republic+of+India+and+the+Peoples+Republic+of+China; Siddharth Varadarajan, "India, China Primed for Energy Cooperation," *The Hindu*, January 13, 2006, http://www.hindu.com/2006/01/13/stories/2006011318821400.htm; "India to Strengthen Energy Cooperation with China," *People's Daily*, January 10, 2006, http://english.people.com.cn/200601/10/eng20060110_234338.html.

29. Yejoo Kim, "Chinese and Indian Cooperation in Africa: The Case of Sudan," Consultancy Africa Intelligence, October 17, 2011, http://www.consultancyafrica.com/index.php?option=com_content&view=article&id=869:chinese-and-indian-cooperation-in-africa-the-case-of-sudan&catid=58:asia-dimension-discussion-papers&Itemid=264.

30. Utpal Bhaskar, "OVL to Resume Drilling in South China Sea," *Live Mint*, January 8, 2012, http://www.livemint.com/Home-Page/FBW7tY2EP3egmwTXji5WjK/OVL-to-resume-drilling-in-South-China-Sea.html.

31. Dipanjan Roy Chaudhury, "India Pulls Out of Choppy Oil Block in Vietnam," *India Today*, May 13, 2012, http://indiatoday.intoday.in/story/india-pulls-out-of-choppy-oil-block-in-vietnam/1/188568.html.

32. "India Affirms Continued Oil and Gas Exploration with Viet Nam," *Vietnam's Sovereign Boundaries*, September 15, 2012, http://123.30.50.199/sites/en/indiaaffirmscontinuedoilandgas-gid--nd-eng81foe.aspx.

33. See the response of Minister of External Affairs Shrimati Preneet Kaur to a question from the lower house of the parliament, "Q No.2147: South China Sea Dispute," Ministry of External Affairs, December 18, 2013, http://www.mea.gov.in/lok-sabha.htm?dtl/22665/Q+NO2147+SOUTH+CHINA+SEA+DISPUTE.

34. Mohan Malik, "China and India Today: Diplomats Jostle, Militaries Prepare," *World Affairs*, July–August 2012, http://www.worldaffairsjournal.org/article/china-and-india-today-diplomats-jostle-militaries-prepare.

35. "Remarks by President Obama and President Xi Jinping of the People's Republic of China Before Bilateral Meeting," White House Office of the Press Secretary, June 7, 2013, http://www.whitehouse.gov/the-press-office/2013/06/07/remarks-president-obama-and-president-xi-jinping-peoples-republic-china-; "Remarks by President Obama and President Xi Jinping of the People's Republic of China After Bilateral Meeting," White House Office of the Press Secretary, June 8, 2013, http://www.whitehouse.gov/the-press-office/2013/06/08/remarks-president-obama-and-president-xi-jinping-peoples-republic-china-.

36. Catherine Beck, "Sunnylands 'Shirt-Sleeves Summit,'" U.S.-China Policy Foundation, June 14, 2013, http://uscpf.org/v3/2013/06/14/sunnylands-shirt -sleeves-summit.

37. See K. Alan Kronstadt, "India-U.S. Relations," *Congressional Research Service*, January 30, 2009, http://fpc.state.gov/documents/organization/120595.pdf.

38. Jeff M. Smith, *Cold Peace: China-India Rivalry in the Twenty-First Century* (Lanham, MD: Lexington Books, 2013); Siddharth Srivastava, "China Looks On at the US-India Lockstep," World Security Network, July 2, 2007, http://www .worldsecuritynetwork.com/China-India/siddharth-srivastava/China-looks-on-at -the-US-India-lockstep; "China Attacks Indo-US Nuclear Deal," *Rediff*, November 4, 2005, http://www.rediff.com/news/2005/nov/04ndeal.htm; "China Reacts Cautiously to First India-US-Japan Meet," *IBN Live*, December 20, 2011, http:// ibnlive.in.com/news/china-reacts-cautiously-to-first-indiausjapan-meet/213618-26 .html; "China Cautions India, US over Patriot Missile Deal" *Economic Times*, February 24, 2005, http://articles.economictimes.indiatimes.com/2005-02-24/ news/27476974_1_patriot-missile-india-and-pakistan-south-asia.

39. Government of India, "PM's Statement to Media After Delegation Level Talks with the Chinese Premier," October 23, 2013, http://pib.nic.in/newsite/ mbErel.aspx?relid=100182.

40. Wang Yusheng, "Who Is Sowing Discord Between China and India?" *People's Daily*, October 23, 2012, http://www.china.org.cn/opinion/2012-10/23/ content_26878808.htm.

41. For more on the claim that India was offered a permanent seat on the Security Council and Nehru's denial, see "UN Seat: Nehru Clarifies," *The Hindu*, September 28, 2005, http://www.thehindu.com/2005/09/28/stories/20050928002 70900.htm.

42. "Joint Statement on the State Visit of Chinese Premier Li Keqiang to India."

43. Mohan Malik, "The East Asia Summit: More Discord than Accord," *Yale-Global Online*, December 20, 2005, http://yaleglobal.yale.edu/content/east-asia -summit-more-discord-accord.

44. Robert H. Wade and Jakob Vestergaard, "The I.M.F. Needs a Reset," *New York Times*, February 4, 2014, http://www.nytimes.com/2014/02/05/opinion/the -imf-needs-a-reset.html.

45. International Monetary Fund, "IMF Members' Quotas and Voting Power, and IMF Board of Governors," May 15, 2015, http://www.imf.org/external/np/ sec/memdir/members.aspx. At the Sixth Financial Dialogue, held in Beijing in September 2013 (a meeting started in 2005), both sides declared again that such reforms are essential. See "India, China for Early Conclusion of IMF Quota Reforms," *Economic Times*, September 28, 2013, http://articles.economictimes

.indiatimes.com/2013-09-28/news/42481748_1_imf-quota-brics-development
-bank-china-and-india.

46. Observer states do not have voting rights at the summit meetings. See "The Regulations on Observer Status at the Shanghai Cooperation Organisation," Shanghai Cooperation Organisation, April 24, 2004, http://www.sectsco.org/EN123/show.asp?id=65.

47. Hypothetically, for instance, to block Indian candidature, China could point to India's unresolved territorial disputes with China, Pakistan, Nepal, Myanmar, Bangladesh, or Sri Lanka. Also, it could cite the UN Security Council resolution 1172 on rolling back South Asian nuclear capability (which it crafted with the United States in the lead in 1998), even though neither India nor Pakistan had violated any treaty that it had signed. This could also be applied to Iran, which is facing sanctions from the international bodies on the nuclear issue.

48. "India Pitches for Full Membership of SCO," *Silicon India News*, October 27, 2005, http://www.siliconindia.com/shownews/India_pitches_for_full_membership_of_SCO-nid-29799.html.

49. See the Indian foreign ministry spokesman's statement, quoted in "India Supports Basic SCO Principles: Official," *Xinhua*, June 13, 2006, http://english .cri.cn/2947/2006/06/13/272@101950.htm.

50. Prime Minister Singh commented, "My decision to attend the Summit is a reflection of the high regard we have for Russia's Presidency of the SCO." See M. Rama Rao, "India Pins Hopes on BRIC, SCO Summits, Singh Likely to Meet Zardari," *Asian Tribune*, June 16, 2009, http://www.asiantribune.com/node/21438; see also "PM to Visit Russia for SCO, BRIC Summits," *Times of India*, June 12, 2009, http://timesofindia.indiatimes.com/India/PM-to-visit-Russia-for-SCO-BRIC -summits/articleshow/4650063.cms.

51. "Seventeenth SAARC Summit, Addu Declaration: 'Building Bridges,'" November 11, 2011, http://www.saarc-sec.org/userfiles/ADDUDECLARATION 11-11-11.doc.

52. For instance, although India supports inclusion of major powers— including extraregional powers—in the SAARC process as observers, China has been somewhat reluctant to agree to expand membership in the EAS and the SCO. Also, on issues of maritime, cyber, and space commons, Indian and Chinese perspectives differ. For example, India has suggested to the United Nations laws promoting freedom of navigation. China, on the other hand, has unilaterally delineated what it believes to be its territory in the South China Sea with a nine-segmented line based on its historical justifications.

# SIX

# Sino-Pakistan Ties
## Trust, Cooperation, and Consolidation

*Syed Rifaat Hussain*

The strength and persistence of China and Pakistan's all-weather friendship confound the predictions of realists and constructivists alike. Realists argue that states enter into an alliance when threatened by a common enemy and that their alliance is likely to atrophy when the threat dissipates.[1] Judged by this realist logic, the Pakistan-China entente cordiale, which was forged in the early 1960s on the basis of shared hostility toward India, should have come undone as the threat from India diminished and Sino-Indian ties have improved since the early 1980s. Contrary to the prediction, Pakistan and China continue to broaden and deepen their bilateral ties.

Social constructivists attribute friendly ties between countries to the existence of commonalities such as identity, culture, values, and religion.[2] None of these fully apply to Pakistan-China strategic cooperation.[3] Regime type also cannot account for the durability of Sino-Pakistan ties, because the relationship has remained solid despite numerous regime changes in Pakistan and periodic upheavals in China's domestic politics.

What, then, explains the longevity of Sino-Pakistan friendship? I offer two reasons that reach beyond realist balance-of-power explanations of the "enemy of my enemy is my friend" variety. The first is the high degree of mutual trust at the leadership level of both countries and the extent to which this has generated good will among their respective publics. The second is China's appreciation of and help in mitigating the security dilemmas resulting from Pakistan's ongoing strategic competition with India. These two factors provide a better explanation for the depth and longevity of Sino-Pakistan ties than do explanations based on international relations theory. Without mutual trust and China's strategic sympathy for Pakistan's security dilemmas, it would be impossible for leaders of both countries to describe the relationship as an "all-weather friendship" that is time tested, "higher than the Himalayas," "deeper than the ocean," and "sweeter than honey."[4] Indeed, it was the weakness and gradual erosion of these two factors in Pakistan's relationship with the United States that caused the demise of their formal alliance.

## The Trust Factor

In his influential work, *Trust and Mistrust in International Relations,* Andrew H. Kydd, defines trust as "a belief that the other side is trustworthy, that is, willing to reciprocate cooperation" and mistrust as "a belief that the other side is untrustworthy, or prefers to exploit one's cooperation." He further observes that states that trust each other sufficiently can cooperate; states that do not may end up in conflict.[5] As a result, states constantly make inferences about one another's motivations. In a similar vein, Aarron F. Hoffman defines trust as an "actor's willingness to place its interests under the control of others based on the belief that those actors will honor their obligation to avoid using their discretion in a harmful manner."[6]

These two definitions capture the essence of trust in interstate relations and underscore its centrality in explaining why states with a high degree of mutual trust would cooperate in an anarchic world. Trust has four noteworthy features. First, trust involves an attitude, a positive disposition toward others. Second, it is marked by an expectation that the trustees will honor their obligations, and third, trustees will act in a manner consistent with their past reputation for trustworthiness. Fourth, trust is neither one sided nor unconditional, and it is a moot point whether cooperation comes before or after trust. In any case, cooperation without trust is like being in a loveless embrace that does not last very long. Andrew Kydd suggests that "costly signaling," defined as "making small but significant gestures that serve to prove that one is trustworthy," is a critical factor in the development of trust between states.[7] States that emit costly signals will be trusted more than those that engage in mere "cheap talk." In conditions of anarchy, states initially are reluctant to trust one another's motives but, through interaction and efforts at cooperation, can update their beliefs about one another's trustworthiness.

The early history of Pakistan-China interaction is critical to understanding the high degree of trust between the two countries. At the time of Pakistan's birth in August 1947, China was in the final throes of a bloody civil war between Communist and Nationalist forces. After the victory of the Communists in October 1949, the new government was empowered to "negotiate and establish diplomatic relations on the basis of equality, mutual benefit and mutual respect for territorial integrity and sovereignty" with powers that "sever relations with the Guomindang reactionaries and adopt a friendly attitude toward the People's Republic of China."[8]

Invitations were sent to foreign powers to recognize the new regime. Welcoming the unfolding shift in power, *Dawn*, the Pakistan national daily, declared that Pakistan would be a part of Asia's rise to greater importance and that "Pakistan would naturally try to establish early diplomatic relations with China."[9] On January 4, 1950, Pakistan became the first Muslim country to recognize the new Chinese government. In September that year, Pakistan, rejecting the Western claim that China's "love of peace" and regard for the UN Charter were "insufficient," supported a resolution to replace the delegation of Nationalist China with that of the People's Republic of China.[10] In June 1950, North Korea, backed by China and the Soviet Union, attacked South Korea in a bid to reunify the country. The failure of this move and subsequent involvement of China in the Korean War convinced many Americans that they faced "a coordinated campaign of militant Communist expansion," and the United States "came to regard the Soviet Union and China as more dangerous, opportunistic, and unpredictable than previously reckoned."[11]

Desperate for external aid and in search of a powerful patron to counterbalance India, Pakistan turned toward the United States, which needed regional allies "to build up positions of strength in areas such as the Middle East that were of crucial strategic value."[12] Pakistan signed a mutual security agreement with the United States in May 1954 and became the most "allied ally" of the United States when it joined the Southeast Asia Treaty Organization (SEATO) in September 1954 and the Baghdad Pact in February 1955. China understood the security pressures that had forced Pakistan to abandon nonalignment in favor of alignment with the West. This is clearly reflected in the conversation held at Bandung, Indonesia, between Pakistani prime minister Mohammed Ali Bogra and his Chinese counterpart, Zhou

Enlai. Zhou subsequently reported to party officials in Beijing that Bogra told him:

> Although Pakistan was party to a military treaty, Pakistan was not against China. Pakistan had no fear that China would commit aggression against her. As a result we achieved a mutual understanding. . . . The Prime Minister further assured that if the United States should take aggressive action under the military treaty or if the United States launched a global war Pakistan would not be involved in it. He said Pakistan would not be involved in it just as it was not involved in the Korean War. I am grateful to him for this explanation, because through these explanations we achieve a mutual understanding. *This creates agreement and harmony amongst us in understanding each other on collective peace and cooperation.*[13]

During their two private meetings at Bandung, Bogra explained to his Chinese counterpart why Pakistan had joined SEATO. The reasons included "fear of India," "her state of defenseless," and the "necessity of strengthening her relative military position even if this must be done through American assistance."[14] The connection between Pakistan's fear of India and her alliance with the United States was well understood by the Chinese premier. By holding out an assurance of Pakistan's benign intent toward China and his country's policy of neutrality in the escalating Sino-American hostility, Bogra won the confidence and trust of Chinese leaders.[15]

The understanding reached between the two prime ministers at Bandung opened the door for further cooperation. Cultural contacts between Pakistan and China expanded rapidly, and these exchanges improved "the general tone of Sino-Pakistan relations."[16] Speaking at the Pakistan Day reception in Beijing on August 14, 1955, Zhou Enlai declared, "In years to come our good neighborly relations will be further promoted and our cultural and economic intercourse will become more and more frequent."[17] In 1956, Prime Minister Hussain Shaheed Suhrawardy and Prime Minister Zhou exchanged state visits and stressed, "Despite different political systems and divergent views on certain international problems, the two countries had no important conflicts of interest and should increase their friendly ties."[18] It was against this backdrop of friendly gestures and mutual desire to promote friendly ties that the two countries concluded the 1963 border agreement that put them on the path to strategic cooperation.[19]

The spirit of accommodation and generosity displayed by the top Chinese leadership while concluding the border agreement had a profound effect on Pakistani leaders. For example, veteran Pakistani diplomat Abdul Sattar captured this impact in his recollection of the negotiations:

> Pakistan remembers with gratitude an extraordinary gesture by Premier Zhou Enlai: after the alignment was agreed, the Pakistan government belatedly realized that some grazing lands along the Mustagh River in the Shimshal Pass on the other side of the watershed were historically used by inhabitants of Hunza. It then appealed for an exception to the watershed principle to save hardship to the poor people. Zhou generously agreed to the amendment of the boundary so that an area of 750 square miles remained on the Pakistan side.[20]

Beijing's spirit of accommodation during boundary negotiations was motivated by more than just the desire to resolve boundary issues with Pakistan. It also wanted to buttress China's credentials as a peace-loving nation. China had concluded similar agreements with Burma and Nepal; the boundary agreement with Pakistan would furnish additional proof of China's peaceful intentions and desire for quiet borders. Another reason is that the Chinese wanted to show the world that their difficulties with India arose largely from the latter's intransigence. It is significant to note that China signed a boundary agreement with Outer Mongolia, an ally of the Soviet Union, on the same day they signed the agreement in principle with Pakistan, an ally of the West.[21] Moreover, by signing the boundary agreement with Pakistan, China removed a potential source of discord between the two neighbors.

In August 1963, the boundary agreement was followed by an air travel agreement, under which Pakistan became the first non-Communist country whose national carrier was granted landing rights in China. This, in turn, was followed by several agreements related to trade and cultural exchanges. China's larger objectives with respect to these agreements were illustrated by the remarks of the Chinese foreign minister when he welcomed the first PIA flight to Shanghai International Airport on April 29, 1964. He said, "We would like to point out that those who tried to isolate and blockade China have failed."[22]

This growing amity between Pakistan and China coincided with a visible cooling trend in Pakistan's relations with Washington. In the wake of the Sino-Indian War of 1962, in which India suffered a major defeat,[23] the United States shipped arms to India without advance notification to Pakistan and ignored Pakistani apprehensions that these arms would be used against Pakistan.[24] To make things worse, the United States urged President Ayub Khan to make a "positive gesture of sympathy and restraint"[25] toward India and advised Pakistan to put its "border talks with China on hold."[26] Ayub did not take advantage of India's vulnerability in its war with China but was disappointed that Pakistani inaction had not been rewarded with a serious negotiation leading to the settlement of the Kashmir dispute. The several rounds of Zulfikar Bhutto–Swaran Singh talks supported by US and British diplomats failed to produce any agreement on Kashmir because India had accused Pakistan of "unlawfully ceding two thousand square miles of 'Indian territory'" to China.[27] Convinced that the only remaining solution was a military one, Pakistan decided to launch Operation Gibraltar, which became the casus belli for a full-scale war between the two countries in September 1965.

After the war, the United States decided to terminate its arms-supply relationship with both India and Pakistan, a decision that caused "anger, bitterness, and disillusionment with the United States."[28] A series of widespread anti-American demonstrations in Pakistan, including the stoning of the US embassy, the burning of the United States Information Service library, and mob attacks on the US consulate in Lahore, provided stark testimony to the depth of anti-American sentiment in Pakistan.[29] For Pakistanis, the prestige and credibility of the United States fell to new depths.

Even before the September 1965 India-Pakistan War, Pakistan's friendship with China had become a bitter bone of contention between Washington and Rawalpindi. The Sino-Indian War rang alarm bells in Washington. To help India "defend itself better should the Chinese Communists renew their attack at an early date," Washington announced an Anglo-American emergency $120 million military aid package for India in December 1962.[30] Overriding Pakistani pleas to link the supply of American military assistance to India to settlement of the Kashmir issue, Kennedy sent a message to Ayub Khan that said the United States believed "the supply of arms to India should not be made contingent on a Kashmir settlement because" Chinese aggression posed "as grave an ultimate threat to Pakistan as to India."[31] Pakistan refused to go along with such "disingenuous" logic. Pakistan's unwillingness to cave in to mounting American demands that "Pakistan should be very careful in dealing with the Chicoms" lest it "jeopardize the relations with the Western world" and cause a "very unfortunate reaction" in the United States only widened the crisis of confidence between the two allies.[32]

Pakistan–United States relations became sharply acerbic during the Lyndon Johnson administration. Viewing China as an "outlaw" state that had become a "near-demonic force," whose "aggressive, adventuristic and unpredictable" behavior needed to be "contained," not courted, President Johnson decided to withdraw his invitation to the Pakistani president as a punishment for "greeting Mao, Zhou and their compatriots with open arms" and for "pledging lasting friendship and fruitful cooperation" between Pakistan and China.[33] In his April 14, 1965, letter to President Ayub, Johnson said that Ayub's proposed visit would "focus public attention on the differences between Pakistan and United States policy toward communist China and might gravely affect continued legislative support for Pakistan's development and defense efforts." Under the circumstances, Johnson concluded, "a postponement of the visit appeared the wisest course of action."[34] Ayub expressed anger over the abrupt cancellation of the visit. Inflexible and unforgiving, Robert Komer, a top National Security Council official, defended the US decision, saying, "Ayub got the signal, though we need to remind him" and that both India and Pakistan would be forced to "reflect on the moral that Uncle Sam should not just be regarded as a cornucopia of goodies regardless of what they do or say."[35]

The 1965 war further consolidated Pakistan's deepening trust in China. As the war escalated following an Indian attack across the international border on September 6, Beijing issued a strong condemnation of Indian aggression and hinted that the PRC might take a more active role in defending Pakistan. The statement said:

> The Indian Government's armed attack on Pakistan is an act of naked aggression . . . and constitutes a grave threat to peace in this part of Asia. The Chinese government sternly condemns India for its criminal aggression, expresses firm support for Pakistan for its just struggle against aggression, and solemnly warns the Indian Government that it must bear full responsibility for all the consequences of its criminal and extended aggression.[36]

Over the course of September, China issued several notes to New Delhi that condemned Indian military provocations along the Sino-Indian border, thereby raising the level of tensions. The September 16 note instructed the Indians to dismantle within three days the fifty-six military installations that had been built on "Chinese territory" in Tibet and to return the four hostages and livestock taken from the area or else "bear full responsibility for all the grave consequences arising there from."[37] The ultimatum was extended shortly thereafter for an additional three days. It was withdrawn when India and Pakistan accepted a UN-sponsored ceasefire agreement on September 22. By issuing its intervention threat, China proved beyond doubt (1) its interest in defending Pakistan; (2) its willingness to stand up to Indian power, which was being supported by both the Soviets and the Americans; and (3) its long-range claim to interests in the South Asian region.[38]

Following the Chinese ultimatum, the American ambassador, on instructions from Washington, met President Ayub. After lecturing about the risks he was running, he bluntly told Ayub that Pakistan faced a critical choice: "If it should directly or indirectly encourage Chinese entry into the conflict, Pakistan would alienate itself from the West, perhaps permanently. This was not a threat, but a reality."[39] Faced with this intense American pressure, Ayub reluctantly acceded to the US-backed UN cease-fire proposal.

The stark contrast between unqualified Chinese support and the bullying tactics of the United States had a profound impact on Pakistani thinking. Pakistan justifiably felt betrayed by Washington. During a "stiff" meeting with the American ambassador on September 29, Ayub "upbraided the United States for its revocation of solemn pledges regarding defense support; decried the lack of cooperation by the United States and the lack of appreciation for Pakistani efforts to moderate Chinese policies toward Vietnam; and accused the United States of bullying a friendly nation."[40] Pakistan needed support, but it wanted friends, not masters. China offered itself as solid anchor, and Pakistani leaders embraced that offer with unmitigated enthusiasm.

## Chinese Strategic Sympathy for Pakistan

China's own experience of foreign invasions, national humiliation, and encounters with colonialism leading to the forcible "opening of China" and loss of territory at the end of the nineteenth century made it extremely sensitive to the security challenges facing postcolonial states, especially small and weak states like Pakistan. Unlike Stalin, who had described the creation of Pakistan as "primitive" and attacked its founding fathers as "running dogs" of British imperialism, China under Mao Zedong never criticized Pakistan's efforts to obtain support from the West. To the contrary, Chinese leaders displayed a remarkable understanding of the security considerations shaping Pakistan's foreign policy—namely, the fear of a larger and hostile India that had led Pakistan to become the most "allied ally" of China's arch-enemy, the United States.

Strategic sympathy may be defined as a feeling of empathy for weak states struggling to survive in an anarchical world dominated by use of brute force by the strong against the weak. Security dilemmas are inherent in anarchical systems where there is no central authority to provide security to small and weak states.[41] In such systems, states typically seek security by forming alliance with others (external balancing), by aligning themselves with stronger powers (bandwagoning) or arms racing (arms buildup). None of these are cost-free strategies, and in pursuing them, the state has to weigh carefully the costs and benefits associated with each. Weak states typically are vulnerable because they can be used as expendable commodities in great power competition for survival and domination. As Thucydides reminded us a long time ago, "The strong do as they can and the weak suffer what they must."[42]

This strategic sympathy for Pakistan as a small developing state, whose two wings were separated by one thousand miles of hostile Indian territory, was reinforced by the general Chinese policy of seeking solidarity and building alliances with the developing world. As part of its effort to build Afro-Asian solidarity at Bandung, the Chinese articulated the concept of Panchshila, the "five principles of peaceful coexistence," as a guiding framework for its foreign policy toward the developing world.[43] This led to a brief period of "Hindi-Chini bhai bhai" (Indians and Chinese are brothers). However, the Chinese soon discovered the emptiness of this slogan through their negotiating experience with India during the effort to settle their border dispute with India in the Himalayas. Not only were the Indians unwilling to accept any adjustment of the boundaries inherited from the British, but they also engaged in "cartographic imperialism" by tampering with old maps on the direct orders of Prime Minister Jawaharlal Nehru in 1954.[44] Nehru's pursuit of the "Forward Policy" provoked the Sino-Indian War in 1962 and led to the unraveling of "Hindi-Chini bhai bhai" phase in their relationship.[45] China's early experiences with India contributed to Beijing's receptivity and sympathy when Pakistani leaders sought Chinese help to counter the perceived Indian threat to their security.

A country's security policy is shaped by its threat perceptions and the capabilities required to cope with perceived challenges. Pakistani threat perceptions have been shaped in what former foreign minister Abdul Sattar has aptly characterized as the "crucible of objective realities" manifested in "threats to its existence [from a hostile India] and the tyranny of imbalance of power."[46] In addition to having to deal with a hostile India in the east, Pakistan had to contend with an "irredentist" Afghanistan in the west. These realities created a security environment in which "strategic options open to Pakistan never were extremely attractive . . . increasingly risky, and limited in number."[47]

Although born as a garrison state, Pakistan did not have sufficient national resources to support military forces that would be capable of defending both wings of a country separated by a hostile neighbor. The American military assistance furnished to Pakistan after the Korean War was barely enough to defend the country. Pakistan's war stamina was less than three weeks when India and Pakistan went to war with each other in September 1965.

Washington's decision to cut off all American military assistance to India and Pakistan during the 1965 war affected the latter disproportionately, because over 80 percent of all military support to Pakistan came from the United States. Pakistan quickly realized the grave mistake it had made by putting all its security eggs in the American basket. The perils of single-source dependency on the United States were exacerbated by shifting American strategic priorities in South Asia, summarized by Robert Komer this way: "If we must choose between Pakistan and India, the latter is far more important."[48] Pakistan was compelled to search for new allies.

China offered itself as a crucial strategic counterweight to a much larger and overbearing India with which Pakistan had already fought a war over Kashmir. China had its own reasons to seek Pakistan's cooperation. The 1960s began with a Sino-Soviet split over ideological and strategic differences that erupted into the open in 1963, marking the beginning of the Coldest War in Asia. The American decision to ship arms to India exacerbated Chinese fear that the United States intended to contain China militarily. Hemmed in by these military and diplomatic pressures, China reached out to Pakistan because it saw both defensive and offensive possibilities. Defensively, a friendly Pakistan "could serve to impede Soviet, American, and Indian actions hostile" to China. Offensively, closer ties with Pakistan "would provide China an entrée into the Islamic world, would serve to improve China's image as a beneficent patron of Third World nations and, over the long term, would open the door for greater Chinese influence in South Asia and the Indian Ocean."[49]

Following the exchange of high level visits in 1964 and 1965, Pakistan and China agreed to common positions on several issues, including a call "for PRC seating in the United Nations, support for Afro-Asian solidarity against imperialism and colonialism, consensus on nuclear disarmament, and the continuation of friendly cooperation between China and Pakistan."[50] Abandoning its former posture of neutrality, China publicly endorsed Pakistan's position on Kashmir. The joint statement issued on February 23, 1964, after Premier Zhou Enlai's visit to Pakistan, expressed hope that the Kashmir issue would be resolved "in accordance with the wishes of the people of Kashmir as pledged to them by India and Pakistan."[51] The most tangible proof of China's appreciation of the security conundrum facing Pakistan came during the 1965 war, when China expressed its readiness to intervene in the conflict by opening a second front "against Indian positions in the Himalayas to reduce the pressure on Pakistan if Pakistan requested such help."[52]

Ayub himself decided against asking China to make such a move because he "feared that both the United States and the Soviet Union would support India" and that "his country would find itself in the unenviable position of facing the hostility of both superpowers."[53] After the war, Pakistan's elite and broader public had a much more favorable view of China. Chinese arms began to flow into Pakistan and were proudly displayed at the National Day parade on March 23, 1966. During Liu Shaoqi's visit to Pakistan in March 1966, China offered a $100 million grant to Pakistan to purchase arms on the international market, thereby freeing the country "from overdependence on the West and allowing it to defend itself against India."[54] In July of the same year, the two countries concluded an arms-supply agreement worth $120 million that included Chinese T-59 tanks, F-6 fighter jets, and IL-28 bombers.[55]

By 1970, Chinese weapons constituted 90 percent of Pakistan's modern fighter planes, one-quarter of Pakistan's tank force, one-third of its air force, and nearly two-thirds of its interceptor bombers. One reason China was willing to provide this weaponry was to bolster Pakistan's capacity for self-defense, which had suffered because of the American arms embargo. A second factor influencing these Chinese decisions was the intensifying Sino-Soviet rivalry in Asia. After suppressing the reform movement known as the Prague Spring in 1968 and enunciating the Brezhnev doctrine under which the Soviet Union arrogated to itself the right to intervene militarily in other socialist countries, Moscow launched its Asian Collective Security Plan in 1969 to contain China. Pakistan objected to the plan because it excluded China and could only be construed as an anti-China alliance. A Pakistani official statement declared that Pakistan would "never join any security arrangement in Asia which may involve her in the Sino-Soviet confrontation."[56]

In 1969, Soviet and Chinese troops clashed along the Ussuri River, provoking fears of nuclear war. Seeking to take advantage of the Sino-Soviet split and to extract the United States from the Vietnam War, the Richard Nixon administration decided to improve relations with China. On August 1, 1969, Nixon visited Pakistan and, in a confidential one-to-one meeting with President Yahya Kahn, stated, "The US would welcome accommodation with Communist China and would appreciate it if President Yahya would let Zhou Enlai know this."[57] The two presidents also discussed China's view of the world. Yahya told Nixon that China felt surrounded by hostile forces and suggested a "dialogue with China to bring China back into the community of nations."[58] Nixon responded, "Asia can not move forward if a nation as large as China remains isolated." He also said that the United States should not participate in "any arrangements designed to isolate China."[59] Yahya arranged a meeting between Henry Kissinger and Air Marshal Sher Ali Khan, who had visited China in July. When asked by Kissinger if there was any perceptible change in China's external behavior, the marshal explained that Zhou maintained that the Soviets were "deliberately provoking" China by trying to extend their territory beyond recognized boundaries.[60] Pakistani officials confirmed that Beijing feared the Soviets might attempt a "preemptive attack on China."[61] Yahya delivered Nixon's message to Zhou in November, and Pakistan continued to play the crucial role of intermediary by delivering secret messages between Washington and Beijing until July 1971, when Kissinger made his secret trip to Beijing.

Pakistan's decision to act as a bridge between the United States and China enraged Moscow.[62] To punish Pakistan for its crucial role in bringing China and the United States closer, Moscow decided to throw its strategic weight behind India. Moscow and New Delhi concluded the Indo-Soviet Treaty of Friendship and Peace in August 1971. The signing occurred while Pakistan's army was fighting a war for the survival of the country against the forces of secession in East Pakistan led by the Awami League, which was being fully backed by India. As the East Pakistan crisis deepened, former Pakistani foreign minister Zulfikar Ali Bhutto traveled to China to seek military assistance.

Bhutto told his Chinese hosts, "In order to intimidate us, India has placed in battle position its armed forces, including heavy armor and artillery and aircraft on the borders of both wings of Pakistan. These feverish military activities lead to one conclusion only. That is, India is planning to achieve its objective against Pakistan through armed conflict."[63] Aware of the presence of nearly forty divisions of Soviet troops on China's borders and the security clauses contained in the Indo-Soviet Treaty, acting foreign minister Ji Pengfei was noncommittal. Reiterating Beijing's established position, he said:

> Our Pakistani friends may rest assured that should Pakistan be subjected to foreign aggression, the Chinese government and people will, as always, resolutely support the Pakistani people in their struggle to defend their state sovereignty and national independence. The Chinese Government and people are greatly concerned over the present tension in the Subcontinent. We maintain that the internal affairs of any country must be handled by its own people. The East Pakistan question is the internal affair of Pakistan and a reasonable settlement should be sought by the Pakistani people themselves, and it is absolutely impermissible for any foreign country to carry out interference and subversion under any pretext.[64]

With the outbreak of the third Indo-Pakistan war in 1971, the Chinese issued statements of outrage condemning the Indians and fully supporting Pakistan. Chinese diplomatic and political support could not help avert Pakistan's military defeat and the dismemberment of the country. But after the creation of Bangladesh, China used its first veto in the Security Council to block the entry of Bangladesh into the UN until the vexed issue of Pakistani "war crimes" in East Pakistan was resolved to the satisfaction of the truncated "new" Pakistan. The decision to veto Bangladesh's entry into the world body was a difficult one for China because of its long-standing opposition to use of the veto and its well-known sympathies for the Bangladeshis. More important, it "defined the extent to which China could go to stand by Pakistan in a situation of crisis."[65] China also voiced its support for the Simla Agreement (1972), which normalized relations between India and Pakistan, and the New Delhi Agreement (1973), which led to the release of over ninety-three thousand Pakistani security personnel who had been taken as prisoners of war by India following Pakistan's military defeat in 1971. After the East-Pakistan military debacle and the birth of Bangladesh in 1971, China took it upon itself to totally rehabilitate the Pakistani armed forces.[66] Between 1971 and 1978, China assisted Pakistan in building two defense-related mega projects: the Heavy Rebuild Factory for T-59 tanks and the F-6 Aircraft Rebuild Factory.[67]

After India detonated its first nuclear device in May 1974, Beijing offered "firm and resolute support in Pakistan's just struggle in defense of its national independence and sovereignty against foreign aggression and interference, including that against nuclear threat and nuclear blackmail."[68] In 1976, Prime Minister Bhutto gained "China's acquiescence in helping Pakistan develop a nuclear weapon, including the provision of uranium for a Pakistani enrichment facility."[69]

The Soviet invasion of Afghanistan in December 1979 raised alarm bells in China. Chinese analysts raised special concerns about Soviet designs on Baluchistan.[70] The seriousness with which Beijing viewed Moscow's military intervention in Afghanistan was reflected in a toughly worded government statement that "vigorously condemned" Moscow's "wanton violation" of all norms of international behavior and warned that its "hegemonistic action" posed a "grave threat to peace and security in Asia and whole world." The statement called the Soviet invasion "a grave step for a southward thrust to the Indian Ocean," and it warned that Moscow's extension of the Brezhnev doctrine of "limited sovereignty" to nonaligned and Islamic countries with which it had signed treaties of friendship and cooperation was an ominous portent.[71]

To contain the Soviet threat, Beijing developed wide-ranging cooperation with Pakistan and formed a quasi alliance with the United States to roll back the Soviet military advance into Afghanistan. China, through Pakistan, "provided covert military supplies worth $200 million to the Afghan resistance and agreed to provide the US with facilities to monitor Soviet activities in its Xinjiang province."[72] Xinjiang was also used as a base for training Afghan Mujahedeen to fight the Soviet Union.[73]

As part of this trilateral strategic cooperation directed against the USSR, Beijing also provided critical help to Pakistan to strengthen its deterrent capability against India. Taking advantage of its role as a front-line state in the Afghan war, Pakistan intensified its quest for nuclear weapons capability.

The lifting of US antiproliferation sanctions against Islamabad gave Pakistan the necessary breathing space to pursue this quest. The United States turned a blind eye to this Pakistani effort because Washington needed Islamabad's cooperation to push the Soviets from Afghanistan. In 1981, President Muhammad Zia-ul-Haq sent Lieutenant-General Syed Zamin Naqvi and Dr. Abdul Qadeer Khan to Beijing to "request bomb-grade fissile material and bomb designs." China obliged and sent "Chinese CHIC-4 weapon design along with fifty kilograms of HEU [highly enriched uranium] to Pakistan."[74] Two years later, American intelligence agencies reported that the Chinese had transferred to Pakistan the complete nuclear weapon design, along with enough weapons-grade uranium for two potential nuclear weapons.

In September 1986, China and Pakistan signed a bilateral agreement governing cooperation in the peaceful uses of nuclear technology. This agreement raised concerns that China was assisting Pakistan to become a nuclear power. Following this agreement, Chinese scientists began "assisting their Pakistani counterparts with the enrichment of weapons-grade uranium."[75] The withdrawal of Soviet military forces from Afghanistan in February 1989 led to the waning of American interest in South Asia, and despite the imposition of American antiproliferation sanctions against Pakistan, Sino-Pakistan cooperation in missile and nuclear fields continued unabated.

In 1989, China and Pakistan signed a military cooperation agreement that envisaged, inter alia, "the purchase of military goods, mutual research and cooperation along with the manufacturing of arms and the transfer of technology."[76] During the same year, "China provided a very small 27 kW (kilowatt) research reactor, the PARR-2."[77]

In 1992, China provided the M-11 missile to Pakistan. Chinese experts provided extensive training to Pakistani technicians so they could become self-reliant for future production of these missiles.[78] More important than these missile transfers was the Chinese decision to set up a "turn-key missile factory" at Fatehjung, which enabled Pakistan to produce M-11 series missiles and "provided Pakistan with tremendous know-how and potential means to develop and produce larger, more capable systems in future." As a result, "Pakistan now has an infrastructure as well as training facility to bring a new generation of missile scientists into the art of solid propellant production."[79]

In return for Chinese help, Islamabad let the Chinese have the American Tomahawk Land Attack Missile (TLAM) when some of them fell on the Pakistani side of the border during the failed American attempt to kill Osama bin Laden in Khost in August 1998. It is widely believed that the Pakistani Babur missile, a subsonic missile that can carry both nuclear and conventional warheads, is a derivative of the recovered TLAMs that was jointly reverse engineered by Chinese and Pakistani scientists.[80]

During President Pervez Musharraf's visit to Beijing in February 2006, China committed to delivering the first small batch of JF-17 Thunder aircraft to Pakistan by 2007. On May 23, 2006, Pakistan and China signed a defense deal worth $600 million, which included the construction of four F-22P frigates for the Pakistan Navy, the upgrading of the Karachi dockyard, and the transfer of technology for the indigenous production of a modern surface fleet. In November 2006, Pakistan's air force signed a memorandum of understanding with the China Electronic Technology Corporation to develop aircraft equipped with long-range early warning radars.[81]

The nuclear deal signed between India and the United States on March 26, 2006, was viewed with alarm by both Beijing and Islamabad. In response, they concluded an agreement to "further deepen cooperation in peaceful application of nuclear power" in February 2006.[82] In November 2009, Beijing announced the $1.4 billion sale to Pakistan of thirty-six J-10B multirole fighters produced by the Chengdu Aircraft Corporation. The sale confirmed China's support for the modernization of Pakistan's conventional-deterrence capability against India. In April 2010, China announced the sale to Pakistan of two nuclear reactors (Chashma 3 and Chashma 4) as part of its "strategic assurance" to Islamabad that "the China-Pakistan partnership is a structural axis of regional politics that will shoulder important responsibilities for regional stability in a post-NATO Afghanistan."[83] A deal for two more Chinese reactors—at 1,000 MWe, the reactors are three times larger than the others—was finalized in 2013. The new reactors are being built in Karachi and they are "a first step toward fulfillment of the Pakistan Atomic Energy Commission's plans for a dramatic expansion of the nation's nuclear-energy infrastructure."[84]

In 2012, more than 50 percent of Pakistan's armaments came from China; only 28 percent came from the United States.[85] Pakistan obtains arms from China at concessional rates and Beijing wants Islamabad to attain a measure of self-reliance in the defense sector. Over the years, it has helped Pakistan to build ordnance factories and most defense deals have entailed direct transfer of technology from China. China's assistance has included supply of spare parts, setting up of local overhaul facilities, licensed production, training facilities, and joint ventures.[86] The provision of large amounts of military hardware and technology from China has accrued to Pakistan "free of charge, or at cost, or under similar highly favorable terms of repayment."[87]

### China's Rise and Its Implications for Pakistan

Having experienced stupendous economic growth, modernization, and social development over the past several decades, China is fast emerging as a powerful country. Led by "fifth-generation leaders" President Xi Jinping and Premier Li Keqiang, China is asserting itself in the global political arena and seeking deeper engagement in the global political economy. China's ascent to a position of greater global influence has evoked envy and fear among its neighbors and peers. To allay these apprehensions, Chinese scholars have advanced the notion of China's "peaceful rise" aimed at creating a harmonious society internally as well as internationally.[88]

In recognition of this ongoing power transition, the United States has announced that it would be pivoting toward the Asia-Pacific region. Other countries are adjusting and adapting to this process of change as well. How would China's rise as a global player affect its relations with Pakistan, which, as documented in the first section of the chapter, have been characterized by close bilateral strategic cooperation? Judging by the long history of their cordial bilateral relationship, shared regional and strategic outlooks, absence of territorial disputes, and high degree of mutual trust, we can predict that the dynamics of Sino-Pakistan entente cordiale would not be fundamentally altered in the foreseeable future. Islamabad views China's stupendous economic growth and its drive for force modernization as additive assets to compensate for its own vulnerabilities.

China views Pakistan as a dependable ally whose military strength is vital for checking India's growing military ambitions and to counter its new doctrine of "two-front war" against China and Pakistan.[89] More importantly, Pakistan does not share Washington and New Delhi's anxiety about the rise of China.[90] Pakistani views on China's rise were well captured by Senator Mushahid Hussain Sayed, who stated categorically that "Pakistan always welcomed the peaceful rise of China since it is a source of strength and security for the small and medium-sized countries in Asia, particularly neighbours like Pakistan."[91]

Pakistan finds itself in total agreement with the three cardinal principles of Chinas' grand strategy—namely, maintaining China's basic system and national security, national sovereignty and territorial integrity, and continued development of the economy and society.[92] To promote these core interests, China's grand strategy emphasizes three objectives: maintenance of a peaceful and stable environment; avoidance of confrontational relationships with most states, especially with China's neighbors; and maximization of its autonomy in the international system to minimize limits of unipolarity.[93]

To achieve peace and development, China has, on many occasions, called for the establishment of a new international political and economic order of peace, stability, justice, and rationality, based on the Five Principles of Peaceful Coexistence and on recognition of the diversity of the world and differences between states. In his speech to the Pakistani Parliament on April 10, 1999, Li Peng, chairman of the Standing Committee of China's National Peoples Congress stated, "China has all along pursued an independent foreign policy of peace and established and developed relations with other countries on the basis of the Five Principles of Peaceful Co-existence."[94]

Almost a decade later, in 2011, President Hu Jintao repeated the same formulation in an interview with the *Wall Street Journal* and the *Washington Post*. He said:

> China has been committed to the independent foreign policy of peace and has developed friendship and cooperation with all countries on the basis of the Five Principles of Peaceful Coexistence. We stand for equality and mutual respect between countries. Like other countries in the world, China must uphold its own sovereignty, territorial integrity, and development interests. At the same time, we are willing to properly handle differences and disagreements in state-to-state relations in accordance with the basic norms governing international relations and the principle of mutual understanding, mutual accommodation, dialogue, and consultation.[95]

These principles were codified in a Treaty of Friendship, Cooperation, and Good-Neighborly Relations during Chinese Premier Wen Jiabao's visit to Islamabad in April 2005. The treaty committed both nations to enhance their mutual cooperation "in accordance with the universally recognized principles and norms of international law and on the basis of the Five Principles of Peaceful Coexistence." Under the treaty, "both nations agreed not to join any alliance or bloc which infringes upon the sovereignty, security, and territorial integrity of the other, nor will either allow its territory to be used by a third country to jeopardize the state sovereignty, security, and territorial integrity of the other party to the pact." They further agreed to enhance their cooperation in "fighting terrorism, separatism, and extremism, as well as organized crime, illegal immigration, and trafficking in drugs and weapons."[96]

Prime Minister Wen Jiabao's 2005 visit to Islamabad occurred against the background of escalating violence in the Chinese province of Xinjiang, which has a 5,500-kilometer-long border with Pakistan. Chinese authorities have blamed the violence on the banned East Turkestan Islamic Movement (ETIM), a separatist group with links to Al-Qaeda. ETIM shifted its base to Afghanistan following the collapse of the Soviet Union in 1991 and then moved into tribal areas of Pakistan in response to the American- and NATO-led International Security Assistance Force military campaign against Taliban-controlled Afghanistan in late 2001. In December 2003, ETIM leader Hasan Mahsum was reported killed in Pakistan. China's mounting security concerns relating to ETIM and subversive activities of other insurgent groups working in Xinjiang necessitated insertion of article V into the treaty. This article committed the signatories to "crack down on terrorism, separatism and extremism."[97]

During his December 2010 visit to Islamabad, Prime Minister Wen praised Pakistan's efforts to fight terrorism and stated, "Pakistan has given great sacrifices and made great efforts in the fight against terrorism. . . . This is a well-known fact." He urged the international community to respect and support Pakistan.[98] His comments were meant to defend Pakistan in the face of mounting US criticism that Islamabad was not doing enough to fight terrorism. Privately, China has been urging Islamabad to ensure that militant groups operating from the federally administered tribal areas (FATA) of the country do not play any role in fomenting trouble in the predominantly Muslim Chinese province of Xinjiang. There have been a number of violent attacks on Chinese workers in Pakistan, particularly in the insurgency-infested area of Baluchistan. In May 2004, three Chinese engineers were killed in a car bomb blast in Gwadar. From 2004 to 2010, there were four separate terrorist attacks on the Chinese workers engaged in development projects in different parts of the country. Twelve Chinese lost their lives in these attacks.[99] That such acts of violence have not discouraged nearly twelve thousand Chinese workers from doing their jobs in Pakistan attests to the strength of Pakistan-China relations. For its part, Pakistan has enhanced its efforts to provide greater protection and security to the Chinese workers by offering "army-backed security" to Chinese firms doing business in Pakistan.[100]

China and Pakistan are acutely aware of the need to broaden the base of their relationship and to develop a cooperative security framework that addresses Pakistan's security dilemmas and creates an environment conducive to China's peaceful rise. Chinese who know about their country's aid to Pakistan's nuclear program firmly believe that assisting Pakistan's quest for the absolute weapon created a level playing field that is a sine qua non for lasting peace in South Asia. That is why Beijing has viewed Pakistan's acquisition of nuclear weapons without the alarm evinced by Western nations and has continued to provide support for Pakistan's nuclear and missile programs.

China's economic success and future growth depend on assured access to hydrocarbons from the Persian Gulf and Africa. This necessity has made Pakistan central to China's energy security strategy and grand strategy for South Asia. Thus, China has steadily expanded its economic ties with Pakistan and helped finance more than two hundred projects in the country, including the expansion and improvement of the Karakoram Highway, the Thar coal project, the Bhasha Dam, and construction of the Gwadar Port on the coast of Pakistan's Baluchistan province. Construction of the Gwadar Port project began in March 2002 and was completed in 2007. China provided $248 million in financial assistance during the first phase and the bulk of the estimated $840 million cost of the second phase. Several hundred Chinese laborers worked on this mega project. Initially, the Singapore Port Authority managed the Gwadar Port, but in 2013 Pakistan terminated this contract and transferred control to China. This is significant because Gwadar is strategically located at the entrance of the Persian Gulf about 390 nautical miles east of the Gulf of Hormuz and about 234 nautical miles west of Karachi. Given its strategic location and the ancillary network of roads surrounding it, Gwadar is supposed to connect the Pakistan economy to Xinjiang via the Karakoram Highway. As observed by Ziad Haider, "It is meant to transform Pakistan into a vibrant hub of commercial activity among the energy rich Gulf and Central Asian states, Afghanistan, and China, and to provide the Pakistan Navy with strategic depth by serving as a naval base. The port will also enable China to diversify its crude oil import routes and extend its presence in the Indian Ocean."[101]

China has also been promoting a transnational network of roads, railways, and ports as a public good that can benefit the region. Behind this advocacy lies a vested Chinese interest; without connectivity, China will not be able to sustain its export-led growth and its emergence as the biggest trading state. Equally impressive has been the progress it has made "in unlocking its hinterland to neighboring countries."[102] For example, in its land-locked western region, China has announced plans to transform the cities of Kashgar and Urumqi into major trade hubs between the eastern and western parts of the Eurasian continent.[103]

Despite its impressive economic growth rates, South Asia remains a segmented region and lacks transborder connectivity. China's interest in helping the region overcome this crippling handicap should be taken seriously. During his first visit to the region, Chinese prime minister Li Keqiang offered a "handshake across the Himalayas" by emphasizing that "there is enough space in the world for the development of India and China" and that "both countries view each other as partners for mutual benefit and not as rivals or competitors."[104] Speaking to the news media, the Chinese premier said, "World peace and regional stability cannot be a reality without strategic mutual trust between India and China. And likewise, the development and prosperity of the world cannot be a reality without the cooperation and simultaneous development of China and India." While in Pakistan, he offered Chinese help to resolve Pakistan's energy crisis, and in their joint statement, both countries pledged to "tap the potential of trade [and] logistics" and agreed to "enhance interconnectivity and jointly develop a long-term plan for a China-Pakistan economic corridor."[105]

The return to power of the Pakistan Muslim League–Nawaz (PML-N) party, led by Mian Nawaz Sharif, following May 2013 national elections brought renewed dynamism to Pak-China economic cooperation. Several agreements have been signed for construction of road and railway links between Xinjiang and the Gwadar Port in Baluchistan. In a meeting with Nawaz Sharif on the sidelines of the Boao Forum in April 2014, Premier Li said the two countries have agreed to make the building of a Pakistan-

China economic corridor the focus of bilateral cooperation and to forge a China-Pakistan "community of shared destiny."[106] In his keynote address to the Boao conference, Pakistan's prime minister called for a collective approach and coordinated effort for economic prosperity. He urged the regional countries to focus on "greater regional connectivity particularly through roads, rails and sea lanes."[107] This would help in promoting mutual relations, which, in turn, would help to achieve development of the region.

China's future political stability and sustainable development depend on continuous economic growth fueled by readily available and affordable energy supplies. China' s advocacy of a Pakistan-China economic corridor must be seen in the context of Beijing's continuing search for access to global energy resources by investing in and deepening political relationships with energy-producing states and the countries on the transit route. In the last decade, China has assisted the construction of deep-sea ports in Pakistan (Gwadar), Bangladesh (Chittagong), and Sri Lanka (Hambantota) and a land port on the border with Nepal. This so-called string-of-pearls strategy—with Gwadar Port situated at the edge of the Arabian Sea bordering the Strait of Hormuz and the Persian Gulf, Chittagong located in the Bay of Bengal, and Hambantota in the Indian Ocean—will help China overcome its "Malacca Dilemma." China envisions connecting these seaports with its different provinces through rail and road networks. Among other goals, these improvements will help supply energy to fuel China's economy.

## Conclusion

This chapter argues that one of the key reasons that the Pak-China entente cordiale forged in the early 1960s has stood like a solid rock across the passage of time and has withstood changes in the international, regional, and domestic environments is the high degree of mutual trust between the two countries. This trust, in turn, has allowed both Beijing and Islamabad to align their respective national interests closely and to pursue policies of strategic assurance toward each other. Pakistan has adjusted itself to the reality of improved Sino-India ties, and Beijing has assured Pakistani leaders, civilians, and military alike of its continued support in dealing with threats to its security. Both sides trust these assurances.

*Notes*

I thank Sharon Freitas for her helpful editorial comments and Janani Ramachandran for her valuable research input. I am particularly grateful to Thomas Fingar for providing guidance and specific suggestions on an earlier draft of this chapter.

1. Realism posits that interstate relations are based on motivations for power. Beyond power, realists stress the analytic centrality of states, their interest in survival, the primacy of material capabilities, and rationality. Realists point to four factors in alliance formation: the level of external threat faced by the allies, the military capabilities of the allied states, the extent to which policy goals are shared by the allies, and the availability of substitute allies. See Stephen M. Walt, "Testing Theories of Alliance Formation: The Case of Southwest Asia," *International Organization* 42, no. 2 (1980): 275–316.

2. Social constructivism argues that state behavior in the international arena is largely a function of social norms and ideas. What states do in the international arena is heavily influenced by their subjective interpretations of the material reality. As Alexander Wendt famously put it, "Anarchy is what states make of it." See Alexander Wendt, "Anarchy Is What States Make of It: The Social Construction of Power Politics," *International Organization* 46, no. 2 (1992): 391–425.

3. As observed by William J. Barnds, "Since China and Pakistan are such different societies their co-operation can hardly be based upon ideological affinity or mutual attraction." See William J. Barnds, "China's Relations with Pakistan: Durability Amongst Continuity," *China Quarterly*, no. 63 (September 1975): 363.

4. "Pakistan and China: Sweet as Can Be?" *The Economist*, May 12, 2011, http://www.economist.com/node/18682839; Sutirtho Patranobis, "China Harps on 'All-Weather Friendship' with Pak," *Hindustan Times*, February 11, 2014, http://www.hindustantimes.com/world-news/ahead-of-pak-president-s-visit-china-harps-on-all-weather-friendship/article1-1182918.aspx; "Felicitations: Pakistan-China Enjoy 'All-Weather' Friendship, Says Zardari," *Express Tribune*, October 1, 2011, http://tribune.com.pk/story/264738/felicitations-pakistan-china-enjoy-all-weather-friendship-says-zardari/2011; Aparna Pande, "All-Weather Friendship," in *Explaining Pakistan's Foreign Policy: Escaping India*, by Aparna Pande, 114–135 (London: Routledge, 2011).

5. Andrew H. Kydd, *Trust and Mistrust in International Relations* (Princeton, NJ: Princeton University Press, 2005), 4.

6. Aaron M. Hofmann, "A Conceptualization of Trust in International Relations," *European Journal of International Relations* 8, no. 3: 394.

7. Kydd, *Trust and Mistrust*, 4.

8. Hafeez-ur-Rehman Khan, "Pakistan's Relationship with the People's Republic of China," *Pakistan Horizon* 14, no. 3 (1961): 134.

9. Ibid.

10. Anwar Syed, "Sino-Pakistan Relations: An Overview," *Pakistan Horizon* 22, no. 2 (1969): 119.

11. Robert J. McMahon, "U.S. Policy Toward South Asia and Tibet During Early Cold War," *Journal of Cold War Studies* 8, no. 3 (2006): 133.

12. Ibid.

13. Cited in Khan, "Pakistan's Relationship," 219–220 (emphasis added).

14. Anwar Hussain Syed, *China and Pakistan: Diplomacy of an Entente Cordiale* (Amherst, MA: University of Massachusetts Press, 1974), 61–62.

15. In April 1963, Premier Zhou Enlai, said in an interview with the Associated Press, "After the formation of SEATO in 1954, the Pakistani Government often declared to the Chinese Government that its participation in that organization was not for the purpose of being hostile to China and would not prejudice Pakistan's friendship for China." Quoted in W. M. Dobell, "Ramifications of the China-Pakistan Border Treaty," *Pacific Affairs* 37, no. 3 (1964): 284.

16. Syed, *China and Pakistan*, 64.

17. Ibid.

18. Barnds, "China's Relations with Pakistan," 468.

19. In September 1959, the government of Pakistan noticed Chinese maps showing parts of Hunza as Chinese territory. Worried that armed patrolling of this undemarcated area could easily provoke a violent clash between Pakistani and Chinese troops, as it had led to armed clashes between the troops of India and China in Longju and at the Kongka Pass in Ladakh, Pakistan proposed border talks in October 1959. The Chinese asked for the parameters of such negotiations. Pakistan replied by identifying three elements: the ground situation, customary law and practices, and mutual accommodation. See Riaz Mohammed Khan, "Pakistan-China Relations: An Overview," *Pakistan Horizon*. 64, no. 4 (2011): 11.

On May 3, 1962, both sides affirmed, "The boundary between China's Sinkiang [Xinjiang] and the contiguous areas, the defense of which is under the actual control of Pakistan, has never been formally delimited and demarcated in history. With a view to ensuring tranquility along the border and the growth of good-neighborly relations between the two countries, they have agreed to conduct negotiations so as to attain an agreed understanding of the location and alignment of this boundary and to sign on this basis an agreement of a provisional nature." Maps were exchanged in July 1962, and talks began in Beijing in October 1962. Soon thereafter it was declared that "upon reaching agreed views on the procedural matters concerning the talks, the representatives of the two parties exchanged plain topographical maps, which were checked technically by map experts of both parties and on which an agreed understanding was attained. Following that, the two parties exchanged maps depicting the boundary line and held formal meetings as well as friendly consultations in a spirit of equality, coopera-tion, mutual understanding, and mutual agreement. And now an agreement in principle has been reached on the location and alignment of the boundary actually existing between the two countries." See K. Sarwar Hasan, ed., *China, India, Pakistan* (Karachi: Pakistan Institute of International Affairs, 1966), 379. The boundary agreement was signed in Beijing on March 2, 1963. For the text of the agreement, see "The People's Republic of China-Pakistan: Agreement on the Boundary Between China's Sinkiang and the Contiguous Areas, Beijing, March 2, 1963," *American Journal of International Law* 57, no. 3 (1963): 713–716.

20. Abdul Sattar, *Pakistan's Foreign Policy, 1947–2005: A Concise History* (Karachi, Pakistan: Oxford University Press, 2007), 71.

21. Syed, *China and Pakistan*, 91.

22. Syed, "Sino-Pakistan Relations," 114.

23. Panicked by the instant meltdown of his army, a desperate Nehru sent two letters to President John F. Kennedy requesting American military help. On November 19, describing India's predicament as "really desperate," he requested the "immediate dispatch of twelve squadrons of all-weather US fighter aircraft and the prompt installation of a sophisticated radar network." In addition, he asked that US personnel not only operate the requested radar stations but also pilot the fighter jets. Robert J. McMahon, *The Cold War on the Periphery: The United States, India and Pakistan* (New York: Columbia University Press, 1994), 292.

24. During Ayub Khan's visit to Washington in July 1961, President Kennedy assured the Pakistani president that "if a Sino-Soviet conflict ever erupted and India asked the United States for military aid, he would consult with Ayub before making any commitments." Ibid. 332.

25. Dennis Kux, *The United States and Pakistan, 1947–2000: Disenchanted Allies* (Washington, DC: Woodrow Wilson Center Press, 2001), 112.

26. Feroz Hassan Khan, *Eating Grass: The Making of the Pakistani Bomb* (Stanford, CA: Stanford University Press, 2012), 40.

27. Jawaharlal Nehru's statement in Indian Parliament on March 5, 1963, quoted in A. G. Noorani, "The Sino-Pak Boundary Agreement," *Criterion* 4, no. 4 (2012): 27.

28. McMahon, *The Cold War on the Periphery*, 332.

29. Ibid.

30. Ibid., 296.

31. Ibid., 308.

32. Ibid., 296.

33. Ibid., 321.

34. Ibid., 322.

35. Ibid., 324.

36. The September 7, 1965, Chinese government statement condemning India's attack can be found in "India's Attack on Pakistan Condemned: Chinese Government Statement," *Peking Review* 37 (1965): 6–7, https://www.marxists.org/subject/china/peking-review/1965/PR1965-37.pdf.

37. R. Bates Gill, *Chinese Arms Transfers: Purposes, Patterns, and Prospects in the New World Order* (London: Praeger, 1992), 145.

38. Ibid.

39. McMahon, *The Cold War on the Periphery*, 332.

40. Ibid.

41. The notion of security dilemma was first articulated by John Herz and later expanded by Robert Jervis as a causal explanation of rational state behavior under conditions of anarchy. A security dilemma refers to a situation wherein two or more states are drawn into a conflict, possibly even war, over security concerns, even though none of the states actually desire conflict. Essentially, the security dilemma occurs when two or more states each feel insecure in relation to other states. As each state acts militarily or diplomatically to make itself more secure, the other states interpret its actions as threatening. An ironic cycle of unintended provocations emerges, resulting in an escalation of the conflict, which may eventually lead to open warfare. See John Herz, "Idealist Internationalism and Security Dilemma," *World Politics* 2, no. 2 (1950): 157–180. See also Robert Jervis, "Cooperation Under the Security Dilemma," *World Politics* 30, no. 2 (1978): 167–214.

42. Thucydides, *History of the Peloponnesian War* (London: Penguin Books, 1972), 400.

43. In his statement in Bandung, Premier Zhou Enlai pledged that China was committed to resolving border disputes with its neighbors peacefully and offered his thoughts on how it should be done: "China borders on twelve countries with some of which the boundary lines remain undefined in certain sectors. We are ready to delimit those sections together with our neighbors. Pending this, we agree to maintain the status quo and recognize the undefined boundary lines as lines yet to be defined. Our Government and people will refrain from stepping over the boundary line. Should such an incident happen, we will be ready to point out our mistake and immediately order the trespassers back into Chinese territory. In defining any boundary line with our neighbors, only peaceful means can be employed and no other alternative should be allowed. Further negotiations can be held if one round of negotiation does not produce any results." Quoted in Neville Maxwell, "Settlement and Disputes: China's Approach to Territorial Issues," *Economic and Political Weekly* 41, no. 36 (2006): 3874.

44. For details of Nehru's direct orders to dispense with historical record and construct a new Indian narrative on the boundary question, see Noorani, "The

Sino-Pak Boundary Agreement," 5–8. See also Maxwell, "Settlement and Disputes," 3873–3881.

45. New Delhi began implementing the Forward Policy in November 1961. This policy involved sending small contingents of lightly armed Indian troops into the disputed areas of both Aksai Chin and Arunachal Pradesh, in the hope that the presence of Indian troops would compel the People's Liberation Army (PLA) to withdraw. This policy backfired disastrously when PLA troops attacked them.

46. Abdul Sattar, "Foreign Policy," in *Pakistan in Perspective, 1947–1997*, ed. Rafi Raza (Oxford: Oxford University Press, 1997), 67.

47. Stephen P. Cohen, *The Pakistan Army* (Berkeley: University of California Press, 1984), 147.

48. McMahon, *The Cold War on the Periphery*, 283.

49. Gill, *Chinese Arms Transfers*, 143. Pakistan has played a key role in shaping a positive image of China in the Muslim world. For example, after the July 2009 Xinjiang riots that resulted in at least 193 deaths because of Beijing's "Strike Hard" policy, Islamabad deployed its diplomatic skills to prevent the issue from being included on the agenda of the Organization of the Islamic Conference annual meeting, thus sparing China a damaged image in the eyes of the Muslim states. See Sajjad Malik, "Pakistan Saved China from Embarrassment on Xinjiang Violence," *Daily Times*, September 5, 2009, http://archives.dailytimes.com.pk/national/05-Sep-2009/pakistan-saved-china-from-embarrassment-on-xinjiang-violence.

50. Ibid.

51. K. M. Arif, ed., *China-Pakistan Relations, 1947–1980* (Lahore, Pakistan: Vanguard Press, 1984), 9.

52. Barnds, "China's Relations with Pakistan," 475.

53. Ibid,. 476.

54. Ibid. During that visit, Liu Shaoqi declared that the "Pakistani people can rest assured that, when Pakistan resolutely fights against foreign aggression in defense of its national independence, sovereignty, and territorial integrity, the 650 million Chinese people will stand unswervingly on their side and give them resolute support and assistance." See Arif, *China-Pakistan Relations*, 102.

55. Gill, *Chinese Arms Transfers*, 146.

56. Aparna Pande, *Explaining Pakistan's Foreign Policy: Escaping India* (London: Routledge, 2011), 123.

57. Yukinori Komine, *Secrecy in US Foreign Policy: Nixon-Kissinger and the Rapprochement with China* (London: Ashgate, 2008), 95.

58. Ibid.

59. Ibid.

60. Ibid.

61. Ibid., 96

62. Soviet pique was reflected in Andrei Gromyko's comment on Pakistan's role as a "dirty broker" following Kissinger's secret trip to Beijing in July 1971. See Khan, "Pakistan-China Relations," 12.

63. "Pakistan Delegation in China," *Peking Review*, November 12, 1971, p. 5.

64. Ibid., 23.

65. Khan, "Pakistan-China Relations," 12.

66. Gill, *Chinese Arms Transfers*, 148.

67. Fazal-ur-Rahman, "Pakistan's Evolving Relations with China, Russia, and Central Asia," in *Eager Eyes Fixed on Eurasia*, vol. 1, *Russia and Its Neighbors in Crisis*, ed. Iwashita Akihiro (Sapporo, Japan: Slavic Research Center, 2007), 213.

68. Gill, *Chinese Arms Transfers*, 150.

69. Ibid.

70. Describing Baluchistan as the "gateway from Central Asia to the Sea," rich in natural resources, and strategically placed at the mouth of the Persian Gulf, a Chinese analyst declared, "Because of its strategic position and rich resources Baluchistan has ever been coveted by the imperialists. Tsarist Russia, in particular, had tried on many occasions to carve a passage south through the Baluchistan area in Afghanistan and Iran to reach the Indian Ocean and secure warm-water harbors on the Arabian Sea and the Persian Gulf. To make the old tsar's dream come true, the new tsars are trying by every means to . . . bring the Baluchistan under their influence." "Moscow covets Baluchistan," *Peking Review*, March 10, 1980, p. 27.

71. Robert G. Sutter, *Chinese Foreign Policy: Developments After Mao* (New York: Praeger, 1986), 114.

72. Shahzad Akhter, "Sino-Pakistan Ties: An Assessment," *Strategic Studies* (2010): 74.

73. Yitzhak Shichor, "The Great Wall of Steel: Military and Strategy" in *Xinjiang: China's Muslim Borderland*, ed. Fredrick S. Starr (Armonk, NY: M. E. Sharpe, 2004), 149.

74. Khan, *Eating Grass*, 188. Confirming this transaction, Dr. Khan, in a letter written to his wife in 2004, revealed, "The Chinese gave us the drawing of the nuclear weapon, gave us 50 kg of enriched uranium, gave us 10 tons of UF6 (natural) and 5 tons of UF6 (3%)." According to Khan's account, the nuclear material acquired from China was kept in storage until 1985. After developing its own highly enriched uranium (HEU), Pakistan wanted to return the borrowed material. China responded that the "HEU loaned was now to be considered as a gift . . . in gratitude for Pakistan's help with Chinese centrifuges." Khan, *Eating Grass*, 188.

75. Pande, *Explaining Pakistan's Foreign Policy*, 126.

76. Claude Rakisits, "Pakistan-China Bilateral Relations, 2001–2011: A Deepening but Cautious Partnership," *Security Challenges* 8, no. 3 (2012): 87.

77. Mark Fitzpatrick, "Overcoming Pakistan's Nuclear Dangers," International Institute for Strategic Studies, Adelphi Paper No. 4432014, p. 14.

78. Khan, *Eating Grass*, 239.

79. Ibid., 242.

80. Ibid.

81. Haris Raqeeb Azeemi, "55 Years of Pakistan-China Relationship," *Pakistan Horizon* 60, no. 2 (2007): 113, quoting an article in *Dawn* (Karachi), November 25, 2006, p. 1.

82. Azeemi, "55 Years of Pakistan-China Relationship," 118.

83. Mathieu Duchatel, "The Terrorist Risk and China's Policy Toward Pakistan: Strategic Assurance and the United Front," *Journal of Contemporary China* 20, no. 71 (2011): 554.

84. Fitzpatrick, "Overcoming Pakistan's Nuclear Dangers," 12.

85. Paul Holtom, Mark Bromley, Pieter D. Wezeman, and Siemon T. Wezeman, "Trends in International Arms Transfers, 2012", *SIPRI Fact Sheet*, March 2013, http://books.sipri.org/product_info?c_product_id=455.

86. Akhter, "Sino-Pakistan Ties," 78.

87. Gill, *Chinese Arms Transfers*, 159.

88. Zheng Bijian, "China's 'Peaceful Rise' to Great Power Status," *Foreign Affairs* 84, no. 5 (2005): 23–24.

89. Rajat Pandit, "Army Reworks War Doctrine for Pakistan, China," *Times of India*, December 30, 2009, http://timesofindia.indiatimes.com/india/Army-reworks-war-doctrine-for-Pakistan-China/articleshow/5392683.cms.

90. Jeffrey W. Logo, "What China Will Want: The Future Intentions of a Rising Power," *Perspectives on Politics* 5, no. 3 (2007): 515. The debate over China threat theory reflects this anxiety. Reflecting the views of those who support the China threat theory, John J. Mearsheimer argues that regardless of China's domestic political situation and engagement with the global capitalist order, the country will seek regional hegemony in East Asia as it becomes more powerful. He notes, "China and the United States are destined to be adversaries as China's power grows." In his view, China's international ascent to power represents a clear and present "threat" to continued US dominance and to the liberal order. G. John Ikenberry, in contrast, sees China as being constrained by the Western-centered liberal order in which it is becoming increasingly embedded: "The rise of China does not have to trigger a wrenching hegemonic transition," he contends. Rather, "the capitalist democratic world is a powerful constituency for the preservation—and, indeed, extension—of the existing international order." For this dichotomous

debate, see Christopher A. McNally, "Sino-capitalism: China's Re-emergence and the International Political Economy," *World Politics* 64, no. 4 (2010): 741–776.

91. Asim Yasin, "Pakistan Always Welcomed Rise of China: Mushahid," *News International,* March 29, 2014, http://www.thenews.com.pk/Todays-News -2-241000-Pakistan-always-welcomed-rise-of-China:-Mushahid.

92. M. Taylor Fravel, "China Views India's Rise: Deepening Cooperation, Managing Difference," in *Asia Responds to Its Rising Powers: China and India,* ed. Ashley J. Tellis, Abraham M. Denmark, and Greg Chaffin (Washington, DC: National Bureau of Asian Research, 2011), 67–68.

93. Ibid., 69.

94. Li Peng's policy statement, *Pakistan Horizon* 52, no. 3 (1999): 95.

95. Quoted in Zafar Jaspal, "Af-Pak and Regional Peace in China's Perspective: A Critical Appraisal," *Pakistan Horizon* 64, no. 4 (2011): 38.

96. M. Akram Zaki, *China of Today and Tomorrow: Dynamics of Relations with Pakistan* (Islamabad, Pakistan: Institute of Policy Studies, 2010), 103.

97. Ibid.

98. Maleeha Lodhi, "Cementing a Strategic Partnership," *News International,* December 28, 2010, http://www.thenews.com.pk/Todays-News-9-22489-Cement ing-a-strategic-partnership.

99. Mathieu Duchatel, "The Terrorist Risk and China's Policy Towards Pakistan: Strategic Reassurance and the United Front," *Journal of Contemporary China* 20, no. 71 (2011): 544

100. Khawar Ghumman, "Chinese Firms to Get Army-Backed Security," *Dawn,* March 3, 2014, http://www.dawn.com/news/1090694.

101. Ziad Haider, "Baluch, Beijing, and Pakistan's Gwadar Port," *Georgetown Journal of International Affairs* 6, no. 1 (2005): 95–96.

102. Jonathan Holslag, "China's Roads to Influence," *Asian Survey* 50, no. 4 (2010): 645.

103. "The Autonomous Region of Xinjiang will become not only a gateway to our Central Asian neighbors, but also to South Asia, Russia, and even Europe," claimed one Chinese scholar at the Chinese Academy of Social Sciences. Quoted in ibid., 642.

104. Frank Jack Daniel and Rajesh Kumar Singh, "China Offers India a 'Handshake Across the Himalayas,'" *Reuters,* May 20, 2013, http://www.reuters .com/article/2013/05/20/us-india-china-idUSBRE94J03820130520; Ministry of External Affairs, Government of India, "Joint Statement on the State Visit of Chinese Premier Li Keqiang to India," May 20, 2013, http://mea.gov.in/bilateral -documents.htm?dtl/21723/Joint+Statement+on+the+State+Visit+of+Chinese++Li +Keqiang+to+India.

105. Daniel and Singh, "China Offers"; "China, Pakistan Issue Joint Statement, Vow to Deepen Cooperation," *Xinhua*, May 24, 2013, http://news.xinhua net.com/english/china/2013-05/24/c_124755957.htm.

106. Mohammed Arif, "China Ready to Start Work on Pakistan China Economic Corridor in 2015: Chinese Premier," Nihao-Salam, April 11, 2014, http://www.nihao-salam.com/news-detail.php?id=NTQzMw==.

107. "PM Underlines Need for Regional Connectivity," *Dawn*, April, 11, 2014, http://www.dawn.com/news/1099083.

# SEVEN

# Rebuilding Lifelines of Its Soft Underbelly
## China Engages Its Southwest Frontiers

*Swaran Singh*

During most of its history, the People's Republic of China has remained skeptical of the peoples inhabiting lands on both sides of its southwestern borders. Beijing's policies have perhaps sought to emphasize differences and minimize contacts among the mostly non-Han peoples, who often had more in common with one another than with China's cultural traditions and contemporary political objectives. These policies not only limited the contacts and cross-border interactions, but they also impeded development and exacerbated the economic and cultural divide between the rest of China and its frontier communities. By the start of the twenty-first century, however, Beijing had concluded that policies previously justified on security grounds were producing consequences that endangered internal stability and limited China's influence on and access to these markets and resources. The result was a paradigm shift in China's perception of and policies toward Afghanistan, Bhutan, Bangladesh, Myanmar, and Nepal.[1] President Xi Jinping's "One Belt, One Road" initiative has only further refined and formally incorporated this reorientation as part of his larger vision at redefining great-power relations. This chapter looks briefly at the logic underlying Beijing's earlier approach to its southwest frontier regions as it examines the reasons why China eventually felt the need for change and what it has done to move in that direction.

Beijing's perceptions of potential problems and possibilities in the region were (and are) shaped by enduring historic linkages between these neighboring states and China's remote and sparsely inhabited provinces on its southwestern frontiers. Most such linkages were between people, not governments or other politico-economic institutions. Indeed, their socio-cultural linkages were worrisome to Beijing because they connected the increasingly restive minorities that populate China's southwest frontier to fellow ethnics on the other side of the border.[2] Beijing's view of the region was, therefore, largely shaped by its security concerns about its "soft under-belly" resulting from colonial legacies of the Great Game competition for control of lands along China's periphery.[3]

Given their distance from China's more developed eastern provinces and their historic linkages to cross-border societies, China did not accord high priority to its southwestern frontier provinces even during the initial de-cades of the "reform and opening" policy launched by Deng Xiaoping in 1978. Neglect both impeded development in the region and exacerbated the alienation of the people who lived there and were already displeased by restrictions on their ability to interact with fellow ethnics on the other side of the border. The situation began to change in approximately 2000, when slow growth in the region began to be perceived as an obstacle to sustained growth elsewhere in the country and incidents of unrest among the mi-norities who lived there became increasingly frequent and widespread. To address these problems, Beijing adopted new measures to promote develop-ment in its southwestern provinces with the twin goals of narrowing the economic gap between China's coastal and interior provinces and reducing the alienation of the minority peoples who lived in its southwestern prov-inces. Because its initial strategy of fostering development by building in-frastructure and infusing Han Chinese only further alienated its southwest minorities, the key element in the new strategy is to build trade, transport, and resource-sharing networks with its southwestern neighbors.

This chapter is organized in four sections. The first outlines the evolu-tion of China's security concerns about its soft underbelly and its histori-cal and cultural engagement with the minority communities living in the southwest. The second section discusses specific triggers for the paradigm shift in China's perception of and policies toward these cross-border link-ages and examines in detail China's recent initiatives vis-à-vis its southwest neighbors. The third section provides an assessment of the success, limita-tions, and challenges of the way China is engaging its southwestern neigh-bors and its impact on China's own minorities. The final section offers some concluding remarks.

## China's Soft Underbelly

This is not the first time that China's destiny has been intertwined with that of its southwest frontiers and their cross-border linkages. Historical interactions go back at least to the time when Chinese emperors ruled from the ancient capitals of Chang'an and Xi'an. These frontiers are situated on the edge of a large plateau, bounded by the Himalayas to the south and west. This sparsely populated plateau has long been considered vulnerable to hostile forces seeking access to the Chinese heartland. This perceived vulnerability influences Chinese judgments about national security and about life and politics inside Tibet and the neighboring territories to the east.[4] In the late nineteenth century, this plateau became the locus and goal of competition among the great powers, a development that exacerbated Chinese concerns about the vulnerability of the country's soft underbelly. As a result, successive Chinese governments concluded that ensuring the physical security of China proper required effective Chinese control of the southwestern periphery. This, in turn, required restricting the ability of hostile foreigners to influence China's minorities.[5] In 1949, Beijing put liberation of Tibet at the very top of its national priorities list because it saw maintenance of control over the southwest as necessary for "consolidating the frontiers and national defense" of the People's Republic.[6]

Historically, China's elite used both physical (e.g., military and bureaucratic power) and cultural means to strengthen their ability to control the southwest peripheries. The cultural control involved the export of what Victor Mair calls the "culture of the capital" to the frontiers and colonies through what Steven Harrell describes as empire's civilizing project.[7] For Sara Davis, "the inequality between the civilizing center and the peripheral peoples had its ideological basis in the center's claim to a superior degree of civilization, along with a commitment to raise the peripheral people's civilization to the level of the center, or at least closer to that level."[8] Perhaps for this reason, spreading the "capital culture" did not include efforts to co-opt local wisdom, rituals, and skills and, therefore, contributed to the alienation of China's minority communities. This imperial approach to consolidating control through cultural chauvinism continued into the Communist period, as reflected in disastrous attempts to export the culture or ideology of the Great Leap Forward and the Cultural Revolution to these peripheries.

Reasons for China's historic neglect of local cultures and aspirations in these southwest frontiers are easy to find. Difficult terrain, severe underdevelopment, and sparse populations consisting mainly of minorities characterize both sides of China's southwest frontiers. The imperial approach adopted by successive central governments alienated minority peoples and fueled occasional religious and political turmoil. China's efforts to engage and assimilate Tibet and the adjacent provinces of Gansu, Qinghai, Sichuan, Yunnan, Guizhou, and Guangxi and to engage with diverse and fragile cross-border ruling regimes entailed formidable challenges for successive Chinese governments. China's recent prosperity and infrastructure-building initiatives have somewhat facilitated engagement with the peoples on its periphery. In addition, regional organizations, like the Indian Ocean Rim Association, the South Asian Association for Regional Cooperation, and the Bay of Bengal Initiative for Multi Sectoral Technical and Economic Cooperation have also provided modern multilateral platforms that facilitate China's economic engagement with its smaller neighboring countries. Nevertheless, Chinese interaction with its minorities and neighboring peoples continues to be constrained and complicated by many of the same physical and attitudinal impediments that shaped interactions in the past.

China's leaders recognize this dynamic and one of the reasons for the paradigm shift in Beijing's policies toward the southwest was their growing understanding of how this vicious cycle of alienation, underdevelopment, and unrest among its minorities on the southwestern frontiers was constraining China's ability to strengthen its cross-border linkages and expand economic relations with its southwestern neighbors. A second factor in the shift to a new paradigm was the change in mind-set that has occurred as a result of China's unprecedented rise and expanding footprint around the world. Increased prosperity and power achieved through interaction with the outside world have caused Chinese leaders to conclude that sustained growth and greater security can better be achieved by expanding contacts with states beyond its borders than by attempting to limit such interaction. Stated another way, frontier regions once valued as a buffer and barrier to invasion and ideas from abroad are now seen as valuable bridges to markets and resources essential for economic growth and political legitimacy. This shift in mind-set helps explain the evolving contours of China's relations with its southwestern neighbors and their implications for minority peoples on the Chinese side.

In his celebrated *Imagined Communities*, Benedict Anderson shows how Chinese "conceived of themselves as cosmically central, through the medium of a secret language linked to a superterrestrial order of power."[9] China's sacred and complex writing system, he says, preserved in a powerful "high center" was seen as fading out to "porous and indistinct" frontiers inhabited by subjects, vassal states, and barbarians in that order of distance from the center.[10] This way of thinking shaped both the mental mapping of imagined geographies and the sociopolitical framework of China's suzerainty over frontier peoples and polities. This enduring framework allowed for flexible policies. For example, fearing that the southwest might fall prey to Mongols, the rulers of the Qing dynasty (1644–1911) adopted a more interventionist approach in its dealings with this "enigmatic and hard-to-access neighbor."[11] Bradley Reed's study of Sichuan shows how the late Qing military campaigns against local powers in the Kham region enabled the state to employ an innovative approach to frontier expansion by replacing indigenous institutions with the establishment of a bureaucratic system of government.[12] All such strategies became less effective over time because local informal staffs were indispensable but also vulnerable to official and public censure.[13]

Competition between the Russian and British empires reenforced China's consciousness of the southwest and shifted attention further afield, from the Yunnan-Guizhou plateau to the larger Tibetan plateau that is bounded by Himalayan ranges.[14] China's feuding warlords became even more paranoid about the situation in the late nineteenth century. After the death of Emperor Qianlong and his decorated generals, the Qing frontier strategy became inward looking and defensive. When the Qing dynasty was replaced by the warlord governments of the Republican era, nonaction again became the hallmark of policies toward the southwest.[15] The frontier agency of the Nanjing-based Republic of China was much better able to assimilate China's problematic southwest minorities than were the warlords who held sway during and after the last years of the Qing dynasty, but the task remained a work in progress.[16] The Japanese invasion of China in 1937–1945 provided the wartime Nationalist government another opportunity to revive China's state-building tasks in the southwest.[17]

Recent studies have demonstrated that such episodic top-down imperial efforts to superimpose capital culture remained incapable of assimilating the southwest minorities. John Herman uses recent ethnohistorical scholarship and archaeological discoveries to examine ancient China's interface with the southwest (*nanzhong*) region demonized by Chinese scholar-officials as "not only an inhospitable frontier populated with uncivilized barbarians (*manyi*), but also as a peripheral part of China where intrepid commanders such as Tang Meng in the second century BCE and Zhuge Liang at the beginning of the third century CE had staked China's claim" to the southwest territories.[18]

Despite episodic efforts by Chinese central governments to exert control over the southwest, neglect was the dominant policy much of the time. Consequently, it was never easy for the People's Republic of China (PRC) to ensure local support and achieve legitimacy in southwest frontier regions. Twentieth-century China's internal turmoil—civil war, Japanese occupation, renewed civil war, the Great Leap Forward, and the Cultural Revolution—exacerbated the continued alienation of its southwest peripheries. Memories of nineteenth century Great Game competition waged along its southwest frontiers were revived by Western policies of containment and the Soviet occupation of Afghanistan from 1979 until 1989.

China's policy of reform and opening and its engagement with the Western powers beginning in the late 1970s led to a gradual shift in China's political discourse as references to liberation were replaced by calls for integration of China's frontier regions. This reflected recognition that continued success of the kind that had produced China's "rise" since the 1990s could not be assured without more balanced development across the country. Continued neglect of the southwest increasingly was seen as an impediment to the continued economic success of China's coastal provinces. The imperatives of future growth made changing the paradigm necessary. The fruits of reform and opening made it possible to change the paradigm and provided clear guidance with respect to how it should change and how that change could be implemented on the ground.

## Triggers of Transformation

China's increasing recognition as a rising power has triggered expectations both at home and abroad for more balanced regional development and better treatment of the country's minorities. Also, the twenty-first-century world is far too interconnected for China to avoid providing better, if not equal, treatment for its minorities. Though important, these factors only partially explain the unprecedented transformation of China's approach to engaging its smaller southwestern neighbors and its southwest frontier minority communities. Other triggers contributing to China's reorientation vis-à-vis its southwest frontier region are listed here (in roughly chronological order):

- Deng Xiaoping's policy of reform and opening led to the restructuring of Mao Zedong's China and unleashed a new trade-led development model that has transformed China's decision-making processes and created a robust implementation machinery.

- The processes unleashed by Deng's reforms have also de-ideologized China. Dogma has been replaced by pragmatism, and justifying any and all departures from orthodoxy as manifesting "Chinese characteristics" has denatured ideology. China's "socialist market economy" has strengthened the country's economic engagement with the outside world and made China an outward-looking nation. This has transformed China's international relationships, including those across its southwest frontiers.

- China's rise has made it more self-confident and willing to be more assertive and to take bold initiatives. A self-assured China is less skeptical and far more willing to engage its neighbors and to allow contacts with its restive internal minorities in the southwest frontiers.

- China now has the financial wherewithal to undertake large-scale projects linking its southwest to the rest of China and to neighboring countries. China's economic success makes such expensive projects seem cost effective in addition to attracting foreign direct investment to these remote regions.

- Technological advances have made it possible for China to overcome historical and geographical impediments to linking the southwest region to prosperous coastal cities in the east and to neighboring states across its southwest frontiers. This has contributed to building mutual trust and ensured better cross-border interactions and understanding.

- China hopes to benefit from the rise of several countries across its southwestern border, and these neighbor states are also far more comfortable in taking advantage of Chinese prosperity. Interest in expanded relationships is mutual because the natural resources of neighboring states make them attractive partners for Beijing.

- Economic growth in China's coastal provinces has exacerbated societal and opportunity gaps between China's eastern and western regions. These inequalities have fueled internal dissension and subjected Beijing to criticism from abroad. Beijing feels increasing pressure to achieve more balanced development and to accelerate progress in the regions that are home to large minority populations.

- Terrorism in Afghanistan and Pakistan has revived China's concerns about possible spillover effects on China's Muslim minorities and their implications for cross-border links with China's southwestern neighbors. China is expected to take the lead in organizing regional alternatives to provide security after the International Security Assistance Force withdraws from Afghanistan in 2016. This will make China's engagement with neighboring countries vital to the success of China's larger regional-security initiatives.

Indeed, China began looking afresh at its southwest frontiers as early as the late 1970s, but some of its major "Go West" initiatives, including mega projects like the Tibet railway, did not pick up speed or produce results until recently. China is attempting to build an extensive social and material infrastructure connecting these remote regions to its booming eastern shores and to rebuild and strengthen its cross-border links with the goals of accelerating growth, increasing prosperity, and making the prosperity of neighboring countries more dependent on their ties to Beijing. The results of policies implemented in accordance with China's new paradigm can be seen in the trade, transportation, and resource-sharing networks that have contributed to a better political atmosphere for addressing more difficult political issues, such as border management, water sharing, and energy pipelines. In addition to the economic benefits they produce, these projects are potent instruments to expand Chinese influence in the region.[19]

The following subsections examine some of China's specific initiatives seeking to transform its engagement with its southwest frontier minorities and cross-border regimes.

### TRADE AND INVESTMENT

Trends in bilateral trade are the most visible and easily measured indicator of the transformation that has occurred in China's engagement with smaller states across its southwest frontier. Historically, trade was an important instrument used by successive Chinese rulers to control the southwest barbarians.[20] The Silk Road, built during the Han dynasty (around 200 BC), was a thriving network connecting people along China's southwest frontier until the 1962 India-China war restricted its scope to a few essential commodities, traded almost exclusively between Nepal and a few Tibetan cities.[21] The importance of the Silk Road had already decreased, however, because the advent of steam engines made sea routes more attractive. The British used the trade in opium to expand their influence in these territories. History seemed to repeat itself in the early 1990s when the opening of cross-border trade produced an upsurge in the transport of drugs into China's southwestern provinces of Yunnan and Guangxi.[22] The prominent role of illicit drugs was, in part, a function of the fact that Yunnan and Guangxi looked initially instead to the Southeast Asian tiger economies. It is only in the last decade that Yunnan and Sichuan have emerged as the most important pioneers in China's economic engagement with its southwestern neighbors.[23]

According to United Nations data, China's exports to the five smaller countries across its southwest frontier (Afghanistan, Bangladesh, Bhutan, Myanmar, and Nepal) rose from $2.6 billion in 2003 to an all-time high of $18 billion in 2012 (see Figure 7.1). China's exports to Bangladesh and Myanmar have grown impressively, but in some respects its trade with turmoil-ridden Nepal and Afghanistan has been even more remarkable. Investments in resources and infrastructure building have been particularly important in the latter two countries. Indeed, China's trade with both Afghanistan and Nepal has increased sixteen-fold in the last ten years. In 2009, China expanded its investments to ensure Afghanistan's internal stability and to diminish the negative impact of instability in Afghanistan on China's own internal security.[24] Although China refused to contribute to

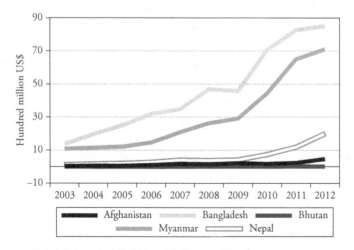

FIGURE 7.1 China's bilateral trade with southwest neighbors, 2003–2012
SOURCE: UNCTADstat database, http://unctadstat.unctad.org

the stabilization force in Afghanistan, it has invested about $4 billion in resource-related projects and pledged more than $1 billion in assistance, giving China a major stake in the post-2014 peace and security of that country.[25]

Nepal has been a major beneficiary of China's growing activism across its southwest frontiers. China-Nepal trade increased approximately fivefold from 2009 to 2012, and China has since opened a direct air link between Lhasa and Kathmandu. The air link has produced spectacular increases in the flow of Chinese visitors into Nepal. However, the number of Tibetans visiting India through Nepal has declined from an average of 2,500 to 3,000 per year to only 600 in 2009, probably in part because His Holiness the Dalai Lama's office in Nepal was closed in 2005.[26] In 2009, China increased its annual grant assistance to Nepal by almost 50 percent, from $19 million to $22 million. When chief of the People's Liberation Army General Staff Chen Bingde visited Nepal in 2011, China pledged $19.9 million for a military hospital, and China's Export-Import Bank extended a soft loan of $97 million for a hydropower project on the Trishuli River. In return, Nepal is expected to ensure better border security and allow Chinese to invest in select sectors.[27] Since then, China has overtaken India to become Nepal's largest trading partner and, on an annual basis, its largest investor. This has had a visible impact on Kathmandu's political orientation, which is shifting in favor of Beijing.

China-Myanmar trade, which was virtually nonexistent before 1988, grew at an impressive 25 percent per year from 1988 to 1995.[28] Although China's trade with Myanmar rose sharply after the imposition of Western sanctions in 1988 and reached its peak of $767 million in 1995, it declined gradually in the wake of the East Asian financial crisis in 1997. But even conservative estimates show a significant increase during last ten years (see Figure 7.1). Statistics on China's border trade are not very reliable because they do not include informal, transit, and barter trade and cannot account for underpricing and smuggling. China regards its border trade with Myanmar as the most successful case of its engagement with its smaller southwest neighbors.

Transit across the Yunnan border accounts for over 55 percent of China-Myanmar trade in value terms. Calculated in terms of volume, more than 80 percent of Myanmar exports to China and about 40 percent of its imports from China cross the Yunnan border, making Myanmar Yunnan's largest trading partner.[29] In the wake of post-2011 reforms, Myanmar media and the public became very critical of China's business practices. It took the Chinese ambassador more than a year to meet Aung San Suu Kyi, who was released from detention in November 2010. But given its high stakes, China has encouraged regular high-level visits and announced the conclusion of a "comprehensive strategic cooperative partnership" in May 2011.[30] China's persistence and the strategic partnership with Myanmar appear to be driven primarily by the US policy shift toward Myanmar and its pivot to Asia and Indo-Pacific strategies.

India was the largest trading partner of Bangladesh until China captured that position in 2004. China's displacement of India had symbolic and political significance for India-Bangladesh relations and for domestic politics in both nations because the ranking of India and China in terms of trade was regarded as a symbolic indicator of whether Bangladesh was closer to Beijing than to New Delhi. Beijing recognized this and used both tariff and nontariff mechanisms to incentivize trade with Bangladesh. Provision of military equipment to Bangladesh was a particularly important incentive; for many years imports from China accounted for as much as 90 percent of Bangladesh's total defense imports.[31] Rapid growth of China's economy made it possible for Beijing to achieve a sharp increase in its exports to Bangladesh. This increase in Bangladesh imports from China led to a formidable trade deficit that, according to the Commerce Ministry of Bangladesh, had increased from $3.3 billion in 2008–2009 to $5.8 billion in 2013.[32] In addition to quickly increasing its exports to Bangladesh, China has also emerged as a major investor in that country and gained much favorable publicity for giving Bangladesh seven friendship bridges, among other symbolically important infrastructure projects. The May 20, 2013, announcement by China and India that they intend to move forward on the Bangladesh-China-India-Myanmar Economic Corridor proposal indicates that there will be additional ways to expand China-Bangladesh economic ties in the years ahead.[33]

Bhutan has gained international recognition for its democratization, for its gross happiness index, and for hosting the sixteenth summit meeting of the South Asian Association for Regional Cooperation (SAARC) in April 2010. It has not, however, achieved significant improvement in its relationship with China. Their border negotiations have come to a virtual standstill, and Bhutan continues to accuse China of border incursions, poaching, and illicit logging and road-construction activities. Though their trade remains negligible, China continues to pursue ways to engage with Bhutan. In April 2010, China sent a high-level delegation led by Executive Vice Minister of Foreign Affairs Wang Guangya to attend the Sixteenth SAARC Summit held at Thimpu. Wang used the opportunity afforded by the visit to hold bilateral talks with Lyonpo Khandu Wangchujk, the minister of foreign affairs. During those talks, the two sides agreed to establish an expert group to discuss modalities for joint field assessment of the boundary question.[34] But even before that, in October 2003, Bhutan had formally joined the World Tourism Organization at its General Assembly meeting in Beijing. Since then, according to the Bhutanese newspaper *Kuensel*, there has been an enormous increase in the number of Chinese tourists visiting Bhutan. China's ranking in terms of tourist visits increased from fifth (1,494 tourists) in 2010 to second (6,005) in 2013.[35] The number of Chinese tourists was less than 100 until 2004. Chinese products are procured in Bhutan via Hong Kong, Nepal, and India. But even if Bhutan sees China as potentially a major trade partner and investor, there are serious physical constraints because most of Bhutan's habitation and infrastructure is in the south (adjacent to India). Steep gorges and high mountains in the north are a major barrier to trade and communication with China.

TRANSPORT NETWORKS

In addition to gaining commercial benefits, China seeks to use its economic power and prowess in building transport networks to forge robust political, societal, and infrastructural links between its southwest frontier provinces and neighboring countries. Although China has tried to maintain a subtle approach when using its influence to ensure that these neighbors toe the line on China's core security concerns (e.g., separatism), it has also undertaken "charm offensives" to mitigate anxieties and underscore the positive spin-offs available from China's initiatives. China also acts to protect its own interests. For example, the Chinese Foreign Ministry sent a delegation to meet with the largely ostracized Taliban regime in early 1999. The reported reason for the delegation was Beijing's concern about rising violence in Xinjiang.[36]

China seeks to expand its transportation networks into all its southwestern neighbors but has achieved the highest degree of integration with Myanmar. One reason for this relatively closer integration is the temporal conjunction of high-profile massacres in 1988 (Yangon) and 1989 (Beijing) that caused the most developed nations to curtail relations with the regimes in Myanmar and China. Their shared isolation from others brought them closer together in ways that led to a special relationship that peaked during the first half of the 1990s.[37] By 2007, China had completed a 651-kilometer four-lane expressway between Kunming and the city of Ruili on the China-Myanmar border. China then assisted Myanmar to upgrade 170 kilometers of road on its side of the border. Other Chinese projects include construction of a rail link from Dali to Lashio and a road link from Lashio to Chiang Mai in Thailand.[38] Inside Myanmar, China has provided loans and credits for the construction of the Sittwe seaport, dams, bridges, and strategic roads along the Irrawaddy River that connect Yunnan province to the Bay of Bengal.[39] Myanmar's entry into the Association of Southeast Asia Nations (ASEAN) in 1997 and it post-2011 political reforms have opened the country to several other interested countries, a development that has slowed China's exclusive infrastructure-building spree of the early 1990s.

Both the difficult physical terrain and the politics of the New Great Game have shaped China's dealings with Afghanistan through its 57-kilometer-long border at the Wakhan corridor. During the Soviet occupation of Afghanistan in the 1980s, the Wakhan corridor became a principal route for arming the Mujahedeen. According to American and Soviet sources, China supplied weapons worth $400 million and trained more than thirty thousand mujahids in Pakistan and Xinjiang.[40] The resultant rise in violence in Xinjiang that began in the late 1980s gradually made China aware of cross-border terrorism linkages and their impact on its Uighur population. From the July 2009 Urumqi riots to the Kunming railway-station massacre in March 2014, various episodes of such violence suggest that China's already serious cross-border terrorism problem could become worse after the slated 2016 departure of International Security Assistance Force (ISAF) troops from Afghanistan. Aware of this possibility, China's Ministry of Defense has been building new supply depots, mobile command and communication centers, and transport infrastructure on China's side of its southwest frontiers. It has also built a 75-kilometer-long road parallel to and 10 kilometers from the Sino-Afghan border.[41] Only time will tell whether China's much-anticipated role in post-2016 Afghanistan will transform China's southwest minorities into barriers, buffers, or bridges.

Transit between China and Nepal is difficult but less difficult than it is between China and Bhutan or Afghanistan. There are eighteen mountain passes between Nepal and Tibet, fourteen of which are in active use.[42] China has advanced ambitious proposals for north-south cross-border projects, the most ambitious of which would build a rail link between Lhasa and Khasa, a town on the Sino-Nepal border, and link Nepal to China's gigantic rail network.[43] Bhutan, in contrast, has no formal diplomatic relations with China, their 470-kilometer-long disputed border remains officially closed, and there are no cross-border rail or road links of any kind. The two countries have, however, been negotiating since their 1998 Agreement on Maintenance of Peace and Tranquility Along the Sino-Bhutanese Border Area. Bangladesh does not border China directly, but during the May 2013 visit of Chinese Premier Li Keqiang to New Delhi, China and India decided to implement proposals for a Bangladesh-China-India-Myanmar Economic Corridor. This has raised hopes that China will consider building physical links to Bangladesh and explore possibilities for access to the Chittagong port on the Indian Ocean.[44]

WATER-SHARING MECHANISMS

Tibet is the ultimate sources of major rivers that flow into Bhutan, Nepal, Bangladesh, and Myanmar.[45] However, unlike trade and transport, China's water-sharing behavior with southwest neighbors has been a mixed bag of distrust and disengagement. Developing mechanisms for cross-border water sharing is complicated by the rapid pace of construction and industrialization and increasing global awareness of the likely outcomes of climate change.

China suffers from major water-scarcity problems despite the fact that the Tibet plateau has been popularly called the "water tank of the world." Owing, in part, to its rapid industrial development in the last three decades, China's water tables have dropped at alarming rates, and many rivers and lakes have been badly polluted by industrial effluent and agricultural run-off. The Yellow River (*Huanghe*) has failed to reach the sea since the early 1990s. The water-shortage problem is so serious in the northern part of the country that China has been planning massive projects to divert river water from south to north. The first such project, known as *Nanshui beidiao gongcheng* (to divert southern water north), was completed in March 2013. This is one of many examples of how China plans to build "engineering solutions to problems of basic environmental scarcity."[46] However, these massive projects in Tibet have direct implications for neighboring countries whose requirements for fresh water have been increasing almost as rapidly.

Bangladesh is the only one of China's five smaller southwest neighbors that depends heavily on river water coming from China. China's longest river originating in Tibet, the Yarlong Tsangbo, is called *Brahmaputra* in India and *Jamuna* as it flows into Bangladesh. China's approach to water sharing in this case is strikingly different from what one might expect from what it says about joint and sustainable development of shared resources. China's rhetorical position proclaims the importance of maintaining "communication and cooperation" to ensure no negative impact on the river's lower reaches. It also claims that China "has always taken a responsible attitude towards cross-border river development."[47] Despite this assurance, lower riparian states are concerned about China's grand plans for northward diversion of river waters and its plans to build several hydropower stations on the Yarlong Tsangpo River. The Chinese government had, in early 2013, formally approved three of these new hydropower projects. This river runs 2,057 kilometers through the far southwest portion of the Tibet plateau at an average altitude of 4,500 meters. Any mega construction on this river could be dangerous to the fragile ecological and environmental life of the Himalayan ranges and have serious consequences for all of China's southwestern neighbors.

ENERGY TRANSMISSION AND PIPELINES

In contrast to water, which flows mainly from China to its southwestern neighbors, energy typically originates in the neighboring countries and flows into China. Indeed, China's engagement with countries on its southwestern periphery is driven, in significant measure, by its desire to access onshore energy resources. Two of China's southwestern neighbors, Bangladesh and Myanmar, have significant reserves of gas and oil. However, violence and religious extremism, poverty and corruption, political instability, and poor governance characterize the complex security environment in these two countries. All of these conditions pose challenges for long-term internal and cross-border investment by Beijing.

Tibetans have maintained close links with Nepal, and China's Muslims have developed links across Afghanistan and even in Bangladesh and Myanmar. These ties were not sufficient to foster energy-related projects, however. The situation changed beginning in the early 1990s and exploitation of these energy resources became more attractive to both sides. What happened next in terms of China's interactions with its immediate neighbors has been described by Stephen Blank as "a pattern of China's leveraging its superior economic position in the current climate [of global slowdown] to induce this accommodation behavior in Asia even if it is all done by purely peaceful and economic means."[48] China has been particularly interested in the natural gas reserves of Bangladesh and Myanmar, and Dhaka has already offered exploration rights to China at Barakpuria.[49]

Myanmar has been China's most sought-after partner not just for its gas but also for building road, rail, navigation, and pipeline links to the Indian Ocean, which remains the lifeline for China's energy imports. Myanmar has extensive gas reserves and, with completion of two 800-kilometer pipelines from Kyaukphy in Myanmar's Rakhine state to Ruili on the Chinese border in May 2013, Myanmar has become China's newest energy supplier. By 2007, three China-based companies had signed contracts for oil and gas explorations in fourteen blocks, including Petro China's contract to buy 6.5 trillion cubic feet of natural gas for a period of thirty years, starting in 2009.[50] Nevertheless, the politics of unrest on the 2,200-kilometer-long China-Myanmar border has been too complicated to be easily resolved. To some extent, that remains true of relations along all of China's southwest frontiers, which means its relative success in trade and transport has not fully facilitated resource-sharing and has not resolved unrest among China's minorities.

## Assessment

Citizens of the smaller countries on China's southwestern border and minority peoples living on the Chinese side of the frontier are happy to take advantage of the economic and other benefits of increased attention and investment from Beijing, but increased cross-border engagement has done little to reduce their distrust of Han Chinese and the Communist Party. Old grievances and suspicions continue to shape perceptions and limit enthusiasm for central government initiatives. China's relationships with people on both sides of the southwestern border are further complicated by new problems and grievances associated with trade, transport, and resource-sharing arrangements encouraged or undertaken by Beijing to achieve Chinese developmental, stability, and security objectives. Greater prosperity and increased interchange with people and places beyond the local community have improved living standards but they have also increased awareness of inequality and repression. Central government expectations of gratitude and approval have often garnered resentment and demands for change. Those living along the frontier know that they benefit from many Chinese initiatives but also know about and resent the fact that Han Chinese often benefit more than they do from increased engagement. Instead of praise and appreciation, greater engagement has sometimes fueled dissatisfaction and unrest. Harsh and sometimes violent repression of dissent in the name of maintaining order often increases the already significant sense of alienation. Increased cross-border interchange sometimes leads minorities in China's southwest to conclude that they have more in common with fellow ethnics and co-religionists across the border than with their political masters in Beijing. For Beijing, the new policies are thus proving to be a two-edged sword.

Some of this distrust, of course, is a function of historical legacies. The British conquest of upper Burma (1885) and Tibet (1905) had made China suspicious of British designs on China's southwest frontiers and the loyalties of those who lived there. Suspicion and distrust were compounded in 1950 when Kuomintang (KMT) General Li Mi and his forces retreated from Yunnan into Burma and, for several years, continued to fight Communist forces from their Burmese redoubt. It was further compounded in 1959 when the Dalai Lama fled to India with thousands of followers who settled in India, Nepal, and Bhutan. Given "New China's" fragile situation at the time, Beijing signed a boundary agreement with Nepal in March 1960 "on the basis of the existing traditional customary line." The boundary agreement it concluded with Myanmar in October 1960 was based on the British McMahon Line, and the November 1963 agreement with Afghanistan marked "China's formal recognition of the existence of the Wakhan Corridor." Although the Sino-Bhutan boundary was rumored to have been settled in a secret agreement in 1961, neither side has ever advertised it.[51] The Sino-Bhutanese boundary remains disputed, but the two sides signed a peace and tranquility agreement in 1998.

China's security calculus with regard to its soft underbelly probably accounts for Beijing's generosity in its border settlements with the smaller southwest neighbors. Facing many other problems associated with the disastrous Great Leap Forward and the rift with the Soviet Union to the northeast, Beijing was eager to conclude agreements that would settle disputes in the southwest and reduce the likelihood of foreign support for disgruntled groups inside China. Factors that made the region attractive as a buffer against outside interference or aggression—the difficult terrain and sparse human habitation—also contributed to its underdevelopment and the alienation of the minority peoples who lived there.

Governments of the countries on the other side of the border faced similar problems. It has always been difficult for Kabul, Kathmandu, and Rangoon (now Yangon) to assimilate the peoples along the frontier and ensure their writ in remote frontier communities. In Myanmar, for example, the so-called Kokang Myanmar National Democratic Alliance Army, a predominantly Han Chinese militia in the Kokang region of the Shan State, has attempted to secede from Myanmar several times. More than fifty thousand of these Han Chinese have fled to China in the last ten years. In 2010, China deployed forces along the border to prevent illegal entry. However, the deployments jeopardize cross-border trade and the pipeline China has proposed to build.[52] Links between Tibetans and their sympathizers in Nepal decrease China's leverage when trying to persuade successive Nepalese governments to take harsh actions against the Tibetans who live there and are alleged to be using the country as a base for anti-China activities in Tibet. Muslim and Buddhist groups are believed to criss-cross China's southwest and the neighboring countries in search of sanctuaries and sympathy.

China has taken important initiatives to assimilate its 110-million-strong indigenous minority population. Minority peoples have been exposed to better economic and educational opportunities, but the process of cultural assimilation by Han China has also resulted in the loss of their languages, identity disarray, and social displacement that threatens to disrupt interethnic coexistence.[53] China's state policy recognizes the special cultural characteristics of ethnic minorities, but little is known about the way the policy is implemented and the policies have been the target of numerous protest demonstrations.[54]

During most of the historical era, Han held the most powerful positions in government institutions and lived in the more highly developed regions of China. Minority peoples lived primarily in China's northwestern and southwestern regions. Both Han and minority groups have moved out of their traditional areas in recent decades, but the minority groups continue to inhabit largely the same areas that they have for centuries. What has changed is that their protests and revolts have become more frequent, violent, and widespread, especially since the late 1980s. The protests are inherently political, but many are characterized as "subsistence expectation protests," centered on language, social identity, and environmental issues and on coerced fund-raising for development projects on which minorities claim to have no share in decision making. The protests are regarded as more than just a reflection of alienation, specific grievances, and historical legacies and have been characterized as "equally reflective of the transitional pains of China."[55] Intermittent protests in Tibet since 2008 have included the self-immolation of more than 125 Buddhist monks. The March 2014 massacre at the Kunming railway station was a rare but equally gruesome form of minorities' protest.[56]

Comparing economic development in China's southwestern provinces to other parts of China yields a similar picture. Per capita income in the five southwestern provinces has continued to lag that of other provinces for the last sixty years (see Table 7.1). Tibet, Yunnan, and Guizhou have actually slipped lower during the period of China's spectacular growth. Of the five, only Sichuan has achieved a noticeable improvement. Guangxi was sliding lower until 2000 but has improved noticeably during the last ten years. Yunnan-Myanmar trade and investment illustrates the achievements and limitations of China's policies toward the southwest frontier. Cross-border engagement has increased, but the content remains primarily economic. China's political influence, especially in Myanmar, has declined sharply. Engagement with Bangladesh and Afghanistan remains strong but is largely guided by China's own strategic interests with little consideration for China's southwest minorities. China and Bhutan have no official relations and their economic engagement continues to be hostage to the state of China-India relations because, for China, the road to Thimpu goes through New Delhi.

TABLE 7.1

Provincial ranks based on per capita GDP (for selected years)

| Province | 1952 | 1980 | 1990 | 2000 | 2010 |
|----------|------|------|------|------|------|
| Guangxi | 27 | 28 | 29 | 29 | 26 |
| Guizhou | 29 | 29 | 30 | 31 | 31 |
| Sichuan | 28 | 26 | 26 | 23 | 24 |
| Tibet | 25 | 23 | 22 | 26 | 28 |
| Yunnan | 26 | 25 | 25 | 28 | 29 |

SOURCE: Rongxing Guo, *Understanding the Chinese Economies* (Waltham, MA: Academic Press, 2013), 150.

## Conclusion

China's expanding engagement with its five smaller southwestern neighbors is primarily a function of China's need to ensure peace and development along frontiers inhabited largely by China's underdeveloped and alienated minorities. This has become an essential part of China's quest for balanced development and international prestige. In pursuing its objectives in the southwest, China has relied primarily on its rapidly growing economic leverage. This has been its greatest strength but also its primary limitation in engaging its neighbors and assimilating its southwest minorities. Especially in politics, China has been showcasing and not really empowering its minority peoples. That China's policies remain insufficiently grounded in local sociopolitical rituals, traditions, and wisdom perhaps partly explains why Beijing continues to encounter difficulties in these frontier regions. Another reason is that these five neighboring states lie between China and India and they must remain sensitive to the concerns and ambitions of these large and rapidly rising neighbors.

China's initiatives also reflect greater appreciation that, in China, economic engagement is the most cost-effective way to address underdevelopment and political unrest along its southwest frontier. But it is also beginning to show China's growing appreciation of the significance of other cross-border linkages to the development and of the need for mutual respect in assimilation of its own minority peoples. This is at the core of China's paradigm shift with respect to engaging its smaller neighbors and is part of China's strategy to ensure that neighboring countries remain comfortable with China taking the lead in efforts to build a subregional development and security architecture. Building such a subregional framework is essential for China's long-term peaceful rise, which remains premised on continued high economic growth to ensure social stability and regime security. China's economic rise, therefore, both facilitates and necessitates reviving these historical cross-border linkages with its southwestern frontiers. The smaller countries across these frontiers have begun to appreciate their own growing stakes in engagement with China, but they are also limited by their own historical baggage and internal catharsis. In the longer term, global trends are likely to facilitate more extensive and holistic engagement to advance the interests of both sides.

*Notes*

1. This chapter does not examine China's relations with Pakistan and India, which are covered elsewhere in this book.

2. The southwest region of China historically included the scenic regions of the Yunnan-Guizhou plateau, inhabited largely by China's minorities that today constitute provinces of Yunnan, Guizhou, and Sichuan. These were incorporated into China in 230 BC by the Qin dynasty emperor Shi Huangdi. This frontier was extended further during the thirteenth-century Yuan dynasty to also include the Tibetan plateau, which defines China's current southwest frontiers.

3. See Taylor M. Fravel, *Strong Borders, Secure Nation: Cooperation and Conflict in China's Territorial Disputes* (Princeton, NJ: Princeton University Press, 2008), 72; Jeff M. Smith, *Cold Peace: China-India Rivalry in the Twenty-First Century* (Lanham, MD: Lexington Books, 2013), 58; and Robert F. Ely, *Candidate for President* (Bloomington, IN: AuthorHouse, 2013), 207.

4. Fravel, *Strong Borders*, 72.

5. Control of Tibet plateau had been central to the Great Game competition involving the nineteenth-century imperial powers of Russia, China, and Great Britain. Western containment of China in the twentieth century involved intervention in Tibet until almost the mid-1970s. Western interference was annoying, but Beijing became even more concerned about Tibet after the Sino-Soviet split because Soviet troops on the Chinese-Mongolian border threatened to close access to Xinjiang through the Gansu corridor, leaving Tibet as China's only reliable link to Xinjiang. For details see Fravel, *Strong Borders*, 72.

6. John W. Garver, *Protracted Contest: Sino-Indian Rivalry in the Twentieth Century* (Seattle: University of Washington Press, 2001), 39.

7. Victor H. Mair, ed., *Contacts and Exchange in the Ancient World* (Honolulu: University of Hawaii, 2006), 63, 215; Steven Harrell, "Introduction: Civilizing Projects and the Reaction to Them," in *Cultural Encounters on China's Ethnic Frontiers*, ed. Steven Harrell (Hong Kong: Hong Kong University Press, 1996), 32.

8. Sara L. M. Davis, *Song and Silence: Ethnic Revival on China's Southwest Borders* (New York: Columbia University Press, 2005), 14.

9. Benedict Anderson, *Imagined Communities*, 3rd ed. (London: Verso, 2006), 13.

10. Ibid., 19.

11. Yingcong Dai, *The Sichuan Frontier and Tibet: Imperial Strategy in the Early Qing*, (Seattle: University of Washington Press, 2009), 3.

12. Xiuyu Wang, *China's Last Imperial Frontier: Late Qing Expansion in Sichuan's Tibetan Borderlands* (Lanham, MD: Lexington Books, 2011), 186.

13. Ibid.

14. Mark Edward Lewis, *China Between Empires: The Northern and Southern Dynasties* (Cambridge, MA: Harvard University Press, 2009), 12.

15. Dai, *The Sichuan Frontier*, 228.

16. Hsiao-Ting Lin, *Tibet and Nationalist China's Frontier: Intrigues and Ethnopolitics, 1928–49* (Vancouver: UBC Press, 2006), x.

17. Ibid., xi.

18. John Herman, "The Kingdoms of Nanzhong: China's Southwest Border Region Prior to the Eight Century," *T'oung Pao* 95, no. 4 (2009): 241; see also Muzaffar Olimov and Saodat Olimov, "Tajikistan and China: Changing Images," *Journal of Central Asian Studies* 19, no.1 (2010): 12.

19. John W. Garver, "Development of China's Overland Transportation Links with Central, South-west and South Asia," *China Quarterly*, no. 185 (2006): 1.

20. Yingshi Yu, *Trade and Expansion in Han China: A Study in the Structure of Sino-Barbarian Economic Relations* (Los Angeles: University of California Press, 1967), 111.

21. Norottam Banskota, *South Asia Trade and Energy Security: The Role of India* (Boca Raton, FL: Universal, 2012), 66.

22. Harry J. Waters, *China's Economic Development Strategies for the 21st Century* (Westport, CT: Quorum Books, 1997), 93.

23. Starting in 2012, Kunming (Yunnan) began holding an annual China-South Asia Exposition, and Chengdu (Sichuan) hosts the Global Fortune Forum.

24. Dezan Shira, *China's Neighbors: Who Is Influencing China and Who China Is Influencing in the New Emerging Asia* (Hong Kong: Asia Briefing, 2012), 7.

25. Artemy M. Kalinovsky, "Sino-Afghani Border Relations," in *Beijing's Power and China's Borders: Twenty Neighbors in Asia*, ed. Bruce A. Elleman, Stephen Kotkin, and Clive Schofield (New York: M. E. Sharpe, 2012), 19.

26. Ian Jeffries, *Political Developments in Contemporary China: A Guide* (New York: Routledge, 2011), 321.

27. Chitra K. Tiwari, "China-Nepal Border: Potential Hot Spot?" in *Beijing's Power and China's Borders: Twenty Neighbors in Asia*, ed. Bruce A. Elleman, Stephen Kotkin, and Clive Schofield (New York: M. E. Sharpe, 2012), 225.

28. David I. Steinberg and Hongwei Fan, *Modern China-Myanmar Relations: Dilemmas of Mutual Dependence* (Copenhagen: NIAS Press, 2012), 208.

29. Maung Aung Myoe, *In the Name of Pauk-Phaw: Myanmar's China Policy Since 1948* (Singapore: Institute of Southeast Asian Studies, 2011), 156.

30. Renaud Egreteau and Larry Jagan, *Soldiers and Diplomacy in Burma: Understanding the Foreign Relations of the Burmese Praetorian State* (Singapore: National University of Singapore, 2013), 291.

31. Pravakar Sahoo, "Economic Relations with Bangladesh: China's Ascent and India's Decline," *South Asia Research* 33, no. 2 (2013): 131.

32. Refayet Ullah Mirdha, "Bangladesh Seeks Expanded Trade Privileges from China," *Daily Star*, March 31, 2014, http://www.thedailystar.net/bangladesh-seeks -expanded-trade-privileges-from-china-17967.

33. Monish Gulati, "Sushma Visit Gives Fresh Impetus to India-Bangladesh Ties: Analysis," *Eurasia Review*, June 30, 2014, http://www.eurasiareview. com/30062014-sushma-visit-gives-fresh-impetus-india-bangladesh-ties-analysis/.

34. Caroline Brassard, "Bhutan: Cautiously Cultivated Positive Perception," in *A Resurgent China: South Asian Perspectives*, ed. S. D. Muni and Tan Tai Yong (New Delhi: Routledge, 2013), 81.

35. Kinga Dema, "Americans Back on Top in Tourist Arrivals," *Kuensel Online*, February 11, 2014, http://www.kuenselonline.com/100811/#.UxTZSvldWbk.

36. Michael E. Clarke, *Xinjiang and China's Rise in Central Asia: A History* (New York: Routledge, 2011), 255.

37. Swaran Singh, "The Sinicization of Myanmar: A Special Relationship," *Issues and Studies* 33, no. 1 (1997): 118.

38. Jonathan Hoslag, *China + India: Prospects for Peace* (New York: Columbia University Press, 2010), 92.

39. Wim Swann, *21st Century China: View and Vision* (New Delhi: Global Vision, 2009), 253.

40. Kalinovsky, "Sino-Afghani Border Relations," 17.

41. Ibid., 19.

42. Pushpa Adhikari, *China Threat in South Asia* (New Delhi: Lancers, 2012), 23.

43. Rajshree Jetly, "India and China: Emerging Dynamics and Regional Security Perspectives," in *Perspectives on South Asian Security*, ed. Shanthie Mariet D'Souza and Rajshree Jetly (Singapore: World Scientific, 2013), 54; Harsh Pant, *China's Rising Global Profile: The Great Power Tradition* (Portland, OR: Sussex Academic Press, 2012), 47.

44. Bi Shihong, "Trade Corridor Helps Rejuvenate Asia," *Global Times*, June 3, 2013, p. 9.

45. Todd Hofstedt, "China's Water Scarcity and Its Implications for Domestic and International Stability," *Asian Affairs: An American Review*, no. 37 (2010): 78.

46. Scott Moore, "China's Massive Water Problem," *International Herald Tribune*, March 29, 2013, p. 8.

47. Yang Lina, "China Communicating with India on Cross-border River Issue: Spokeswoman," *Xinhua*, February 4, 2013, http://news.xinhuanet.com/ english/china/2013-02/04/c_132150620.htm.

48. Stephen Blank, "Chinese Energy Policy in Central and South Asia," *Korean Journal of Defence Analysis* 21, no. 4 (2009): 449.

49. Pravakar Sahoo, "Economic Relations with Bangladesh: China's Ascent and India's Decline," *South Asia Research* 33, no. 2 (2013): 123.

50. Maung Aung Myoe, *In the Name of Pauk-Phaw: Myanmar's China Policy Since 1948* (Singapore: Institute of Southeast Asian Studies, 2011), 159.

51. Byron N. Tzou, *China and International Law: The Boundary Disputes* (New York: Praeger, 1990), 68–72.

52. Brendan Whyte, "The Sino-Myanmar Border," in *Beijing's Power and China's Borders: Twenty Neighbors in Asia*, ed. Bruce A. Elleman, Stephen Kotkin, and Clive Schofield (New York: M. E. Sharpe, 2012), 295.

53. Gulbahar H. Beckett and Gerard A. Postiglione, eds., *China's Assimilationist Language Policy: The Impact on Indigenous/Minority Literacy and Social Harmony* (New York: Routledge, 2012), 1.

54. Gerard A. Postiglione, ed., *China's National Minority Education: Culture, Schooling, and Development* (New York: Routledge, 1999), 4–5.

55. Yanqi Tong and Shaohua Lei, *Social Protest in Contemporary China, 2003–2010: Transitional Pains and Regime Legitimacy* (New York: Routledge, 2014), 134, 143.

56. Jonathan Kaiman, "Kunming Knife Attack: Xinjiang Separatists Blamed for 'Chinese 9/11,'" *The Guardian*, March 2, 2014, http://www.theguardian.com/world/2014/mar/02/kunming-knife-attack-muslim-separatists-xinjiang-china.

# EIGHT

# Central Asia in Chinese Strategic Thinking

*Zhao Huasheng*

China has a long and rich history of political, cultural, and commercial relations with Central Asia. For many centuries, Chinese have referred to the vast region west of the Silk Road gates at Jade Pass and Yangguan Pass in Gansu province as *Xiyu*, which means the "Western Regions." Exactly what lands were subsumed under the term *Xiyu* have varied over time and have been more a function of extant political conditions than features of geography, but they always included territory in the modern-day Chinese province of Xinjiang and what is now referred to as Central Asia.[1] In 138 BC, Han dynasty emperor Hanwu sent an envoy named Zhang Qian to Xiyu to forge a partnership intended to mitigate the threat from the Huns, a nomadic people living in northern regions of China since ancient times.[2] Zhang Qian's search for allies took him as far as Fergana and Samarkand (located in present-day Uzbekistan) and Afghanistan. Zhang failed to achieve his political objective, but his journey to the west paved the way for centuries-long interactions between China and Central Asia.[3]

China established its first military-administrative office in Xiyu in 60 BC. The office, which was responsible for present day Xinjiang and parts of Central Asia, marked the beginning of China's administrative control of Xiyu. The degree to which China exercised effective control in the territories over which it claimed jurisdiction was greater in some dynasties than in others. In the nineteenth century, Russia annexed all of Central Asia and by the early twentieth century most of Xiyu was controlled by Russia and its successor, the Soviet Union.[4]

After the dissolution of the Soviet Union in 1991, China rekindled its memory of past ties and sought to restore its relationships with Central Asia. However, Central Asia had changed greatly after one and a half centuries under Moscow's sway. Moreover, the international situation and political aspirations are very different now than when China last exercised suzerainty in the region. As a result, China had to rediscover Central Asia and rebuild its relationships with the region on a new foundation.

In fashioning relations anew, China's policies and actions toward Central Asia have been shaped by the priority Beijing ascribes to self-strengthening through modernization and sustained economic growth and Chinese perceptions of security challenges and economic opportunities in the region.[5] They have also been shaped by the perceptions, priorities, and policies of states in the region and a limited number of external actors. This chapter examines China's interests and priorities in Central Asia and the policies it has adopted to achieve them.

### Evolution of Chinese Strategic Thinking About Central Asia

China's strategic thinking with respect to Central Asia has evolved since the establishment of formal diplomatic relations in early 1992. In the first years after the collapse of the Soviet Union, China's top priorities were to normalize state-to-state relations; settle the border problems that China and the USSR had been unable to resolve; and ensure safety along its borders with Kazakhstan, Kyrgyzstan, and Tajikistan.

China also had other concerns and interests in the region, but they were not high on Beijing's agenda. Terrorism originating in the Xinjiang Uighur Autonomous Region (separatist and terrorist groups refer to it as *East Turkestan*) had already become a problem, but at the time there was no political or practical framework for counterterrorism cooperation between China and Central Asian states. Economic contacts, particularly along the border, were increasing, and cheap Chinese commodities were pouring into thirsty Central Asian markets. But trade between China and Central Asia was still trivial in comparison to China's overall foreign trade volumes. The trade turnover of China and Central Asia from 1992 to 1997 was $460 million, $600 million, $570 million, $770 million, and $870 million, respectively. For the same period, China's foreign trade with all nations totaled

$165.5 billion, $195.7 billion, $236.6 billion, $280.8 billion, $289.8 billion, and $325.1 billion, respectively.[6]

Energy from Central Asia was not yet significant to China, which became a net oil importer only in 1993. China imported very little oil; the world energy market was characterized by low prices, limited competition, and sufficient supply; and China did not feel compelled to find new sources of supply. Purchasing oil in the world market was easier then and also more economically appealing than investing in expensive pipelines from Central Asia to China. It was not until 1997 that China and Kazakhstan signed an agreement to build the first pipeline from Central Asia to China. That project was proposed by Kazakhstan, not China.[7]

Relations moved to a higher level in April 1996, when the leaders of China, Russia, Kazakhstan, Kyrgyzstan, and Tajikistan gathered in Shanghai to sign an agreement to enhance military trust in border areas. The agreement was regarded as a logical and appropriate step to improve relations after the five states had settled their border disputes. The special purpose meeting received widespread international attention and evolved into a regular forum for the five presidents—dubbed the "Shanghai Five"—to meet annually to discuss issues of common concern.[8] Formation of the Shanghai Five opened the door for China to engage Central Asia in a multilateral format that included Russia. The existence of this new multilateral mechanism enhanced China's interest in the region and boosted its enthusiasm for additional forms of cooperation with the region.

The following year, the five states signed an agreement on mutual reduction of military forces along their common borders.[9] Settlement of border disputes and enhanced border security reduced concern about border security and cleared the way for China to broaden and deepen its relations with Central Asia. As border issues receded in importance, Beijing accorded higher priority to enhancing economic cooperation and the fight against the "three evil forces" of terrorism, separatism, and extremism. Since 1997, these new objectives have been at the top of China's diplomatic agenda for Central Asia.

The terrorist attacks of September 11, 2001, changed geopolitics everywhere, especially in the Central Asian region. The attacks also changed China's view of Central Asia. The region acquired higher priority in Chinese strategic thinking because of its actual and potential importance to China's growing worries about terrorism, separatism, and extremism. But the attacks also had an indirect impact on Chinese thinking about the region because they triggered a sharp rise in the price of oil and increased competition for available supplies. This occurred at precisely the time that China's imports of oil increased substantially and it became ever more dependent on overseas sources of energy to fuel its growing economy.[10] The changed situation caused China to reconsider its energy strategy and to attach higher priority to securing reliable supplies from Central Asia. One result of this recalculation of China's energy strategy was that work on the Kazakhstan-China pipeline that had been approved in 1997 was restarted in 2003.

Central Asia gained increased geostrategic importance for other reasons as well. The conflict in Afghanistan added new levels of uncertainty about the region's future and triggered numerous moves and countermoves by regional and external actors. Foreign military forces poured into the region. The United States gained access to military bases in Uzbekistan and Kyrgyzstan. Nearly all the major powers came to the region with the shared goal of fighting transnational terrorism and often widely divergent visions of what the postconflict situation should look like. Russia both supported and worried about the developments occurring on its southern periphery. China quickly recognized that it could not remain a disinterested or disengaged observer in a region that was fast becoming an arena of cooperation and competition of all the great powers.[11]

Precisely how China would become engaged was not preordained by historical precedents or an overarching "grand strategy" to achieve Chinese objectives. More than a decade later—after the Obama administration had announced its "Pivot to Asia"—a group of Chinese academics proposed a hypothetical "March West" strategy to balance US moves to strengthen its position in the Western Pacific by expanding China's presence in Central Asia, South Asia, West Asia, and the Middle East.[12] Whatever the merits of this proposal, which has not achieved the status of official policy, it was formulated long after Beijing had begun to respond to the changing situation in Central Asia.

The absence of a grand strategy did not mean that China's efforts to shape developments were nothing more than knee-jerk or opportunistic responses to what was happening in the region. To the contrary, they were logical, even predictable steps to ameliorate perceived threats to China's security and to sustain the high rates of economic growth judged necessary to achieve prosperity, internal stability, and the strength to deter and influence real and imagined adversaries. However, when Chinese President Xi Jinping referred to the idea of a "Silk Road economic belt" during his visit to Kazakhstan in September 2013, many interpreted his words as an indication of China's grand strategy for this region.[13] The sections that follow provide brief summaries of the way China's policies toward Central Asia evolved in response to new dangers and opportunities.

## Security

Concerns about security have been central to China's policies toward Central Asia throughout the more than two thousand years of relationships with Xiyu. All Chinese dynasties from the Qin (221 BC–207 BC) to the Qing (1644–1911) accorded high priority to maintaining stability and unity, and all worried about threats from the northwest. These concerns continued into the modern era. During the reign of the Republic of China (1911–1949), while the country suffered continuous domestic conflict and Japanese aggression, the central government exercised only loose and limited control over Xinjiang and the region was in a state of constant chaos. In 1933, influenced by pan-Islamism and pan-Turkism, separatists in Xinjiang proclaimed the establishment of an "Islamic Republic of East Turkestan" in Kashgar.[14] This was the first time that separatists in Xinjiang had used the name *East Turkestan* to identify their "state." The "constitution" of the Islamic Republic of East Turkestan imposed Sharia law and declared establishment of a "permanent independent state."[15]

Although this "state" was short-lived—it existed for only three months and was not recognized officially by any country—it remained the goal of separatists in Xinjiang. It was reincarnated with backing from the Soviet Union in 1944 as the "East Turkestan Republic." This time the separatist regime was located in Yining, a city near the northwestern border between Xinjiang and Soviet Central Asia. It proclaimed the end of Chinese rule in Xinjiang and creation of an independent "state." The East Turkestan Republic existed for a little more than eighteen months—that is, only until the Soviet Union withdrew support in June 1946. However, the negative legacy of the two "republics" continues until today because the current East Turkestan separatists claim to be fighting to restore these former "republics."

The establishment of independent Central Asian states in the space of the former Soviet Union coincided with the new wave of separatist and terrorist activities in Xinjiang perpetrated by East Turkestan terrorists. The close geographical, ethnic, and religious links between Xinjiang and Central Asia permit the latter region to serve as a refuge and outpost for the East Turkestan activists who flee from and penetrate into Xinjiang. This made it natural and necessary for China to seek cooperation with the states of Central Asia in order to safeguard security and stability in Xinjiang. China's policy priorities were and are to ensure that the Central Asian states continue to recognize Chinese sovereignty in Xinjiang; to limit the space for activity of the East Turkestan organizations; to establish institutionalized bilateral and multilateral regimes of security cooperation; and to form a common security space between China and Central Asia in which to contain terrorism, separatism, and extremism.

One of the first steps taken by China to address this problem was to take the lead in organizing the group of states that evolved into the Shanghai Cooperation Organisation (SCO). Originally formed as the "Shanghai Five" (China, Kazakhstan, Kyrgyzstan, Russia, and Tajikistan) in 1996, the grouping was renamed in 2001 after the addition of Uzbekistan. The SCO also has five observer states (Mongolia, Pakistan, India, Iran, and Afghanistan) and serves as China's principal multilateral platform in the region. It uses this platform to address China's security concerns in the region through cooperation to combat "the three evil forces": terrorism, separatism, and extremism.[16] This is accomplished through both bilateral arrangements and the Regional Antiterrorist Structure that was established in 2003 to coordinate antiterrorist activity.

In addition to signing bilateral agreements with Central Asian states, China initiated the 2007 Treaty on Long-Term Good-Neighborliness, Friendship, and Cooperation, in which SCO members pledged not to allow activities of the "three evil forces" in their territory that could be harmful to any third state and to cooperate in searching, detaining, extraditing, and repatriating terrorists, separatists, and extremists.[17] Within the framework of the SCO, China, and other member states conduct joint antiterrorist military exercises. As of 2013, the SCO had conducted eleven military exercises. China was the only member state to take part in all the joint drills.

Ensuring the security and stability of Xinjiang will be a long-term challenge for China. The terrorist events that have occurred in Xinjiang in recent years illustrate how difficult it will be to meet this challenge. The large-scale riot that occurred in Urumqi, the provincial capital, on July 5, 2009, was the biggest and most violent riot in Xinjiang in the last sixty years.[18] The April 2013 terrorist attack in Bachu county caused the death of fifteen public servants and policemen, including ten Uighurs, three Hans, and two Mongols. Three of the dead were women.[19] Two months later, in June 2013, there was another violent attack, this time in Shanshan county in the eastern part of Xinjiang. The attack killed twenty-four innocent people, sixteen of them Uigurs.[20] According to Zhang Chunxian, the secretary of the Xinjiang Party Committee, 96 percent of planned terrorist attacks were detected and eliminated before the attacks were executed.[21] This demonstrates the effectiveness of China's counterterrorist campaign, but it also shows that the East Turkestan separatists are still very active in preparing and organizing terrorist activities. It is also clear that it will be impossible for China to eradicate terrorism, separatism, and extremism in the foreseeable future.

## Energy

Energy was added to the list of China's priorities in Central Asia in 2001. In the 1990s, the price of energy was only about ten to twenty dollars a barrel. The world energy market had ample supply and limited competition. Moreover, China had only recently become a net oil importer and had not yet experienced a serious shortage of energy. As a result, assuring access to energy had not yet become a pressing issue. Before 1997, overseas oil constituted no more than 10 percent of China's domestic consumption. However, China's dependence on imported oil had been growing steadily, and the steady increase soon caused China to rethink its energy policy. In 2000, imported oil crossed the 30 percent of consumption threshold, and all indications were that the percentage would continue to rise. The following year, the Chinese government referred to the need for an "oil strategy" for the first time and initiated work to develop a national oil strategy for the twenty-first century.[22] The resultant calibration of need was one of the factors that led the government to proclaim the "go out" strategy to ensure supply through active involvement in worldwide exploration and exploitation of energy (and other) resources.[23]

The events of September 11, 2001, occurred in the midst of heightened concern about energy security and the admonition to seek resources abroad.

In addition to many other consequences, the terrorist attacks radically changed the world energy landscape. Global energy supplies became tight, energy prices began to soar, and worldwide competition for energy became more intense. China suffered more than others from this energy shock. The situation was made even worse by the fact that Russia walked away from negotiations with China for the construction of an oil pipeline from Angarsk (in Russia) to Daqing (in northeastern China). China and Russia had been negotiating to build this pipeline for about seven years when Russia suddenly abandoned the talks after Japan indicated that it was prepared to compete with China for the pipeline deal.

Under the changed circumstances, Central Asia acquired unprecedented importance in China's energy strategy. From that point forward, the region was perceived to be a strategically important source of energy to fuel China's drive for sustained economic growth and one of the regions that could make a significant contribution to the diversification of China's energy import structure. The first concrete manifestation of this change of perception was renewed pressure from China to restart construction of the China-Kazakhstan pipeline project. In June 2003, during President Hu Jintao's visit to Kazakhstan, the two leaders expressed political support for building the China-Kazakhstan oil pipeline.[24] In May 2004, the China National Petroleum Corporation (CNPC) and Kazmunaigaz signed the agreement to build an oil pipeline from Atasu, Kazakhstan, to Alashankou, China.[25] The pipeline was completed in 2005 and put into operation the following year.

China's energy interests in Central Asia broadened to include gas as well as oil in approximately 2005. The major factor driving China's decision to make this shift was the desire to transform the structure of domestic energy consumption with the goal of increasing the proportion of clean energy through greater use of natural gas. To achieve this goal, China decided to partner with Turkmenistan, the largest producer of natural gas in Central Asia. In 2006, China and Turkmenistan agreed to a deal under which Turkmenistan will provide thirty billion cubic meters of gas to China annually for thirty years beginning in 2009. Construction of the Turkmenistan-Uzbekistan-Kazakhstan-China gas pipeline began in 2008 and was completed at the end of 2009. China's president, Hu Jintao, and Turkmenistan's president, Gurbanguly Berdymukhamedov, were present for the ceremonial opening of the gas pipeline. Another gas agreement was signed in 2011, during the Turkmenistan president's visit to China.[26] According to that agreement, Turkmenistan will increase gas deliveries to China by twenty-five billion cubic meters annually, increasing the total amount of gas that Turkmenistan will supply to China to sixty-five billion cubic meters per year.

China also seeks to arrange gas cooperation with Kazakhstan, Uzbekistan, and Tajikistan. Kazakhstan and Uzbekistan each have sizeable gas reserves and could provide gas to China. China and Uzbekistan concluded a gas deal in 2010 under which Uzbekistan will supply ten billion cubic meters of natural gas to China every year.[27] Uzbekistan's gas began to flow to China in 2012.

Supplying 11.98 million tons, Kazakhstan was China's eighth largest oil supplier in 2013. This figure constituted about 4.2 percent of the 282.1 million tons China imported that year.[28] In 2012, the Central Asia–China gas pipeline delivered approximately twenty billion cubic meters of gas to China. This was less than had been agreed on and constituted a little less than half the total volume of China's yearly gas imports.[29] The volume was expected to reach thirty billion cubic meters in 2013 but reached only 24.7 billion cubic meters that year. However, Turkmenistan accounted for 46 percent of China's gas import structure, and it remains the largest among all the gas exporters to China.[30] Adding the fifteen billion cubic meters of gas that could be provided by Uzbekistan and Kazakhstan made Central Asia China's most important supplier of natural gas.

## Economic and Transportation Interests

China's trade with Central Asia has increased steadily since 2002 but still represents only a small share of China's total foreign trade. Before Central Asia acquired greater strategic importance, as described in the previous section, two-way trade with China had never exceeded $2 billion per year. A decade later, in 2012, the total had climbed to a record high $45 billion but still represented just a little more than 1 percent of China's overall foreign trade volume of more than $3,866 billion in the same year. That low percentage understates Central Asia's economic importance to China, however.

Trade with Central Asia is important nationally primarily because of its importance to Xinjiang's economy. Xinjiang is China's largest province (in terms of territory). It is located far from the eastern, most developed provinces of China, but it is close to Central Asia; shares more than three thousand kilometers of common borders with Kazakhstan, Kyrgyzstan and Tajikistan; and is only a short distance from Uzbekistan.

Most (consistently more than 60 percent) of Xinjiang's foreign trade has been with Central Asia. For example, in 2012, $17.5 billion of Xinjiang's $25 billion foreign trade volume was with countries in Central Asia (approximately 70 percent).[31] This is not surprising, because ten of the fifteen authorized border crossings in Xinjiang are located on borders with Central Asia (seven to Kazakhstan, two to Kyrgyzstan, and one to Tajikistan).

Economic development of Xinjiang is a national priority. In 2000, the Chinese government released its strategy for "development of the western regions."[32] Xinjiang is one of the focal points of this policy, which aims to accelerate economic development in the western provinces in order to keep pace with the eastern part of China. Accelerated development of Xinjiang is intended to achieve multiple objectives, such as narrowing the economic gap between Xinjiang and the more developed eastern provinces and reinvigorating modernization and economic development of the country as a whole. It also has the additional important goal of helping alleviate discontent and security problems in Xinjiang. By eliminating poverty and improving the living standard of local residents, sustained development could help reduce the ability of East Turkestan separatists to manipulate the population.

Stated another way, fostering economic development through trade with Central Asia is considered an important way to alleviate the conditions that allow terrorism, separatism, and extremism to flourish. This objective has acquired even greater importance after the riot in Urumqi on July 5, 2009.[33] The central government issued another developmental strategy for Xinjiang in 2010 with the announced goal of promoting accelerated development and long-term stability. Later that year, Beijing designated two cities in Xinjiang (Kashi in the south and Horgos in the north) as special economic zones. The central government hopes that the two new special economic zones will serve as economic locomotives that drive development in the province. The central government took an additional step in 2011, when it decided to upgrade the status of the Urumqi Fair, a yearly economic and trade exhibition that began in 1992, from that of a local exposition to a national level one. The fair, renamed the China-Eurasia Expo, will be held annually in Urumqi. Then vice premier Li Keqiang attended the first session of the China-Eurasia Expo in 2011, and Premier Wen Jiabao took part in the second China-Eurasia Expo the following year.

As indicated by the examples just cited, Beijing has a strong interest in promoting economic integration between China and the states of Central Asia. China first put forward the idea of creating a free economic zone in the framework of the Shanghai Cooperation Organization in 2003.[34] Eight years later, China formally proposed conducting a feasibility study for the formation of a free economic zone.[35] China made this proposal because it sought to expand economic cooperation with the Central Asian states in ways similar to what had been achieved through cooperation with the Association of Southeast Asia Nations (ASEAN) and other states.[36] However, it is important to note that although economic cooperation between China and Central Asian states has grown quickly, and trade volumes have increased steadily, the integration project has stagnated.

The region also has abundant supplies of metals and minerals, and Chinese companies are actively engaged in cooperative projects to develop them. These projects are mutually beneficial, adding to the revenues of the producer countries and providing China with resources needed by its growing economy.

Another reason Central Asia is important to China is because it is the geographic bridge connecting China with South Asia, West Asia, the Middle East, the Caucasus, and Europe. This makes it a crucial link in China's plan to create a transportation network to connect China with those regions. In other words, the region is important not only because of what it has in the way of resources and markets desired by China but also because of where it is.

## Geostrategic Perspectives

China considers the Central Asian region to be a strategic rear area. Currently, and for the foreseeable future, China's primary strategic pressure lies to its east. This makes Central Asia part of China's strategic rear area, but that characterization in no way diminishes the region's importance to China. China's interests are well served if the region remains stable because that allows Beijing to concentrate on areas of greater immediate strategic concern without distraction of its attention and resources.

Securing Central Asia as China's stable strategic rear area required meeting certain conditions, such as resolving disputed border issues and maintaining peace and security in border areas. Border disputes had festered for a long time and were irritants in China's relations with neighboring Central Asian states. Without solution of the border disputes and guaranteed security along the border, cooperation could not go forward on a solid foundation. Both of these prerequisites have been satisfied. China's task now is to ensure that the Central Asian nations adopt goodwill foreign policies toward China and enable China to maintain good bilateral relations with all of the Central Asian states. Another requirement is to ensure that Central Asia does not fall under the sway of any big power or group of big powers that have unfriendly strategic relations with China.

Central Asia is unique in that it is the only place where all the great powers converge. All the great powers declare that they favor cooperation with one another. However, despite avowals of desire to work together, the only cooperation that has occurred in recent years has been bilateral, such as that between China and Russia and between the United States and the European Union. As a matter of fact, cooperation among the great powers in Central Asia has been more rhetorical than real. Even in those areas where the great powers are supposed to have common interests and where, theoretically, cooperation should occur (such as combating terrorism and narcotics), no major cooperative framework has been formed. The reasons are strategic distrust and geopolitical competition among the great powers, particularly between Russia and the United States. However, although the great powers are reluctant to engage in close cooperation, they have been able to avoid direct confrontations. All the great powers publicly deny that they are engaged in a new version of the Great Game. That said, China is especially attentive to the geopolitical moves of the United States and Russia. China does not consider the United States to be a rival in Central Asia and generally seeks to work cooperatively with the United States to achieve shared objectives. China has expressed this attitude many times.[37] The principal objective of the Afghanistan war, in which the United States was the major actor, was to destroy Al-Qaeda and the Taliban regime. Achieving this objective contributed to the security of nearby states, including China. The US military presence in Central Asia is not welcomed by China, but it is not regarded as a pressing security threat. Moreover, the United States is considered unlikely to pose a serious challenge to China in the region or to impede its engagement with the Central Asian states. China believes that Beijing and Washington share a series of common interests in the region and could cooperate to combat terrorism and drug trafficking. It is China's judgment that cooperation with the United State can advance the interests of both countries and that confrontation will harm the interests of both.[38]

Nevertheless, China has found it difficult to work with the United States as a strategic partner. China and the United States disagree on many issues and have different approaches toward Central Asia, particularly in regard to political development. China especially dislikes what it regards as efforts by the United States to achieve regime change in the states of Central Asia by fostering and supporting "color revolutions." The 2005 color revolution in Central Asia caused serious concern in China. China does not want versions of the Arab Spring to spread into Central Asia, and it does not welcome the prospect of a long-term US military presence. Most worrisome to China is its suspicion that the United States applies a double standard with regard to East Turkestan. However, despite all these problems, China and the United States were able to create the subdialogue on Central Asia, the purpose of which, according to Assistant Secretary for South and Central Asian Affairs Robert O. Blake, Jr., was "to explore . . . and to discuss how we [the United States and China] can collaborate and coordinate our efforts in Central Asia in areas of mutual interest."[39]

Russia's actions and intentions in Central Asia are of particular importance to China, and Sino-Russian relations have the most significant impact on China's diplomacy in the region. The reason is not simply that Russia is the biggest player in the region but also, and more importantly, that Russia regards the region as part of its zone of influence.[40]

China considers Russia to be a strategic partner in Central Asia and tries hard to maintain a positive relationship. It is in China's interest to maintain good relations with Russia because doing so enhances the China-Russia strategic partnership and creates a favorable environment for China to develop cooperation with the Central Asian states. In this regard, Sino-Russian relations have been a great success. China and Russia have maintained a cooperative relationship for more than twenty years. They actively collaborate to combat terrorism, fight drug trafficking, and maintain regional stability. The Shanghai Cooperation Organization has played a useful facilitating role by providing a unique platform for China and Russia to work together as partners in Central Asia.

Commentators frequently express pessimism about the ability of China and Russia to avoid conflicts of interest in Central Asia and it is true that their relationship is complicated by a number of issues.[41] It would be unwise to pretend that there are no disagreements or that the differences are not important, but there have been no clashes between China and Russia in Central Asia for more than twenty years. The reason, as the director of the Graduate Institute of Slavic Studies and Literature at Tamkang University has noted, is that Russia and China are strategic partners in Central Asia, and when they disagree, the disagreements are tactical.[42]

China has no intention of trying to impede Russia in Central Asia. It does not oppose Russia's integration project, the Eurasian Union. Indeed, it seeks to collaborate with it. The political and economic plans that China is promoting in the region are beneficial for both countries. All these projects address domestic development needs; none of them target Russia, or step on Russia's toes. China regards its economic presence in Central Asia as a positive factor that contributes to regional development and stability, which are in Russia's interests as well as in China's. A. V. Malashenko, a professor with the Moscow Carnegie Center, shares this view and has observed that China does not pose a political challenge to Russia in Central Asia. On the contrary, he argues, China tries to avoid politics as much as possible. To the extent that there is a challenge, it is an economic one.[43]

To be sure, China and Russia do compete in some areas in Central Asia, particularly in the economic arena, but the competition takes place within the ordered structure of the international system. When it does occur, it is usually a product of circumstances, not the result of deliberate attempts to contain one another. At the moment, the character of Sino-Russian competition is benign. Each country has pursued its own interests, but there have been no malicious attacks, and neither seeks to defeat or destroy the other. Their competition is bounded by rules of the global order that reduce the danger that competition will escalate into conflict.

Despite the existence of disagreements, Russia and China do not threaten each other's security in Central Asia. This point is very important because security is the most important concern of both countries. Maintaining a strategic partnership with Russia in Central Asia is China's long-term policy, and it will continue into the future.

## Conclusion

China has many and diverse interests in Central Asia. They include security, energy, economic growth, and geostrategic politics. Trends indicate that all of China's interests in the region will continue to grow and that China's Central Asia diplomacy will intensify. The scheduled withdrawal of US and International Security Assistance Force troops from Afghanistan will increase the severity of regional security challenges. As a result, China's security concerns about the region are likely to increase for many years. One reason is that China's oil and gas imports from Central Asia will continue to rise. Another is that economic cooperation and trade between China and Central Asia will also increase, creating greater vulnerabilities for all parties. Finally, Central Asia has a significant role to play in the Silk Road Economic Belt, to which China attaches great importance. These developments will increase the geopolitical significance of the region, and China will assign even greater importance to Central Asia. In addition to wanting to ensure that its strategic rear area is secure, China will want to use the region as an important strategic asset on the diplomatic chessboard.

## Notes

1. See, for example, James Millward, *Eurasian Crossroads: A History of Xinjiang* (London: C. Hurst, 2007), and the works cited therein.

2. See Wang Zhilai, *Zhongya tongshi* [A complete history of Central Asia] (Urumqi, China: Renmin Press, 2004), 97.

3. See Miao Pusheng and Tian Weijiang, *Xinjiang shigang* [A survey of Xinjiang history] (Urumqi, China: Renmin Press, 2004), 64.

4. China was forced to sign the agreement with Russia on demarcation of the northwest border in 1864. It was the basic document describing the China-Russia border in the region until the collapse of the USSR. See She Taishan, *Xiyu tongshi* [A complete history of western regions] (Zhengzhou, China: Zhongzhou Guji Press, 2003), 470–471.

5. For information on China's strategy for sustained development, see, for example, Li Lanqing, *Breaking Through: The Birth of China's Opening-Up Policy* (New York: Oxford University Press, 2009).

6. See Zhao Huasheng, *Zhongguo de Zhongya waijiao* [China's Central Asia diplomacy] (Beijing: Shishi Press, 2008), 45.

7. In his speech on the opening of the China-Kazakhstan oil pipeline, Kazakhstan president Nursultan Nazarbayev said that when he proposed the pipeline in 1997, it was viewed as utopian, but now the utopia has been turned into reality. See Dmitry Kim, "'Kazakhstan prevraschaet utopiu v realnost'" ["Kazakhstan turns utopia into reality"], *NV.kz*, December 21, 2005, http://www.nv.kz/2005/12/21/8448.

8. See, for example, Jia Qingguo, "The Shanghai Cooperation Organization: China's Experiment in Multilateral Leadership," in *Eager Eyes Fixed on Eurasia*, vol. 2, *Russia and Its Eastern Edge*, ed. Iwashita Akihiro (Sapporo, Japan: Slavic-Eurasian Research Center, 2007), 113–123, https://src-h.slav.hokudai.ac.jp/coe21/publish/no16_2_ses/05_jia.pdf.

9. "The Agreement Between the Russian Federation, the Republic of Kazakhstan, the Kyrgyz Republic, the Republic of Tajikistan and the People's Republic of China About Mutual Reducing Armed Forces Around Border," April 24, 1997, http://cis-legislation.com/document.fwx?rgn=3872.

10. China's imports of oil increased from 90.13 million barrels in 1994 to 512.94 million barrels in 2000. See Jin Liangxiang, "Energy First: China and the Middle East," *Middle East Quarterly* 12, no. 2 (2005): 3–10, http://www.meforum.org/694/energy-first.

11. See Alexander Cooley, *Great Games, Local Rules: The New Great Power Contest in Central Asia* (Oxford: Oxford University Press, 2012).

12. Wang Jisi, "'Xi Jin,' Zhongguo diyuan zhanluede zai pingheng" ["March West," China's geostrategic rebalance], *Huanqiu* [Global Times], October 17, 2012, http://opinion.huanqiu.com/opinion_world/2012-10/3193760.html.

13. See Tang Danlu, "Xi Suggests China, C. Asia Build Silk Road Economic Belt," *Xinhua*, September 7, 2013, http://news.xinhuanet.com/english/china/2013-09/07/c_132700695.htm.

14. James A. Millward, *Eurasian Crossroads: A History of Xinjiang* (New York: Columbia University Press, 2007), 201–206.

15. Ibid., 205.

16. See "SCO Cooperation to Combat 'Three Evil Forces,'" *Xinhua*, September 22, 2006, http://www.china.org.cn/english/2006/Sep/181910.htm. "The Shanghai Convention on Combating Terrorism, Separatism and Extremism" was signed on June 15, 2001, the same day the SCO was established. In the convention, the three evil forces of terrorism, separatism, and extremism are defined in terms of behavior and intention, not in reference to specific groups. The convention is available on SCO's website at http://www.sectsco.org/EN123/show.asp?id=68.

17. See Hu Jintao, "Enhance Good Neighborliness and Mutual Trust and Promote Peaceful Development," *China News and Report*, August 16, 2007, http://www.china.org.cn/english/report/227544.htm.

18. See Edward Wong, "Riots in Western China amid Ethnic Tension," *New York Times*, July 5, 2009, http://www.nytimes.com/2009/07/06/world/asia/06china.html.

19. "Xinjiang Bachu Xian '4-23' yanzhong baoli kongbu fanzui anjian gaopo" [Xinjiang Bachu County "4/23" act of terrorism case solved], *Xinhua*, April 29,

2013, http://news.xinhuanet.com/legal/2013-04/29/c_115594447.htm; "11 More Terrorist Suspects Captured After Xinjiang Deadly Attack," *China Weekly*, April 29, 2013, http://news.xinhuanet.com/english/china/2013-04/29/c_132349574.htm.

20. "Xinhua Insight: Investigations Reveal Details of Xinjiang Terror Attack," *China Weekly*, July 6, 2013, http://news.xinhuanet.com/english/indepth/2013-07/06/c_124966189.htm.

21. "96% Xinjiang Terrorist Attacks Foiled: Official," *China Daily*, May 17, 2013, http://usa.chinadaily.com.cn/china/2013-05/17/content_16508172.htm.

22. The concept of an "oil strategy" was first used by then Prime Minister Zhu Rongji in his report to the National People's Congress on June 6, 2001. The following year China produced the framework for its oil strategy for the twenty-first century under the auspices of the Economic and Commercial Committee and the Planning Committee of the Chinese government. See "Zhongguo buju xin shiyou zhanlue" [China sets out a new oil strategy], *Sohu*, November 11, 2002, http://business.sohu.com/01/47/article204254701.shtml; Forest Lee, "China's 21st Century Oil Strategy Outlined," *People's Daily Online*, November 14, 2002, http://en.people.cn/200211/14/eng20021114_106819.shtml.

23. See Aaron L. Friedberg, *"Going Out": China's Pursuit of Natural Resources and Implications for the PRC's Grand Strategy* (Seattle, WA: National Bureau of Asian Research, 2006).

24. See "Hu Jintao and Kazakh President Nursultan Nazarbayev Signed the Joint Statement (Full Text)," *China News*, June 3, 2003, http://www.chinanews.com/n/2003-06-03/26/310091.html.

25. See "Hasakestan he Zhongguo qianshu Atasy-Alashankou shiyou guandao jianshe xieyi," [Kazakhstan and China signed Atasu-Alashankou oil pipeline construction agreement], China National Oil and Gas Exploration and Development Corporation, May 31, 2004, http://www.oilchina.com/cnodc/syxx/cnodc_xl.jsp?bsm=040BA8B8E.000028D5.6102&db=cnodcsykj.

26. See "Hu Jintao tong Tukumansitan zongtong huitan" [Hu Jintao talks with Turkmenistan president], *People's Daily*, November 24, 2011, http://politics.people.com.cn/GB/1024/16367083.html.

27. See "CNPC Signs Gas Supply Agreement with Uzbek Oil Company," *Sina*, June 10, 2010, http://english.sina.com/business/2010/0609/324077.html.

28. Tian Chunrong, "2013 nian Zhongguo shiyou tianranqi jinchukou zhuang-kuang fenxi" [An analysis of China's import and export of oil and gas in 2013], *International Petroleum Economics*, no. 3 (2014): 34.

29. "Xinjiang cheng Zhongya youqi jinru Zhongguo zhongyao huanjie" [Xinjiang is serving as an important link for delivery of Central Asia's oil and gas to China], *Xinhua*, December 20, 2012, http://news.xinhuanet.com/fortune/2012-12/20/c_114099054.htm.

30. "CPC Central Committee's Recommendations for Formulating the Tenth Five-Year Plan for National Economic and Social Development," *People's Daily*, October 11, 2000, http://cpc.people.com.cn/GB/64162/71380/71382/71386/48379 46.html.

31. "2012 nian Xinjiang waimao jin chukou zong zhi shou po 250 yi meiyuan" [Xinjiang's total 2012 import/export value exceeds $25 billion for the first time], *Tianshanwang*, January 22, 2013, http://news.ts.cn/content/2013-01/22/content_ 7711333.htm.

32. "CPC Central Committee's Recommendations."

33. Wong, "Riots in Western China."

34. "Shanghai Hezuo Zuzhi chengyuan guo Zongli huiwu Wenjiabaoti san changyi" [At the meeting of Shanghai Cooperation Organization member states Prime Minister Wen Jiabao brought forward three initiatives], *People's Daily*, September 23, 2013, http://www.people.com.cn/GB/shizheng/1024/2104056.html.

35. "Jiang Yaoping Fu Buzhang lu tuan chuxi Du shang bie Shanghai Hezuo Zuzhidi shici jingmao buzhang huiyi" [Vice Minister Jiang Yaoping heads delegation to attend the Dushanbe tenth economic and trade ministers' meeting of the Shanghai Cooperation Organization], Shanghai Cooperation Organization Regional Economic Cooperation Network, November 11, 2011, http://www.sco-ec .gov.cn/crweb/scoc/info/Article.jsp?a_no=276704&col_no=48.

36. In July 2002, China and ASEAN signed an agreement to create a free economic zone. The leaders of China and the ASEAN states were determined to implement the agreement by 2010. See "Zhonghua Renmin Gongheguo yu Dongmeng lingdaoren lianhe xuanyan" [Joint declaration of the leaders of PRC and ASEAN states], *Xinhua*, October 9, 2003, http://news.xinhuanet.com/world/ 2003-10/09/content_1114267.htm.

37. As early as October 2002, on the eve of President Jiang Zemin's visit to the United States, China's vice foreign minister, Li Zhaoxing, said China was willing to cooperate with the United States in bilateral consultations and cooperation on international and regional issues, including regarding China in Central Asia. See "Zhongmei guanfang meiti ruhe kandai Bushi fanghua" [How the media in China and the United States view Bush's visit], *People's Daily*, February 20, 2002, http:// www.people.com.cn/GB/guoji/501639.html.

38. Sino-American energy cooperation was later proposed by China. Beginning in August 2005, energy cooperation was one of the principal issues discussed in the Sino-American Strategic Dialogue.

39. U.S. Department of State, "Media Roundtable: Press Conference, Robert O. Blake, Jr.," March 18, 2011, http://www.state.gov/p/sca/rls/rmks/2011/158583 .htm.

40. See Chapter 11; and Roman Muzalevsky, "Russia's Strategy in Central Asia: An Analysis of Key Trends," *Yale Journal of International Affairs*, Winter 2009, pp. 26–42, http://yalejournal.org/wp-content/uploads/2011/01/094103muzalevsky .pdf.

41. For example, Professor Sergey Lousianin, the vice director of the Moscow-based Institute of Far East Studies, observed, "Although there have been numerous elements cementing Russian and Chinese cooperation, there have been growing sentiments of competition in the Central Asian sphere. As China's influence begins to undermine Russia's, the two key players become entangled in confrontation." Sergey Lousianin, "Russia, China and Central Asia: Energy Aspects," *New Eastern Outlook*, June 15, 2011, http://www.ar.journal-neo.com/node/7115.

42. Alexander Pisarev, "Russia and China in Central Asia," *ISPI Analysis*, no. 131 (2012), http://www.ispionline.it/it/documents/Analysis_131_2012.pdf.

43. A. V. Malashenko, "Kto brosaet vyzov Rossii v Zentralnoi Asii?" [Who challenges Russia in Central Asia?], *Nezavisimaya Gazeta*, March 3, 2012, http:// www.ng.ru/courier/2012-03-05/11_challenge.html.

# NINE

# China as a Balancer in South Asia
## An Economic Perspective with Special Reference to Sri Lanka

*Saman Kelegama*

China's rise as an economic superpower over the past two decades has been remarkable. With growth rates averaging 10 percent annually and strong indications that it will soon overtake all other major powers in economic terms, China has also increased its diplomatic influence. Smaller South Asian countries welcome China's increased economic and diplomatic power as a counterbalance to that of the United States and India.

The implications of China's rise for the regional and international order are enormous. The extent to which China's rise offers opportunities or threatens national interests varies from country to country and, within South Asia, countries have responded to China's rise in different ways. Many countries have chosen to foster close diplomatic and economic ties in order to leverage China's growth to accelerate their own economic development. Others, notably the region's larger economies—particularly India—are apprehensive about China's vast size, exporting capacity, and massive inflows of foreign direct investments (FDI). The South Asian democracies are more apprehensive about China's increasing political and military power than about its economic challenge. They worry that the emergence of an authoritarian world power will have a detrimental impact on the global system. Their concern is heightened by the modernization of China's armed forces, which is viewed with suspicion because of uncertainty about China's future role and intent in world affairs.

South Asia feels the effects of China's rise with particular intensity because of its geographic proximity. For example, China's need to secure the flow of energy resources from the Persian Gulf and ensure the security of sea lanes for trade of all kinds has prompted China to build surveillance and support facilities and to maintain a substantial naval presence in the Indian Ocean. The People's Liberation Army Navy has established relations with Indian Ocean rim countries and has offered to sell military equipment to South Asian countries at attractive prices. It has also established a foothold in major ports including Chittagong in Bangladesh, Hambantota in Sri Lanka, and Gwadar in Pakistan.

For many South Asian countries, the principal reason for fostering deeper integration with China is to capitalize on the potential for economic gains. China's remarkable transition from extreme poverty to impressive growth has sparked regional interest in learning from China's experience since the adoption of reforms in 1978. Moreover, China's rapid economic growth creates new trade and investment opportunities for South Asian countries. Such opportunities are welcome because spillover benefits from India's economic growth have been limited and the South Asian Association for Regional Development (SAARC) has been ineffective in achieving enhanced regionalism during its twenty-five-plus years of existence. As a result, China's engagement with individual South Asian countries is widely perceived as potentially beneficial.

For India, however, China's increasing presence in the region has produced serious concerns. Although Sino-Indian relations have improved significantly over the last decade, especially in the economic arena, this has not prevented the emergence of politically contentious issues. Moreover, because India sees itself as the dominant power in South Asia, it is suspicious of and discomforted by China's growing involvement in the region.[1] Some analysts have observed that India sometimes views China as posing a "formidable constraint" to its influence in smaller neighboring economies.[2] Factors that have contributed to this view include China's vast foreign exchange reserves, increasing presence in Africa, veto power in the UN Security Council, acknowledged emphasis on noninterference, and aversion to holding others accountable on human rights and governance issues. China's historical friendship with India's unfriendly neighbor Pakistan also contributes to India's growing suspicions. Taken together, these developments have "transformed the region from India's 'near abroad' into China's own backyard."[3]

Much has been written about China's strategic interests in the South Asian region and the dynamics and complexities involved in China's relationships with India and Pakistan, the two largest economies in the region. The views of the smaller economies in South Asia have received much less attention, and the studies that do exist focus on security and political issues.[4] The manner in which relationships are developed, both bilaterally and multilaterally, will have a significant impact not only on the political and security issues but also on the economic dynamics of the region. Do these countries view China as an important contributor to realization of their own economic development agendas or as a threat to their own development? More importantly, do they see the increasing Chinese presence as a counterbalance to India's leading position and role in the region, both economically and diplomatically? This chapter addresses these questions in part, but it focuses on how the smaller South Asian countries view economic issues related to China's rise by using Sri Lanka as a case study.

## China's Rise: Perspective of Smaller South Asian Countries

China's rise has been driven by a combination of factors, including three decades of sustained and outstanding economic growth, fast military modernization, and the ability to participate in multilateral institutions and organizations and contribute to international efforts to resolve conflicts. This has earned appreciation from countries around the world, including South Asia. This point is noteworthy because South Asia is one of the regions closest to China and because the way the smaller South Asian countries view China's rise is influenced by the simultaneous rise of India, the largest economy in their own region.

The smaller South Asian countries are generally more comfortable with a rising China than is India and tend to view China in a more positive light. However, the smaller economies do not all perceive China's rise in the same way. Bangladesh, Sri Lanka, Maldives, and Nepal view China as an important source of economic and noneconomic assistance and also as an increasingly important counterbalance to India's role in the region. When China applied for observer status in SAARC in 2007, these four countries joined Pakistan in enthusiastically supporting the application. Ultimately, the other South Asian members agreed to go along, but the others did not support China with the same degree of enthusiasm.

Afghanistan and Bhutan perceive China somewhat less positively. Although Afghanistan regards China as a friendly neighbor, it does not view

China as a counterbalance to India and would probably prefer that Beijing do more to constrain Pakistan.[5] Bhutan's strong historical ties to and heavy reliance on India for its foreign policy and domestic economic performance constrain its relationship with China. The following section examines the contrasting perceptions of these two groups in greater detail.

Judging the way one country perceives another is a complicated task for several reasons. One is that diverse constituencies and stakeholders do not have identical interests and, therefore, do not perceive other countries in the same way. Also, perceptions, although often based on reality, are not necessarily identical with reality because they are shaped by factors such as experience, exposure, and the nature of engagement and thus are also subject to change depending on circumstances.[6] The perceptions discussed in this chapter are based on the general overarching perceptions prevalent in each country at the current point in time.[7]

## Economic Opportunities

The smaller states of South Asia view China's rise primarily in terms of the opportunities it creates for their own economies. China's phenomenal economic growth during the first decade of the twenty-first century has made it significantly better able to respond to their trade and investment needs, and China has gradually strengthened its links with growing South Asian markets to support its own export-led growth. Three examples illustrate the kinds of changes now taking place:

- In 2000, membership in the former Bangkok Agreement was expanded to include China and renamed Asia Pacific Trade Agreement (APTA). APTA includes three South Asian members.[8]
- China and Pakistan signed a free trade agreement in late 2006, and it came into operation in 2007.[9]
- China obtained Dialog Partner status in the Indian Ocean Rim Association for Regional Cooperation in 2001; India, Sri Lanka, and Bangladesh were already members.[10]

By 2012, China had become the largest trading partner of three South Asian countries (Pakistan, Bangladesh, and Nepal) and the second largest trading partner of Sri Lanka. Although China has no free trade agreement with India, Sino-Indian trade increased from $1.5 billion in 2001 to $50 billion in 2011, and

China has become India's second largest trading partner (second to the United Arab Emirates [UAE]).[11] Partly as a result of these institutional arrangements but primarily because of China's rapid growth, trade between China and the smaller regional countries has evinced steady increases in recent years, increasing from $5.7 billion in 2001 to $97 billion by 2011.[12]

This growth in trade with China is in marked contrast to the trade of smaller countries with India. As noted earlier, historical rivalries and political tensions have been a constant obstacle to expanding trade flows within the region, despite the existence of the SAARC Preferential Trade Arrangement (SAPTA) since 1995 and the South Asia Free Trade Agreement (SAFTA) since 2006. Some of India's neighbors complain that India has adopted heavily protectionist measures that hamper regional integration and the ability of other SAARC members to realize the benefits of better integration. Moreover, since SAARC countries traditionally have produced similar goods, they compete with one another for access to Western markets. This sense of competition and rivalry has hindered cooperation as trade partners in pursuit of mutual economic gain. Despite working out free trade agreements with Nepal (1996), Sri Lanka (1998), and Bhutan (over many years), India still has not provided significantly greater market access to the smaller regional economies. Trade growth is also impeded by the inadequate supply capacity of the smaller countries.

China, in contrast, is relatively unburdened by such competitive rivalries (except in a few product areas such as ready-made garments and toys) and, therefore, is emerging as a less problematic trading partner for South Asia. China and India have the highest degree of trade complementarities, but China's trade with the smaller economies, such as Bangladesh, Sri Lanka, and Nepal, is growing, albeit not yet as fast as trade with India.[13] Better utilization of the APTA preferential tariff lines is important in this context.

Constraints on the extent to which smaller countries in the region have been able to benefit from India's growth have been partially compensated by the increasing trade opportunities offered by China's rise. Figures 9.1 and 9.2 illustrate the ratio of imports from smaller regional countries imported by India and China as a share of their imports from the world. As can be seen, India's share of imports from the region has shown a declining trend in many of the countries, whereas the share imported by China has been on the rise, particularly in the cases of Bangladesh and Sri Lanka.

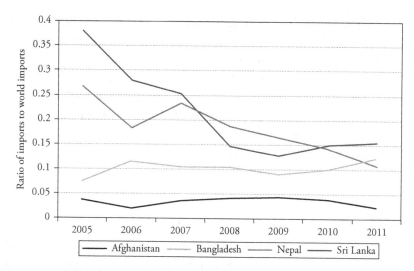

FIGURE 9.1 India's share of imports from small South Asian countries, 2005–2011

SOURCE: Author's calculations using data from International Monetary Fund, *Direction of Trade Statistics Yearbook, 2012* (Washington, DC: IMF, 2012)

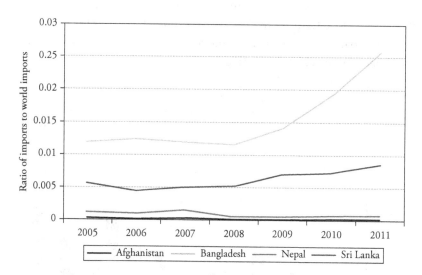

FIGURE 9.2 China's share of imports from small South Asian countries, 2005–2011

SOURCE: Author's calculations using data from International Monetary Fund, *Direction of Trade Statistics Yearbook, 2012* (Washington, DC: IMF, 2012)

China is Bangladesh's largest trade partner. Under the APTA, a range of Bangladeshi products have received duty-free access to the Chinese market. Furthermore, despite a history of competition between the two countries for the manufacture of ready-made garments, China has taken steps to ease tensions by outsourcing some ready-made garment jobs to Bangladesh, where labor costs are lower. In return, Bangladesh has offered China exploration rights to its reserves of coal, natural gas, and oil.[14] China's share of Sri Lankan exports has also increased from 0.4 percent in 2006 to 1.2 percent in 2012.[15]

### Investment

Chinese outward FDI has increased at an exceptional average growth rate of 49.9 percent per year, from $2.7 billion to $68.8 billion during the period from 2002 to 2010. The South Asian region has been an important recipient of such FDI flows; the share of Chinese outward FDI to South Asia has risen from a mere 0.08 percent in 2004 to 60 percent in 2010.[16] Although the bulk of these flows go to Pakistan and India, Chinese FDI into smaller countries, particularly Sri Lanka and Bangladesh, has been on an upward trajectory in more recent years (Figure 9.3).

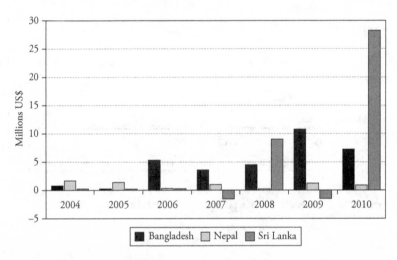

FIGURE 9.3 China's outward FDI flows to selected South Asian countries, 2004–2010
SOURCE: People's Republic of China Ministry of Commerce, "2010 Statistical Bulletin of China's Outward Foreign Direct Investment," September 16, 2011, http://images.mofcom.gov.cn/hzs/accessory/201109/1316069658609.pdf

In Bangladesh, until 2010 the volume of Chinese investment was not significant (only $250 million between 1977 and 2010), but in 2011 alone, China invested $200 million.[17] The main areas of Chinese investment are in the agro-based, food, textile, chemical, glass and ceramics, engineering, and service industries.[18] China has pledged to increase investment in Bangladesh, particularly in the textile sector, despite concerns about industrial safety standards.[19] China (together with Hong Kong) is also an important source of FDI in Sri Lanka, albeit at levels much lower than FDI from India.

Hostility toward intraregional investments has long been a major obstacle in South Asia. The situation has changed somewhat in recent years as India has become a more important source of outward FDI, but outflows to other South Asian countries still are not very significant.[20] In 2006–2007, South Asia accounted for a mere 0.1 percent of India's total FDI.[21] There are, however, some indications that India is gradually increasing its investments in the region. For example, India is now Sri Lanka's fourth largest source of FDI, in part because of the existence of a free trade agreement. A second example is that, after a failed attempt in 2004, Tata reopened discussions with Bangladesh on investment in the country's telecom, power, and automobile sectors.

## Financial Assistance

China has become an increasingly important source of economic and technical assistance, interest-free loans, interest-subsidized preferential loans, and grants for projects in infrastructure development, power, communication, telecommunications, energy exploration, and mineral extraction in many smaller countries in the region. Such projects, particularly in infrastructure, energy, and mineral extraction, benefit the recipient countries but also assist China's efforts to gain a strategic foothold in the Indian Ocean region. Several scholars assert that financial support for the development of ports in Pakistan (Gwadar), Bangladesh (Chittagong), Sri Lanka (Hambantota), and Myanmar (Sittwe) is an important part of China's naval strategy (more than 85 percent of China's energy imports from the Middle East and mineral resources from Africa transit through the "string of pearls" ports of Hambantota, Gwadar, Chittagong, Cocoa Island and Sittwe in Myanmar, Sihanoukville in Cambodia, Marao in the Maldives, and Seychelles.[22] China is also establishing rail and road connections with Pakistan, Nepal, Bhutan, and Myanmar.[23] Other activities now under way include exploration of oil and gas resources in Sri Lanka and Myanmar and possible energy pipelines linking China with Myanmar, Bangladesh, Pakistan, Afghanistan, India, and Iran.

In Sri Lanka, China has been an important provider of financial assistance for infrastructure development since the end of the separatist war in 2009. The most notable projects receiving Chinese assistance are the Hambantota Sea Port Development Project, construction of the Norochcholai energy power station, exploration for oil in the Cauvery Basin sea, a second international airport in Mattala, the building of an expressway from the airport to Colombo, and modernization of the island's railway carriages. Nepal has also benefited from increased Chinese aid, including financing of a railway line from the Tibetan capital of Lhasa to Kathmandu.[24]

China is playing an increasingly vital role in Bangladesh, where it is building six major "friendship bridges" and has provided assistance to the development of two 210 MW power plants in Chittagong and 250 MW Barapukuria Coal-fired Thermal Power Plant.[25] China runs a trade surplus with each of these countries and the provision of aid is perceived to be a way of ensuring that the relationship is beneficial to both parties. Indian financial assistance to other countries in South Asia is smaller and less significant.

Since the late 1980s, South Asia has been looking for an external investor to create a stimulus for intraregional trade.[26] It is worth recalling that Japanese FDI during the 1980s played a key role in stimulating intraregional trade among East Asian countries. South Asia failed to attract Japanese FDI in the 1990s because of policy uncertainty and conflict in the region. In the mid-2000s, however, Chinese financial assistance for infrastructure development began to play a significant role in enhancing the supply capacity in the South Asian region, especially in the small South Asian countries. Although the impact of this aid may not be felt immediately, it will stimulate more trade in the long run. Smaller South Asian countries value this stimulus from China because there is no other large source of investment in the region, and there is little resistance to the terms of Chinese financial assistance, including the use of Chinese labor.[27]

## China as a Model of Economic Development

China is viewed by most South Asian states as an important model of economic development because of its success in making the transition from extreme poverty to impressive growth since adopting market reforms in 1978. The reforms introduced to improve agricultural productivity in the 1980s were studied with keen interest by South Asian countries even before they had begun to produce sustained results. Even though many of these countries had very different socioeconomic conditions than did China and lacked strong political systems to streamline rural labor and agricultural productivity, they undertook to learn from Chinese best practices.[28] China's phenomenal success in mobilizing FDI to build a robust manufacturing sector has attracted the attention of the smaller South Asian countries. So, too, have China's high rates of domestic savings and financial and banking reforms to facilitate the availability of credit for manufacturing and export ventures. Interest in learning lessons from China's experience increased even further after the 2008 global financial crisis and China's impressive performance in its aftermath.

South Asian observers attribute China's success to its combination of economic liberalization and political stability, with the latter coming from an authoritarian political system. Indeed, some of the smaller regional states, such as Bangladesh, Sri Lanka, and Maldives, seem to be moving toward more authoritarian systems.

Despite SAFTA, India's imports from the region constitute only 4 percent of its total imports, and India's FDI into the region is still not very significant. India's limited involvement within the region has not only hindered the initiation of meaningful projects for regional integration but also limited the potential spillover benefits that India could offer its neighbors, including knowledge and technology transfers from its booming services sector. The plethora of nontariff barriers and other impediments associated in doing business with India make it difficult for other countries to enter its market despite advantages afforded by geographical proximity. Moreover, Indian manufacturing processes have not become as fragmented and globalized as those observed in China and other East and Southeast Asian countries and, therefore, do not enable neighboring countries to use SAFTA provisions to enter Indian supply chains.[29] Studies of vertical industry links in South Asia show that intra-industry trade remains at an extremely low level compared to other regional groupings like the Association of Southeast Asia Nations.[30] In contrast, China's manufacturing sector is strongly linked to global supply chains, particularly in Asia.

The tendency of the smaller regional states to look to China—rather than India—as the economic role model, leader, and catalyst for achieving integrated growth has prompted India to adjust its own approach to regional integration. The shift can be seen by the following gestures by India:

- On January 1, 2008, India offered duty-free-market access to the Indian market for exportable products of less developed SAARC member states (subject to a negative list).
- In 2010, India contributed $100 million to the Social Window of the SAARC Development Fund.
- In 2011, India unilaterally reduced its SAFTA negative list at the Seventeenth SAARC Summit in Adu City.[31]

Clearly, China has indirectly galvanized SAARC, with India taking an active role.

## Military Assistance

China has also emerged as a significant provider of military equipment. Pakistan has traditionally looked to China for the import of arms, but now smaller countries like Bangladesh, Sri Lanka, and Nepal also rely more heavily on China. As indicated in Table 9.1, Bangladeshi imports of arms from China have been increasing at rapid rates in recent years.

Defense cooperation between China and Bangladesh began soon after China accorded recognition to Bangladesh in 1975. This cooperation includes personnel training, material support and production, and equipment and armaments upgrades. Over the years, China has emerged as the largest and most important provider of Bangladesh's military hardware and training of its armed forces.[32] In Sri Lanka, Chinese-supplied arms were instrumental in winning the separatist war with the Liberation Tigers of

TABLE 9.1
China's arms trade with South Asian countries, 1990–2012 (millions of US$)

| Country | 1990 | 1995 | 2000 | 2005 | 2006 | 2007 | 2008 | 2009 | 2010 | 2011 | 2012 |
|---|---|---|---|---|---|---|---|---|---|---|---|
| Bangladesh | 96 | 9 | 11 | 1 | 184 | 55 | 10 | — | 12 | 161 | 301 |
| Nepal | — | — | — | 2 | — | — | — | — | — | — | — |
| Pakistan | 325 | 261 | 68 | 78 | 98 | 144 | 250 | 803 | 864 | 760 | 852 |
| Sri Lanka | — | 15 | 29 | 28 | 49 | 42 | 53 | — | 5 | — | — |

SOURCE: Stockholm International Peace Research Institute, "International Arms Transfers," in *SIPRI Yearbook 2013* (Oxford: Oxford University Press, 2013), http://www.sipri.org/yearbook/2013/05.

Tamil Eelam (LTTE) during 2008 and 2009. In the face of India's inability to supply the needed arms, China became an important supplier.[33] It also gave Sri Lanka the freedom from political conditionality being imposed by India, the United States, and other members of the international community.[34] Nepal has also approached China for the supply of arms at times of rebellion against the government, in part because of India's refusal to do so. Some notable instances in which China has come through for Nepal are in the 1960s, 1988, and 2005. China has thus emerged as a reliable partner in the field of security, specifically rising to the occasion in the face of India's inability to oblige because of domestic political imperatives. This is yet another manifestation of the balancing role being played by China in the South Asian region.

## *Upholding Sovereignty and Independence*

China's diplomatic relations with smaller South Asian states is another interesting area of study. Through the use of both multilateral institutions and bilateral relations, China has politically assured smaller states that it supports their sovereignty and independence.[35] Multilaterally, China has used its veto power and political clout in the UN Security Council to its advantage. As far back as 1972, China used its first veto in the UN Security Council to block Bangladesh's admission to the United Nations and to indicate solidarity with Pakistan and show that it did not approve the breakup of Pakistan's territorial integrity.[36] When the West criticized the Sri Lankan government for its conduct with respect to the humanitarian crisis during the last phase of the separatist war against the LTTE, China provided support and assistance to Colombo.

Rightly or wrongly, the smaller South Asian states believe that China is an important counterbalance to political pressure from India and other countries. In return, China has always sought reiteration of their "one China" policy and support for the principle of noninterference. Bilaterally, China has produced statements to show unity and support to smaller states in the region whenever they face pressure from the West and, more significantly, from India. In 1962, the then Chinese defense minister made a statement assuring Nepal that any attack on Nepal would also be treated as an attack on China and would be defended accordingly.[37] China subsequently issued similar statements pledging support for the sovereignty and independence of

Pakistan, Bangladesh, Nepal, and Sri Lanka when they were under pressure from India.[38]

In contrast, India has largely failed to establish enduring political and diplomatic ties in the region, and ties that traditionally have been considered strong have been deteriorating. The case of Nepal illustrates India's counterproductive diplomacy and lack of political vision. New Delhi had earned significant goodwill in Nepal for its positive role in the 2006 Jana Andolan-II (People's Movement II), but it dissipated this goodwill in a period of two to three years.[39] By 2009, India was one of the most unpopular countries in the eyes of the main Nepalese communities.[40] India's support for the former Maldives president Mohamed Nasheed caused the successor government to regard India with suspicion, so much so that India's GMR Group lost a contract to run the Male airport.[41] The tensions between South India and Sri Lanka since the end of Sri Lanka's war, which became more intense in the recent past, is another example of failed Indian diplomacy. These developments were not caused or shaped by China, but China has been a beneficiary of Indian missteps in the region.

One reflection of perceptions that China is benefiting from and seeks to take advantage of Indian mistakes in the region is the prevalence of speculation in India that China was wresting projects from India in smaller regional states. For example, a well-known Indian reporter noted that contracts for power projects in Sri Lanka and Bangladesh initially awarded to India might be taken over by China.[42] One project is the joint venture between India's state-run National Thermal Power Corporation (NTPC) and the Ceylon Electricity Board to build a 500 MW power plant in Sri Lanka's Eastern Province, which had been subject to substantial delays. The speculation proved unfounded.[43] Similarly, NTPC's proposal to set up coal-based power projects in partnership with the Bangladesh Power Development Board has not been so far successful. Although NTPC may ultimately proceed with the Khulna project, its fate is highly uncertain because of disagreements over tariffs and the use of Chinese equipment. Meanwhile, the Chinese are aggressively seeking to build a 1,320 MW project in Chittagong. Even if unfounded, speculation and suspicion about Chinese intentions are widespread in India.

## Concerns and Apprehensions

As noted previously, Bhutan's perceptions of a rising China are somewhat different than those of the other small regional states. The reason is that

Bhutan's economy is heavily dependent on India. For example, its currency, Ngultrum, is pegged to the Indian rupee. A free trade agreement that has been in effect for many years facilitates preferential trade and allows Bhutan's imports and exports from other countries to transit via India.[44] Bhutan's military is trained in India. Bhutan and China have had friendly exchanges, especially in the recent past, but trade between them is minimal and there are no economic aid or investment flows from China into Bhutan. China's economic incentives for engaging with Bhutan are increasingly apparent, but Bhutan's dependence on India precludes using relations with China as a counterbalance to India.[45] The strength of the relationship between India and Bhutan has constrained ties between Bhutan and China to a level of friendship rather than intimacy.[46] Even if Bhutan sees China as a more important future trade partner, tensions between China and India will constrain how far Bhutan is willing to go.

Even though most of the smaller regional states see many potential advantages from a rising China, they also see reasons for concern. One such concern arises from their trade relationships. The expanding trade and investment relations between China and the smaller regional states unquestionably have many positive effects, but the large trade imbalance in favor of China has become a source of worry even though running a trade deficit with a country as large as China is unavoidable.[47] Given the vast difference in size and economic power, China's exports to the region naturally far exceed its imports from the region. Moreover, many of the small regional countries export primary products to China and import value-added manufactured goods from China. However, unable to compete with imported Chinese consumer goods, regional states have been compelled to close industries manufacturing similar products. Examples include India's toy industry, Sri Lanka's umbrella industry, and Pakistan's ballpoint pen industry. In response, regional countries have imposed nontariff barriers to shield the effects of the influx of Chinese consumer durables. Some have also resorted to antidumping legal action.[48]

The current account deficits of the smaller regional states are largely offset by significant capital inflows from China into their capital accounts, and the concerns noted earlier are far outweighed by the overall economic benefits and soft support offered by China.[49] For example, Bangladesh has made its trade deficit with India a political issue but addressed its deficit with China through diplomatic channels.[50] Indeed, when visiting China in the last week of May 2013, Sri Lanka's president suggested appointing a team to study the possibility of working out a free trade agreement between China and Sri Lanka.[51]

China's military modernization is not viewed as a threat by the smaller regional states. In fact, as beneficiaries of Chinese arms transfers, they look to China for newer and cheaper weapons. China's military support to the smaller states does not prevent it from seeking a strategic foothold in the region by exercising its political and economic clout. As S. D. Muni and Tan Tai Yong have shown, the principal cause of anxiety among the smaller states is the possibility that China will become more assertive and intimidating when it becomes a major world power.[52] All small regional states support the "one China" policy, but they are somewhat uncomfortable about the treatment of the minority peoples in Tibet and Xinjiang. The small South Asian countries also worry about a possible military conflict between China and India but do not have a strategy to hedge against possible adverse effects.

## China as a Balancer to India: The Case of Sri Lanka

Encircled by the two emerging global powers, Sri Lanka increasingly looks to China as a counterbalance to India.[53] Sri Lanka has had important cultural, historic, and religious ties to both India and China since ancient times. However, the relationship with India was naturally the closer one, given geographical proximity and greater cultural similarities. China was perceived as a huge, powerful, and distant Asian power. In recent times, however, Sri Lanka's relationship with these two emerging economic powers has changed. For political reasons, Sri Lanka increasingly looks to China for both political and economic support. Assistance from India is gradually declining relative to that from China.[54]

Since achieving independence, Sri Lanka has appreciated the importance of its relationship with India but remained wary of New Delhi's unilateral and authoritarian tendencies in the region. Accordingly, it has often sought to balance its relationship with India by reaching out to other powers. The significant role played by India in Sri Lanka's postindependence political life has sometimes strained Indo-Sri Lanka relations. From Indira Gandhi's decision to arm Tamil militants in the early 1980s and Rajiv Gandhi's decision to send the Indian Peacekeeping Force to implement the 1987 India-Lanka Political Accord, to India's support for Sri Lanka's war against the LTTE in 2009, the violent conflict between Tamil nationalist activists and the Sinhalese-dominated Sri Lankan state has always been influenced by policies and attitudes in New Delhi and in the southern state of Tamil Nadu. Such interventions by India have created a sense of distrust, which has affected socioeconomic relations between the two countries. Many Sinhalese view India as favoring Tamils and as wanting to weaken or divide the country. Tamils, on the other hand, see India as having continually broken promises to defend their rights and protect their lives, especially during the final phase of the war in 2009. India's unwillingness to supply the requested arms during the war paved the way for China to gain a foothold in Sri Lanka. Beijing has been Sri Lanka's largest arms supplier for some time, but the amount of its support escalated from a few million dollars in 2005 to approximately $1 billion in 2008.[55] Beijing's support enabled Sri Lanka to win the war with less support from India while ignoring concerns of the West. India's 2009, 2012, and 2013 votes in Geneva in support of the US-sponsored UN resolution on Sri Lanka for promoting reconciliation and accountability and China's vote against the resolution are important cases in point.

Several factors constrain economic relations between Sri Lanka and India. One is the reemergence of fishing disputes. Since January 2011, there have been numerous reported cases of fisherman from both sides being arrested, and in some cases killed, after crossing maritime boundaries. The 2012–2013 harassment of Indian fisherman by Sri Lanka's navy and attacks on Sri Lankan pilgrims and Buddhist monks in Tamil Nadu triggered protests and intense anger that further strained relations between the two countries.[56]

India has offered substantial humanitarian assistance and reconstruction aid to rebuild the war-torn Northern and Eastern provinces of Sri Lanka, but implementation has been slow. One example is the previously mentioned construction of a 500 MW coal-fired power plant in Trincomalee. That project has been subject to substantial delays that take on added significance because of the contrast to the speedy completion of the first phase of the Chinese-built power plant in Puttalam. Delays in India's project to build and repair fifty thousand houses, mostly in the North, are both cause and reflection of Sri Lankan reluctance to deepen its engagement with India, even in instances such as reconstruction where Sri Lanka stands to gain.[57]

The Sri Lankan government can afford to decline Indian financial assistance because it has been increasingly successful in obtaining assistance from China. In addition to serving as a provider of political and military support, China has emerged as an increasingly important source of economic support in Sri Lanka. In the immediate aftermath of the war, the country was in dire need of assistance to avoid further humanitarian crises, protect war refugees, support postconflict reconstruction, and guarantee overall economic development. In contrast to the various forms of conditionality imposed by international lenders such as the World Bank and the International Monetary Fund (IMF), China has attached few—or no—conditions to its loans (i.e., no structural adjustments, policy reforms, competitive biddings, transparency, or accountability requirements).[58] China thus emerged as the ideal option for the Sri Lankan government, which was more inclined toward Populist measures than structural reform. As a result, Chinese aid in the form of donations, grants, and loans rose dramatically.

Between 1971 and 2012, China provided $5.1 billion to Sri Lanka, of which $4.8 billion came from 2005 to 2012. In other words, close to 94 percent of China's loans and grants were provided during the last decade. Approximately 81 percent of this financial assistance was provided through the Exim Bank of China, 17.6 percent by the China Development Bank, and the rest from the Industrial and Commercial Bank of China and other agencies. From 2008 to 2012, 40 percent of the Chinese loans/grants were for roads and bridges, 31 percent for power and energy, 23 percent for ports and shipping, and 6 percent for the aviation sector (Figure 9.4).[59]

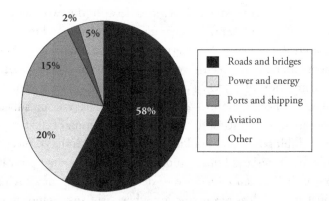

FIGURE 9.4 Distribution of Chinese assistance in Sri Lanka, 2011

SOURCE: Sri Lanka Ministry of Finance and Planning, Department of External Resources, "Performance Report 2011," http://www.erd.gov.lk/files/Performance%20Report%202011%20-%20English%20Version.pdf

China is currently the primary source of foreign finance in Sri Lanka, amounting to $784.7 million in 2011, equal to 38 percent of total commitments, compared to 12.4 percent in 2006. The weighted average interest rate of the $3.6 billion loans from the Exim Bank of China is 2.3 percent. This includes concessional loans to the government ($0.56 billion) and preferential buyers credit totaling $1.8 billion, both at an annual interest rate of 2 percent with repayment periods of twenty years, including a five-year grace period. However, there is also a $1.3 billion buyers credit at an annual interest rate of the London Interbank Offered Rate (LIBOR) plus 2.4 percent with repayment period of fifteen years with a three- to four-year grace period. The China Development Bank Corporation has higher rates of LIBOR plus 2.9 percent. Clearly, some of the Chinese loans carry high interest rates that could become a heavy burden on Sri Lanka's foreign reserves.[60]

The construction by China of the massive port at Hambantota on the southeastern coast of Sri Lanka has been the most significant development and a major cause of concern to India.[61] This project is part of a $1.5 billion development zone that also features a fuel bunkering facility and oil refinery. The invitation to build the port was initially given to India, but bureaucratic and other procedural delays prompted the Sri Lankan government to look to China instead. This strategic investment has also brought many benefits to China, which could use the seaport as a refueling and docking station for the Chinese Navy. Some argue that Sri Lanka has become a jewel in China's "string of pearls" naval strategy in the Indian Ocean region.[62]

China has also undertaken the task of building the Lotus Tower in Colombo, an ultramodern telecommunications structure that will be South Asia's tallest structure. Other major projects funded by China, include an expansion of the main port in Colombo, the construction of a second international airport at Mattala, also near Hambantota, the extension of the Southern Expressway from Galle to Matara, and the reconstruction of railways.

Using cheap commercial credit and imported Chinese labor, Beijing has been heavily involved in the building of roads in war-torn northern Jaffna and the eastern Trincomalee and Batticaloa regions, while also constructing a modern performing arts theater in Colombo. The inflow of Chinese funds, particularly to the North and East of Sri Lanka, which is both geographically and culturally closer to India, is yet another indication

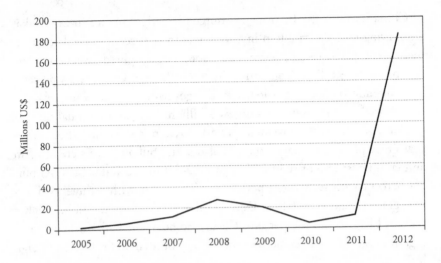

FIGURE 9.5 Chinese FDI in Sri Lanka, 2005–2012
SOURCE: Board of Investment of Sri Lanka, Research Department, investment database, 2013

of China's emergence as a major competitor to India's influence in Sri Lanka and the wider South Asian region.

As indicated in Figure 9.5, the year 2012 witnessed a spectacular surge in Chinese FDI flows into Sri Lanka, increasing from $10.5 million in 2011 to $185 million in 2012. Consequently, China now ranks as the third largest source of FDI in Sri Lanka, up from the fifteenth position in 2011. India, on the other hand, has dropped from second to fourth position in the same time period. Chinese investment has also spread to the electronic and garment industries, for which the Sri Lankan government has established a special free trade zone exclusively for China in Mirigama.[63]

Trade relations between China and Sri Lanka, which date back to the historic China-Sri Lanka Rubber-Rice Agreement signed in 1952, are also on the rise.[64] China's share in Sri Lanka's total exports has tripled from 0.4 percent in 2006 to 1.2 percent in 2012, and China (including Hong Kong) has become Sri Lanka's second largest source of imports, accounting for 13.9 percent of the total.[65] India remains the principal import source and third most important export destination for Sri Lanka, but the share of imports gap between India and China is gradually narrowing. In 2008, India accounted for 24.5 percent of imports, whereas China accounted for only 7.9 percent. By 2012, the shares had changed to 19 percent and 13.9 percent, respectively. Sri Lanka recently proposed a free trade agreement with China similar to the one that already exists with India.[66]

## Conclusion

This chapter examines China's growing presence and involvement in the South Asian region and the possibility of China emerging as a balancer to the role played by India. Most of the smaller states in the region see benefits in maintaining closer ties with China, especially in the context of India's failure to meet their needs. This has contributed to the improvement in China's image and position in the region.[67] The smaller South Asian states will continue to regard China as a counterbalance to India unless and until political tensions and the large imbalances characteristic of relations between India and the smaller states change. India's policy in the region is challenged and influenced by multiple historical and cultural links as well as by political, social, and economic considerations, but China's situation is far less complex with little if any areas of friction and conflict. This creates a "natural comfort level" with a more distant but generous and accommodating power.[68] In the context of limited integration under SAARC, a distinct shift in approaches to regionalism in South Asia is becoming apparent, with smaller states beginning to look to China, rather than India, for assistance in achieving integrated and sustainable growth.

From China's standpoint, increased funding and investments in South Asia's smaller economies are crucial to gaining a strategic foothold in the Indian Ocean region. It thus appears to be a win-win situation, with mutual benefits for both parties. Resolving contentious issues with countries like Pakistan and ensuring that India's economic success is carried forward into other neighboring countries are the only means of reducing the tendency for smaller states to look outside the region for support and assistance. Given China's strong interest in cultivating relationships, the small South Asian economies are likely to continue to enhance their engagements with China bilaterally and through multilateral channels, such as the APTA.

China's image in the South Asian region is thus far unspoiled. Although one could speculate that the smaller South Asian countries might take an increasingly negative view of China's state controlled and one-party-dominated policy, this seems unlikely because perceptions in the modern world are driven more by economic interests than by political ideologies.

*Notes*

1. The South Asian region is clearly dominated by India, in terms of both its size and its economic influence. Currently, India accounts for about 80 percent of the region's GDP, whereas Pakistan accounts for only 10 percent, Bangladesh 6 percent, Sri Lanka 2 percent, and the rest less than 2 percent.

2. International Crisis Group, "India and Sri Lanka after the LTTE," *Asia Report*, no. 206 (2011), http://www.crisisgroup.org/en/regions/asia/south-asia/sri-lanka/206-india-and-sri-lanka-after-the-ltte.aspx.

3. Tarique Niazi, "China's Foot in India's Door," *Asia Times*, August 24, 2005, http://www.atimes.com/atimes/South_Asia/GH24Df05.html.

4. See, for example, S. D. Muni and Tan Tai Yong, *A Resurgent China: South Asian Perspectives* (New Delhi: Routledge, 2012).

5. S. D. Muni, "An Overview: Positive Perceptions, Anxious Undercurrents," in Muni and Yong, *A Resurgent China*, 268–286.

6. These points are developed more fully in Muni, "An Overview."

7. Jianyong Yue, "Peaceful Rise of China: Myth or Reality," *International Politics*, no. 45 (2008): 439–456.

8. Bangladesh, India, Laos, the Republic of Korea, Sri Lanka, the Philippines, and Thailand signed the Bangkok Agreement in 1975. China is the only country to join subsequently. See Ravi Ratnayake, "Impact of China's Accession to the Bangkok Agreement on Intraregional Trade Flows," *South Asia Economic Journal* 3, no. 2 (2002): 147–164.

9. See "Free Trade Agreement Between the Government of the Islamic Republic of Pakistan and the Government of the People's Republic of China," http://wits.worldbank.org/GPTAD/PDF/archive/China-Pakistan.pdf.

10. See Indian Ocean Rim Association, "Formation," http://www.iora.net/about-us/formation.aspx (accessed May 18, 2015); Saman Kelegama, "Can Open Regionalism Work in the Indian Ocean Region Association for Regional Cooperation?" *ASEAN Economic Bulletin* 15, no. 2 (1998): 153–167.

11. The UAE is the largest trading partner of India because Dubai has become an entrepot for Indian trade, and most India-Pakistan trade takes place via the UAE.

12. Emily Brunjes, Nicholas Levine, Miriam Palmer, and Addison Smith, "China's Increased Trade and Investment in South Asia (Spoiler Alert: It's the Economy)," paper prepared for Workshop in International Public Affairs, Spring 2013, Robert M. La Follette School of Public Affairs, University of Wisconsin–Madison, https://www.lafollette.wisc.edu/images/publications/workshops/2013-China.pdf.

13. China has developed as a key manufacturing hub, whereas India has emerged as the key hub for knowledge-based services such as pharmaceuticals, infromation technology (IT), and engineering. A particular area of importance in

this regard has been in the IT sector, where China specializes in the manufacturing of computer hardware, and India is involved in software development.

14. Saman Kelegama, "China-SAARC Economic Cooperation: The Emerging Scenario," *Policy Perspectives* 9, no. 1 (2012): 97–110, http://www.ips.lk/staff/ed/publications_ed/international/china_saarc/economic_cooperation.pdf.

15. Central Bank of Sri Lanka, *Annual Report 2007* (Colombo, Sri Lanka: Central Bank of Sri Lanka, 2008); Central Bank of Sri Lanka, *Annual Report 2013* (Colombo, Sri Lanka: Central Bank of Sri Lanka, 2014), http://www.cbsl.gov.lk/pics_n_docs/10_pub/_docs/efr/annual_report/AR2013/English/content.htm.

16. Ministry of Commerce, People's Republic of China, "2010 Statistical Bulletin of China's Outward Foreign Direct Investment," 2011, http://images.mofcom.gov.cn/hzs/accessory/201109/1316069658609.pdf.

17. C. M. Shafi Sami, "Bangladesh: A Partner for Peace and Prosperity," in Muni and Yong, *A Resurgent China*, 8–42.

18. Islam Shariful, "Emerging Trends in Chinese Investments in Bangladesh: Challenges and Opportunities," *ICS Analysis*, no. 12 (2013), http://www.icsin.org/uploads/2015/04/07/3a1f826bfc9c06bd80aeod2d7372e535.pdf.

19. The collapse of the Rana Plaza in January 2013, a fire at a ready-made garment factory, and similar incidents have raised issues related to safety standards. See, for example, Amy Westervelt, "Two Years After Rana Plaza, Have Conditions Improved in Bangladesh's Factories?" *The Guardian*, April 24, 2015, http://www.theguardian.com/sustainable-business/2015/apr/24/bangladesh-factories-building-collapse-garment-dhaka-rana-plaza-brands-hm-gap-workers-construction; and Emily Jane Fox, "The Cost of Cheap Clothes at Wal-Mart, Sears," *CNN Money*, November 30, 2012, http://money.cnn.com/2012/11/30/news/companies/walmart-bangladesh-factory-fire.

20. Outflows of FDI from India increased from $5 billion in 2005–2006 to $14.8 billion in 2010. See United Nations Conference on Trade and Development, *World Investment Report 2012* (New York: United Nations, 2012).

21. Prema-chandra Athukorala, "Intra-regional FDI and Economic Integration in South Asia: Trends, Patterns and Prospects," *South Asia Economic Journal* 15, no. 1 (2014): 1–36.

22. Patrick Mendis, "Destiny of the Pearl: How Sri Lanka's Colombo Consensus Trumped Beijing and Washington in the Indian Ocean," *Yale Journal of International Affairs* 7, no. 2 (2012): 68–76, http://yalejournal.org/wp-content/uploads/2012/09/articles/Patrick%20Mendis.pdf.

23. Muni, "An Overview."

24. Anita Inder Singh, "China's Expanding Influence in South Asia," *The Tribune*, October 13, 2010, http://www.tribuneindia.com/2010/20101013/edit.htm#6.

25. Muni and Yong, *A Resurgent China*.

26. External investment on a large scale stimulates the trade-investment nexus and contributes to enhancing intraregional trade. See World Institute for Development Economics Research (WIDER), "Mobilizing International Surpluses for World Development: A WIDER Plan for a Japanese Initiative," Study Group Series, no.2, United Nations University, Helsinki, 1987.

27. According to figures submitted to the Sri Lankan parliament, there were close to twenty-five thousand Chinese workers in Sri Lanka. The excessive presence of Chinese labor in Chinese funded projects is of concern to Sri Lanka and other small countries, but nothing can be done about it because it is the only condition that comes with most Chinese loans. Technology transfer from Chinese projects thus remains limited, and this inadequate technology transfer was clearly seen during the frequent breakdown of the Norachchalai Power Plant when Chinese engineers had to be summoned for repairs. See Rohan Gunasekera, "India, China in Investment 'Great Game' over Lanka," *Echelon*, August 2013, pp. 48–56, http://www.ips.lk/staff/ed/latest_essays/downloads/ips_great_game_kelegama.pdf.

28. Muni, "An Overview."

29. Sirimal Abeyratne, "Integration of Sri Lanka into Indian Supply Chains Under the Bilateral Free Trade Agreement," *South Asia Economic Journal* 14, no. 2 (2013): 275–292.

30. Deshal De Mel and Suwendrani Jayaratne, "Vertical Integration of Industries in South Asia," in *Regional Integration and Economic Development in South Asia*, ed. Sultan Hafeez Rahman, Sridhar Khatri, and Hans-Peter Brunner (Cheltenham, UK: Edward Elgar, 2012), 45–99.

31. Nihal Rodrigo, "The 17th SAARC Summit in Addu City, Maldives," in *SAARC: Towards Meaningful Cooperation*, ed. Tomislav Delinic and Nishchal N. Pandey (Kathmandu, Nepal: Centre for South Asian Studies and Konrad Adenauer Stiftung, 2012), 13–20, http://cosatt.org/Book-SAARC.pdf.

32. Sami, "Bangladesh."

33. India finds it difficult to supply arms to combat separatist movements or political rebellions in the neighboring countries, especially if the insurgent group has some ethnic affiliation to Indian citizens in bordering states.

34. Conditions on human rights, political devolution of power, and so forth were not imposed by the Chinese for the supply of arms. Moreover, China supplied military equipment on a long-term installment-payment basis, which was not readily available from other suppliers.

35. Here sovereignty and independence mean noninterference in domestic affairs and respecting the territorial integrity of the nation.

36. For a somewhat different interpretation of China's veto, see Joel Wuthnow, *Chinese Diplomacy and the UN Security Council: Beyond the Veto* (New York: Routledge, 2013), 17–18.

37. Nepal was facing difficulties with India because of King Mahendra's dismissal of the democratic system on December 15, 1960. The Nepali Congress Party was fighting against the king's actions using Indian support and territory.

38. Muni, "An Overview."

39. For more on the Jana Andolan movement, see Krishna Hachhethu and David N. Gellner, "Nepal: Trajectories of Democracy and Restructuring of the State," in *Handbook of South Asian Politics: India, Pakistan, Bangladesh, Sri Lanka, and Nepal*, ed. Paul R. Brass (New York: Routledge, 2010), 131–146.

40. Shambhu Ram Simkhada, "Nepal: A Benign Neighbourhood Power," in Muni and Yong, *A Resurgent China*, 145–175.

41. S. Venkat Narayan, "Is China Trying to Wrest Power Projects in Sri Lanka and Bangladesh from India?" *The Island*, March 25, 2013, http://www.island.lk/index.php?page_cat=article-details&page=article-details&code_title=75550.

42. Ibid.

43. Ifham Nizam, "India Urged to Get Sampur Project Going," *The Island*, August 22, 2013, http://www.island.lk/index.php?page_cat=article-details&page=article-details&code_title=86387.

44. Caroline Brassard, "Bhutan: Cautiously Cultivated Positive Perception," in Muni and Yong, *A Resurgent China*, 72–95.

45. China's Kunming region in Yunnan Province is advocating a gateway from southwestern China to the Indian subcontinent to facilitate cross-border trade and investment. See Ananth Krishnan, "China Plans 'South Asia Gateway' to Boost Regional Links," *The Hindu*, March 3, 2013, http://www.thehindu.com/news/international/south-asia/china-plans-south-asia-gateway-to-boost-regional-links/article4472267.ece.

46. Brassard, "Bhutan."

47. This is a traditional fear that persists even though in a globalized trading environment trade deficits with partner countries should not be a major worry.

48. Uditha Jayasinghe, "China's FTA Should Be Handled with Care: Expert," *Daily FT*, August 30, 2013, http://www.ft.lk/article/183144/China-FTA-should-be-handled-with-care:-Expert.

49. *Soft support* refers to various exchange programs (cultural, sports, etc.) that China has with the smaller South Asian countries.

50. Muni and Yong, *A Resurgent China*.

51. The fair trade agreement was completed in 2014. See "Sri Lanka-China FTA Feasibility Study Completed," *China Daily*, March 21, 2014, http://www.chinadaily.com.cn/business/2014-03/21/content_17368015.htm.

52. Muni and Yong, *A Resurgent China*.

53. India's balkanization of Sikkim, heavy control over neighboring Bhutan, and growing influence in Nepal, together with open support for the state of Tamil

Nadu on issues pertaining to the minority Tamil community in Sri Lanka, have caused the Sri Lankan government to view China as a desirable counterbalance.

54. With the defeat of Tamil separatist group LTTE in mid-2009 and the long delay in offering a political solution to the Tamil minority community, international opinion gradually turned against Sri Lanka, especially in the West and in India. China has stood by the Sri Lankan government on the Tamil minority issue and human rights, as was visible during UN Human Rights Council meetings in March 2012 and 2013.

55. Robert D. Kaplan, *Monsoon: The India Ocean and Future of American Power* (New York: Random House, 2010), cited in International Crisis Group "India and Sri Lanka."

56. D. B. S. Jeyaraj, "Attacks on Two Sri Lankan Buddhist Monks in Tamil Nadu," *Daily Mirror*, March 23, 2013, http://www.dailymirror.lk/27102/attacks -on-two-sri-lankan-buddhist-monks-in-tamil-nadu.

57. A leading Sri Lankan minister stated in India that Sri Lanka no longer needs the India–Sri Lanka Comprehensive Economic Partnership Agreement (IL-CEPA), which was to be the second stage of the existing India–Sri Lanka Bilateral Free Trade Agreement (signed in 1998). The IL-CEPA was negotiated between the two countries for nearly five years, and the Sri Lankan government abandoned it, presumably to reduce Indian influence over the Sri Lankan economy. See Meera Srinivasan, "We Don't Need CEPA Any Longer: Basil Rajapaksa," *The Hindu*, July 19, 2013, http://www.thehindu.com/business/we-dont-need-cepa -any-longer-basil-rajapaksa/article4928411.ece.

58. Examples include structural adjustment programs such as the IMF Standby Arrangement of $2.6 billion negotiated in July 2009. The conditionality of the policy prescriptions included a standard set of macroeconomic reforms known as the Washington Consensus.

59. Data pertaining to Chinese and Indian loans are available in Sri Lanka Ministry of Finance and Planning, *Annual Report, 2012* (Colombo: Ministry of Finance and Planning, 2013), http://www.treasury.gov.lk/publications/under -fiscal-management-responsibility-act/annual-reports/26-national-planning/fiscal -policy/482-annual-report-2012-structure.html; and Sri Lanka Ministry of Finance and Planning, "Mid-year Fiscal Position Report, 2013," http://www.treasury.gov .lk/depts/fpd/reports/fmr/2013/midyearreport-2013.pdf. See also Gunasekera, "India, China."

60. Sri Lanka Ministry of Finance and Planning, *Annual Report, 2012.*

61. Hambantota is located about fifty kilometers from the major sea-lanes of the Indian Ocean. With the presence of the Chinese technicians, the Chinese Navy could always find ways to use the port for its own security purposes in the region, which causes concern in India.

62. See, for example, Patrick Mendis, "Destiny of the Pearl."

63. Saman Kelegama, "China-Sri Lanka Economic Relations: An Overview," *China Report* 50, no. 2 (2014): 131–149.

64. The China–Sri Lanka Rubber-Rice Agreement, signed in April 1952, is viewed as the first step in a long journey of Sri Lanka–China relations. Rubber, which had dropped in price worldwide, was one of Sri Lanka's key exports at that time, and China had difficulties obtaining rubber because of US sanctions. China had an abundance of rice, which had increased sharply in price, that it could export to Sri Lanka, creating an ideal environment for an agreement that benefited both countries.

65. Central Bank of Sri Lanka, *Annual Report, 2012* (Colombo: Central Bank of Sri Lanka, 2013), http://www.cbsl.gov.lk/pics_n_docs/10_pub/_docs/efr/annual_report/AR2012/English/content.htm.

66. Gunasekera, "India, China."

67. India has still not reached a state of development that would enable it to provide generous loans to the small South Asian countries, as China is now able to do. Moreover, India has not been successful in providing the required leadership to SAARC, which has become vulnerable to Indo-Pakistani conflicts. These facts are seen by the smaller South Asian countries as limitations of what India can do for them.

68. Muni, "An Overview," 283.

# TEN

# China and Central Asia

*Sebastien Peyrouse*

With the collapse of the Soviet Union, China was quick to become aware of the unique opportunities contained in this new geopolitical situation, as well as new risks, particularly in relation to its north and northwest borders. In the 1990s and 2000s, China gained increasing influence, which it has used to affect the political and geopolitical situation of Central Asia. More importantly, China has profoundly changed the economic situation in the region. In 1991, however, China could not foresee what would happen and was anxious about the future. Despite the apparent satisfaction of seeing a superpower such as the Soviet Union disappear, and with it the historical Sino-Soviet conflict, Beijing was very concerned about the risks of conflict linked to the unresolved disputes over territorial borders.

As in other regions of the world where Beijing works to establish itself, its settlement strategies addressed many objectives, all of which were seen by Chinese authorities as intrinsically related. First, China consolidated its geopolitical influence in Central Asia by creating economically based good-neighborly relations aimed at diffusing potential tensions. Second, it contributed to regional development in order to avoid political and social destabilization, which could have domestic consequences in Xinjiang and slow down Chinese economic growth. Third, the Central Asian states provided new markets for Chinese products, which could expand to the whole of Russia, Iran, and Turkey. For landlocked Central Asia, the Chinese economic engine opened the prospect of new trans-Eurasian corridors and was seen as a unique historical opportunity.

China's increasing influence has sparked many debates in Central Asia, and no one has an unequivocal response to it. Unlike debates over whether to favor the West or Russia, which tend to be ideological (one is pro-Western or pro-Russian not on account of one's interests but out of conviction), those about China are viewed in an exclusively pragmatic fashion. Many Central Asian economic leaders whose interests are tied to relations with Beijing support the pro-Chinese policies of their government officials. However, anti-Chinese lobbies are also forming. The latter tend to criticize their own governments for having too often subordinated their nation's interests to Beijing's political demands and to decry the economic impact of doing so.

Tensions caused by Chinese activity are growing in several sectors. In Kazakhstan, several members of parliament, including members of the presidential party Otan, have denounced China's expansion in the oil sector and asserted that the country was about to lose its energy independence. Chinese companies operating in Central Asia have generally bad reputations. They are often accused of giving preferential employment to Han Chinese over local personnel (and thereby not helping solve local unemployment problems), of operating in accordance with Chinese and not Kazakh labor regulations, and of offering local workers lower salaries than those of Han immigrants. The growing presence of Chinese immigrants has also raised much concern. Relations between Chinese and Central Asian businesspeople are often strained, and there have been many popular revolts against Chinese petty traders in Kyrgyz bazaars. The Central Asian states are very concerned about Chinese migrants settling in their territories, all the more so as many of their own citizens are emigrating to Russia. The migration issue receives prominent attention in the press, which is keen to emphasize the increasing dangers of the "yellow peril" threatening the country. The issue resonates with the public. Contrary to widespread belief, Central Asian states are not unqualifiedly enamored with China or what it is doing in the region. Exactly how China expands and utilizes its presence in Central Asia will depend, in part, on the approaches and attitudes of the Central Asian states.

This chapter examines China's engagement with the region by looking first at the negotiation of border disputes between China and Central Asia republics and then at the thorny question of water sharing between Kazakhstan and the Middle Kingdom. The final section of the chapter examines the economic and security stakes raised by migration and the movement of people across the borders.

## Border Treaties

In December 1991, Kazakhstan, Kyrgyzstan, and Tajikistan suddenly had to patrol new international borders that were disputed by China. Despite the decade of Sino-Soviet friendship that began when the People's Republic of China was proclaimed in October 1949 and ended with the break in relations between Moscow and Beijing in 1959, the two Communist states had failed to settle the nineteenth century border disputes inherited from the Russian and Qing empires. China played the victim card and accused Moscow of attempting to validate the borders of the czarist empire.[1] The ideological conflict personalized by the clash between Mao Zedong and Nikita Khrushchev manifested itself in frequent border tensions and, in 1969, as the quasi-war between the two countries that occurred on Damanski/Zhenbao Island in the Ussuri River in the Russian Far East and at the Alatau pass in Kazakhstan.[2] Despite meetings between the authorities of the two countries in 1969 and 1978, no demarcation agreement was signed, and the conflicting parties were able to agree only on a declaration of intent to settle the dispute in a peaceful way.

The question of the border disputes was not raised again until Mikhail Gorbachev took up the position of First Secretary of the Communist Party of the Soviet Union. In 1988, a warming in bilateral relations made possible the creation of a working group to prepare for negotiations on the western sector of the Sino-Soviet border. In May 1991, only a few months before the Central Asian states achieved independence, Chinese president Jiang Zemin and Gorbachev claimed that they had reached agreement on the eastern sector of the Sino-Soviet border but not on the western one. Upon independence, the three Central Asian republics bordering China inherited the border disputes that the Soviet Union had failed to settle and began their own negotiations with Beijing. Lacking the history of acrimonious relations that had complicated negotiations between China and the Soviet Union, the newly independent republics and China began the search for a solution in a more cordial atmosphere.

According to Mao, the "unequal treaties" China had been forced to sign excised some 1.5 million square kilometers from China to the advantage of czarist and then Soviet Russia. Close to two-thirds of this territory, or 910,000 square kilometers, was in Central Asia; the other third was in Siberia and the Far East.[3] Chinese documents claimed 22 percent of Central Asia—territory stretching from Semirechie to Lake Balkhash in Kazakhstan, almost all of Kyrgyzstan, and some 28,000 square kilometers in the Pamir region of Tajikistan. However, when the new negotiations began, the Chinese reduced their claims and adopted a "good neighbor" strategy toward the newly independent states. Still under international sanction for the violent repression in Tiananmen in June 1989, Chinese authorities reduced their territorial claims to "only" 34,000 square kilometers. They did so primarily to secure allies in Central Asia. Kazakhstan, Kyrgyzstan, and Tajikistan announced their desire to negotiate with China on the basis of the various agreements made between Moscow and Beijing prior to 1991 as well as on the principles of international law.[4]

The post-Soviet balance of forces afforded China advantages as well as inconveniences. Whereas previously it had to negotiate with a single country, the particularly powerful Soviet Union, now it had to negotiate with much weaker partners, which enabled it to use its power and divide-and-conquer techniques. But negotiating with each new country separately limited possibilities for mutual exchanges of territory. Beijing laid claim to 2,235 square kilometers in Kazakhstan, distributed across eleven zones (some of which were just 10 square kilometers in length), and five segments totaling 3,728 square kilometers in Kyrgyzstan. China stuck to almost all its original claims against Tajikistan, from which it wanted a large part of the Pamir (28,430 square kilometers), territory equivalent to one-fifth of the country's total surface area. In 1992, a working group comprising the four Commonwealth of Independent States (CIS) countries and China was created to enable the Central Asian states to engage China from a somewhat stronger position. These first multiparty meetings helped the Central Asian states, with Moscow's support, to start negotiations with Beijing, as did the creation of the Shanghai Five group in 1996. Nevertheless, all the border agreements were signed on a bilateral basis.[5]

Kazakh president Nursultan Nazarbayev made every effort to obtain rapid progress on this issue during a visit to Beijing in 1993.[6] A first agreement was reached on the delimitation of nine of the eleven contested sectors. The negotiations were facilitated by the nature of the terrain near the border, which made the demarcation less complex than it was in the case of the mountainous zones separating China from Kyrgyzstan and Tajikistan. The territorial demarcation treaty covering these nine sectors, which totaled 1,700 square kilometers, was signed in March 1994. The two segments that were not resolved at that time—namely, the districts of Sardy-Cheldy and the Chagan-Obo Valley, which made up an area of 946 square kilometers and a nondelimited border of about 120 kilometers—were settled in 1998, and a treaty was ratified a few months later.[7] Although the opposition criticized this decision, Kazakh authorities were satisfied with it, as they were granted 57 percent of the territories that China had claimed before the negotiations.[8] Astana at last felt liberated from Chinese threats over Lake Balkhash.

The negotiations with Bishkek lasted longer, for several reasons. Beijing was more distrustful toward the regime of Askar Akayev, who presented himself as resolutely pro-Western. China exerted more direct pressure on the small Kyrgyz state than it did on Kazakhstan, which it was more eager to accommodate. In addition, the border negotiations led to domestic problems that frustrated the ability of the Kyrgyz regime to ratify the agreements it had made.[9] During the 1994 CIS-China meetings, Chinese and Kyrgyz officials released a preliminary document detailing the border sections on which they had already agreed. The first Sino-Kyrgyz border treaty was signed in 1996 (and ratified in 1998). The treaty detailed the demarcation of about 900 kilometers of the 1,011 kilometers of common borders, and both countries agreed to begin demarcation within the already shared zones. In 1999, Jiang Zemin and his Kyrgyz counterpart signed a second agreement in which China was granted 90,000 hectares in the Uzengi-Kuush region in exchange for control by Bishkek of two-thirds of the 7,000-meter-tall Khan Tengri peak, the second highest point in the country, and Victory Peak.[10]

In ceding Uzengi-Kuush, however, Kyrgyzstan lost rich arable lands, exacerbating its dearth of agricultural areas. In addition, the treaty undermined Kyrgyz border security because the territory transferred to China contained the only road link between the three Kyrgyz border posts. The treaty gave China control of the Sarydzhaz and Uzengi-Kuush Rivers, as well as some of the glaciers that made up an important part of Kyrgyzstan's water resources, and mineral deposits such as tungsten. Despite the massive protests and repression that resulted in the deaths of several demonstrators, President Akayev secured ratification of the treaty in 2002.[11] But settling the border disputes with China created an upheaval in domestic Kyrgyz politics, which contributed to undermining Askar Akayev's legitimacy and lead to the Tulip Revolution of March 2005.

The negotiations between China and Tajikistan over their 400-kilometer border turned out to be the longest and most difficult. They began in 1993 under the auspices of the CIS-China joint group. In the middle of a civil war at the time, Tajikistan was in no position to make progress on resolving the issue. It was not until 1999 that negotiations resulted in the signing of an initial agreement on the Karazak Pass region and the Markansu River, which had already been mentioned in the czarist protocol of Novyi Margelan, signed in 1884. The entire section from the Uz-Bel pass to the Afghan border, however, still had to be negotiated. On the margins of a Shanghai Group meeting in Dushanbe in 2000, a treaty was signed on the triborder between China, Kyrgyzstan, and Tajikistan, but the status of the remainder of the Pamir was left unresolved. Only in May 2002 did China and Tajikistan finally manage to reach agreement on all their border disputes. The Tajik authorities ceded to China 1,000 square kilometers of mountainous terrain situated east of Murghab. The Kyrgyz Parliament did not ratify this agreement until early 2011.[12] The territory Beijing obtained represented only 3 percent of that claimed under the Soviet regime; Tajikistan managed to retain 97 percent of the 28,000 square kilometers under dispute.

*Unresolved Water Issue*

Settling border issues did not, however, lead Kazakhstan and China to reach agreement on the thorny question of water and cross-border river management, an issue that today remains one of the main stumbling blocks to better relations between the two countries. Two of Kazakhstan's main rivers, the Ili and the Irtysh, originate in China, the former in the Tian Shan Mountains and the latter in the Chinese Altay Mountains. The Chinese regularly draw water from both rivers without seeking agreement from Kazakhstan, a practice that increased with the implementation of China's "Far West" development programs (*xibu dakaifa*).

These programs aim to foster the rapid expansion of the agricultural industry in Xinjiang province, particularly for cotton and wheat, both of which are water-intensive crops. Moreover, the development of oil reserves and programs to increase the Han population in both rural and urban areas are accelerating population growth throughout Xinjiang, leading to greater water consumption. To complete these projects, Beijing decided to increase the amount of water it extracts from the Ili and Irtysh Rivers. In the 1990s, it announced the construction of the 300-kilometer-long and 22-meter-wide Kara Irtysh-Karamay Canal, which is intended to redirect between 10 and 40 percent of the Irtysh to Ulungur Lake. The objective was twofold: first, to irrigate 140,000 new hectares of agricultural fields and, second, to transport water to the Junggar Basin oil fields, which hold 21 billion tons of oil, a fifth of China's discovered reserves.[13] The canal currently diverts around 500 million cubic meters of water per year, but the figure should increase to more than a billion cubic meters when it reaches full operating capacity in 2020. These extractions have adversely affected Kazakhstan's agricultural and industrial development, and could affect regions as far away as Siberia because the Irtysh is the main tributary of the Ob River, which traverses the Omsk region.[14]

Kazakhstan is concerned about the falling level of these rivers in its territory because it also requires a large amount of water to support its own economic development. According to the Kazakh government, the Irtysh is the main source of water for approximately four million out of the country's total population of fifteen million people.[15] Important towns in the northeast, such as Karaganda, Semei, and Pavlodar, all draw water directly from the Irtysh. Developing the capital, Astana, also requires additional supplies of water. To meet the demands of this bourgeoning city, the authorities must divert part of the Irtysh-Karaganda Canal to supplement the Ishim, the Irtysh's main tributary, which supplies Astana. In addition to threatening urban development in Kazakhstan, the fall in river levels constrains industrial development. Three hydroelectric stations in the northeast—in Bukhtarma on Lake Zaysan, in Ust-Kamenogorsk, and in Shulbinsk—depend on Soviet-era reservoirs that rely on the effluence of the Irtysh. The river is navigable during summer months and is one of the chief means of commercial exchange between this part of Kazakhstan and the Russian town of Omsk.[16] Like the Ili, it feeds the Kapchagay hydroelectric station, which supplies energy to the south of Kazakhstan, where energy shortfalls are still a problem. Between the Chinese border and Lake Balkhash, the Ili is the chief source of irrigation for the fields lining the length of the Grand Almaty Canal and is crucial to rice growing in the Akdalinsk region.[17]

In addition to these economic concerns, Kazakhstan—along with international environmental organizations—is worried about potential ecological risks from China's upstream diversions of water. A reduction in the flow of the Irtysh would degrade the entire region's already fragile ecosystem because the river is already polluted with nitrates, petroleum products, and several heavy metals.[18] If this situation worsens, it could cause significant damage to Lake Zaysan, which, according to some sources, would be threatened with disappearing.[19] A reduction in the flow of the Ili would have even more serious consequences. It provides Lake Balkhash with more than 50 percent of its water supply, but by the time it reaches the lake, the river already carries a large number of agricultural chemical pollutants. Lake Balkhash was ecologically damaged in the 1960s and 1970s by the construction of the Kapchagay reservoir. The lake—the fifteenth largest in the world—plays a key role in maintaining the climatic balance of southeastern and central Kazakhstan. Regular increases in the lake's salinity, however, adversely affect its fresh water levels.[20] Moreover, with the combination of dropping water levels, a deteriorating ecosystem, reduction in the number of fish species, and declining fishing yields, the living conditions of the local population have been detrimentally affected. The United Nations Development Program warned that the fall in the water supply from the Ili to the lake "could become an environmental tragedy comparable to the Aral Sea disaster."[21] If the river levels continue to drop, the ensuing climatic transformation of the region could become irreversible.

International treaties do not adequately regulate the use of water resources and Kazakhstan has had difficulties because the power differential favors its Chinese neighbor.[22] The first Kazakh ambassador to Beijing, Murat Auezov, raised the problem, but he did not succeed in gaining the attention of Chinese leaders.[23] Kazakhstan then attempted to convince Russia to become interested in the problem, pointing to the dangers that exploiting the two rivers would have for the Omsk region. But Moscow has preferred not to get involved in tripartite negotiations. With alarmist articles about the Kara Irtysh-Karamay Canal being published regularly in the Kazakh press, the threat of souring diplomatic relations eventually compelled Beijing to consent to superficial negotiations with Astana. Five rounds of discussion took place from 1999 to 2001.[24] In September 2001, both countries finally signed a framework agreement for the protection and use of cross-border rivers.[25] However, the agreement does not stipulate rules for sharing the Ili or the Irtysh. It merely calls for the "measured" use of common waters. Beijing has refused to set up a joint authority to manage the Irtysh, accepting only the creation of a Sino-Kazakh consultative commission, which has met only a few times.

In 2006, the commission completed a draft agreement concerning the dissemination of information about water quality and submitted it to Beijing for approval. Only in 2010 did the two countries finally declare themselves ready to sign an agreement for the protection of both cross-border rivers, but China is unlikely to agree to any restriction on its right to upstream pumping.[26] The problem has, therefore, yet to be properly addressed. As long as the negotiations remain bilateral, Kazakhstan will have difficulty making itself heard, and China's attitude will continue to reinforce Kazakh concerns about its intentions in the region.[27]

### The Thorny Border Question: Resolution or Stalemate?

Central Asian and Chinese diplomats consider the border litigation cases to have been settled.[28] In all bilateral and multilateral conferences, there is a general satisfaction that these questions were resolved peacefully, as well as an expectation of greater cooperation. Nevertheless, some Kazakh, Kyrgyz, and Tajik experts express different views on this matter than do their political leaders. However, the experts agree on the importance of the principle of diplomatic reciprocity—if they did not subscribe to the "one China" policy, their border disputes with Beijing would be transformed into instruments of coercion.

When it comes to interpreting the history of Sino-Soviet border disputes, most Central Asian experts use Soviet-era arguments. They accuse China of being the instigator of the 1969 confrontations by its incursions into Soviet territory, which they argue gave Moscow no option but to defend itself. They recall that for many years China seemed satisfied with the border situation but then, all of a sudden, unilaterally decided to claim that various parcels situated in Soviet territory were "under dispute," whereas Moscow itself never laid any claim to land on Chinese territory.[29] A book on Kazakhstan's borders published in 2006 caused quite a stir because it claims that China alone was responsible for the violence in 1969 and that the majority of China's claims were unfounded. The authors argue that, despite a Soviet commission dispatched to the region in the 1970s, Moscow actually agreed to negotiate with Beijing on the basis of China's claims, not its own observations.[30]

In Kyrgyzstan, some experts judge that the relatively quick settlement of border disputes helped consolidate the pragmatic atmosphere of Sino-Central Asian relations. Although the territorial disputes were settled to Beijing's advantage, they can now truly be considered a thing of the past as China's top priority has been to stabilize its northwestern border.[31] Others are nonetheless critical of the inequality of the land swap negotiated in 1999. Though Bishkek obtained a large part of the Khan Tengri peak, a national symbol, it lost the Uzengi-Kuush agricultural zone. In Tajikistan, the majority of experts are likewise pleased that Beijing claimed much less land than it had originally wanted. Nonetheless, some of them have stated off the record that the border agreements signed in 2002 have deferred resolution to an unknown point in the future. They suspect that Emomali Rakhmon's regime has tried to appease China by postponing the transfer of territories without revealing it publicly, only to leave it to his successors to manage a likely scandal.[32]

In Kazakhstan, many experts consider that Chinese claims made during the 1966–1976 Cultural Revolution were merely a product of that turbulent time. That page of history having been turned, they urge the public not to dwell on lost territories.[33] Some of their colleagues nonetheless believe that Beijing did take advantage of the weakness of the newly formed independent states to obtain a settlement more favorable to China than to Kazakhstan.[34] They therefore reproach their leader for the fact that, while triumphantly professing to have succeeded in keeping 53 percent of the contested territories, he unilaterally ceded the remaining 47 percent. Objections have also been raised in response to official claims that the lands surrendered were of no strategic value, pointing out, for example, that Kazakh border guards are now stationed in valleys that are dominated by Chinese counterparts who have taken up position on the ridges.[35] Konstantin Syroezhkin has observed, correctly, that the refusal of the Kazakh, Kyrgyz, and Tajik governments to publish the complete texts of border agreements sows seeds of doubt in the public mind and leads it to surmise that certain aspects have been deliberately hidden.[36] The question of cross-border water resources alone gives Kazakhstan a major stake in what was decided. There is broad unanimity on this subject; all the experts consider that China's attitude is indicative of the low regard in which it holds Kazakhstan's legitimate concerns. Even the most Sinophile experts are convinced that the Kara Irtysh-Karamay Canal is going to have a negative impact on Kazakhstan's economic and ecological situation.[37]

Xinjiang's intensive development also raises ecological issues. Winds carry nuclear particles from the Lop Nor test site as far as Central Asia, and a number of other Chinese actions also have a negative impact on Kazakhstan's soil quality, water supplies, and forests.[38] Experts with Sinophobe tendencies like Murat Auezov argue that the draining of water supplies is one of China's primary means to pressure Kazakhstan and limit its autonomy.[39] More moderate experts recognize that China is doing its utmost to modify the river flow in its favor, as well as to exclude Russia from the negotiating table, in order to take the greatest possible advantage of its power differential with Kazakhstan.[40] Konstantin Syroezhkin formulated his point of view on the future of the cross-border river issue unambiguously: "China speaks as an equal only with those that are stronger than it, or with those from whom it wants concessions."[41] Kazakhstan's hopes of procuring an equitable share of water from the Ili and the Irtysh, then, would seem to be futile.

## More Open Borders and Migration

Experts and publics might not be completely happy about the border agreements, but there is no question that they have eased crossings and increased population movements. Several trends in migration and border crossing have developed since independence. Cross-border minorities are rediscovering their historical role as go-betweens, and shuttle traders reinforce the image of China as a land of plenty. Chinese migrants and expatriates now occupy a new place in the Central Asian imagination, and youth attracted by China's success are on a quest to find new professional opportunities.

### CROSS-BORDER MINORITIES: REVIVING A HISTORICAL GO-BETWEEN ROLE

In 1991, most Central Asians regarded China as a strange and distant world even though there have always been population exchanges between the two zones. From the 1870s until the 1960s, hundreds of thousands of people crossed the border from Xinjiang to settle in the Soviet Union, a phenomenon that continued throughout the 1990s and 2000s with the repatriation programs for coethnics living abroad. Today, old and new cross-border minorities play, each in its own way, the role of cultural and economic mediators. Even if their trade-related niche remains modest in comparison to the overall Sino-Central Asian commercial flow, it constitutes an important element in the social strategies of officials on both sides of the border.

There were limited exchanges between the Soviet and Chinese Uighurs in the 1980s, but the opening of the borders at the end of *perestroika* enabled many more to visit family and to engage in a modest level of shuttle trade. In China, Soviet products were considered of higher quality than the national ones, whereas the Central Asians expressed an interest in Chinese household appliances and plastics that could not be found in the Soviet Union. Despite strong suspicions on the part of the central authorities, Beijing then had every interest in playing the Uighur card because it wanted to make its border economy more dynamic. Moreover, Deng Xiaoping's reforms encouraged the ethnic minorities, not to mention the Han Chinese, to set up small private companies for the transit of commodities and to enter into retailing or the restaurant business.

From the start of the 1990s, several markets in Kyrgyzstan and Kazakhstan were transformed into places for the resale of Chinese goods transported from Xinjiang. This trade was quickly taken over by Dungan and Uighur traders. Approximately one hundred thousand Dungans live in Central Asia, mainly in Kyrgyzstan and Kazakhstan. Approximately 30 percent in both these countries engage in trade with China.[42] Some of them, especially those from the border towns, have set themselves up in the shuttle trade. The geographical proximity to China exempts them from having to obtain a visa, so they are able to visit the Chinese shopping centers situated on the other side of the border. There they can buy products for resale when they return home. Uigurs in Central Asia, who maintained close familial relations with Xinjiang, established themselves in the cross-border trade by investing in these markets.

However, many factors soon stood in the way of the new Uighur trade. First of all, the cross-border character of the trade diminished as it increased in magnitude at regional and then state levels with the development of official Sino-Central Asian commercial relations. Kazakh businessmen quickly became aware of the economic stakes and put pressure on the authorities to alter the rules of the game in their favor. Hence, beginning in 1995, the Kazakh government passed a series of laws aimed at making cross-border trading more difficult for small traders and preventing the importation of specific products to safeguard local production. Uighur traders were rapidly displaced by the arrival of companies owned by Han Chinese, who received their supplies directly from large production centers in southeastern China. Others tried to open larger enterprises in collaboration with Chinese and

Central Asian authorities, but the general suspicion to which the Uighurs are subjected has limited their success, as has the fact that the Dungans, the Hans, and the titular nationalities of Central Asia have all targeted the same market.

Fueled by the cross-border trade, the development of links among Uighur communities was quickly seen to be a dangerous phenomenon by Beijing and the Central Asian capitals. China has dissuaded many Uighurs, whom it suspects of harboring separatist sympathies, from engaging in cross-border trade. In the 2000s, good relations between China and Central Asia, not to mention the presence of other transnational communities in the same commercial niche, meant that the Uighurs became marginalized. They found it increasingly difficult to find a Central Asian or Han part-ner willing to associate with them. They have, therefore, been reduced to engaging in very small-scale, low-profit trading or working as assistants or translators for Central Asian businessmen who trade with Xinjiang or Han businessmen settled in Central Asia. And they face particularly tough com-petition from the Dungans.

In two decades, the Uighurs have lost part of the unique niche that was available to them. This has occurred for at least three reasons. First, Sino-Central Asian trade has been brought under state control, with the greatest share going to the titular nationalities—Hans and Central Asians—and not to the minorities. Second, even among the cross-border minorities them-selves, the Uighurs have been marginalized by political suspicion that has impeded their ability to make use of the transnational networks customary among diasporic peoples. Third, in Xinjiang the Uighurs have been out-stripped by the Hans, who themselves now enjoy the advantages of border-ing Central Asia. The extreme political sensitivity of Uighur separatism, which Beijing considers more dangerous than Tibet separatism, has dispos-sessed the Uighurs of their historical trader role and left the field open for other cross-border minorities who are taking advantage of opportunities for trade between China and Central Asia.

## CENTRAL ASIAN PETTY TRADERS AND "SHOP TOURISTS"

The flows from Central Asia to China consist mainly of small traders and "shop tourists" who have no intention of settling in China for the long term. Salaries in China are considered too low, the legal conditions for for-eigners too complicated, and the cultural context somewhat unpropitious for integration. Some Central Asian citizens are employed in Xinjiang, where they work in agricultural, mining, and processing industries. They hope to take advantage of the "Far West" development programs that make it possible for foreign nationals to enjoy tax exemptions.[43] Migrants of this kind are a small minority. The main population movements are temporary. Ever since the *perestroika* years, Central Asian petty traders, mainly Kazakh and Kyrgyz, have traveled to China, mostly to Xinjiang, to compensate partially for the collapse of goods flows coming from Moscow. Upon independence, they benefited from the collapse of the local industries to export scrap metal, nonferrous products containing rare metals, and plastic waste to China and returned with consumer products. This shuttle trade points to a major upheaval in the social fabric, because it has enabled the professional redeployment of engineers and industry workers who lost their employment when the Soviet industries collapsed.

In the summer of 1991, China and Kazakhstan signed their first agreement to encourage the development of shop tourism. The following year, approximately seven hundred thousand Kazakh citizens crossed the border to buy everyday consumer items in China with the intention of reselling them back home.[44] The structuring of trade of greater magnitude quickly eroded the profitability of this shuttle trade, but in 2002, it reportedly still provided employment for nearly half a million Kazakh citizens.

In Kyrgyzstan also, shuttle trade increased quickly with the end of *perestroika*, but in Uzbekistan, Tajikistan, and Turkmenistan, shuttle trade with China remained small until the 2000s. Turkmen and Uzbek petty traders had previously traveled in much larger numbers to Turkey, Iran, and the United Arab Emirates (Dubai in particular). Xinjiang remained a less fashionable destination. Today the situation has changed. Opportunities have increased with the growing numbers of flights from Ashgabat, Tashkent, and Dushanbe to Urumqi, Beijing, Shanghai, and Guangzhou, as well as shop tours by bus that leave from the Ferghana Valley or Tajikistan on trips to Kashgar and Urumqi.[45]

CHINESE MIGRANTS: BEYOND THE CLICHÉS

Migrant flows in each country are extremely different. Beginning in the early 1990s, emigration from China had the greatest impact on Kyrgyzstan and Kazakhstan. In 1988, the Soviet Union and the PRC signed an accord enabling citizens living in border areas to travel without visas. But cross-border travel without a visa was revoked by Kazakhstan in 1994, when the government, which was concerned about its inability to regulate migration flows, decided to curtail the presence of Chinese. In Kyrgyzstan, the system of travel without visa was abolished in 2003; until then, Chinese citizens were able to move freely across the Kyrgyz border and from there to Kazakhstan or Russia thanks to the intra-CIS free circulation agreement. In Tajikistan, simplified procedures for border crossing were put in place only in the mid-2000s. The goal was to energize cross-border exchanges at Kulma-Kalasu pass. Uzbekistan and Turkmenistan have particularly restrictive entry policies and have not yet experienced any significant Chinese migration.

Migration flows, especially of Hans, are difficult to measure reliably. The Central Asian governments are reluctant to collect and publish any statistics and they fail to distinguish between expatriates and migrants. In addition, a large portion of this migration, especially in Kyrgyzstan, is illegal. However, the notion of illegality is complex. The Chinese migrants come to Central Asia either on tourist visas or on thirty-day work invitations, which they obtain from Central Asian or Chinese companies that specialize in this type of service. Once there, they extend their stays for ninety days. Some then choose to stay on and work illegally; others leave for Russia or return to China to start the administrative procedures that will allow them to come back again.[46] These migrants, therefore, do not enter the country illegally, but they stay in it longer than their papers allow and so become illegals. In such a context, the migration figures are very imprecise. Russian experts often declare that Kazakhstan has upward of 150,000 permanently settled Chinese and 300,000 migrants who regularly cross the Chinese border, but these numbers appear to be inflated.[47] In Kazakhstan, the customs services of the Interior Ministry registered 30,000 Chinese citizens crossing the border in 2006.[48] The same year, the customs service of the Committee of National Defense estimated that the flow was around 170,000 people per year.[49] In Kyrgyzstan, the chairman of the Border Service declared that there were about 60,000 Chinese persons living in the country at the beginning of 2008.[50] In Tajikistan, according to the Interior Ministry Migration Service, there were a little more than 10,000 Chinese laborers in 2008.[51] No figures are available for Uzbekistan or Turkmenistan.

These migrants can be classified into several ethnic and professional categories. China includes Central Asian minorities, recognized as ethnic groups in the Chinese system of national classification. There are about

16,000 Chinese Uzbeks; about 44,000 Tajiks, who are based mainly in the Tajik autonomous district of Tashkorgan; and about 181,000 Kyrgyz, settled mainly in the autonomous district of Kyzylsu. China's Kazakhs, two-thirds of whom live in a compact manner in the Ili Kazakh autonomous prefecture, are the most numerous with about 1.5 million persons. These Central Asian minorities benefit only a little from the economic and cultural niche that has opened up with the proximity of the Central Asian states, and are barely involved in cross-border commerce. They mostly live in remote areas, their mobility is confined to their region, and the Chinese authorities are very reluctant to issue passports to them. Passports are required to cross borders and obtain a commercial export license. In addition, they are mainly farmers and stockbreeders who do little business in urban environments.

Opening borders made possible the development of more long-term migratory flows from China to Central Asia. Some members of the Central Asian minorities of China have taken advantage of the opening of borders to emigrate to the two neighboring republics. In Kazakhstan, the majority of the official migrants from China are Oralmans—that is, Chinese Kazakhs who have taken advantage of Astana's repatriation program. Nearly 100 percent of the Chinese citizens who request Kazakh citizenship or permanent residency have been Oralman.[52] In Kyrgyzstan, too, Kairylmans make up a significant percentage of the official Chinese migration, but the percentage is smaller because the country's economic situation is relatively unattractive.

Although no extant statistics record the ethnic origin of migrants, it appears that about half the migrants from China have a Central Asian or Uighur background, and the other half are Han Chinese. The regional and ethnic origins of the Chinese private entrepreneurs have changed dramatically since the beginning of the 1990s. Since the beginning of the 2000s, the number of traders from Xinjiang has dwindled, and about twice as many Hans have come from China's maritime provinces.

In the case of Kazakhstan, only about five thousand Chinese citizens (non-Oralmans) are officially registered as working in the country. They can be divided into three groups. The first category includes employees of the large Chinese companies operating there, mostly in the energy sector. Most in this group are high-salaried graduate engineers who live in Kazakhstan as expatriates with their families for the duration of their contracts. The second subgroup comprises workers in the construction sector, mostly on real estate and energy projects, who, for the most part, are poorly paid employees, few of whom have graduated from high school and who come alone. They live mainly in encampments close to the building sites and do not integrate into the host society. Kazakhstan is reported to be the CIS country that registers the most Chinese in this sector, primarily because many Russian construction companies employ them. The third group is composed of retailers and private businessmen, whose businesses can be either large or small in scale. The most modest arrive as individuals who come to sell their goods to Kazakh retailers. Such individuals are rather rare in Kazakhstan because the laws require that foreigners be part of a joint venture with a Kazakh partner. Wealthier members of this group have developed local intermediary networks and are relatively well integrated.

In terms of the labor market, Han migrants and expatriates occupy specific professional niches. The engineers and technicians invited to work by Chinese companies or joint ventures have skills that the Central Asians often do not have. Chinese migrants who work in poorly paid positions—in particular in construction—have to compete with Uzbek, Kyrgyz, and Tajik migrants who have established themselves in the same sectors. Chinese traders in Kyrgyzstan—estimated to number about thirty thousand—can be divided into two broad categories. The small operators often make the trips between China and Kyrgyzstan themselves and do not seek to obtain long-stay entry permits. They rent one or two containers, in which they stock and resell their goods, and employ one or two local workers, often Dungans or Kyrgyz students who want to practice their Chinese.

The wealthiest Chinese businessmen, referred to as *loben* or *bashlik*, work only in wholesale, not retail. In addition to their sites in the markets, some Chinese entrepreneurs have opened small factories, often on the ruins of old Soviet industries, and produce a diverse array of products. Workers on road construction sites are almost exclusively Chinese who have little contact with locals. Last, some Chinese work seasonally on vegetable or cereal farms, but the agricultural sector is politically sensitive, and the Chinese migrants are not welcome there. In Tajikistan, bazaar trade has only begun to develop, a decade later than in Kyrgyzstan. Chinese traders are less numerous than in the neighboring republic, but they are beginning to set up new wholesale markets in Dushanbe and in Khujand, Kayrakkum, and Istaravshan in the Sogd region, where the local markets are directly supplied from Karasuu.

Most Chinese migrants in Tajikistan are workers and engineers employed by large Chinese companies such as the Sinohydro Corporation, China Roads, and the Chinese Railways. Others are employed in brick factories, such as that in Hissar, a foundry factory in Dushanbe, and concrete-producing companies or chemical factories at Yavan and Kurgan-Tyube. In most cases, these workers live in closed camps with poor sanitary conditions and are fed on site by Chinese cooks. They have very little interaction with the local population, especially because they do not speak Russian or any of the national languages.

Very few Chinese migrants wish to reside permanently in Central Asia, so they do not apply for permanent work visas or nationalization. The length of their stays abroad is generally from a few months to a few years, with the sole aim of accumulating enough capital to start a private business in China, Russia, or Western Europe. Their rates of marriage with Central Asians are low, a reflection of their low levels of integration into the host country. However, there has been a notably quick development of infrastructure to manage this diaspora, including tourist agencies to organize administrative formalities; special banks that cater to Chinese citizens; and restaurants, medical centers, hotels, dry cleaners, and hotels or residences. All these suggest that the number of migrants who decide to remain in Central Asia for a long period will increase and that interaction with the host societies is likely to grow.

## Conclusion

During the first years after the states of Central Asia gained independence, they and China learned to understand one another and the state of their relationships. Though the amount of territory that Beijing obtained in the border settlements was far smaller than stipulated in its original claims, it obtained what it wanted most: recognition that the czarist treaties were unequal and the good will of the new Central Asian states. This facilitated the establishment of pragmatic, good neighborly relations, and the avoidance of conflict. Trust was created where little had existed in the past. Moreover, the territory Beijing acquired in Kazakhstan, Kyrgyzstan, and Tajikistan has real economic and strategic value because it includes access to rivers, subsoil resources, and high-mountain passes.

The Central Asian states, for their part, learned several lessons. First and foremost, as the border disputes threatened the very existence of Kazakhstan, Kyrgyzstan, and Tajikistan, the relationship to China was understood to be vital for the survival of the nations as independent states. Central Asians overwhelmingly give China credit for the fact that they were able to settle their border disputes peacefully within a decade of independence— indeed, within only a few years for Kazakhstan. If the Chinese authorities had wanted to deliver a fatal blow to the young states, which were negotiating for their survival after the collapse of the Soviet Union, the fragile states would not have been able to withstand it. However, concern that the peaceful settlement might be temporary is widespread. Not one of the territorial treaties has been published, a fact that fuels speculation about the existence of secret clauses. Many wonder, for example, if the treaties are definitive or have validity only for a period of twenty years, as is the case with some of the Sino-Russian treaties signed in the 2000s.[53] The possibility of having to renegotiate some of the territorial agreements in the years to come, when the power differential in favor of China will be even greater, is a legitimate public concern in Kazakhstan, Kyrgyzstan, and Tajikistan. Such suspicions are reinforced by the fact that China does not hesitate to violate the demilitarization agreements that are supposed to limit exercises in border regions.[54]

Second, the way the borders were settled demonstrated the complete absence of any post-Soviet unity in their dealings with China. This was a bitter lesson for the Central Asian governments, which had hoped that Russia would weigh in on their side. Despite the meetings of the CIS-China group in 1992–1994, all technical negotiations were conducted bilaterally; no post-Soviet state obtained support from its neighbors. Thus, Kazakhstan and Russia failed to present a common front on the question of the key Sino-Kazakh-Russian rivers, and Kazakhstan and Kyrgyzstan were unable to negotiate together in the showdown with Beijing over water use by upstream and downstream states.

Central Asian experts are highly pessimistic about long-term relations with China and the impact the relationship will have on cultural questions. Contrary to widespread opinion, the Central Asian states are not unqualified fans of China. Experts think that the states of the region will have inherent difficulties in trying to work the overall power differential with China to their advantage. They consider China's ultimate objective with respect to the independence of Central Asia to be particularly unclear and worry that nothing can ensure that the current situation will endure. The suspicion that China still has imperial designs on Central Asia and merely wants to conceal or delay them is predominant. Even those who consider Beijing's economic and geopolitical presence a guarantee of stability for Central Asia turn out not to be Sinophiles on cultural matters. China currently lacks the symbolic means to compete with Russia for conquest of the Central Asian mind. Most regional experts continue to think of Moscow as their main ally and as the ally whose partnership is most natural and least dangerous.

## Notes

1. Byron N. Tsou, *China and International Law: The Boundary Disputes* (New York: Praeger, 1990).

2. George Ginsburgs and Carl F. Pinkele, *The Sino-Soviet Territorial Dispute, 1949–64* (New York: Praeger, 1978); E. D. Stepanov, *Politika nachinaetsia s granitsy: Nekotorye voprosy pogranichnoi politiki KNR vtoroi poloviny XX v* [Politics begin with borders: Some questions about the PRC's border policy in the second half of the twentieth century] (Moscow: Institut Dal'nego Vostoka RAN, 2007).

3. Ying-hsien Pi, "China's Boundary Issues with the Former Soviet Union," *Issues and Studies* 28, no. 7 (1992): 63–75.

4. For more details, see Thierry Kellner, *L'Occident de la Chine: Pékin et la nouvelle Asie centrale (1991–2001)* [China's West: Beijing and the new Central Asia (1991–2001)] (Paris: Presses Universitaires de France, 2008), 539–588.

5. Necati Polat, *Boundary Issues in Central Asia* (Ardsley, NY: Brill Transnational, 2002).

6. A. M. Aunasova and A. M. Suleimenov, "Iz istorii delimitatsii gosudarstvennykh granits Respubliki Kazakhstan" [History of delimitation of state borders of the Republic of Kazakhstan], *Evraluzh* [Eurasian Law Journal] 4, no. 23 (2010), http://www.eurasialaw.ru/index.php?option=com_content&view=article&id=652%3A2010-06-03-09-21-06&catid=99%3A2010-06-02-08-56-30&Itemid=124; "Kazakhstan-Kitai," http://karty.narod.ru/claim/kzcn/kzcn.html (accessed December 16, 2010); Vitalii Khliupin, *Geopoliticheskii treugol'nik: Kazakhstan-Kitai-Rossiia; Proshloe i nastoiashchee pogranichnoi problemy* [A geopolitical triangle: Kazakhstan-China-Russia; The past and present of the border issues] (Moscow: International Eurasian Institute for Economic and Political Research, 1999).

7. Zulfiia A. Amanzholova, Murat M. Atanov, and Bugakuku S. Turarbekov, *Pravda o gosudarstvennoi granitse respubliki Kazakhstan* [The truth about the state

borders of the Republic of Kazakhstan] (Almaty, Kazakhstan: Zhibek Zholy, 2006); K. L. Syroezhkin, *Kazakhstan-Kitai: Ot prigranichnoi torgovli k strategicheskomu partnerstvu* [Kazahkstan-China: From border trade to strategic partnership] (Almaty, Kazakhstan: KISI, 2010), 1:122–132.

8. Ckaes Levinsson and Ingvar Svanberg, "Kazakhstan-China Border Trade Thrives After Demarcation Treaty," *The Analyst*, February 16, 2000, pp. 63–75.

9. Nurgul Kerimbekova and Vladimir Galitskiy, "On the State Border Between Kyrgyzstan and China," *Central Asia and the Caucasus*, no. 5 (2002): 108–113.

10. For more details, see S. K. Alamanov, *Kratkaia istoriia i opyt resheniia pogranichnykh problem Kyrgyzstana* [A short history of solving border issues in Kyrgyzstan] (Bishkek, Kyrgyzstan: Friedrich Ebert Foundation, 2005).

11. Elena Buldakova, "Conflicting Views on Land Issue Between Kyrgyzstan and China," *CIMERA*, no. 24 (2002).

12. S. Smirnov, "Kitai otshchepil chast' Tadzhikistana" [China seized a part of Tajikistan], *Gazeta*, January 12, 2011, http://www.gazeta.ru/politics/2011/01/12_kz_3489206.shtml.

13. Center for Energy and Global Development, "Xinjiang Oil Industry Development," *China Security*, Autumn 2006, http://www.isn.ethz.ch/Digital-Library/Publications/Detail/?ots591=0c54e3b3-1e9c-be1e-2c24-a6a8c7060233&lng=en&id=29404; Marion Dakers, "Lighting Up the New Silk Road, the Chinese Town Built on Oil," *The Telegraph*, July 12, 2015, http://www.telegraph.co.uk/finance/economics/11732939/Lighting-up-the-new-Silk-Road-the-Chinese-town-built-on-oil.html.

14. G. Zholamanova, "Rol' ShOS v uregulirovanii transgranichnykh rek mezhdu Kazakhstanom i Kitaem" [The role of the SCO in the regulation of cross-border rivers between Kazakhstan and China], *Analytic*, no. 1 (2007): 34–42.

15. Bruce Pannier and Edige Magauin, "China Discusses Future of Irtysh River," *Asia Times*, June 5, 1999, http://www.atimes.com/c-asia/AF05Ag01.html.

16. L. N. Kozlov and A. A. Beliakov, "Irtyshsko-obskaia glubokovodnaia magistral' ot Kitaia do severnogo morskogo puti v sostave transportno-energicheskoi vodnoi sistemy Evrazii" [The Irtysh-Ob road from China to the Northern Sea, as part of the hydro-system of transport and energy in Eurasia], *Evraziiskaia Ekonomicheskaia Integratsiia* [Eurasian Economic Integration] 3, no. 4 (2009): 132–143.

17. For more details, see Sebastien Peyrouse, "Flowing Downstream: The Sino-Kazakh Water Dispute," *China Brief* 7, no. 10 (2007): 7–10, http://www.jamestown.org/single/?no_cache=1&tx_ttnews%5Btt_news%5D=4131.

18. B. Temirbolat, "Mezhdu Kazakhstanom i Kitaem mozhet nachat'sia konflikt iz-za vody" [A water-related conflict might occur between Kazakhstan and China], *Saiasat* [Politics], no. 8 (2000): 97–98.

19. Sergei Schafarenko, "Black Irtysh River [E]ndangered by Irrigation Channel," European Rivers Network, November 1999, http://www.rivernet.org/ob/irtysh.htm.

20. Balkhash Lake has the peculiarity of being divided into two parts, the western part being made up of fresh water and the eastern part of salt water.

21. United Nations Development Program, *Water Resources of Kazakhstan in the New Millennium* (Almaty, Kazakhstan: UNDP, 2004), 41.

22. Eric W. Sievers, "Transboundary Jurisdiction and Watercourse Law: China, Kazakhstan, and the Irtysh," *Texas International Law Journal* 37 (Winter 2002): 7.

23. "Murat Auezov rassuzhdaet ob ekologicheskikh problemakh, i ne tol'ko o nikh" [Murat Auezov addresses ecological problems and other issues], *Megalopolis*, no. 3 (2000): 7.

24. A. Mukhamberdiiarova, "Kazakhstan-Kitai: reshenie vodnoi problemy opiat' otkladyvaetsia" [Kazakhstan-China: The solution to water issues is put on hold again], Institut Voiny i Mira [The Institute of War and Peace], April 10, 2001.

25. A. D. Riabtsev, "Sushchestvuiushchii opyt vodnymi resursami na transgranichnykh rekakh" [Existing experience on water resources in transborder rivers], Central Asian Water, April 2006, http://www.cawater-info.net/library/rus/ryabtsev_rus.pdf.

26. "Kazakhstan nameren podpisat' soglashenie s Kitaem o transgranichnykh rekakh" [Kazakhstan will sign an agreement with China on transbondary rivers], *Ria Novosti*, February 24, 2010, http://www.rian.ru/world/20100224/210592367.html.

27. A. D. Riabtsev, *Ugrozy vodnoi bezopasnosti v Respublike Kazakhstan v transgranichnom kontekste i vozmozhnye puti ikh ustraneniia* [Threats to water security of the Republic of Kazakhstan in the cross-border context and possible ways of solving them], Interstate Commission for Water Coordination of Central Asia, 2008, http://www.icwc-aral.uz/workshop_march08/pdf/ryabtsev_ru.pdf.

28. See, for example, B. K. Sultanov and L. M. Muzaparova, eds., *Stanovlenie vneshnei politiki Kazakhstana: Istoriia, dostizheniia, vzgliad na budushchee* [The establishment of Kazakhstan's foreign policy: History, successes, vision for the future] (Almaty, Kazakhstan: IWEP, 2005); and M. Imanaliev, *Ocherki o vneshnei politike Kyrgyzstana* [Essays on the foreign policy of Kyrgyzstan] (Bishkek, Kyrgyzstan: Sabyr, 2002). See also Steven Parham, *Narrating the Border: The Discourse of Control over China's North-West Frontier* (Bern, Switzerland: Institut für Ethnologie at the Bern University, 2004).

29. Konstantin Syroezhkin, "Central Asia Between the Gravitational Poles of Russia and China," in *Central Asia: A Gathering Storm?* ed. Boris Rumer (Armonk, NY: M. E. Sharpe, 2002), 182; Ablat Khodzhaev, *Kitaiskii faktor v Tsentral'noi Azii* [The Chinese factor in Central Asia] (Tashkent, Uzbekistan: FAN, 2007), 133–134.

30. Amanzholova, Atanov, and Turarbekov, *Pravda o gosudarstvennoi granitse respubliki Kazakhstan*, 40–44.

31. Orozbek Moldaliev, interview by the author, February 15, 2008, Bishkek, Kyrgyzstan.

32. Anonymous interviews by the author, March 2008, Dushanbe, Tajikistan.

33. Basen Zhiger and Klara Khafizova, "Kazakhstan i Kitai v XXI veke: Strate-giia sosedstva" [Kazakhstan and China in the 21st century: Neighborhood strategy], *Ekonomicheskie Strategii—Central'naia Azia* [Economic Strategies—Central Asia], no. 2 (2007): 15–17.

34. Konstantin Syroezhkin, *Problemy sovremennogo Kitaia i bezopasnost' v Tsentral'noi Azii* [Problems of contemporary China and security in Central Asia] (Almaty, Kazakhstan: KISI, 2006), 204.

35. "Murat Auezov o vremeni i o sebe" [Murat Auezov on the time and himself], *Ekspress K.*, no. 161 (2000), https://zonakz.net/articles/11699.

36. Konstantin Syroezhkin, interview by the author, March 4, 2008, Almaty, Kazakhstan.

37. Zhiger and Khafizova, "Kazakhstan i Kitai v XXI veke."

38. K. T. Talipov, "Prirodnye resursy Sin'tszian-uigurskogo avtonomnogo raiona Kitaia: Problemy na fone optimisticheskikh prognozov" [Natural resources of the Uyghur Autonomous Region of Xinjiang in China], *Shygyz*, no. 1 (2005): 95–100.

39. Murat Auezov, "Istoriia i sovremennost' v kitaisko-kazakhstanskikh otnosheniiakh" [History and current standing of Sino-Kazakh relations], *Tsentral'naia Aziia i Kavkaz* [Central Asia and the Caucasus], no. 4 (1999), http://www.ca-c.org/journal/cac-04-1999/st_20_auezov.shtml.

40. Zholamanova, "Rol' ShOS v uregulirovanii transgranichnykh rek mezhdu Kazakhstanom i Kitaem."

41. Syroezhkin, "Central Asia Between the Gravitational Poles of Russia and China," 196.

42. Nurik Ma (representative of the Dungan Association of Kazakhstan at Xi'an), interview by the author, October 11, 2008, Xi'an, China.

43. Sadykzhan Ibraimov, "China-Central Asia Trade Relations: Economic and Social Patterns," *China and Eurasia Forum Quarterly* 7, no. 1 (2009): 55.

44. V. Babak, "Astana v treugol'nike Moskva-Vashington-Pekin: Kazakhstansko-kitaiskie otnosheniia" [Astana in the triangle Moscow-Washington-Beijing: Kazakhstan-China relations], *Tsentral'naia Aziia i Kavkaz* [Central Asia and the Caucasus], no. 1 (2000), http://www.ca-c.org/journal/cac-07-2000/19.babak.shtml.

45. Anonymous interviews by the author with Central Asians in the main commercial malls devoted to post-Soviet traders in Kashgar, Urumqi, and Beijing, May and September 2008.

46. Konstantin Syroezhkin, interview by the author, September 29, 2010, Almaty, Kazakhstan.

47. K. Borishpolets and A. Babadzhanov, "Migratsionnye riski stran Tsentral'noi Azii" [The risks of migrations in Central Asian countries],

*Analiticheskie Zapiski MGIMO* [Analytical Proceedings MGIMO], no. 2 (2007):
9–19; V. A. Korsun, *Vneshniaia politika Kitaia na poroge XXI veka* [China's foreign
policy on the threshold of the twenty-first century] (Moscow: MGIMO, 2002), 50.

48. S. Kozhirova, "Vnutrennie i vneshnie aspekty sovremennoi kitaiskoi
migratsii" [Domestic and foreign aspects of contemporary Chinese migration],
*Analytic*, no. 6 (2007): 51.

49. E. Sadovskaia, "Sovremennaia kitaiskaia migratsiia v Kazakhstane:
Osnovnye tendentsii, problemy i perspektivy" [The current Chinese migration in
Kazakhstan: Main tendencies, problems and perspectives], in *Tsentral'naia Aziia
i Kitai: Sostoianie i perspektivy sotrudnichestva* [Central Asia and China: Current
status and prospects for cooperation], ed. B. Sultanov and M. Laruelle (Almaty,
Kazakhstan: KISI, 2008), 130–156.

50. "V Kyrgyzstane nakhoditsia bolee 60,000 grazhdan Kitaia" [There are
more than 60,000 Chinese citizens in Kyrgyzstan], *24.kg*, January 30, 2008.

51. Saodat Olimova, "The Multifaceted Chinese Presence in Tajikistan," *China
and Eurasia Forum Quarterly* 7, no. 1 (2008): 71.

52. Konstantin Syroezhkin, "Kitaiskaia migratsiia v Kazakhstane: Voobraz-
haemye i real'nye ugrozy i vyzovy" [Chinese migration in Kazakhstan: Imagined
and real threats and challenges], *Mezhdunarodnye Issledovaniia* [International
Surveys], no. 1 (2009): 122.

53. Neville Maxwell, "How the Sino-Russian Boundary Conflict Was Finally
Settled: From Nerchinsk 1689 to Vladivostok 2005 via Zhenbao Island 1969," in
*Eager Eyes Fixed on Eurasia*, ed. Akihiro Iwashita (Hokkaido, Japan: Slavic
Research Center, Hokkaido University, 2007), 47–73.

54. This was the case, for example, in January 2007 after Chinese security
forces attacked a training camp of the East Turkestan Islamic Movement in the
Tashkurgan region, situated about twenty-five kilometers from the Tajik-Chinese
border, an attack in which some eighteen persons were killed and seventeen others
arrested. See "Kyrgyz Border Guards Say China Tightening Security," *Radio Free
Europe/Radio Liberty*, January 11, 2007, http://www.rferl.org/content/article/
1073932.html.

# ELEVEN

# Managing Imperial Peripheries
## Russia and China in Central Asia

*Igor Torbakov*

Most rulers of the great world empires tended to believe that their vast realms would exist eternally, and court poets went out of their way to give artistic support to the rulers' hubris. Virgil once famously contended that Romulus had been granted the "gift of empire without end." But as Michael Mann points out—correctly—that was a delusionary idea. All empires actually end, and Rome fell, as did many other great powers before and after it.[1] But an empire's fall does not mean there cannot be a new rise; as William McNeill suggests, "The forces that so persistently restored . . . empire . . . in the past" have retained their "cogency."[2] Historians—from Edward Gibbon to Leopold von Ranke to Paul Kennedy—have long been intrigued by the "rise and fall" dynamic. In his magisterial exploration of the rise and fall of the great powers in the modern era, Kennedy came to three important conclusions. First, in the long run, there appears to be a strong correlation between a great power's strategic emergence and the robustness of its economy. Similarly, economic decline inevitably leads to the strategic demise. Second, in the international system, economic clout and military might are always relative—that is, the key is not to be strong in absolute terms but to be stronger than your main geopolitical competitors. Third, the historical record demonstrates that the great powers' relative strength never stays constant but rather fluctuates, mainly because of the uneven development of different societies that in itself is the result of the workings of multiple factors—not least the organizational and technological breakthroughs that give one state an edge over the others.[3]

These reflections have a direct bearing on the topic of this chapter; over the last twenty years, the world's distribution of power has been fundamentally modified because of the unprecedented growth of China's economic wealth and political influence. In the introduction to his magnum opus, Kennedy approvingly cites the seventeenth-century Austrian author Philipp von Hörnigk. "Whether a nation be today mighty and rich or not," this mercantilist thinker asserted, "depends not on the abundance or security of its power and riches, but principally on whether its neighbors possess more or less of it."[4] Remarkably, von Hörnigk was resurrected again very recently by a leading Sinologist who referred to his cogent argument and then noted that the West's "decreasing comparative power generates a perception of decline and an irrational fear of China."[5] One could argue, however, that Russia should have even more grounds for concern: "The reversal of China's and Russia's fortunes at the close of the 20th century could not have been more dramatic. For the first time in their recent history Russians have to deal with a China which is more powerful and more dynamic than their own country."[6]

This chapter investigates how China and Russia are adjusting to the new situation that arises from the profound shift in the balance of power caused by the former's rise and the latter's relative decline. The main focus is on Moscow's and Beijing's interaction in Central Asia—the area that for the last three hundred years has been a contested borderland sandwiched between expanding Russian and Chinese imperial states. Over the last several years, the body of literature devoted to the analysis of Russia's and China's policies in the region has grown exponentially.[7] Much of this scholarly work gets the story right, presents uncontroversial facts, and is very informative and insightful. However, most of the studies tend to explore the Russian and Chinese conduct in Central Asia separately, without investigating complex linkages between the two countries' actions. Broader historical context, the differences between the Russian and Chinese perceptions of bilateral relationship, and the imperial dimension have not received sufficient scrutiny.

This chapter seeks to fill these lacunae, and to this end it advances several key arguments. First, I argue that the notions of empire and "postimperium" are crucial for the understanding of Russia's and China's policies in the region.[8] True, all empires end, but they end differently, and here we are dealing with two quite different types of postimperial situations. Russia's case appears to be that of a country that is going through a particularly tortuous process of postimperial readjustment. To borrow Dean Acheson's famous characterization of postwar Great Britain, Moscow "has lost an empire, and has yet to find a role."[9] Post-Soviet Russia's international identity remains uncertain, its geopolitical orientation on the west-east axis is as contested as ever, and its approach toward the lost borderlands is a mix of pragmatic policies and the moves driven by the longing to restore its great-power status. By contrast, China seems to represent a rather unique case of quite successful transformation of empire into a nation-state. Its principal objective in Central Asia is both strategic and pragmatic: to keep the volatile region stable to help Beijing consolidate the center's rule in the country's far-flung northwest province of Xinjiang and finalize its incorporation into the Han-dominated Chinese national state. Second, I argue that the complex interface between Russia and China in Central Asia is best conceptualized as the one that has led—under the Romanovs and the Qing—to the formation of a kind of Sino-Russian condominium as the two imperial states divided the steppes between themselves. In fact, historically, the parallel expansions were mutually reinforcing as the conquests from the west and the east denied regional peoples the room for maneuver. It was the Soviet Union's collapse that marked the end of the erstwhile condominium: the former Soviet dominion has been suddenly transformed into the five independent states. Yet geostrategically, Central Asia remains primarily Russia and China's neighborhood. As America's "Central Asian moment" is drawing to a close as it prepares to exit Afghanistan, Sino-Russian competition in the region is likely going to intensify. Finally, I argue that in this new geopolitical situation China has found itself in a stronger position: although Moscow has lost its Central Asian possessions, Beijing has retained its own (Xinjiang) and is now only happy to expand its influence at the expense of the weakened Russia. Yet under the new conditions, the two historical overlords of Central Asia—the Bear and the Dragon—are mostly preoccupied with security issues and thus are faced with their perennial challenge: how best to manage the (former) imperial peripheries.

### Russia's Postimperium: A Quest for Great Power Status amid Strategic Uncertainty

Russia may have dumped its empire voluntarily (as the official narrative would have it), but what followed this "act of liberation" was quite unusual indeed. Unlike some other former imperial polities, this "rump Russia" did not immediately exit the international arena; nor did it reinvent itself as a "regular" national state with more modest geopolitical ambitions. Instead, since the early 1990s, Moscow has been tenaciously seeking the leadership role in post-Soviet Eurasia—the former empire's borderlands now composing the "new Eastern Europe" (Belarus, Ukraine, and Moldova), the three nations of the South Caucasus, and the five "-stans" of Central Asia. Russia's craving the dominant position in what the Eurasianist thinkers called its natural *mestorazvitie* (developmental space) is intimately connected with the country's self-understanding. Moscow's geopolitical control over the bulk of Eurasian landmass that is organized as a Russia-led distinct "civilizational space" appears to constitute a key element in Russia's claim to great-power status.[10]

Indeed, Russia's prized geographical location and its bi-continental (Euro-Asian) dimension have long been perceived as "objective factors" that make the country predestined for geopolitical preeminence. Not a small number of Russian strategists and policy makers took pride in the nineteenth-century Russian thinker Petr Chaadaev's memorable description of Russia as a vast realm spread "between two great divisions of the world, between the East and the West, resting one elbow on China and the other on Germany."[11] Yet the last two decades saw profound changes—both in Russia and in those "two great worlds" that flank it—that resulted, in the words of Perry Anderson of UCLA, in the "drastic alteration" in Russia's geopolitical setting:

> Russia is now wedged between . . . [the] European Union, with eight times its GDP and three times its population, and a vastly empowered China, with five times its GDP and ten times its population. Historically speaking, this is a sudden and total change in the relative magnitudes flanking it on either side. Few Russians have yet quite registered the scale of the *ridimensionamento* of their country.[12]

Worse still, Anderson argues, this brutal redistribution of power cannot fail to negatively affect Russia's traditional sense of itself. In the past, Russia could join a group of European nations as a member of an ad hoc coalition or, following the Congress of Vienna, be a part of the Concert of Europe, enjoying at times—as the largest and most powerful country—a position of primus inter pares. Yet now Russia faces in Europe not a bunch of individual countries but a continental bloc, which it is not going to join. Russia's exclusion from the United Europe of 28, however, makes its European identity quite problematic; "Russia—in being what cannot be included in the Union—is now formally defined as *what is not Europe*, in the new, hardening sense of the term."[13] The Russian elites, of course, are enraged by what they see (arguably, with some justification) as an injustice and a snub, yet the European Union's position on the matter cannot be altered and will continue to poison the relationship between Moscow and Brussels for years to come. The situation Russia is faced with in the East appears to be no less dramatic and potentially even more damaging for the national self-image. Since the eighteenth century, the Russian governing elites have perceived their country as being charged with a special *mission civilisatrice*, destined to bring enlightenment and modern civilization to the benighted multitudes in Asia—both within Russia's "own Orient" and further afield, including China. This Russian version of the "white man's burden" rested—not unlike similar attitudes of the British and French colonial administrators—on the racist assumption of the Russians' superiority vis-à-vis the "yellow peoples." The spectacular reversal of China's and Russia's roles has turned upside down the Russians' long-standing perceptions of what is "civilized" and what is "backward" and acted as a kind of reality check that the Russian public finds particularly difficult to adjust to.

The upshot of the momentous transformation of Russia's geopolitical environment and of its impact on the very sense of what Russia is appears to be a growing sense of Russia's strategic isolation. Being cold-shouldered in the West by the arrogant attitude of the European Union, which is reluctant to see Russia as part of the Brussels-centered Europe, and overshadowed in the East by the increasingly assertive giant of China, Moscow appears doomed to a kind of geopolitical loneliness. Russia, as the Princeton historian Stephen Kotkin notes, "doesn't really belong to very much. . . . It doesn't belong in the West and it doesn't belong anywhere in the East. It hasn't found a place in the international order where it can pursue its own interests and enhance its interests in partnerships with other countries."[14]

It would thus appear that the foreign policy course of nonalignment—otherwise known as "strategic independence"—that the Russian leadership is currently pursuing is not so much a carefully designed and forward-looking strategy as a reaction to the fundamentally altered geopolitical landscape around Russia. In a way, it seems to be both a reflection of and an attempt to adapt to the situation of geopolitical loneliness. Russia's ruling elites believe that in these new unfavorable circumstances the country can reinvent itself as a great power only if it holds a leadership position in post-Soviet Eurasia. As the lands that used to be part of the "historic Russia," ex-Soviet republics of Central Asia constitute an important element of this geopolitical equation.

## Central Asia: Living Dangerously Between the Two Empires

Central Asia is conventionally understood as an area comprising five ex-Soviet republics: Kazakhstan, Kyrgyzstan, Tajikistan, Uzbekistan, and Turkmenistan. Yet from historical and geocultural standpoints the Central Asian region is much larger; it includes also China's province of Xinjiang as well as Inner and Outer Mongolia (i.e., Inner Mongolian Autonomous Region of China and the Republic of Mongolia).[15] This vast area's historic dynamic (with its "long cycles" of expansion and contraction) is best conceptualized as the protracted process of partition of what effectively became, in the words of Owen Lattimore, the "Inner Asian Frontier" populated largely by nomadic Turkic and Mongolian tribes between the two expanding sedentary empires—Russia and China—throughout the last three centuries.[16] The Soviet Union's breakup has released the western portion of historic Central Asia from its colonial bondage and thus created a geopolitical void that the other, more successful "nationalizing" empire—now called the People's Republic of China (PRC)—has hastened to fill in. The PRC's policies in Central Asia and its interaction with Russia in the region can be adequately understood only if China is perceived the way its governing elites perceive it: not as an outside actor but as a power both historically and strategically firmly imbedded in the region—primarily through Xinjiang, a huge chunk of Central Asia lying within the borders of the Chinese state. Xinjiang, as one Western analyst has aptly noted, "has [a] dual identity, being both 'China in Central Asia' and 'Central Asia in China.'"[17] It is precisely this historical and geographical reality that is behind Beijing's strategic interest in the other part of Central Asia that used to be a colonial possession of its imperial competitor—Russia/the USSR.

There are numerous parallels (as well as some significant divergences) between Russia's and China's advance and subsequent conduct in their respective zones of Central Asia.[18] The two imperial powers started penetrating the region from the opposite sides—one from the west, the other from the east—almost simultaneously. Although the three Kazakh Hordes accepted Russian protection in the 1730s to 1740s, in 1759 the Qing crushed the Mongol Zunghar state and conquered Xinjiang. This dual expansion set in motion a momentous process of the "closure of the steppe," to borrow Peter Purdue's felicitous phrase, that ultimately shaped the present-day borders of Russia, China, and the Central Asian states wedged between those two giants.[19]

By the end of the nineteenth century, most of the territory of Central Asia was under Russian or Chinese rule, and the frontiers between the two imperial domains were negotiated. Both the Qing and Romanov Russia were pursuing typically colonial policies in their Central Asian possessions, deploying cartographic and ethnographic knowledge to reorder the region and bring it under their administrative control. The two empires were initially seeking to govern the newly conquered peoples at a distance through indirect rule, relying mostly on local chieftains and preserving traditional ways. But as the nineteenth century was drawing to a close, the first attempts were made at more formal integration. In 1884 Xinjiang was given a provincial status and Qing officials were charged with the administration of the empire's "Western Frontier," and the Russian government launched in the mid-1890s a massive campaign of agricultural colonization of Turkestan and Southern Siberia. Between 1896 and 1916 more than one million colonists—mostly Russian and Ukrainian peasants—came into possession of one-fifth of the land in the Russian Turkestan.[20]

The first decades of the twentieth century saw Central Asia in a state of flux, following the nearly simultaneous demise of the Qing and the Romanov dynasties. However, the former imperial overlords managed to restore their control over the breakaway provinces. The Soviets reconquered their part of Central Asia in the early 1920s and soon afterward launched an unprecedented program of social engineering that involved the institutionalization of ethnic federalism, the realization of state-territorial delimitation, and the creation of the new national identities for the Central Asian peoples. For their part, the Chinese Communists reestablished China's sovereignty over Xinjiang in 1949, following their victory in the civil war with the Nationalists. Remarkably, although the PRC's "nationality policy" was informed by Marxist-Leninist ideology and influenced by Soviet practices, the Chinese Communist Party significantly modified its Soviet mentor's template of how to manage multiethnicity. Unlike the Soviets, who territorialized ethnicity by creating federal republics with their "titular nations" and the right (that was deemed would never be exercised) to secede from the Union, the PRC introduced a system of limited "regional national autonomy." The latter was envisioned as a tool to strengthen "unified, multiethnic" China. All autonomous regions were considered integral parts of the territory of the Chinese state, and regional organs of government operated under the unified leadership of the central government.[21] As David Kerr reminds us, "China is now the largest country in the world not to practice meaningful federalism. Instead it pursues an informal, ad hoc federalism of 'one country, many systems' that is supposed to solve problems as different as those of Taiwan, Hong Kong, Tibet, and Xinjiang."[22] The Sino-Soviet Cold War in the 1960s–1980s led to the extreme militarization of the border between the Soviet and the Chinese parts of Central Asia, the latter being completely insulated from one another and reoriented solely toward their respective "imperial centers"—Moscow or Beijing.

The Soviet implosion marks a crucial watershed in the history of the three-way interaction between Russia, China, and Central Asia as it appears to have come full circle. "The re-establishment of part of Central Asia's political independence with the collapse of the Soviet Union in 1991," Michael Clarke argues, "has resulted in the return of the region to a situation similar in a number of important respects to that which characterized the region during the 1700 to 1900 period." That was, Clarke says, "an era of the gradual apportionment of the region between the imperial states of Russia and China."[23] The sense that all three actors—Russia, China, and the now-independent states of Central Asia—are again in the process of transition does suggest a certain similarity with the past. Yet there is also an important distinction: the obvious fact that the Central Asian nations now enjoy full sovereignty and international recognition of their independence signifies a profound reversal of Russia's and China's roles in the region. While Moscow is trying to build new relations with ex-Soviet colonial possessions in Central Asia, Beijing is using Xinjiang—"China in Central Asia"—as a strategic asset and a bridgehead to project power and influence into the former domains of its old new rival.[24]

## Mutual Perceptions and the Burden of History

"Russia and China don't possess a 'difficult historical legacy' that would fuel mutual hostility," one Russian analyst argues in a recent article published in the leading Moscow policy journal. He goes on to say, "Along Russia's borders there isn't a single large state with which [our] country had less military conflicts throughout its history than with China." By contrast, he adds, Russo-Chinese cooperation aimed against the West has much deeper historical roots.[25] This statement reflects a dual misperception characteristic of the Russians' way of viewing their relationship with China. First, it claims that, by and large, the relationship has been of a friendly (if not cordial) nature—a view that once gave rise to the famous myth of the "unbreakable" Russo-Chinese friendship.[26] Second, it seems to suggest that Russia's relations with China had a certain moral character—one that the West's policies toward China definitely lacked.

True, skirmishes along the Russo-Chinese frontier were not nearly as gory as the wars Russia waged in the European theater. But this was largely because throughout the nineteenth century—the period of Russia's aggressive eastward expansion, including into Central Asia—China was a much weaker power, a clear underdog that could easily be pressured into making geopolitical concessions without resorting to raw force. It is worth remembering that the Chinese historiography characterizes a hundred years of the country's history—roughly between 1842 and 1949—as a "century of humiliation" precisely because the Chinese see this period as a time of troubles when their enfeebled country was unceremoniously pushed around by haughty Western powers, including Russia. In fact, following the Opium Wars, many Qing bureaucrats came to consider Russia as a more dangerous enemy than other major European powers because, unlike Western Europeans, the Russians were interested not in trade but in territorial aggrandizement. The distribution of Chinese foreign policy documents, as S. C. M. Paine's research has demonstrated, confirms Beijing's particular preoccupation with Russia. "Nearly half of all these materials relate to Russia, while less than a third deal with Great Britain, and less than a tenth concern Japan or the United States." Moreover, Paine notes,

> In these archival documents, Chinese officials, over and over again, describe Russian designs on Chinese territory, using such terms as "gnawing away like a silkworm," "gobbling up," "eyeing predatorily like a tiger," "drooling at the mouth," "insatiable," "having evil intentions," "desiring that which belongs to others," and "unfathomable" behavior.[27]

As Russia pushed deeper and deeper into Central Asia, it never hesitated to encroach on China's interests—or even undermine China's sovereignty over borderland territories—when its own strategic interests so demanded. Under the 1864 Treaty of Tarbagatai the Qing had to transfer to Russia 440,000 square kilometers of territory in the region northwest of Xinjiang—up to and including Lake Balkhash.[28] In 1871 the Russians deployed troops into the Ili Valley in Xinjiang to prevent local rebels from spreading the Muslim Uprising raging in the region in 1862–1878 across the border and joining forces with their religious brethren in the Russian-held part of Central Asia. Russia would withdraw its forces from most occupied territories only after the Chinese agreed—under the 1881 Treaty of St Petersburg—to make considerable trade concessions and pay a substantial indemnity. Following the Qing dynasty's fall in 1911, Russia did not waste much time before expanding its influence into Chinese Outer Mongolia. Although Russia itself was soon shaken by the 1917 Revolution, the Red Army's presence in Mongolia during the Russian civil war was instrumental in the transformation of this Chinese protectorate into a Soviet one—a process that culminated in the establishment of the Mongolian People's Republic in 1924.[29] Now, a quick look at the map shows that "China's northern border wraps around Mongolia, a giant territory that looks like it was once bitten out of China's back."[30] The period of the 1930s–1940s saw further expansion of Soviet influence in Xinjiang as the region was constantly rocked by Turkic-Muslim rebellions and local Han warlords were increasingly compelled to rely on the Soviet Union's support, military and otherwise.[31] In 1944, a revolt supported by the Soviets led to the establishment of the East Turkestan Republic (ETR) in the Ili Valley in the far northeast part of Xinjiang and the division of the region into the two parts controlled, respectively, by the Uighur nationalists of the ETR and the Chinese nationalist government of Chiang Kai-shek.[32] It was only in 1949 when the People's Liberation Army marched into the region that Beijing's sovereignty over Xinjiang was fully restored.

China's ruling elites' disdain at the Russian/Soviet heavy-handed treatment of their country's sovereignty and vital security interests can be clearly sensed in the remarkable exchange between Soviet leader Nikita Khrushchev and Mao Zedong. During their conversation in July 1958, Khrushchev asked Mao—apparently half-jokingly—if the Chinese "really consider us as red imperialists." To this the Great Helmsman gave a rather caustic reply: "There was a man by the name of Stalin, who took Port Arthur and turned Xinjiang and Manchuria into semi-colonies, and he also created four joint-stock companies [under the terms that proved very unfavorable for the Chinese]. There were all his good deeds."[33]

The gap between Russian and Chinese perceptions of the bilateral relationship is truly remarkable and appears to reflect the extent of mutual misunderstandings—particularly in Russia's case. Bobo Lo seems to be painting a more accurate picture when he writes in his analysis of the Chinese perceptions of Russia that "for much of the last three hundred years, Sino-Russian interaction has been tense, awkward, and occasionally confrontational."[34] Lo notes that policy makers on both sides may indeed claim that they "have consigned past antagonisms to the metaphorical dustbin of history." But this is false: "Historical memory continues to play a crucial role. Its impact is understated but unmistakable. . . . Its presence is all-pervasive, touching on every aspect—political, economic, strategic, and civilizational."[35]

### Central Asia (Re)Discovered: Redrawing the Fences in Russia's Backyard

There is a popular trope one often encounters in analytic literature these days—that of Central Asia's "discovery" at the turn of the twenty-first century. It looks something like this: following the Soviet empire's collapse and the subsequent emergence from under its rubble of five independent "-stans," the world suddenly became aware of the new Central Asian region and of its growing strategic importance. Although this may well be true for *some* parts of the world, it is certainly *not* true as far as Russia and China are concerned. For Moscow or Beijing, the 1991 Soviet meltdown did not produce previously hidden terra incognita; rather, it resulted in the dramatic shift in their respective geopolitical positions in the region where they have been interacting for the last three centuries. In a nutshell, what actually happened is this: The loss of the Soviet empire left Moscow without its Central Asian dominion. This region has now been reconfigured—with five brand-new states claiming Westphalian sovereignty. Russia's task then was to find new ways to reconnect with its former vassals and reassert its regional leadership. For its part, Beijing stood looking in amazement and bewilderment at what happened to its erstwhile rival. The overwhelming sentiment in China was not one of triumphalism but of anxiety: What did all this mean for the security of China's own Central Asian domain? How should it respond to new threats and challenges emanating from this huge geopolitical void across the border and affecting the stability of Beijing's rule in Xinjiang?

I argue that Russia's and China's differing policies in Central Asia have ultimately been shaped by historical legacies, by the two countries' sense of what they are, as well as by the need to find pragmatic solutions to numerous problems mostly pertaining to the spheres of security and energy. Last but not least, there is an important task of accommodating the two countries' interests in the region. It is also useful to keep in mind that Central Asia is only one element—and not necessarily the most important one—of Moscow and Beijing's strategic universes. Russia's evolving approach to Central Asia reflects a complex interplay of three broad perspectives or "agendas": the notion of "great power-ness" (*derzhavnost*) coupled with a historical tradition of the centuries-long regional hegemony, the security imperatives stemming from the region's volatility and potential instability spillover, and the domestic dimension that is embodied in the Russian public's growing concern about what it sees as the most negative consequence of "Eurasian" integration—namely, the massive influx of labor migrants from Central Asia.

Russia's most recent programmatic documents—the latest update of the Foreign Policy Concept and Foreign Minister Sergei Lavrov's article titled "The Philosophy of Russian Foreign Policy"—provide a good snapshot of the governing elite's strategic thinking.[36] The cornerstone of Russia's geopolitical vision is the notion of multipolarity.[37] Russia's fundamental interest is declared to be the "formation of a stable—ideally, self-regulating—polycentric system of international relations, in which Russia by rights plays the role of one of the key centers." It is the firm conviction of the Russian leadership that the main essence of the current period of global history lies in the "consistent development of multipolarity." The main building blocks of what Russian strategists call the "new international architecture" are regional integration associations. It is noteworthy that the "regionalist trend" is given a clear civilizational connotation. It is asserted that under the current conditions the significance of "civilizational identity" is being enhanced—a factor that, in its turn, prompts the world's leading powers to form "various civilizational blocs."[38]

Russia's top politicians have long argued for closer integration between Russia and several other post-Soviet countries—a process that should ultimately lead to the formation of the "Eurasian Union." As the analyst

Igor Okunev of Moscow State Institute of International Relations notes, the "restoration of a single Eurasian space, the former geopolitical niche of the Russian Empire and the Soviet Union," is the "main messianic idea of [Russian president] Vladimir Putin."[39] From Moscow's standpoint, the vision of the emerging Eurasian Union is strategically very important. According to the Kremlin's geopolitical outlook, Russia can successfully compete globally with the United States, China, and the European Union only if it acts as a leader of the regional bloc. By bringing Russia and its ex-Soviet neighbors into a closely integrated community of states, Russian strategists contend, would allow this Eurasian association to become one of the major centers of power that would participate on par with other such centers in global and regional governance. Remarkably, the ambition to build the "Eurasian Union" is also viewed as a remedy to Russia's unresolved problem of its international identity—what Kotkin describes as Russia being neither of the West nor of the East. The "Eurasian vision" appears to be the way out of this painful dilemma: Russia does not need to make a choice between West and East because it is a world unto itself—the center of Moscow-sponsored Eurasian civilization. In this context, Putin's pet project is an attempt to advance an alternative model of sociopolitical *and* civilizational development.[40]

The language of Russian policy papers should not be seen as just the rhetorical flourish. In fact, it reflects the huge importance the Kremlin attaches to the concepts of status, prestige, and privilege. As great power status lies at the heart of Russia's international identity, it is striving to achieve regional primacy in post-Soviet space, particularly in Central Asia, which is believed to be probably the only area left where Moscow can still act as a leader.[41] What matters is not just Russian influence per se but also the recognition of this influence by other major actors—something that is closely related to Russia's image and ranking in the international pecking order. For the country's governing elites, this is a very sensitive issue indeed, given the radical shift in the global balance of power over the last two decades. The thing is that there is a direct link between Russia's international status and the elites' ability to govern. As the former weakens, so does the latter's hold on power. The upshot of all this is that the Kremlin considers the reassertion of its regional dominance as no less important a task than pursuing some concrete and tangible material interests. However, as some Russian and international experts argue, in Central Asia, Moscow is seeking to pursue not a neo-imperial but, rather, a postimperial policy.[42] Its ultimate goal is not to rebuild a Russian empire or resurrect Soviet ties but to achieve indirect control over the regional countries and maximize Russia's interests there through deploying a still formidable arsenal of soft power (trade, investment, culture). Furthermore, to enhance international legitimacy and allay the suspicions of its weaker neighbors, Moscow operates in the region via a raft of multilateral organizations—such as the Eurasian Economic Union, the Customs Union, the Single Economic Space, and the Collective Security Treaty Organization (CSTO)—the bulk of which it sponsors itself, and one, the Shanghai Cooperation Organization (SCO), that it cosponsors with Beijing.

It is worthwhile to note at this point that Moscow's approach to Central Asia (including the integration blueprints for post-Soviet Eurasia) is part of Russia's broader strategy toward East Asia—an area that also comprises Russia's vast Far Eastern periphery. This strategy appears to pursue a three-pronged objective: (1) to enhance Moscow's strategic footprint in East Asia, (2) to better integrate into the region's prosperous economic networks and make good use of the economic potential of the dynamic Asia Pacific to revitalize Russia's depressed Far Eastern provinces, and (3) to use East Asia as a hedge against a stagnant Europe as well as to decrease Russia's overdependence on trade with European Union countries. For all the talk of Russia as a Euro-Asian country par excellence, there is a clear imbalance in terms of Russia's European and Asian trade; while the bulk of Russia's landmass lies beyond the Urals, less than a quarter of its trade is with Asia and more than a half with Europe. The Kremlin's goal seems to be to correct the excessive tilt toward Europe and transform Russia into what some commentators call a two-faced "Eurasian Janus that looks both ways"—to the west and to the east.[43] Thus, Putin wants the Eurasian Union to "become one of the poles in [the] contemporary world and at the same time to play the role of the efficient 'link' between Europe and the dynamic Asia Pacific region."[44] China, which Putin has characterized as a "paramount center of global economy,"[45] is seen by the Kremlin strategists as a key partner that would facilitate Russia's realizing its ambitious pivot to Asia.[46] "I am convinced that China's economic growth is by no means a threat, but a challenge that carries colossal potential for business cooperation—a chance to catch the Chinese wind in the sails of our economy," in particular by "smartly using Chinese potential for the economic development of Siberia and the Far East," Putin stated in his recent programmatic policy paper.[47] At the same time, the Kremlin leadership, being well aware of the growing power differential, is loath to find itself in the position of Beijing's junior partner in world affairs. The Eurasian Union that would comprise at least several Central Asian nations is meant to serve as a balance against China's formidable economic and political clout.[48] In a recent move meant to emphasize Moscow's status as Beijing's equal partner, the leaders of Russia and China made an agreement in May 2015 to link their countries' key integration projects: the Russia-led Eurasian Economic Union and China's Silk Road Economic Belt. "Essentially, we seek ultimately to reach a new level of partnership that will create a common economic space across the entire Eurasian continent," Putin said of the landmark accord.[49]

It would appear, though, that in its attempts to realize what one Western analyst calls "Putin's grand plan for Asia"—including Moscow's objective to reassert its regional primacy in Central Asia—Russia is being increasingly challenged by three formidable factors.[50] First is Moscow's own chronic inability to properly articulate its interests in Central Asia. Second is the profound shift in Russian public attitudes—namely, the growing prominence of what some analysts call a "Russia First" stance.[51] Its adherents strongly support the policies focused directly on "homeland security" and are clamoring for the country's disengagement from culturally "alien" lands. Finally, the factor whose impact on Russia's regional role is likely going to be the strongest in the long term is the steady expansion of China's influence in the region.

Russia's problems with elaborating a coherent policy toward the Central Asian countries flow out of Moscow's ambiguous approach to all its ex-Soviet dominions. The portrayal of post-Soviet space in civilizational terms—as a "natural geopolitical niche" of the "historic Russia," or as a "community of fate" striving to achieve its "historical destiny"—prompts Russian strategists to work out various integration schemes whereby Central Asia (or at least some regional countries such as Kazakhstan, Kyrgyzstan, and Tajikistan) would be locked into the Russia-led regional organizations, and their political and economic interactions with the outside world would be limited to the minimum. Such an arrangement, however, is impractical, and this appears to be recognized by the Russian leadership. As a Moscow top diplomat declared recently, "Russia does not claim an exclusive role in Central Asia and it is open for cooperation."[52] Yet the Kremlin cannot forgo its claim to the "privileged position" in the region because only this, it is assumed, would afford Moscow its coveted great-power status, which, in its turn, would help it play a significant role in global governance and strike bargains with the world's other great powers on matters unrelated to Central Asia. The outcome of such strategic ambivalence is a policy that is inconsistent, contradictory, and largely reactive, rather than proactive.

In the course of the recent discussion of Russia's Central Asia policy at the Moscow-based Institute of World Economy and International Relations (IMEMO), most participants agreed that "so far, we don't have any clearly articulated policy toward Central Asia whatsoever."[53] Analysts note that the country's leaders neither formulated what Russia's overall interests in the region were nor spelled out what the "zone of privileged interests" really meant. Aleksei Arbatov, one of Russia's most prominent security experts, puts it best:

> What are our economic interests in Uzbekistan or Tajikistan in concrete terms? What are our security interests? What do we want from them [Central Asians]? Finally, what are our military interests? Do we want our bases to be stationed there? What for? Which destinations to fly from those bases? We don't fly any-where—[we] just sit there for the sake of state prestige. We do have our base in Kant [Kyrgyzstan]. Where do our airmen fly from this base? By contrast, the Americans do fly from Manas [US air base in Kyrgyzstan; American troops va-cated the base in 2014]—they carry out certain operations connected with [their military effort in] Afghanistan. But our [airmen] simply sit on the ground. This is what our policy actually boils down to.[54]

Notably, while Russia is striving for the leadership role within the CSTO, its leaders seem reluctant to take up political and moral obligation to maintain peace and security, conduct peacekeeping operations, prevent the outbursts of mass violence and suppress pogroms no matter which eth-nic group is targeted. The 2010 interethnic riots in southern Kyrgyzstan laid bare the weakness of the CSTO as an institution that is incapable of either preventing such conflicts from happening or quickly resolving them when they erupt. It is also true, however, that when the CSTO was founded in 2002, its charter did not envision the possibility of the organization's inter-ference into the member-states' domestic affairs in case of internal crises. It was only at the end of 2011 that the decision was taken to allow the CSTO's Collective Rapid Reaction Force to be involved when there is a domestic crisis situation that a member-state is unable to deal with on its own.

Similarly, a deficit of clarity and coherence is characteristic of Russia's approach to Afghanistan.[55] Most Russian experts agree that the potential deterioration of the Afghan situation following the 2016 planned withdrawal of US armed forces from the country would pose a serious threat to some particularly fragile Central Asian regimes and as a result endanger Russia's security as well. However, they seem to disagree in their assessments of the concrete parameters of this potential threat and, consequently, of the scale of Russia's possible involvement. Although some analysts (e.g., Arbatov) are convinced that "in case of the Taliban's revanche we'll have to fight" to defend Central Asia and ultimately Russia's 7000 kilometers-long porous border with Kazakhstan, other specialists (e.g., Aleksei Malashenko) argue that the *direct* "Islamist threat" to Russia proper does not exist and that "the Taliban march on Kazan" is a figment of sickly imagination.[56] At the same time, these experts say, a persistent threat to the Central Asian nations "from the South" is a leverage that Moscow tries to make good use of to press regional strongmen preoccupied with their own political survival to exclusively align themselves with Russia on security matters.[57] Likewise, the Russian leadership appears to be of two minds regarding the US military presence in Central Asia. For sure, Moscow's main worry is that, following the drawdown of Western military involvement in Afghanistan, the situation in this fractious country might become even more chaotic with the turmoil spilling over into the volatile Central Asian region. There seems to be an understanding in the Kremlin that such development would seriously jeopardize the realization of Moscow's pet geopolitical project—the formation of the Eurasian Union. "We have a strong interest in our southern borders being calm," Putin said recently. "We need to help them [US and coalition forces]. Let them fight. . . . This is in Russia's national interests."[58] Yet the Russian leaders remain deeply suspicious of American designs. "Having announced their exit from Afghanistan in 2014, Americans are busy setting up there and in the neighboring [Central Asian] states their military bases without any clear-cut mandate, aims, and terms of their operation," Putin noted in his detailed analysis of the Russian foreign policy strategy. "To be sure, we don't like this."[59] Some of Russia's senior officials express their opinion on the matter in a much blunter manner. "If the price for security in Central Asia is a continued US presence there," one senior Russian diplomat recently said, "that price is unacceptable for us."[60] In spring 2013, Russian top brass announced the formation of a Special Operations

Command. The move, which apparently reflects the sense of Central Asia's potential vulnerability, involves the creation of a special force that will be used exclusively outside Russian territory.[61] The jury is still out, however, on how efficient this new command might be.

Thus a key strategic issue—how far Moscow is prepared to go to maintain security in Central Asia—remains unresolved. Russia appears to be facing a difficult dilemma: either to take up a mission of providing comprehensive stability and security to the volatile region, or to voluntarily disengage from the region's security field and focus solely on what might threaten Russia directly. Some scholars suggest that at the end of the day Moscow is likely going to make a choice in favor of the second option and characterize this shift as the emergence of a "Russia First" strategy.[62] The trend toward disengagement seems to be further strengthened by the profound shift in Russian public attitudes. In the minds of the growing numbers of Russians, millions of Central Asian labor migrants working in the large Russian cities came to be increasingly associated with drug smuggling, other types of criminal offense, and violence. Migration is a complex phenomenon across the board, and it plays a particularly controversial role in the relations between Russia and the Central Asian nations. On the one hand, migration provides one of the strongest links connecting the Russian and Central Asian societies. But on the other hand, it acts as a major irritant, fostering alienation and enmity between different ethnic communities and giving a boost to Russian nationalist sentiment and xenophobia.[63] It is noteworthy, however, that the social forces engaged in the critique of migration are much broader than the pockets of Russian skinheads. In fact, the discussion of migration's impact on Russian society is increasingly becoming an important element of the discourse on Russian foreign policy and of Russian identity. As they analyze this sensitive aspect of Russia—Central Asia relations, Russian political thinkers ranging from moderate nationalists to Westernizing liberals challenge the economic, political, and ideational premises of the Kremlin strategy.[64]

Here is the thrust of their argument. Because of Central Asia's relative poverty and low purchasing power of its population, the region cannot be considered as an important export market for Russian businesses. The volume of Russian exports to the Central Asian countries is lower than the amount of money transferred to those countries from Russia by migrant workers. Closer integration will compel Russia to support the countries whose living standards are six to fifteen times lower than Russia's. That's why Russia's joining any integration associations with the Central Asian nations is counterproductive and fraught with huge financial losses. Instead of integrating with Central Asia Moscow's priority should be to limit the inflows of migrants through the introduction of visa regime with regional countries. Furthermore, the system of "geopolitical subsidizing"—whereby the Central Asian states earn more through exploiting the visa-free regime with Russia than Russia makes through doing trade with those countries—has negative political consequences. This system effectively provides the backing for the region's authoritarian, corrupt, and parasitical regimes. With Russia readily absorbing the next contingent of the region's surplus labor, the local rulers are given a booster shot; potential rebels get out, and additional money gets in. Finally, domestic critics of the Kremlin strategy point out its compensatory, "quasi-imperial" function. Instead of resolutely rethinking Russia as a nation-state and sorting out the country's "true" national interest, Moscow continues to be mired in the ambiguous phase of "postimperium"—still desperate to assert its regional privilege and attain great power status. Yet the "Eurasian integration" that results in "swamping" Russia with millions of Central Asian laborers is precisely what prevents Russia from transcending the postimperial stage and reasserting its European identity. While radical demographic changes that the massive migration is bringing in its wake make the task of building the Russian nation ever more difficult, the "Eurasian" geopolitical orientation distracts Russia from what some critics consider to be the country's "historical choice"—the European civilization.[65] Thus, one Russian analyst notes, "domestic considerations dictate the need to control, contain, erect protective barriers, and detach from the region, with which Russian society no longer feels a cultural continuity."[66]

But the factor that arguably will have the strongest impact on the geopolitical landscape of Central Asia in the long run is China. The reversal of China's and Russia's roles in the region as a result of the steady growth of Beijing's influence and the decrease of Moscow's is nicely captured in a pithy Western comment: "Central Asia once may have been Russia's backyard, but China has redrawn the fences."[67] Indeed, the difference between the outcomes of Russia's and China's policies in the region cannot be more glaring. Russia has famously declared that its key objective is to restore its regional primacy and become one of the main centers of power in a multipolar system. But how exactly are we to measure a country's success in attaining primacy or privileged role? International relations specialists note that these are relative notions: a sense of a state's own status is ultimately a function of its relations with the other states.

By contrast, China has never said that it seeks a leadership role and always deferred to Russia as a principal power in Central Asia. What Beijing did say is that its intent was to pursue a policy of "engaging the periphery" as an important element of its overarching strategy of "peaceful rise."[68] Remarkably, China's success in implementing this policy is relatively easy to measure. Over the last several years, the PRC has become Central Asia's main trading partner (having pushed Russia out of this position); deeply penetrated the region's commodities sector as dozens of Chinese businesses cut lucrative deals with local companies; made regional states dependent on China by providing large-scale credits to local governments; played a key role in the major overhaul of the region's infrastructure, seeking to enhance interdependency between ex-Soviet Central Asia and Chinese Central Asia; and, last but not least, tapped into the region's rich hydrocarbon resources by constructing two major energy pipelines—the ones that for the first time in many decades do not traverse Russian territory. This development that effectively broke Moscow's stranglehold on the region's energy market deserves special mention as it has reshaped a Sino-Russian energy relationship in a way that greatly benefits Beijing (and the energy-rich Central Asian nations). Previously, as a monopolist controlling fuel transportation networks, Russia had much stronger bargaining position vis-à-vis both China (as an energy consumer) and the Central Asian countries (as energy producers forced to export the fuel exclusively in westerly direction through the pipes they did not control). Now, the opening of the new Beijing-sponsored export routes for oil and gas leading eastwards to China makes it possible for the Chinese and Central Asians to haggle Moscow down.

Being in no position to prevent China's expansion into its former backyard, the Kremlin had to quietly acquiesce to the move. Recent Sino-Russian energy mega deals—on the supply of oil with Rosneft and of gas with Gazprom—have amply demonstrated Beijing's subtle modus operandi. The strategic partnership with China appears to help Moscow realize its two strategic goals—to reorient its energy export flows away from Europe and toward East Asia while receiving multibillion-dollar loans from Beijing and to secure long-term supply contracts with China accompanied by lavish

Chinese prepayments. Yet there is a downside: China is keen to obtain Russian oil and gas at below world market prices.[69] The true outcome of Sino-Russian energy cooperation, according to Stephen Kotkin, is that it "confirm[s] Moscow's real status as largely a supplier of raw materials."[70]

Why did Russia and China perform so differently in Central Asia? The main reason is that following the Soviet Union's disintegration, Russia's and China's positions relative to Central Asia were drastically altered. After 1991, Russia and the five Central Asian nations emerged as the *new* states that never existed as sovereign polities within their *new* borders at any time in history. Russia ceased to be an empire, but it did not become a regular nation-state. Instead, it has found itself in an ambivalent postimperial situation and has been faced with a difficult task of postimperial readjustment, which is a very complicated and essentially an open-ended process. That is why Moscow keeps looking at Central Asia with a proprietary eye and its policies toward the region are informed by the strong sense of historical entitlement. As the control (if only a symbolic one) over former imperial periphery is seen as a marker of great power status and the latter is deemed inseparable from Russia's identity, there is no wonder that in Moscow's approach to Central Asia the issues of prestige and privilege often took precedence over concrete economic and political matters.

China, however, is a very different geopolitical animal. Unlike Moscow, Beijing did not lose its *own* Central Asian periphery. In fact, the PRC has managed to keep most of the Qing dynasty's imperial domains. It could be argued that, in a certain sense, today's China is still an imperial polity—but one of a very special kind. Unlike a classical empire whose system of government and legitimacy rest on *diversity*, the PRC's ruling elites consistently used the institutions of modern states to attain societal *cohesion* and forge the Chinese nation. They unapologetically consider nationalism as a cornerstone of their legitimacy.[71] Thus, in the words of Dominic Lieven, China "is an empire that has been more successful than others in making a transition toward national state."[72]

Beijing's approach to ex-Soviet Central Asia after 1991 has been essentially a "comprehensive security project."[73] Given the fact that China's Central Asian dominion—Xinjiang Uighur Autonomous Region (XUAR)—is not an ordinary far flung border region but a former imperial periphery with its special ethno-religious characteristics and a long tradition of political unrest, the central government's primary task was to secure its rule in XUAR.

Here we have a good example of the irony of history: the collapse of one empire (and the rise of new security threats that accompany such collapse) served as a powerful incentive for the other imperial polity to consolidate its rule in its own peripheries and to tie them up ever closer with all other territories that in their totality constitute China's national "geobody."[74] Thus Beijing's Central Asia policy should be understood as an extension of its "Go West" policy that has primarily been driven by domestic considerations. But there is a high degree of interconnectedness between the two. The PRC's elites hold that the best way to keep XUAR stable is to deliver economic growth, and the opening up to Central Asia is seen as key to sustain steady economic development of Xinjiang.[75] Basically, Beijing is pursuing a two-pronged strategy seeking to increase economic interdependency between Central Asia and XUAR and to make the Central Asian rulers dependent on China to such an extent that they would never ever risk playing the Uighur card.

The PRC is implementing this strategy by cultivating bilateral relations with the Central Asian nations and also through its multilateral instrument of choice—the so-called China's "new regionalism" embodied in the SCO. Here again the difference between the Chinese and Russian practices is remarkable. Although the Russian-sponsored regionalism in its form emulates the Western templates (such as the European Union and North Atlantic Treaty Organization), the way it actually works diverges from that of the Western organizations as its main goal is to serve as an instrument of Russia's regional hegemony or at least as a marker of its primacy. China's "new regionalism" appears to be a more subtle operation. It is defined by "open, functional, interest-based cooperation among contiguous states" that rests on a solid foundation of a mutual respect for the member-states' sovereignty.[76] In this definition, the principle of sovereignty is key, and it refers above all to China's own sovereignty and control of XUAR. Yet the "new regionalism" helps Beijing reach some other goals as well: it makes the expansion of Chinese businesses into Central Asia much smoother, and it is often deployed to counter what the Chinese elites call US unilateralism. Interestingly, however, some Chinese and Central Asian scholars suggest that it would be a mistake to believe that China interprets international relations concepts—such as multilateralism—in the same way the Western nations do. They argue that China's "new regionalism" is in fact a result of the modernization, transformation, and adaptation of the model of interstate relations that was formed during the imperial epoch as an element of the Chinese overall concept of the world order.[77] China's practice of multilateralism, then, is an attempt to deploy the transformed and modified tributary system/vassalization to project its power and influence into the region and ultimately have the Central Asian nations recognize Beijing's primacy—in a way similar to the way the Middle Kingdom dealt with "barbarians" on its western frontier.[78]

## Conclusion

So are we witnessing the emergence of the new regional hegemon in Central Asia? The tentative answer is, well, not yet. First, most observers agree that Beijing is not interested in playing such a role. "China has little interest in becoming the regional hegemon, but it aspires to recognition as a strategic principal in Central Asia."[79] Second, even if the Chinese governing elites were more ambitious, the realization of their hegemonic plans would encounter serious obstacles. For starters, hegemons are usually not well liked. Although Beijing is not yet a hegemon and vigorously denies having the aspirations of becoming one, China's phenomenal rise, tremendous wealth, and formidable military muscle have already bred a lot of suspicions, resentment, and fear in Central Asia. As they say, success breeds its own challenges. It also does not help when the Chinese—ranging from big time politicians to petty traders—behave in the region in an overbearing and arrogant manner. In summer 2006, a Western scholar doing a field research on the Chinese-Kyrgyz border met a Chinese businessman from Kashgar who bluntly told him, "The people here know who makes the decisions these days and ever since the Russians left: it's us."[80] But history is never short of ironies, and this dramatic reversal of roles (the Russians are out; the Chinese are in) has definitely produced another one. As Niklas Swanstrom has nicely put it, "China has now taken many of the roles that Russia once played, including that of being feared and distrusted."[81] It is precisely because China is feared today in Central Asia, probably more than Russia, that the local rulers would not want to see Russia exit completely. Instead of being left one-on-one with the giant of China, they want their weakened former overlord to stay so that they can continue happily playing Beijing and Moscow off against one another and thus maximizing their strategic room for maneuver.[82] For the short to medium term, Russia, vacillating between the desire to reassert itself and the pressure to disengage, will be nervously watching what used to be its Central Asian backyard, where China will continue to methodically redraw the fences. The crucial question, of course, is how far the fences will be moved. "The frontiers of China are moving even if its boundaries are not," one Indian analyst has said recently.[83] But this is not exactly true. As a result of border negotiations between the PRC and the four post-Soviet states—Russia, Kazakhstan, Kyrgyzstan, and Tajikistan—China's boundaries did move. Remarkably, Beijing's weakest neighbor, Tajikistan, had to surrender almost one percent of its territory to China. This brings us back to von Hörnigk's astute comment that postulated the decisive role of power differential in relations between states. What will happen if the asymmetry of the relationship deepens? Will the existing border regime survive? This is a moot question: "No border, after all, is immutable and the logic of history is that over time, borders drift with local and national self-interest."[84]

*Notes*

1. Michael Mann, "Introduction: Empires with Ends," in *The Rise and Decline of the Nation State*, ed. Michael Mann (Oxford: Basil Blackwell, 1990), 1.

2. William H. McNeill, "Introductory Historical Commentary," in *The Fall of Great Powers: Peace, Stability, and Legitimacy*, ed. Geir Lundestad (New York: Oxford University Press, 1994), 7.

3. Paul Kennedy, *The Rise and Fall of the Great Powers: Economic Change and Military Conflict from 1500 to 2000* (New York: Vintage, 1989).

4. Ibid., xxii.

5. David Gosset, "Xi Jinping's Long March to Defeat the West's Fear of China," *World Post*, March 15, 2013, http://www.huffingtonpost.com/david-gosset/xi-jinpings-long-march-to_b_2881145.html.

6. Dmitri Trenin, *True Partners? How Russia and China See Each Other* (London: Center for European Reform, 2011), 1.

7. See Marlene Laruelle and Sebastien Peyrouse, *Globalizing Central Asia: Geopolitics and the Challenges of Economic Development* (Armonk, NY: M. E. Sharpe, 2013); Marlene Laruelle and Sebastien Peyrouse, *The Chinese Question in Central Asia: Domestic Order, Social Change and the Chinese Factor* (London: Hurst, 2012); Alexander Cooley, *Great Games, Local Rules: The New Great Power Contest in Central Asia* (New York: Oxford University Press, 2012); Robert E. Bedeski and Niklas Swanstrom, eds., *Eurasia's Ascent in Energy and Geopolitics: Rivalry or Partnership for China, Russia and Central Asia* (New York: Routledge, 2012); S. Enders

Wimbush, "Great Games in Central Asia," in *Strategic Asia 2011–12: Asia Responds to Its Rising Powers—China and India*, ed. Jessica Keough, Travis Tanner, and Ashley J. Tellis, (Seattle, WA: National Bureau of Asian Research, 2011), 259–282; Niklas Swanstrom, "China and Greater Central Asia: New Frontiers?" Central Asia-Caucasus Institute and Silk Road Studies Program, Silk Road Papers, December 2011, http://www.silkroadstudies.org/resources/pdf/SilkRoadPapers/2011_12_SRP_Swanstrom_China-Central-Asia.pdf; Niklas Swanstrom, "China and Central Asia: A New Great Game or Traditional Vassal Relations," *Journal of Contemporary China* 14, no. 45 (2005): 569–584; Emilian Kavalski, ed., *The New Central Asia: The Regional Impact of International Actors* (Singapore: World Scientific, 2010); Marlene Laruelle, Jean-Francois Huchet, Sebastien Peyrouse, and Bayram Balci, eds., *China and India in Central Asia: A New "Great Game"?* (New York: Palgrave Macmillan, 2010); Vladimir Boyko, "Endangered Heartland: Russian Central Asia Between Domestic and External Geopolitics," in *Eurasian Perspectives: In Search of Alternatives*, ed. Anita Sengupta and Suchandana Chatterjee (New Delhi: Shipra, 2010), 1–14; Eugene Rumer, Dmitri Trenin, and Zhao Huasheng, *Central Asia: Views from Washington, Moscow, and Beijing* (Armonk, NY: M. E. Sharpe, 2007); Anita Sengupta, *Russia, China and Multilateralism in Central Asia* (New Delhi: Shipra, 2005); Martin Spechler and Dina Spechler, "Russia's Lost Position in Central Asia," *Journal of Eurasian Studies* 4 (2013): 1–7; Stephen Blank, "Whither the New Great Game in Central Asia?" *Journal of Eurasian Studies* 3 (2012): 147–160; Stephen Blank, "The End of Russian Power in Asia?" *Orbis* 56, no. 2 (2012): 249–266; Yelena Zabortseva, "From the 'Forgotten Region' to the 'Great Game' Region: On Development of Geopolitics in Central Asia," *Journal of Eurasian Studies* 3 (2012): 168–176; Rouben Azizian and Elnara Bainazarova, "Eurasian Response to China's Rise: Russia and Kazakhstan in Search of Optimal China Policy," *Asian Politics and Policy* 4, no. 3 (2012): 377–399; Julie Wilhelmsen and Geir Flikke, "Chinese-Russian Convergence and Central Asia," *Geopolitics* 16, no. 4 (2011): 865–901; James MacHaffie, "China's Role in Central Asia: Security Implications for Russia and the United States," *Comparative Strategy* 29, no. 4 (2010): 368–380; James Bosbotinis, "Sustaining the Dragon, Dodging the Eagle and Barring the Bear? Assessing the Role and Importance of Central Asia in Chinese National Strategy," *China and Eurasia Forum Quarterly* 8, no. 1 (2010): 65–81; V. V. Naumkin, I. D. Zvyagel'skaya, and A. V. Grozin, *Interesy Rossii v Tsentral'noi Azii: Soderzhanie, perspektivy, ogranichiteli* [Russia's interests in Central Asia: Contents, perspectives, constraints] (Moscow: Rossiiskii Sovet po Mezhdunarodnym Delam [Russian International Affairs Council], 2013); Aleksei Malashenko, *Tsentral'naia Aziia: Na chto rasschityvaet Rossiia?* [Central Asia: What is Russia's calculus?] (Moscow: ROSSPEN, 2012); G. I. Chufrin, *Rossiia v Tsentral'noi Azii* [Russia in Central Asia] (Almaty, Kazakhstan: KISI, 2010); D. B. Malysheva, *Tsentral'noaziatskii uzel mirovoi politiki* [The Central Asian nexus of global politics] (Moscow: IMEMO, 2010); A. Bogaturov, ed., *Mezhdunarodnye otnosheniia v Tsentral'noi Azii: Sobytiia i dokumenty* [International relations in Central Asia: Developments and documents] (Moscow: Aspekt Press, 2011); A. Bogaturov, A. S. Dundich, and E. F. Troitskly, *Tsentral'naia Aziia: "Otlozhennyi neitralitet" i mezhdunarodnye otnosheniia v 2000-kh godakh* [Central Asia: "Delayed neutrality" and international relations in the 2000s] (Moscow: NOFMO, 2010); and S. V. Zhukov and O. B. Reznikova, *Tsentral'naia Aziia i Kitai: Ekonomicheskoe vzaimodeistvie v usloviiakh globalizatsii* [Central Asia and China: Economic interaction in globalization era] (Moscow: IMEMO, 2009).

8. I borrow the term from Dmitri Trenin; it refers to a relatively long period of imperial exit and postimperial condition. See Dmitri Trenin, *Post-imperium: Evraziiskaia istoriia* [Post-imperium: A Eurasian story] (Moscow: ROSSPEN, 2012).

9. Quoted in L. J. Butler, *Britain and Empire: Adjusting to a Post-imperial World* (London: I. B. Tauris, 2002), 167.

10. David Kerr, "Dilemmas of the 'Middle Continent': Russian Strategy for Eastern Eurasia," *International Spectator* 44, no. 2 (2009): 76.

11. Petr Chaadaev, "Letters on the Philosophy of History," in *Russian Intellectual History: An Anthology*, ed. Marc Raeff (Amherst, NY: Humanity Books, 1999), 166–167.

12. Perry Anderson, "Russia's Managed Democracy," *London Review of Books* 29, no. 2 (2007), http://www.lrb.co.uk/v29/n02/perry-anderson/russias-managed -democracy.

13. Ibid. (emphasis added).

14. Stephen Kotkin, "Soviet Collapse and Russia's Path to the Present," *Washington Profile*, March 13, 2009. Kotkin's view appears to be widely shared by other Western analysts who describe Russia's current position as strategic/civilizational isolation. According to Fiona Hill and Bobo Lo, Russia is "caught between an East to which it does not belong and a West in which it does not easily fit." See Fiona Hill and Bobo Lo, "Putin's Pivot: Why Russia Is Looking East," *Foreign Affairs*, July 31, 2013, http:// www.foreignaffairs.com/articles/139617/fiona-hill-and-bobo-lo/putins-pivot.

15. See Peter B. Golden, *Central Asia in World History* (New York: Oxford University Press, 2011); S. A. M. Adshead, *Central Asia in World History* (London: Macmillan, 1993).

16. See Owen Lattimore, "Inner Asian Frontiers: Chinese and Russian Margins of Expansion," in *Studies in Frontier History: Collected Papers, 1928–1958* (Paris: Mouton, 1962), 134–159; and Owen Lattimore, *Pivot of Asia: Sinkiang and the Inner Asian Frontiers of China and Russia* (Boston: Little, Brown, 1950).

17. David Kerr, "Central Asian and Russian Perspectives on China's Strategic Emergence," *International Affairs* 86, no. 1 (2010): 140. For a more detailed

discussion of Xinjiang's history, see Michael Clarke, *Xinjiang and China's Rise in Central Asia: A History* (New York: Routledge, 2011); James A. Millward, *Eurasian Crossroad: A History of Xinjiang* (New York: Columbia University Press, 2007); S. Frederick Starr, ed., *Xinjiang: China's Muslim Borderland* (New York: M. E. Sharpe, 2004); and Gardner Bovingdon, "The History of the History of Xinjiang," *Twentieth Century China* 26, no. 2 (2000): 95–139.

18. For the discussion of some of these parallels during the early modern period, see Victor Lieberman, "The Qing Dynasty and Its Neighbors," *Social Science History* 32, no. 2 (2008): 281–304.

19. See Peter C. Perdue, "Boundaries, Maps, and Movement: Chinese, Russian, and Mongolian Empires in Early Modern Central Eurasia," *International History Review* 20, no. 2 (1998), 263.

20. Golden, *Central Asia*.

21. Colin Mackerras, *China's Minorities: Integration and Modernization in the Twentieth Century* (New York: Oxford University Press, 1994).

22. Kerr, "Central Asian and Russian Perspectives," 128.

23. Michael Clarke, "The 'Centrality' of Central Asia in World History, 1700–2008: From Pivot to Periphery and Back Again," in *China, Xinjiang and Central Asia: History, Transition and Crossborder Interaction into the 21st Century*, ed. Colin Mackerras and Michael Clarke (New York: Routledge, 2009), 29.

24. Amy Kardos, "A New 'Frontier Thesis' for the Northwest Chinese Borderland? The Reinvention of Xinjiang from a Place of Chinese Exile to a Land of Opportunity," *Central Eurasian Studies Review* 7, no. 2 (2008): 7–12.

25. Vasily Kashin, "Summa vsekh strakhov: Factor kitaiskoi ugrozy v rossiiskoi politike" [The sum total of all fears: The factor of the Chinese threat in Russian politics], *Rossiia v Global'noi Politike* [Russia in Global Affairs], no. 2 (2013), http://eng.globalaffairs.ru/number/The-Sum-Total-of-All-Fears-15935.

26. As one line from the Soviet song of the 1950s "Moscow-Beijing" had it, "A Russian and a Chinaman are brothers forever."

27. S. C. M. Paine, *Imperial Rivals: China, Russia, and Their Disputed Frontier* (New York: M. E. Sharpe, 1996), 10–11.

28. This and the other two "unequal treaties"—of Aigun (1858) and of Peking (1860)—saw the Qing emperor surrendering to Russia a staggering 1.5 million square kilometers of territory. See Paine, *Imperial Rivals*.

29. However, the Chiang Kai-shek government would recognize Outer Mongolia's independence from China only in 1945, following Stalin's promises to provide Soviet support to the Nationalists.

30. Robert D. Kaplan, "The Geography of Chinese Power," *Foreign Affairs* 89, no. 3 (2010): 28.

31. Andrew D. W. Forbes, *Warlords and Muslims in Chinese Central Asia: A Political History of Republican Sinkiang, 1911–1949* (Cambridge: Cambridge University Press, 1986).

32. Linda Benson, *The Ili Rebellion: The Muslim Challenge to Chinese Authority in Xinjiang, 1944–1949* (New York: M. E. Sharpe, 1989).

33. Vladislav M. Zubok, "The Mao-Khrushchev Conversations, July 31–August 3, 1958 and October 2, 1959," *Cold War International History Project Bulletin* 12–13 (2001): 254.

34. Bobo Lo, "How the Chinese See Russia," *Russie.Nei.Reports*, no. 6 (2010): 6. A contemporary Russian perspective is well represented in Aleksandr V. Lukin, ed., *Rossiia i Kitai: Chetyre veka vzaimodeistviia* [Russia and China: Four centuries of interaction] (Moscow: Ves' Mir, 2013). See also Gilbert Rozman's review of this study: "Russian Perceptions of Sino-Russian Relations," *Asan Forum*, July 19, 2013, http://www.theasanforum.org/russian-perceptions-of-sino-russian-relations/.

35. Bobo Lo, *Axis of Convenience: Moscow, Beijing, and the New Geopolitics* (Baltimore: Brookings Institution Press, 2008), 17–18.

36. Ministry of Foreign Affairs of the Russian Federation, "Kontseptsiia vneshnei politiki Rossiiskoi Federatsii" [Concept of the foreign policy of the Russian Federation], February 18, 2013, http://www.mid.ru/foreign_policy/official_documents/-/asset_publisher/CptICkB6BZ29/content/id/122186?p_p_id=101_INSTANCE_CptICkB6BZ29&_101_INSTANCE_CptICkB6BZ29_languageId=en_GB; Sergei Lavrov, "Vneshnepoliticheskaia filosofiia Rossii" [The philosophy of Russian foreign policy], *Mezhdunarodnaia Zhizn'* [Foreign Affairs], no. 3 (2013), http://archive.mid.ru//brp_4.nsf/o/8D9F4382C2ACD54744257B400 05117DF.

37. For more on the interpretation of the notion of multipolarity in Russia and China, see V. Ya. Portyakov, "Videnie mnogopoliarnosti v Rossii i Kitae i mezhdunarodnye vyzovy" [Perspectives on multipolarity in Russia and China and international challenges], *Sravnitel'naia Politika* [Comparative Politics], no. 1 (2013): 86–97.

38. See Lavrov, "Vneshnepoliticheskaia filosofiia Rossii." For an interesting discussion of Russia's "civilizational turn," see Andrei Tsygankov, "Vladimir Putin's Civilizational Turn," *Russian Analytic Digest*, no. 127 (2013): 5–7.

39. Igor Okunev, "Vneshniaia politika dlia bol'shinstva?" [A foreign policy to suit the majority?], *Rossiia v Global'noi Politike* [Russia in Global Affairs], no. 2 (2013), http://eng.globalaffairs.ru/number/A-Foreign-Policy-to-Suit-the-Majority-16049.

40. Ibid.

41. Malashenko, *Tsentral'naia Aziia*, 7.

42. Trenin, *Post-imperium*; Lo, *Axis of Convenience*; Cooley, *Great Games*.

43. David Pilling, "Russia Begins Its Slow Pivot to Asia," *Financial Times*, September 12, 2012, http://www.ft.com/intl/cms/s/0/512ddcba-fc3c-11e1-acof -00144feabdco.html. For a critical perspective on Russia's Asian pivot, see Hill and Lo, "Putin's Pivot."

44. Vladimir Putin, "Novyi integratsionnyi proekt dlia Evrazii: Budushchee, kotoroe rozhdaetsia segodnia" [A new integration project for Eurasia: The future in the making], *Izvestiia* [News], October 3, 2011, http://izvestia.ru/news/502761.

45. Vladimir Putin, "Rossiia i meniaiushchiisia mir" [Russia and the changing world], *Moskovskie Novosti* [Moscow News], February 27, 2012, http://valdaiclub .com/politics/39300.html.

46. See Dmitri Trenin, "From Greater Europe to Greater Asia? The Sino-Russian Entente," Carnegie Moscow Center, April 2015, http://carnegieendow ment.org/files/CP_Trenin_To_Asia_WEB_2015Eng.pdf.

47. Putin, "Rossiia i meniaiushchiisia mir."

48. For detailed discussions of the Eurasian Union project, see S. Frederick Starr and Svante E. Cornell, eds., *Putin's Grand Strategy: The Eurasian Union and Its Discontents* (Washington, DC: Central Asia-Caucasus Institute, 2014), http:// www.silkroadstudies.org/resources/1409GrandStrategy.pdf; and Sean Roberts, Anais Marin, Arkady Moshes, and Katri Pynnoniemi, *The Eurasian Economic Union: Breaking the Pattern of Post-Soviet Integration?* (Helsinki: Finnish Institute of International Affairs, 2014), http://www.fiia.fi/en/publication/439/the_eurasian _economic_union.

49. Ivan Nechepurenko, "Russia-China Alliance Could Launch New World Order," *Moscow Times*, June 15, 2015, http://www.themoscowtimes.com/news/ article/russia-china-alliance-could-launch-new-world-order/523711.html.

50. Richard Weitz, "Putin's Grand Plan for Asia," *The Diplomat*, March 13, 2012, http://thediplomat.com/2012/03/putin-grand-plan-for-asia/.

51. Anna Matveeva, for example, has suggested recently that "a 'Russia First' strategy" may be in the making. See Anna Matveeva, "Selective Engagement: Russia's Future Role in Central Asia," *Central Asia Policy Brief*, no. 3 (2012): 1, http:// centralasiaprogram.org/blog/2012/07/08/selective-engagement-russias-future-role -in-central-asia.

52. Cooley, *Great Games*, 72.

53. See "Tsentral'naia Aziia v kontekste afganskoi situatsii" [Central Asia in the context of the situation in Afghanistan], *Mirovaia Ekonomika i Mezhdunarodnye Otnosheniia* [World Economy and International Relations], no. 5 (2011): 9.

54. Ibid., 12.

55. For a more detailed discussion of Russia's Afghanistan policy, see Ekaterina Stepanova, "Afghanistan After 2014: The Way Forward for Russia," *Russie.Nei.Vi-*

*sions*, no. 71 (2013), https://www.ifri.org/sites/default/files/atoms/files/ifristepa
novanatoafghanistanrussiaengmay2013.pdf; Alexander Lukin, "Central Asia and
Afghanistan in Russia's Strategy," *International Affairs* 57, no. 5 (2011): 57–63; and
Dmitri Trenin and Alexei Malashenko, *Afghanistan: A View from Moscow*
(Washington, DC: Carnegie Endowment for International Peace, 2010).

56. See Arbatov's remarks in "Tsentral'naia Aziia v kontekste afganskoi
situatsii," 13; and Malashenko, *Tsentral'naia Aziia*, 87.

57. Malashenko, *Tsentral'naia Aziia*, 87–88.

58. Michael Bohm, "Why Putin Wants U.S. Bases in Afghanistan," *Moscow
Times*, May 17, 2013, http://www.themoscowtimes.com/opinion/article/why
-putin-wants-us-bases-in-afghanistan/480087.html.

59. Putin, "Rossiia i meniaiushchiisia mir."

60. Alexander Golts, "Alone Against the Taliban," *Moscow Times*, May 14,
2013, http://www.themoscowtimes.com/opinion/article/alone-against-the-taliban/
479917.html.

61. See Dmitri Trenin, "Russia's New Tip of the Spear," *Foreign Policy*, May 8,
2013, http://www.foreignpolicy.com/articles/2013/05/08/russia_new_special_ops_
command_afghanistan.

62. See Matveeva, "Selective Engagement."

63. Marlene Laruelle, "Russian Policy on Central Asia and the Role of Russian
Nationalism," Central Asia-Caucasus Institute and Silk Road Studies Program,
Silk Road Papers, April 2008, http://www.silkroadstudies.org/resources/pdf/
SilkRoadPapers/2008_04_SRP_Laruelle_Russia-Central-Asia.pdf.

64. See Vladislav Inozemtsev, "Gde russkim zhit' khorosho" [The place where
Russians live happily], *Vedomosti* [News], May 14, 2013, http://www.vedomosti
.ru/opinion/articles/2013/05/14/gde_russkim_zhit_horosho; Vladislav Inozemtsev,
"Rossii pora otdelit'sia ot byvshego SSSR" [Russia should secede from the former
Soviet Union], *Moskovskii Komsomolets* [Moscow Young Communist League Mem-
ber], April 22, 2013, http://www.mk.ru/specprojects/free-theme/article/2013/
04/21/844895-rossii-pora-otdelitsya-ot-byivshego-sssr.html; Vladimir Milov, "Kar-
tochnyi domik evraziistva" [The Eurasianism's house of cards], *Gazeta*, April 22,
2013, http://www.gazeta.ru/comments/column/milov/5267145.shtml; and Kirill Rodionov, "Samolikvidatsiia Rossii" [Self-liquidation of Russia], *Nezavisimaia
Gazeta* [Independent Newspaper], May 17, 2013, http://www.ng.ru/ideas/2013-05-17/
5_samolikvidatsia.html.

65. See Kirill Rodionov, "Tabuirovannyi vopros nashego vremeni: Pochemu
mul'tikul'turalizm nesovmestim s demokratiei" [The question of our time that
is taboo: Why multiculturalism is incompatible with democracy], *Nezavisimaia
Gazeta* [Independent Newspaper], September 25, 2013, http://www.ng.ru/
ideas/2013-09-25/5_tabu.html; and Kirill Rodionov, "Mezhdu imperiei i

natsional'nym gosudarstvom" [Between the empire and the national state], *Nezavisimaia Gazeta* [Independent Newspaper], June 24, 2013, http://www.ng.ru/ideas/2013-06-24/9_democracy.html. For a more detailed discussion of the attitudes toward migration in Russia, see A. Gorodzeisky, A. Glikman, and D. Maskileyson, "The Nature of Anti-immigrant Sentiment in Post-Socialist Russia," *Post-Soviet Affairs* 31, no. 2 (2015): 115–135; Vladimir Malakhov, "Russia as a New Immigration Country: Policy Response and Public Debate," *Europe-Asia Studies* 66, no. 7 (2014): 1062–1079; and Mikhail Alexseev, "Societal Security, the Security Dilemma, and Extreme Anti-migrant Hostility in Russia," *Journal of Peace Research* 48, no. 4 (2011): 509–523.

66. Matveeva, "Selective Engagement," 3.

67. Cooley, *Great Games*, 96.

68. See Michael Clarke, "'Making the Crooked Straight': China's Grand Strategy of 'Peaceful Rise' and Its Central Asian Dimension," *Asian Security* 4, no. 2 (2008): 107–142.

69. Assessing the Sino-Russian oil deal, Aleksei Maslov, head of the School of Asian Studies at the Higher School of Economics in Moscow, noted that "maybe the most striking point is not just [that there was] a new agreement with Rosneft, but first of all, it is the price of this oil, which is much lower than average world prices." See Richard Solash, "Despite Wariness, China-Russia Relations Warming," *Radio Free Europe/Radio Liberty*, August 9, 2013, http://www.rferl.org/content/russia-china-relations-warming/25070935.html. See also Erica S. Downs, "Money Talks: China-Russia Energy Relations After Xi Jinping's Visit to Moscow," Brookings Institution, April 1, 2013, http://www.brookings.edu/blogs/up-front/posts/2013/04/01-china-russia-energy-relations-downs; and Nina Poussenkova, "Russia's Eastern Energy Policy: A Chinese Puzzle for Rosneft," *Russie.Nei.Visions*, no. 70 (2013), http://www.ifri.org/sites/default/files/atoms/files/ifrirnv70poussen kovarosneftengapril2013.pdf.

70. Stephen Kotkin, "Mr. Xi Goes to Moscow," *New York Times*, March 27, 2013, http://www.nytimes.com/2013/03/28/opinion/global/mr-xi-goes-to-moscow .html.

71. Magnus Fiskesjo, "Rescuing the Empire: Chinese Nation-Building in the Twentieth Century," *European Journal of East Asian Studies* 5, no. 1 (2006): 15–44; Zheng Yongnian, *Discovering Nationalism in China: Modernization, Identity and International Relations* (Hong Kong: Cambridge University Press, 1999).

72. Dominic Lieven, "Imperiia, istoriia i sovremennyi mirovoi poriadok" [Empire, history and contemporary world order], in *Mify i zabluzhdeniia v izuchenii imperii i natsionalizma* [Myths and misconceptions in the study of empire and nationalism], ed. Ilia Gerasimov, Marina Mogilner, and Aleksandr Semyonov

(Moscow: Novoe Izdatel'stvo [New Publishing House], 2010), 311. Some scholars, however, would argue that China's transition to nation-state has not been completed and that it will yet have to deal with its own "imperial exit." Thus, McNeill notes that "China . . . continue[s] to preside over an old-fashioned polyethnic empire, though stirrings of discontent in Tibet and along China's inner Asian borderlands are not far to seek." McNeill, "Introductory Historical Commentary," 7. See also Dru C. Gladney, *Dislocating China: Muslims, Minorities and Other Subaltern Subjects* (London: Hurst, 2004); and Thomas Heberer, *China and Its National Minorities: Autonomy or Assimilation?* (Armonk, NY: M. E. Sharpe, 1989).

73. Steven Blank, "Kazakhstan's Border Relations with China," in *Beijing's Power and China's Borders: Twenty Neighbors in Asia*, ed. Bruce A. Elleman, Stephen Kotkin, and Clive Schofield (Armonk, NY: M. E. Sharpe, 2013), 103; Russel Ong, "China's Security Interests in Central Asia," *Central Asian Survey* 24, no. 4 (2005): 425–439.

74. For more on the concept of "geobody," see William A. Callahan, "The Cartography of National Humiliation and the Emergence of China's Geobody," *Public Culture* 21, no. 1 (2009): 141–173.

75. Zhao Yueyao, "Pivot or Periphery? Xinjiang's Regional Development," *Asian Ethnicity* 2, no. 2 (2001): 197–224.

76. Chien-peng Chung, "The Shanghai Cooperation Organization: China's Changing Influence in Central Asia," *China Quarterly* 180 (2004): 993.

77. For a discussion of Central Asia in the context of traditional China's world order, see Joseph F. Fletcher, "China and Central Asia," in *The Chinese World Order: Traditional China's Foreign Relations*, ed. John K. Fairbank (Cambridge, MA: Harvard University Press, 1968), 206–224.

78. Kushtarbek Shamshidov, "Podkhod Kitaia k mul'tilateralizmu v kontekste ego otnoshenii so stranami Tsentral'noi Azii" [China's approach toward multilateralism in the context of its relations with Central Asian countries], *Tsentral'naia Aziia i Kavkaz* [Central Asia and the Caucasus] 15, no. 4 (2012): 25–50; Zheng Yongnian, ed., *China and International Relations: The Chinese View and the Contribution of Wang Gungwu* (New York: Routledge, 2011); Chung Chien-peng, *China's Multilateral Cooperation in Asia and Pacific: Institutionalizing Beijing's "Good Neighbor Policy"* (New York: Routledge, 2010); Chung Chien-peng, "The Shanghai Cooperation Organization: China's Changing Influence in Central Asia," *China Quarterly* 180 (2004): 989–1009. Some Western scholars cautiously agree with this interpretation of China's "new regionalism." Thus, Michael Clarke has advanced a "nuanced view of the 'vassalization' of Central Asia, whereby China provides Central Asia with certain economic or political/security goods, for example through SCO, in return for guarantees regarding the issue of Uighur

'separatism' in Xinjiang." See Michael Clarke, "China and the Shanghai Coopera-tion Organization: The Dynamics of 'New Regionalism,' 'Vassalization,' and Geopolitics in Central Asia," in Kavalski, ed., *The New Central Asia*, 135.

79. Lo, *Axis of Convenience*, 101.

80. Steven Parham, *Controlling Borderlands? New Perspectives on State Peripher-ies in Southern Central Asia and Northern Afghanistan* (Helsinki: Finnish Institute of International Affairs, 2010), 59.

81. Niklas Swanstrom, "Central Asia and Russian Relations: Breaking Out of the Russian Orbit?" *Brown Journal of World Affairs* 19, no. 1 (2012): 112.

82. Lattimore commented on Central Asia's peculiar geopolitical position half a century ago: "The Inner Asian frontier has great and powerful peoples [Russians and Chinese] on more than one side. Its peoples therefore have some degree of choice. Whether their ultimate fate be subjugation or association and alliance, they can try to influence the decision by their own action." See Lattimore, "Inner Asian Frontiers," 157.

83. Kerr, "Central Asian and Russian Perspectives," 127.

84. Mark Galeotti, "Sino-Russian Border Resolution," in *Beijing's Power and China's Borders: Twenty Neighbors in Asia*, ed. Bruce A. Elleman, Stephen Kotkin, and Clive Schofield (Armonk, NY: M. E. Sharpe, 2013), 263.

# TWELVE

# China and South Asia
## The Economic Dimension

*Vivek Arora, Hui Tong, and Cristina Constantinescu*

China and South Asia are home to three billion people and account for a substantial and growing portion of the global economy. The magnitude and character of their economic linkages and interactions are changing in ways that could have a profound impact on the region and the world. This chapter examines two such linkages: the extent of trade and financial integration and the extent of competition and complementarities in China's economic interaction with the countries of South Asia. *South Asia,* as used in this chapter, refers to Afghanistan, Bangladesh, Bhutan, India, Maldives, Nepal, Pakistan, and Sri Lanka.

The chapter is organized as follows. The first section discusses the rapidly growing roles of China and South Asia in the global economy and, in this context, the trade and financial linkages between China and South Asia. These linkages have increased significantly since 2000, but there is still substantial scope for mutual benefit from closer economic integration. The second section discusses the benefits of closer economic integration between China and South Asia for the countries involved. The third section examines issues related to competition and complementarities in their labor-abundant economies in order to illustrate the extent to which they are competitors in global export markets for labor-intensive goods and their ability to complement each other by performing different functions in transnational supply chains or because they specialize in different niches. A brief final section identifies some of the challenges that China and South Asia will face in the decades ahead. These challenges include harnessing the benefits of closer integration while managing the risks; further rebalancing demand in order to sustain strong growth; developing adequate social safety nets; dealing with changing demographics, such as population aging in China; developing financial systems that support economic development while being well supervised and regulated; and developing an appropriate strategy for capital account liberalization. How these challenges are handled will have significant consequences for individual countries, the region, and the world.

## China, South Asia, and the Global Economy

China and South Asia are growing rapidly and playing increasingly important roles in the global economy. But they could play an even bigger role if still-limited trade and financial linkages among the constituent nations were expanded to unlock gains from trade, knowledge spillovers, risk sharing, and diversification. The benefits of doing so would have potentially profound consequences for the region and the more than 40 percent of the world's people who live there.

As of 2012, China and South Asia had a combined gross domestic product (GDP) of $10.5 trillion (at market exchange rates) and accounted for 15 percent of world GDP (Tables 12.1 and 12.2). Two decades ago, their share of world GDP was less than 4 percent. On a purchasing power parity (PPP) basis, they accounted for 22 percent of world GDP in 2012; in 1990 it was only 8 percent. Together, China and South Asia contributed nearly 2 percentage points to the 4.5 percent average annual growth rate of the global economy during 2008–2012. This is a marked change from the less than 1 percentage point contribution they made to the 7 percent annual world growth during 1990–1994 (Table 12.3).

China's contribution to global GDP during recent decades has been substantially larger than that of South Asia. In 1990, China and South Asia each accounted for nearly 2 percent of world GDP. But by 2012, China's GDP of $8.2 trillion (market exchange rates) accounted for 11.5 percent of world GDP. In contrast, South Asia's $2.3 trillion GDP accounted for 3.2 percent. Within South Asia, India is by far the largest economy, accounting for 80 percent of regional GDP. Pakistan, the next largest regional economy, contributes 10 percent. Comparable figures for other states in the

TABLE 12.1

China's and South Asia's shares in the world GDP

| Country | 1990 | | 2012 | |
|---|---|---|---|---|
| | At market exchange rate (%) | At purchasing power parity (%) | At market exchange rate (%) | At purchasing power parity (%) |
| **China** | 1.8 | 3.9 | 11.5 | 14.9 |
| **South Asia** | 1.9 | 4.1 | 3.2 | 6.9 |
| Afghanistan | 0.0 | 0.0 | 0.0 | 0.0 |
| Bangladesh | 0.1 | 0.3 | 0.2 | 0.4 |
| Bhutan | 0.0 | 0.0 | 0.0 | 0.0 |
| India | 1.5 | 3.2 | 2.5 | 5.6 |
| Maldives | 0.0 | 0.0 | 0.0 | 0.0 |
| Nepal | 0.0 | 0.0 | 0.0 | 0.0 |
| Pakistan | 0.2 | 0.6 | 0.3 | 0.6 |
| Sri Lanka | 0.0 | 0.1 | 0.1 | 0.2 |

SOURCE: IMF *World Economic Outlook* database, October 2012, http://www.imf.org/external/pubs/ft/weo/2012/02/weodata/index.aspx.

NOTE: South Asia totals may be off by 0.1 percent because of rounding.

TABLE 12.2

China and South Asia: GDP and regional shares, 2012

| Country | AT MARKET EXCHANGE RATE | | AT PURCHASING POWER PARITY | |
|---|---|---|---|---|
| | Billions of US$ | Percentage of total | Billions of $ | Percentage of total |
| **China** | 8,227 | | 12,406 | |
| **South Asia** | 2,283 | 100 | 5,714 | 100 |
| Afghanistan | 20 | 1 | 34 | 1 |
| Bangladesh | 123 | 5 | 306 | 5 |
| Bhutan | 2 | 0 | 5 | 0 |
| India | 1,825 | 80 | 4,684 | 82 |
| Maldives | 2 | 0 | 3 | 0 |
| Nepal | 19 | 1 | 41 | 1 |
| Pakistan | 232 | 10 | 515 | 9 |
| Sri Lanka | 59 | 3 | 126 | 2 |

SOURCE: IMF *World Economic Outlook* database, April 2013, http://www.imf.org/external/pubs/ft/weo/2013/01/weodata/index.aspx.

NOTE: Totals for South Asia may be slightly off because of rounding.

TABLE 12.3
China's and South Asia's contributions to world GDP
growth (in percent, PPP basis)

|  | 1990–1994 | 2008–2012 |
|---|---|---|
| **World** | 7.0 | 4.4 |
| **China** | 0.6 | 1.4 |
| **South Asia** | 0.3 | 0.5 |
| Afghanistan | — | 0.0 |
| Bangladesh | 0.0 | 0.0 |
| Bhutan | 0.0 | 0.0 |
| India | 0.2 | 0.4 |
| Maldives | 0.0 | 0.0 |
| Nepal | 0.0 | 0.0 |
| Pakistan | 0.0 | 0.0 |
| Sri Lanka | 0.0 | 0.0 |

SOURCE: IMF *World Economic Outlook* database, http://www
.imf.org/external/ns/cs.aspx?id=28.

NOTE: South Asia totals may be off by 0.1 percent because of
rounding. Dash indicates unavailable data.

region are 5 percent for Bangladesh; 3 percent for Sri Lanka; and less than 1
percent each for Afghanistan, Nepal, Bhutan, and Maldives (see Table 12.2).

TRADE INTEGRATION

Trade linkages between China and South Asia have increased in recent
years, but they are still relatively small in comparison with comparable linkages in other parts of the world and with the predictions of trade theory.
The role of China in South Asia's trade increased substantially after China's
accession to the World Trade Organization (WTO) in 2001. Merchandise
trade with China accounted for around 10 percent of South Asia's external
trade in 2012, up from only 3 percent in 2000 (Table 12.4 and Figures 12.1
and 12.2), and was equivalent to 4 percent of South Asia's GDP. China is
much more important to South Asia as a source of imports than as a destination for exports, accounting for 12 percent of South Asia's imports but
only 5 percent of its exports.

The importance of trade with China varies across South Asian countries (see Figure 12.1). For each country, the share of trade with China has

TABLE 12.4
China and South Asia: bilateral merchandise trade

|  | 1990 | 2000 | 2012 |
|---|---|---|---|
| Share of China in South Asia's trade (%) | 1.2 | 2.7 | 9.6 |
| Trade with China as a share of South Asia's GDP (%) | 0.2 | 0.7 | 4.1 |
| Share of South Asia in China's trade (%) | 1.3 | 1.2 | 2.5 |
| Trade with South Asia as a share of China's GDP (%) | 0.3 | 0.5 | 1.1 |

SOURCE: IMF *Direction of Trade Statistics* database, http://elibrary-data.imf.org/finddatareports.aspx?d=
33061&e=170921; IMF *World Economic Outlook* database, http://www.imf.org/external/ns/cs.aspx?id=28.
NOTE: GDP is evaluated at market exchange rates.

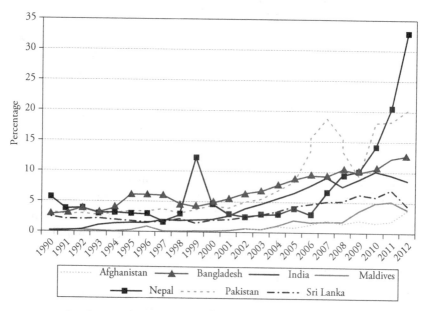

FIGURE 12.1 South Asia's trade with China as a percentage of each country's trade
SOURCE: IMF *Direction of Trade Statistics* database, http://elibrary-data.imf.org/finddatareports.aspx?d=
33061&e=170921; IMF *World Economic Outlook* database, http://www.imf.org/external/ns/cs.aspx?id=28

increased gradually over the past two decades, with the path becoming
steeper since 2001. The share has increased particularly sharply for Pakistan
and Nepal since 2006, doubling to 20 percent in 2012 for Pakistan and rising sixfold to over 30 percent for Nepal. For Pakistan, the increase reflects a
rise in both exports and imports after the China-Pakistan free trade agreement (FTA) was signed in November 2006.[1] In Nepal, the increase reflects

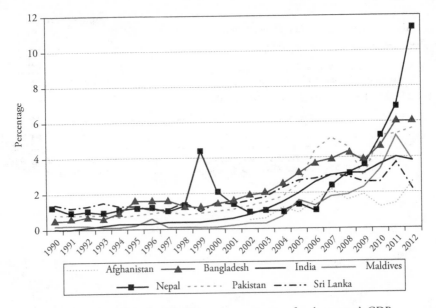

FIGURE 12.2 South Asia's trade with China as a percentage of each country's GDP
SOURCE: IMF *Direction of Trade Statistics* database, http://elibrary-data.imf.org/finddatareports.aspx?d=
33061&e=170921; IMF *World Economic Outlook* database, http://www.imf.org/external/ns/cs.aspx?id=28

mainly a substantial uptick in imports from China, which may be related to a rise in foreign direct investment (FDI) from China in construction and energy projects. China's share of total trade with South Asian countries ranges from around 5 percent in the case of Afghanistan, Maldives, and Sri Lanka to more than 30 percent for Nepal.

The commodity composition of trade between China and South Asia comprises mainly exports of intermediate products and raw materials from South Asia to China and exports of more advanced capital goods and man-ufactures from China to South Asia. For example, Table 12.5 shows the top five exports from China to India and from India to China. A feature of the trade composition is its high concentration; in each direction, the top five exports account for nearly two-thirds of total bilateral exports. The high concentration in intermediate and raw materials, which are relatively undif-ferentiated products, may make South Asian exports to China quite vulner-able to cyclical volatility.[2]

The role of South Asia in China's trade is much smaller than the role of China in South Asia's trade. South Asian countries accounted for only

TABLE 12.5

China and India: five most important exports, as a percentage of total exports, 2011

| Product category | | Share of bilateral exports |
|---|---|---|
| **China's exports to India** | | |
| 84 | Nuclear reactors, boilers | 25.0 |
| 85 | Electrical mchy equip parts thereof | 20.7 |
| 29 | Organic chemicals | 9.2 |
| 31 | Fertilisers | 7.0 |
| 73 | Articles of iron or steel | 4.3 |
| **India's exports to China** | | |
| 26 | Ores, slag and ash | 25.8 |
| 52 | Cotton | 16.8 |
| 74 | Copper and articles thereof | 11.2 |
| 27 | Mineral fuels, oils | 9.7 |
| 29 | Organic chemicals | 5.2 |

SOURCE: *United Nations Commodity Trade Statistics Database* (UN Comtrade), http://comtrade.un.org.

NOTE: Product category codes and names use the Harmonized System (HS) 1988/92 tariff nomenclature.

2.5 percent of China's external merchandise trade as of 2012, equivalent to just 1 percent of China's GDP (see Table 12.4 and Figure 12.3). It is true, however, that the share of South Asia in China's trade rose sharply after 2000, when it had stagnated at just over 1.2 percent of the total for at least a decade. India accounts for the largest share of China's trade with South Asia (70 percent), followed by Pakistan and Bangladesh.

Although the trade linkages between China and South Asia have increased substantially since 2001, they are still relatively small. For example, the United States accounts for approximately 40 percent of the external trade of the rest of the Western Hemisphere countries (North and South America and the Caribbean) and Germany for around 15 percent of the trade of other European countries (Figures 12.4 and 12.5). These shares substantially outweigh that of China in South Asia. In Africa, it is true that South Africa accounts for only around 5 percent of the trade of other sub-Saharan African countries, but its share in the trade of other South African

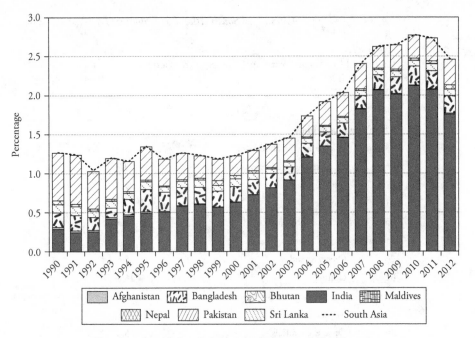

FIGURE 12.3 China's trade with South Asia as a percentage of China's trade

SOURCE: IMF *Direction of Trade Statistics* database, http://elibrary-data.imf.org/finddatareports.aspx?d=33061&e=170921; IMF *World Economic Outlook* database, http://www.imf.org/external/ns/cs.aspx?id=28

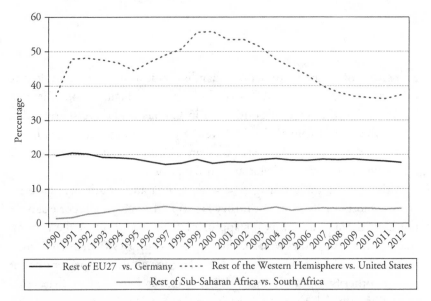

FIGURE 12.4. Trade linkages for select economies: share of trade with largest regional economy (percentage of regional trade)

SOURCE: IMF *Direction of Trade Statistics* database, http://elibrary-data.imf.org/finddatareports.aspx?d=33061&e=170921; IMF *World Economic Outlook* database, http://www.imf.org/external/ns/cs.aspx?id=28

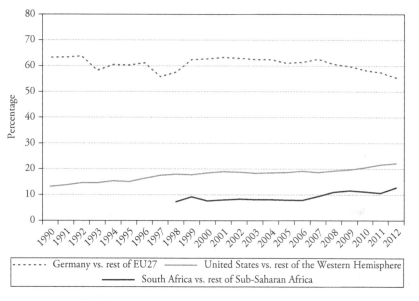

FIGURE 12.5 Trade linkages for select economies: trade with the region (percentage of total trade)

SOURCE: IMF *Direction of Trade Statistics* database, http://elibrary-data.imf.org/finddatareports.aspx?d= 33061&e=170921; IMF *World Economic Outlook* database, http://www.imf.org/external/ns/cs.aspx?id=28

Development Community and Southern African Customs Union countries is much larger.

China-South Asia trade is also small in comparison with even simple predictions such as those based on the gravity model, which holds that trade between two entities is directly related to the product of their economic size (GDP) and inversely related to the distance between them. Historical estimates in the literature suggest that a decade ago China-India trade was only 15 to 40 percent of its potential based on gravity considerations.[3] Our own estimates, based on more recent data, bear out these conclusions, particularly with respect to South Asia's exports to China.

Before turning to the estimation, however, it is instructive to note that even an informal inspection of the data suggests that gravity considerations would predict far greater trade than actually exists between the two regions. The share of individual South Asian nations in the region's trade with China directly reflects their relative sizes (Figures 12.6 and 12.7). India is by far the largest South Asian economy, and correspondingly, it accounts for the bulk

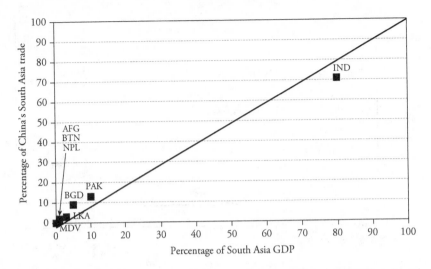

FIGURE 12.6 The size of selected economies in South Asia and the value of their trade with China, 2012

SOURCE: IMF *Direction of Trade Statistics* database, http://elibrary-data.imf.org/finddatareports.aspx?d= 33061&e=170921; IMF *World Economic Outlook* database, http://www.imf.org/external/ns/cs.aspx?id=28

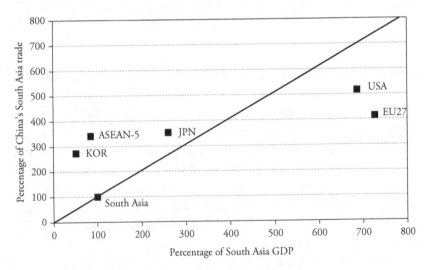

FIGURE 12.7 Selected groups' and countries' economic size and trade with China, 2012

SOURCE: IMF *Direction of Trade Statistics* database, http://elibrary-data.imf.org/finddatareports.aspx?d= 33061&e=170921; IMF *World Economic Outlook* database, http://www.imf.org/external/ns/cs.aspx?id=28

of South Asia's trade with China. Pakistan is next, although its share is substantially smaller than India's, followed by Bangladesh and the other smaller economies.

How much does geographical distance limit China-South Asia trade? A crude way to take distance into account is to compare China's trade with South Asia and its trade with other economies or groups of economies that share two characteristics. First, they must be roughly the same size as South Asia and, second, they must be roughly the same distance from China as is South Asia. Korea is roughly half the size of South Asia in terms of GDP, and the ASEAN-5 group (five of the members of the Association of Southeast Asian Nations—Indonesia, Malaysia, the Philippines, Singapore, and Thailand) is roughly equivalent in size to South Asia. Both being in Asia, their distance from China is more comparable than the distances from the United States or Europe. However, the ASEAN-5 group's trade with China, as well as Korea's trade with China, is much larger than is South Asia's trade with China.

To be sure, several considerations that influence bilateral trade are not reflected in the figure. Korea is geographically closer to China than South Asia and, therefore, may be expected to trade more extensively with China than South Asia does. It is also true that the short direct distance from China to South Asia may understate the effective distance for many types of trade, because sea routes are much longer. That is, topography and distance from China's major production centers may contribute significantly to the shortfall in South Asia's trade with China relative to what considerations of size and distance alone would suggest. Moreover, ASEAN, which might be more similar to South Asia in terms of distance, has an FTA with China. Exports of vertically integrated electric and electronic components to China have come to play an important role in the exports of many ASEAN countries. Notwithstanding all of these considerations, the difference in trade shares seems still to be very large, with Korea's and the ASEAN-5's trade with China being nearly three times and more than three times, respectively, the size of South Asia's trade with China.

Geopolitical and foreign policy factors probably inhibit trade, but we do not attempt to estimate the role of these factors, even though it has been suggested that they are so important that it can seem naïve to ignore them. In our view, however, gravity-type assessments remain useful because they help answer the important question of how large trade between partner countries *could* be if these factors were absent and trade barriers were low. They represent, in other words, a notion of what could be possible.

More formally, one can estimate the effect of size and distance on China's trade and examine how its trade with South Asia, in particular, looks in comparison with the overall picture. To estimate the gravity model for China, we examined 2,313 observations on trade in goods between China and 180 countries from 2000 to 2012 (annual data). The trade data are taken from the International Monetary Fund's Direction of Trade Statistics database. The dependent variable is the log of the US dollar value of China's exports (imports) of goods to (from) all its partner countries, with missing values treated as zero. Consistent with standard estimation of gravity models, we control for log GDP and log GDP per capita (both in PPP dollars) of both China and its partner countries and for bilateral distance weighted by population. A dummy for South Asia is added to examine whether China-South Asia trade is higher or lower than gravity-model predictions.

The results are shown in Table 12.6 (a pooled OLS estimation). In column 2, which examines other countries' imports from China, the coefficient for partner countries' log GDP is positive and significant, and that for distance is negative and significant. These findings are consistent with gravity considerations. The dummy variable for South Asia is negative and significant. In particular, based on the point estimate, South Asia's imports from China are roughly 33 percent lower than the gravity model would predict.[4] In column 3, a dummy variable added separately for India also turns out to be negative but insignificant. Based on the point estimate, Indian imports from China are 50 percent lower than gravity model predictions. In column 4, which examines other countries' exports to China, the South Asia dummy again has a negative coefficient, suggesting that South Asia's exports to China are 90 percent lower than gravity model predictions. In column 5, a dummy for India suggests that Indian exports to China are 85 percent lower than gravity considerations alone would suggest. The results indicate, therefore, that compared with non-Asian countries, South Asian countries have smaller imports and exports with China than predicted by the gravity model. By contrast, Table 12.6 also shows that *Southeast* Asia's trade with China is *larger* than predicted by the gravity model.

Before ending the discussion of the gravity model estimation, it is worth noting a matter of interpretation. The underlying factors driving gravity models may be different in Asia than in Europe and North America.

TABLE 12.6

Gravity model for trade of goods between China and the world

| | LOG IMPORTS FROM CHINA | | LOG EXPORTS TO CHINA | |
|---|---|---|---|---|
| | Without control for India | With control for India | Without control for India | With control for India |
| Log GDP (China's partner) | 0.977*** (80.08) | 0.979*** (79.13) | 1.478*** (60.73) | 1.473*** (59.60) |
| Log GDP (China) | 11.76 (0.83) | 11.73 (0.83) | 52.01* (1.90) | 52.18* (1.90) |
| Log GDP per capita (China's partner) | 0.0222 (1.07) | 0.0206 (0.99) | −0.0759* (−1.91) | −0.0724* (−1.82) |
| Log GDP per capita (China) | −10.57 (−0.71) | −10.55 (−0.71) | −53.09* (−1.85) | −53.27* (−1.86) |
| Weighted distance | −0.0182** (−2.45) | −0.0180** (−2.42) | −0.0577*** (−4.09) | −0.0580*** (−4.11) |
| 1 for South Asia | −0.376*** (−3.05) | −0.332** (−2.55) | −2.564*** (−10.94) | −2.656*** (−10.75) |
| 1 for India | | −0.360 (−1.08) | | 0.731 (1.18) |
| 1 for East Asia | 1.942*** (11.56) | 1.940*** (11.54) | 1.923*** (6.11) | 1.928*** (6.12) |
| 1 for Southeast Asia | 0.685*** (6.24) | 0.684*** (6.23) | 0.940*** (4.54) | 0.943*** (4.55) |
| Constant | 2.780 (1.60) | 2.787 (1.61) | 8.911*** (2.68) | 8.915*** (2.68) |
| Observations | 2,313 | 2,313 | 2,226 | 2,226 |
| R-squared | 0.832 | 0.832 | 0.720 | 0.720 |

NOTE: *t*-statistics in parentheses; *$p < 0.1$, **$p < 0.05$, ***$p < 0.01$.

Whereas in Europe and North America the relevance of size and distance is motivated by the search for new markets and lower production costs, in Asia the motivation is often to establish new bases for the production of exports. Abundant labor supply and low wages initially attracted a wave of Japanese FDI to Hong Kong Special Administrative Region, Korea, Taiwan Province of China, and Singapore during the 1960s and 1970s. Subsequently, as the latter economies developed, their FDI as well as Japan's sought out the abundant supply of low-cost labor, first in Southeast Asia and then in China. As incomes rose in Asia, final demand in the region began to play a greater role in determining the composition and volume of intra-Asian trade. China's FDI and trade relationships have followed this general pattern with the important exception that securing supplies of natural resources has been a major additional factor.[5]

FINANCIAL INTEGRATION

Another aspect of the economic linkages between China and South Asia is financial integration. Data on bilateral capital flows are not available on as systematic or comprehensive a basis as they are for trade flows, making it hard to ascertain the extent of financial integration with any precision. However, the picture that can be pieced together from anecdotal evidence and the little available data is that financial integration is very limited in size and is confined largely to FDI. Portfolio flows are minimal across the two regions and so are bank loans, although anecdotal reports suggest that, on occasion, South Asian corporations have relied on Chinese bank financing.

In 2011, China's direct investment flows to South Asia amounted to less than $1 billion. Pakistan accounted for 37 percent of the total and Afghanistan and India for 33 percent and 20 percent, respectively (Figures 12.8, 12.9, and 12.10). China's FDI has been concentrated in the energy, construction, and transport sectors. Conversely, South Asian direct investment flows to China amounted to just under $60 million, of which about three quarters came from India. A development in more recent years is the growing role of China in financing public investment in South Asia through, for example, lending to the public sector and through private-public partnerships.[6] Overall, the level of financial integration is low relative to that in other comparable cases globally. For example, US financial integration with other Western Hemisphere countries and German integration with other European countries are several orders of magnitude larger than China-South Asia financial integration.

Tourism and remittances are examples of other types of economic linkage. These linkages too are relatively small between China and South Asia. Remittances are very small in both directions. Although their share has increased in recent years, Chinese tourists still account for only around 2 percent of tourist arrivals in the three largest South Asian countries, and the large South Asian countries account for a similarly small share of tourist arrivals in China (Figures 12.11 and 12.12). For the Maldives, Nepal, and Bhutan, however, the share of China in tourist arrivals has increased substantially since the mid-2000s.

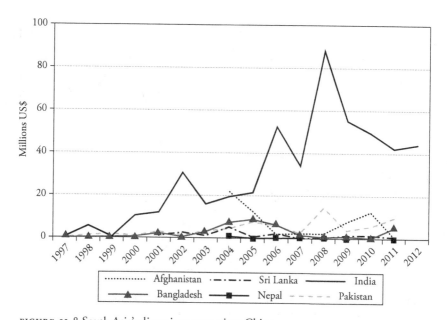

FIGURE 12.8 South Asia's direct investment into China

SOURCE: CEIC Data, *China Economic and Industry Data Database*, https://www.ceicdata.com/en/countries/china

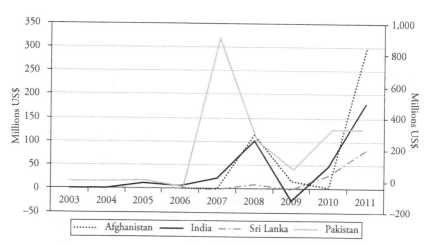

FIGURE 12.9 China's direct investment into Afghanistan, India, Sri Lanka, and Pakistan

SOURCE: CEIC Data, *China Economic and Industry Data Database*, https://www.ceicdata.com/en/countries/china

NOTE: Right-hand axis applies to Pakistan; left-hand axis applies to other countries.

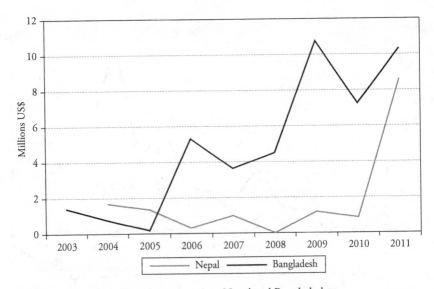

FIGURE 12.10 China's direct investment into Nepal and Bangladesh
SOURCE: CEIC Data, *China Economic and Industry Data Database*, https://www.ceicdata.com/en/countries/china

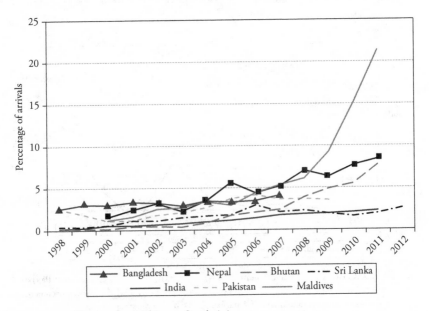

FIGURE 12.11 Tourists from China to South Asia
SOURCE: United Nations World Tourism Organization, *Yearbook of Tourism Statistics*, various editions

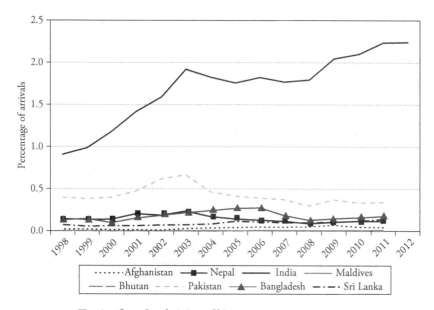

FIGURE 12.12 Tourists from South Asia to China

SOURCE: United Nations World Tourism Organization, *Yearbook of Tourism Statistics,* various editions

## More Integration Would Be Beneficial for All

Closer integration of China and South Asia, not to mention among South Asian countries themselves, could have substantial benefits for all countries involved.[7] Senior leaders in China and South Asia regularly acknowledge and affirm the benefits of closer economic relations.[8] This recognition is reflected, for example, in increasing cooperation between China and India through the dialogue among BRICS nations (Brazil, Russia, India, China, and South Africa). Trade expansion in recent years has regularly outstripped the objectives that leaders have set.

Integration is useful not as an end in itself but as a means of achieving the broader economic goals of growth and development. It can allow countries to realize mutual gains from trade, help smaller countries overcome the limitations posed by the small size of national markets, expand the markets of firms from all countries, and focus countries' attention on common economic challenges.

Regional integration could help small countries that would otherwise be isolated to achieve a minimum scale of production and to increase their access to world markets. In East Asia, for example, rapid economic growth in recent decades has been greatly facilitated by the expansion of trade that was fueled by falling trade barriers and transport costs.[9] Closer integration could also foster "supply chain" development, with different components of a good being produced in different countries. As Uwe Deichmann and Indermit Gill point out, a small, low-income country "may not be able to build computers or cars, but it can produce the cables or wires that will be used in assembly lines in China. Through this 'vertical disaggregation' . . . growth and prosperity [can] spread."[10] The limited integration that has occurred between South Asia and China is striking in view of the potential benefits of closer integration.

Analysts and policy makers recognize several factors as contributing to the relatively limited economic integration between China and South Asia. Many of the same factors contribute to limited integration within South Asia. Key economic factors include trade barriers, infrastructure constraints, and transport costs. In particular:

- *Trade barriers* still exist in the form of both tariffs and regulatory procedures. Procedures and regulations are, moreover, disparate across the different countries. Asian countries have been making progress on regional integration through a variety of trade agreements, with the ASEAN-China FTA being but one example. South Asia, however, with the exception of Pakistan, does not have an FTA with China. Although effective tariff rates on Chinese imports from South Asia and from the ASEAN were very similar through 2001, they are now substantially smaller for ASEAN countries (Figure 12.13).
- *Infrastructure* development has been remarkable in China, which has good roads, railways, ports, power, and telecommunication coverage. South Asia, by contrast, falls short in many of these areas.[11] Greater regional connectivity would help reduce trade costs, encourage investment, and promote other economic linkages such as tourism. Power shortages have widespread effects on growth, public finance, and trade.[12] Numerous studies show that better infrastructure and logistics generally contribute significantly to trade.[13]
- Infrastructure constraints contribute to high *transport costs*, which are also driven up by high fees and regulatory burdens.[14] Experience in the rest of the world over the past several decades suggests that falling transport costs can have a profound impact on trade. Where such costs have fallen, they have often led to new opportunities for scale economies and specialization and, thereby, contributed to substantial expansion of trade.[15] Transport costs are particularly important for intra-industry trade in parts and components. This aspect can provide opportunities even for small countries that, even if they do not have

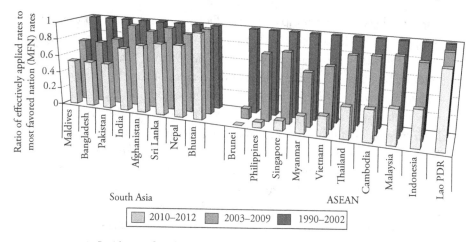

FIGURE 12.13 Incidence of preferential tariffs applied on imports into China from South Asia and ASEAN

SOURCE: UNCTAD *Trade Analysis Information System* (TRAINS) database, http://databank.worldbank.org/data/reports.aspx?source=UNCTAD---Trade-Analysis-Information-System-%28TRAINS%29

NOTE: Tariffs weighed by trade values.

the capacity to build advanced final products, can produce the inputs for such products. A declining cost of transportation between Southeast Asia and China may also reflect China's resource needs and Southeast Asia's growing openness to FDI, especially in Vietnam, Cambodia, Laos, and Myanmar.

Closer integration creates opportunities but also carries risks that must be managed. Such risks include greater potential for contagion, as trade and financial systems become more closely connected, and the need to develop adequate safety nets for those who may be displaced or disadvantaged as integration changes the pattern of trade. As the global financial crisis shows, even countries that have long been open and benefited from global trade and financial flows are vulnerable to shocks and volatility. The lesson from these experiences is not that a closed system is preferable to an open one but that closer integration needs to be supported by sufficiently strong financial and other institutions to manage the greater volatility that might result.

## Complements or Substitutes?

Given the similarities between the Chinese and South Asian economies, a natural question is whether, on balance, they are more likely to compete in world markets or to be complementary. Do China and India, for example, compete in world trade because both are labor-abundant low-wage economies? Or do they complement each other, say, because China's production tends to be relatively capital intensive or because of supply-chain-type arrangements whereby India (along with other South Asian countries) supplies inputs to China for the production of exported goods? The question is ultimately an empirical one, and an ongoing one for further study, but our preliminary conclusion is that there is not a great deal of substitutability between Chinese and Indian production.[16] In particular, trade in specific products reflects no negative correlation in recent years between the growth rates of Indian and Chinese exports to third countries.

Arvind Virmani has argued that China and India specialize in somewhat different types of exports, based on their natural resource endowments, skills, and policies. For example, although both countries export textiles and garments, they specialize in different types of products. India's exports are heavily concentrated in cotton textiles and garments, in part reflecting the abundance of cotton in India, whereas China's exports are relatively more concentrated in man-made fibers. The two countries' exports have, therefore, been noncompeting. In terms of skills, the workforces in both China and India include a large number of people with strong mathematics and science training. India's relatively more common use of English and experience dealing with a diverse workforce may facilitate an advantage in services such as advertising and entertainment. China's policies have tended to enable high investment in manufacturing on a large scale. Labor policy may also influence these differences, with India's rigid labor laws for organized industry contributing to a greater use of educated labor and focus on higher value-added niche products.[17]

A priori, one may expect that, as a labor-abundant economy, China would specialize in production of labor-intensive manufactures and, being relatively less well endowed with capital and natural resources, would import capital-intensive manufactures, intermediate goods, and primary products including energy. Such a pattern of trade would benefit countries that export capital-intensive products such as electronic components (e.g., Korea and Singapore) or natural resources (e.g., Australia and Indonesia). But it may not benefit exporters of similar labor-intensive manufactures, as the countries of South Asia may be because of their labor abundance.

On the other hand, in China the cost of capital relative to labor is low in comparison with other countries.[18] The low cost of capital has led to high-capital-intensity investment-led growth, reflected in job creation that is relatively limited in relation to growth.[19] That is, notwithstanding its large population, China's production and exports may, unlike South Asia's, be capital- rather than labor-intensive. In addition, with labor costs rising in China, South Asian nations have an opportunity to link into supply chains with China, undertaking those stages of production where their relatively low labor costs give them a comparative advantage.

The question of whether China and South Asian economies compete with or complement each other in world markets is, therefore, an empirical one. Some light can be shed on this question by examining whether the growth of China's exports of specific categories of goods appears to have forced a reduction or slowdown in India's exports of the same goods. In general, the answer is no. Of course, one does not know the counterfactual in the sense that it is possible India's export growth might have been even faster in the absence of Chinese exports. India's export growth in specific goods has, however, not changed substantially as Chinese exports have picked up, particularly after China's accession to the WTO in 2001.

In particular, detailed export data from the United Nations Comtrade database allow one to divide exports into the following four categories based on their global technological intensity:[20]

- *High-technology products*, including computers, office machinery, electronics communications, and pharmaceuticals
- *Medium-high-technology products*, including scientific instruments, motor vehicles, electrical machinery, chemicals, other transport equipment, and non-electrical machinery
- *Medium-low-technology products*, including rubber and plastic goods, shipbuilding materials, other manufacturing materials, nonferrous and ferrous metals, nonmetallic mineral products, fabricated metal products, and petroleum refining
- *Low-technology products*, including paper printing; textiles and clothing; food, beverages, and tobacco; and wood and furniture

In addition to examining these four categories of products, it is worth examining separately two specific types of goods—*electronics-communications* and *textiles-clothing*—because China is the world's largest exporter of these goods.

Figures 12.14–12.19 show the growth in Chinese and Indian exports of the aforementioned product categories since 1990. That is, the starting point for each country is the level of its exports in 1990. Of particular interest is a comparison between the period before and after 2001, when China joined the WTO and saw a boom in its overall exports.

Overall, exports in the various sectors do not suggest that China's rapid export growth has crowded out India's exports. In *high-technology products*, China's export expansion has outstripped India's, but neither country's export growth rate changed substantially after 2001. In *medium-high-technology products*, export growth picked up for both countries after 2001. The same pattern is repeated in *medium-low-technology exports* and *low-technology exports*. The picture is not different when one looks more narrowly at the electronics-communications and textile and clothing subsectors. In *electronics-communications*, China's export growth picked up after 2001, but India maintained its already rapid growth. In *textiles and clothing*, China's export growth again picked up after 2001, whereas India's relatively sluggish pace continued unchanged.

Trends in bilateral China-India trade mirror those in the exports of China and India to the world (Figures 12.20–12.23). In *high-technology* products, export growth in either direction did not change markedly after 2001.

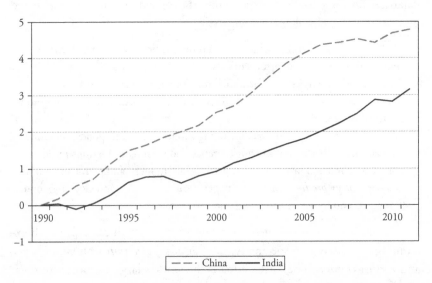

FIGURE 12.14 China and India: high-technology exports, 1990–2011 (log scale, 1990 = 0)
SOURCE: *United Nations Commodity Trade Statistics Database* (UN Comtrade), http://comtrade.un.org

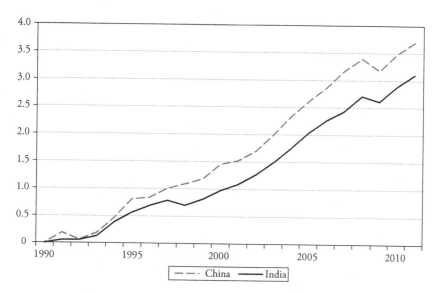

FIGURE 12.15 China and India: medium-high-technology exports, 1990–2011 (log scale, 1990 = 0)

SOURCE: *United Nations Commodity Trade Statistics Database* (UN Comtrade), http://comtrade.un.org

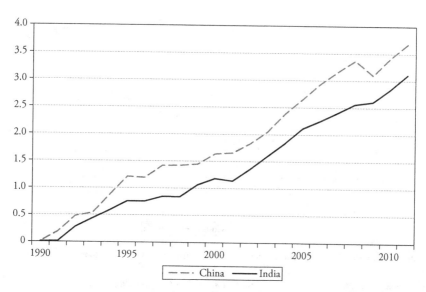

FIGURE 12.16 China and India: medium-low-technology exports, 1990–2011 (log scale, 1990 = 0)

SOURCE: *United Nations Commodity Trade Statistics Database* (UN Comtrade), http://comtrade.un.org

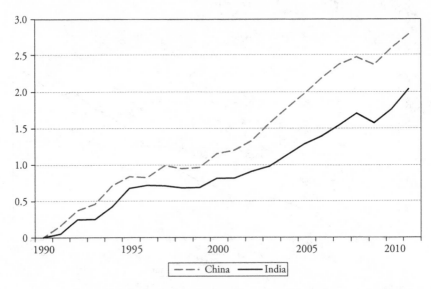

FIGURE 12.17 China and India: low-technology exports, 1990–2011 (log scale, 1990 = 0)
SOURCE: *United Nations Commodity Trade Statistics Database* (UN Comtrade), http://comtrade.un.org

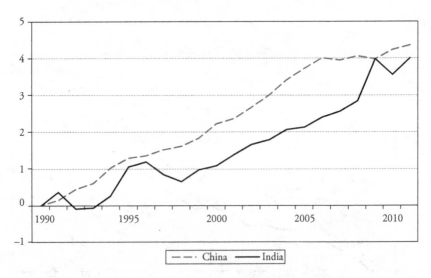

FIGURE 12.18 China and India: electronic communications exports, 1990–2012 (log scale, 1990 = 0)
SOURCE: *United Nations Commodity Trade Statistics Database* (UN Comtrade), http://comtrade.un.org

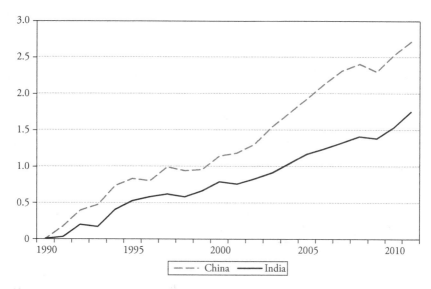

FIGURE 12.19 China and India: textiles and clothing exports, 1990–2012 (log scale, 1990 = 0)

SOURCE: *United Nations Commodity Trade Statistics Database* (UN Comtrade), http://comtrade.un.org

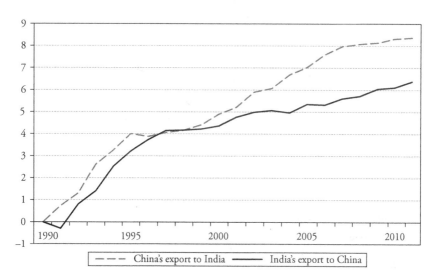

FIGURE 12.20 China and India: bilateral trade in high-technology products, 1990–2012 (log scale, 1990 = 0)

SOURCE: *United Nations Commodity Trade Statistics Database* (UN Comtrade), http://comtrade.un.org

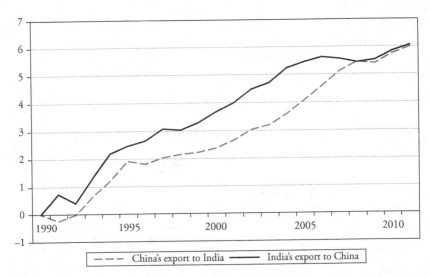

FIGURE 12.21 China and India: bilateral trade in medium-high-technology products, 1990–2012 (log scale, 1990 = 0)
SOURCE: *United Nations Commodity Trade Statistics Database* (UN Comtrade), http://comtrade.un.org

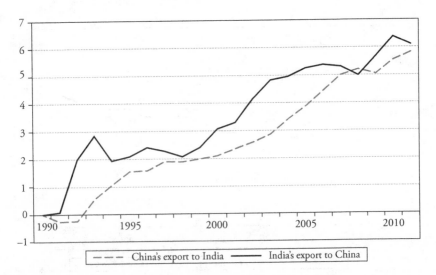

FIGURE 12.22 China and India: bilateral trade in medium-low-technology products, 1990–2012 (log scale, 1990 = 0)
SOURCE: *United Nations Commodity Trade Statistics Database* (UN Comtrade), http://comtrade.un.org

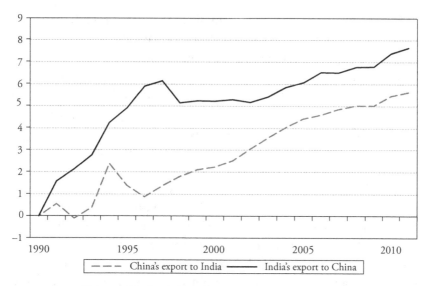

FIGURE 12.23 China and India: bilateral trade in low-technology products, 1990–2012 (log scale, 1990 = 0)

SOURCE: *United Nations Commodity Trade Statistics Database* (UN Comtrade), http://comtrade.un.org

In *medium-high-technology* products and *medium-low-technology* products, China's exports to India picked up significantly after WTO entry, but India's exports to China also continued to grow. *Low-technology* export growth from China did not change much after 2001, but India's exports to China accelerated. Overall, although one does not know the counterfactual, it is hard to see how China's exports have crowded out those from India. In global markets for inputs (e.g., commodities) the share of China and South Asia has been increasing.

## Future Challenges

China has achieved in significant measure the rebalancing from external to internal demand that has been under way for several years, but it still needs to achieve a better internal rebalancing from investment to consumption. In South Asian countries, the rebalancing challenge differs. In India, for example, there is a need to boost investment. The rebalancing of demand in different countries will have consequences for others.

Demographics will change profoundly in the years ahead. In particular, the age profile of the population will rise substantially in China, and the dependency ratio is projected to rise from around 12 percent now to over 40 percent by 2050 (Figure 12.24). South Asia, by contrast, has a more benign outlook. In China, the rising dependency ratio will pose challenges for the pension system,[21] for productivity and growth, and for the labor supply.[22] The working-age population will reach a peak in the next few years, and then China may cross the so-called Lewis Turning Point and move from a vast supply of low-cost workers to a labor shortage.[23]

As China and South Asia develop, it is likely that their financial systems will need to become more open in order to support the level of development. Capital account liberalization will have implications for themselves, for each other, and for the world. Tamim Bayoumi and Franziska Ohnsorge discuss in broad terms the likely global implications.[24] Also, an appropriate strategy for capital flow liberalization is needed to maximize the benefits of capital flows and mitigate the risks.[25]

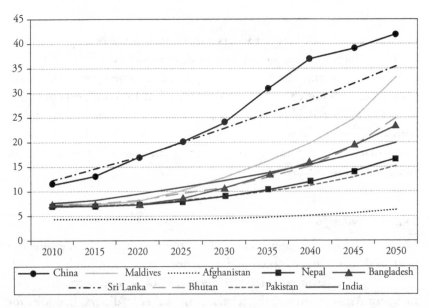

FIGURE 12.24 Demographic outlook for China and South Asia: old-age dependency ratio

SOURCE: United Nations, *World Population Prospects: The 2010 Revision* (New York: United Nations, 2011)

NOTE: Old-age dependency ratio is the ratio of people age 65 and over to those of working age (15–64); estimates from 2015 to 2050 are based on assumptions of medium fertility.

Finally, China's remarkable success since 1978 in lifting living standards for a greater number of people in a shorter span of time than ever before in human history surely offers lessons for other countries. With GDP having grown by an average of 10 percent annually since 1978, it has doubled every seven years and implied an eightfold increase in income in just a single generation. China's policy of reform and opening up involved a reform of incentives to encourage more private participation and less state involvement in production and an opening up of external trade and direct investment. Particular aspects of China's strategy and implementation may be useful for other developing countries. In turn, some lessons from South Asia's development may be useful for China. Such lessons may include, for example, the relatively successful development of financial markets in India, particularly equity markets.[26]

## Notes

We appreciate the useful discussion by Tom Fingar, Rafiq Dossani, Dan Sneider, and other participants at the June 2013 "China and the World" workshop at the Shorenstein Asia-Pacific Center at Stanford University. We are grateful to Steven Dunaway, Rahul Anand, Steven Barnett, K. Eapen, and Rodrigo Cubero for helpful comments. We are, however, solely responsible for the contents of this chapter, which represents the views of the authors and not those of the International Monetary Fund, its executive board, or its management.

1. Pakistan is the only South Asian country with which China has an FTA. A China-India FTA remains the subject of a discussion between the two countries.

2. For a discussion of this point and its causes and implications, see Arvind Virmani, "India-China Economic Cooperation," in *China and India: Learning from Each Other*, ed. Jahangir Aziz, Steven Vincent Dunaway, and Eswar S. Prasad (Washington, DC: International Monetary Fund, 2006), chap. 13.

3. Ibid.

4. This conclusion can be drawn from Table 12.6. The coefficient on the South Asia dummy in the second column is −0.376. This is the amount by which the log of actual imports from China is less than the log of what South Asian countries' imports from China would have been based on gravity factors alone (rather than on gravity factors *plus* the fact that these countries are in South Asia). That is, if the former factor is $M$ and the latter is $F$, then $\log M - \log F = -0.376$, or $\log (M/F) = -0.376$. Therefore, $M/F = \exp(-0.376)$, and $(M - F)/F$ (which is just the percentage difference between $M$ and $F$) $= \exp(-0.376) - 1$, which turns out to be 0.33. The translation from Table 12.6 to the rest of the paragraph in the text is based on the same logic.

5. A related but separate question is whether the limited extent of trade integration within South Asia also limits the size of China-South Asia trade. If so, greater subregional integration in South Asia could help smaller countries achieve a minimum scale of production and increase their access to larger regional markets.

6. Data on such financing are not readily available.

7. There is a large literature on the benefits of regional economic integration and the issues to be overcome in achieving it. For a recent discussion in an Asian context, see Asian Development Bank, *Asian Economic Integration Monitor, March 2013* (Manila, Philippines: Asian Development Bank, 2013), http://www.adb.org/sites/default/files/publication/30181/aem-201303.pdf.

8. See Ministry of External Affairs, Government of India, "Joint Statement on the State Visit of Chinese Premier Li Keqiang to India," May 20, 2013, http://mea.gov.in/bilateral-documents.htm?dtl/21723/Joint+Statement+on+the+State+Visit+of+Chinese++Li+Keqiang+to+India.

9. See Uwe Deichmann and Indermit Gill, "The Economic Geography of Regional Integration," *Finance and Development*, December 2008, pp. 45–47.

10. Ibid., 46.

11. For discussion of infrastructure needs in Asia, including South Asia, see International Monetary Fund, *Regional Economic Outlook: Asia and Pacific*, (Washington, DC: International Monetary Fund, 2011).

12. For an examination of the implications of power shortages for the Indian economy, see Kalpana Kochhar, Utsav Kumar, Raghuram Rajan, Arvind Subramanian, and Ionnis Tokatlidis, "India's Pattern of Development: What Happened, What Follows?" IMF Working Paper WP/06/22, January 2006.

13. John S. Wilson and Tsunehiro Ostuki, "Cutting Trade Costs and Improved Business Facilitation in South Asia," in *South Asia: Growth and Regional Integration*, ed. Sadiq Ahmed and Ejaz Ghani (Washington, DC: World Bank, 2007), 236–270, http://siteresources.worldbank.org/SOUTHASIAEXT/Resources/Publications/448813-1171648504958/SAR_integration_ch9.pdf. John Wilson and Tsunehiro Otsuki argue that, if South Asian countries were to raise the port efficiency, customs environment, regulatory environment, and service-sector infrastructure halfway to average East Asian levels, the gains from trade to South Asia would be equivalent to nearly one-third of the region's trade with the rest of the world and 60 percent of the intraregional trade in South Asia. Alberto Behar, Phil Manners, and Benjamin Nelson conclude that a 1-standard-deviation improvement in logistics raises exports by about 46 percent for an average-sized developing country. See Alberto Behar, Phil Manners, and Benjamin Nelson, "Exports and International Logistics," World Bank Policy Research Working Paper 5691, June 2011, http://elibrary.worldbank.org/doi/pdf/10.1596/1813-9450-5691.

Other research finds significant effects on trade from bilateral telecommunications prices and traffic. See Carsten Fink, Aaditya Mattoo, and Ileana Cristina Neagu, "Assessing the Impact of Communication Costs on International Trade," *Journal of International Economics* 67, no. 2 (2005): 428–445; and Richard Portes and Helene Rey, "The Determinants of Cross-Border Equity Flows," National Bureau of Economic Research Working Paper 7336, September 1999.

14. In 2013, the average cost of transporting a container from India was $1,170, nearly double the cost in China ($620). See World Bank, "Trading Across Borders," http://www.doingbusiness.org/data/exploretopics/trading-across-borders (accessed May 20, 2015).

15. For a review of the experience in recent decades, see Paul Krugman, "The Increasing Returns Revolution in Trade and Geography," *American Economic Review* 99, no. 33 (2009): 561–571.

16. This section focuses on India, rather than South Asia as a whole, because of data constraints and because of India's large size in South Asia.

17. Virmani, "India-China Economic Cooperation."

18. For a discussion that develops this argument, which remains valid, see International Monetary Fund, "People's Republic of China: 2006 Article IV Consultation," July 11, 2006, https://www.imf.org/external/pubs/ft/scr/2006/cr06394.pdf.

19. Jahangir Aziz and Steven Dunaway note that on an annual basis in most countries 3 to 4 percent GDP growth is associated with 2 to 3 percent employment growth, but in China 10 percent GDP growth in recent decades has tended to generate only about 1 percent employment growth. See Jahangir Aziz and Steven Dunaway, "China's Rebalancing Act," *Finance and Development* 44, no. 3 (2007), http://www.imf.org/external/pubs/ft/fandd/2007/09/aziz.htm.

20. The breakdown according to technological intensity follows Thomas Hatzichronoglou, "Revision of the High-Technology Sector and Product Classification," OECD Science, Technology and Industry Working Papers 1997/02, January 1, 1997.

21. See Steven V. Dunaway and Vivek B. Arora, "Pension Reform in China: Cutting the Gordian Knot," *China Economic Quarterly* 2, no. 3 (2007): 43–47.

22. See Mitali Das and Papa N'Diaye, "Chronicle of a Decline Foretold: Has China Reached the Lewis Turning Point?" IMF Working Paper WP/13/26, January 2013.

23. Mitali Das and Papa N'Diaye assess that on current trends, the Lewis Turning Point will emerge between 2020 and 2025. See ibid.

24. Tamim Bayoumi and Franziska Ohnsorge, "Do Inflows or Outflows Dominate? Global Implications of Capital Account Liberalization in China," IMF Working Paper WP/13/189, August 2013.

25. International Monetary Fund, "The Liberalization and Management of Capital Flows: An Institutional View," November 14, 2012, http://www.imf.org/external/np/pp/eng/2012/111412.pdf.

26. David Dollar draws some lessons from China for Africa that may apply to a broader range of countries. See David Dollar, "Lessons from China for Africa," World Bank Policy Research Working Paper 4531, February 2008, http://elibrary .worldbank.org/doi/pdf/10.1596/1813-9450-4531. For a discussion of lessons from China for India and from India for China, see Klaus Gerhaeusser, Yoshihiro Iwasaki, and V. B. Tulasidhar, eds., *Resurging Asian Giants: Lessons from the People's Republic of China and India* (Manila, Philippines: Asian Development Bank, 2010), http://www.adb.org/sites/default/files/publication/28001/resurging-asian -giants.pdf. For a discussion of how China and India have addressed common policy challenges, see Aziz, Dunaway, and Prasad, *China and India.*

# THIRTEEN

# China's Engagement with South and Central Asia
## Patterns, Trends, and Themes

*Thomas Fingar*

The primary objective of this book is to describe and explain China's interactions with selected countries in South and Central Asia. It is not and does not seek to be comprehensive in its coverage of countries, issues, or modes of interaction. Each contributor was asked to examine specific bilateral and/or regional manifestations of China's engagement with the region in a way that would illuminate China's objectives and actions to achieve them; to discuss the concerns and goals of the South or Central Asian country or countries examined and how those concerns and goals are addressed through the country's relationship with China; and, as appropriate, to identify patterns and trends in the way China interacts with the countries and region. The result is both a snapshot that captures key elements in China's relationship with the region in the second decade of the twenty-first century and a collection of case studies that facilitate comparisons and identification of patterns and learning curves.

In addition to providing a snapshot of current types of engagement and analyses of how relationships and interactions evolved from what they were thirty-five years ago to what they are today, the book is intended to facilitate comparisons among regions and over time. As the first volume in a series, this book alone is inadequate to make empirically based judgments about whether, how, and why China's engagement with countries in South and Central Asia resembled and differed from those with countries in other regions. That task must await completion of additional regional studies. The single region studies do, however, allow for preliminary judgments about the utility of the "threats to security" and "contributions to development" framework described in Chapter 1.

Several chapters examine or touch on relationships between security concerns and engagement intended to facilitate continued development and economic growth in China. Chapters 2, 4, 5, 8, and 10 note security concerns as impediments to engagement that had to be addressed, recalibrated, or removed to clear the way for increased economic interaction and/or continue to limit and shape specific forms of engagement. Chapters 7 and 8 also examine ways in which the priority attached to sustained economic growth is linked to concerns about living standards and instability in areas inhabited by minority peoples in China's frontier provinces. Taken together, the chapters in this book describe a dynamic in which external security concerns impeded engagement while India was aligned with the Soviet Union and the Central Asian states were part of the USSR (Chapters 2, 5, 10, and 11) and internal security concerns centered on discontent among minority peoples in western and southwestern China prodded Beijing to expand contacts with countries in the region (Chapters 7 and 8).

The findings presented also are consistent with the framework's prediction that the states of South and Central Asia would not be among the first countries targeted by China when it began to pursue modernization through increased engagement with the outside world. The security threat they posed to China apparently was judged by officials in Beijing to be high enough to impede developmental cooperation but not so high as to require immediate or concerted efforts to counter or reduce the threat. The exception to this generalization is the continued importance of relations with Pakistan to China's strategy for managing the perceived threats posed by the Soviet Union and India (Chapters 3 and 6). This situation changed not because of anything that China or countries in the region did but because the Soviet Union collapsed.

The findings presented here are also consistent with the framework's judgment that Beijing would not make a major effort to engage the region in the 1980s because what the region could provide was less important to the first phase of reform and opening than were the potential contributions of other regions, especially North America, Western Europe, and Northeast Asia. The potential contribution of countries in the region changed in the early to mid-1990s because the success of China's developmental strategy had increased the demand for commodities that were available in the region and because changes in the economic policies of India and other South Asian countries made them more attractive trade and investment partners. Because they had more to offer China, China became more active in promoting engagement (Chapters 7, 8, 10, and 12).

A third feature of the framework outlined in Chapter 1 is its assumption that the countries in a given region (or, in this case, two subregions) have much in common and that decision makers in Beijing would tend to view them as part of an interconnected whole rather than as entirely discrete entities. China's decision to engage with the region appears to have been a decision to engage with all the countries at the same time, not a decision to engage sequentially or in very different ways. The exception, again, is Pakistan. This did not mean that China sought always or primarily to engage the countries in a multilateral forum. Chapter 10 makes clear that China deliberately dealt with the newly independent states of Central Asia individually (even though they had hoped Moscow would back them to increase their collective bargaining power on border and water issues). But direct bilateral interactions had numerous spillover effects within the region (Chapters 9, 11, and 12).

Consistency does not constitute confirmation of the utility of the framework; that will require, at a minimum, its examination in additional regions and at different phases of China's post-1978 engagement with the outside world. But it does suggest that viewing Chinese actions through the twin lenses of security concerns and contributions to development may be a useful way to anticipate and explain China's objectives, priorities, and interactions with particular countries and regions. It also suggests that other factors noted by contributors to this volume and many others who have analyzed the dynamics of China's international relations (e.g., geography, history, culture, and ideology) are generally less important determinants of what happens than are security and economics. Although such other factors condition and shape all China's dealings with other countries and assume preeminent importance in specific cases, the assessments in this volume suggest that they operate largely within parameters defined by security and economic calculations.

The envisioned series, of which this book is the first installment, is intended to facilitate comparisons across space and time and discovery of patterns within and among regions (e.g., were regions engaged at the same time and in more or less the same way, and depending on whether the answer to that questions is yes or no, what accounts for the pattern?). Such comparisons must be deferred until work on other regions has been completed, but the studies presented in this volume suggest a number of intraregional patterns and dynamics that are important, even if confined to South and Central Asia, and that can be tested in other regions of the globe. The most important of these patterns are summarized in the following sections.

## The Importance of Geography and Geopolitics

As Robert Kaplan reminds us, the precise impacts of geography have changed in the era of instant communications and high-speed travel, but they have not been eliminated. Indeed, they continue to shape perceptions and the possibility spaces of countries, firms, and individuals.[1] Whether countries are adjacent or distant from one another; separated by high mountains, vast deserts, navigable rivers, or dangerous seas has shaped the magnitude and patterns of interaction for centuries. Geography, perhaps more than any other factor, explains why China has—and has had—very different relationships with the peoples and polities of Central Asia than it has with those in South Asia. The impact of geography and geopolitics is a leitmotif that runs through all the chapters in this volume but is most prominent in Chapters 7, 8, 10, and 11.

China's assessment of the international situation and strategy of development are global in scope but the way in which Beijing addresses security concerns and development-related possibilities is partly a function of geography. The same is true of the regional states examined in this book. With the exception of India, they do not share China's global perspective or ambitions and are even more constrained by location, terrain, demography, and other dimensions of geography than is the People's Republic. All are to some extent "prisoners of geography," but they have very different abilities to capitalize on or mitigate the inherent constraints.

The world's highest mountain range severely limited China's interaction with South Asia until the modern era. The resultant isolation was compounded by the fact that China was not a maritime nation and India's seaborne activities were oriented primarily across the Indian Ocean (because of the Monsoon) and into parts of Southeast Asia. In contrast to China's relations with countries in Northeast Asia, which were marked by centuries of Chinese suzerainty, extensive cultural penetration, and strong memories of interaction with the Middle Kingdom, and Southeast Asia, where China regarded most states as vassals, its relations with South Asia were minimal.[2] Among other consequences, this relative isolation meant that China and states in the region do not have to overcome the kinds of historical memory problems that complicate relationships in Northeast Asia.[3] But it also means that there is little history to build on when attempting to forge new relationships. To the extent that history is a factor, it plays a much greater role in shaping the way other regional countries perceive and interact with India than with China.

Geography plays a very different role along China's northwestern frontier. Natural barriers, mainly deserts, are less formidable obstacles than the Himalayas, and the "boundary" between China and its neighbors is both more recent and less meaningful to the ethnic groups living on both sides of the line. The northwestern territories on China's side of the border constitute a large percentage of China's total landmass but only a small percentage of its population. Through much of history, this frontier region was regarded more as a buffer and barrier to invasion by peoples from the west than as an integral part of the Chinese empire. Han chauvinism and benign—and sometimes not so benign—neglect were long a hallmark of the way China's central governments treated the area. Conditions that once were thought to make the region a good buffer zone have recently been recognized as contributing to unbalanced development and growing unrest among the minority peoples living there.[4]

In the nineteenth century, the region's location at the nexus of the Russian, British, and Chinese empires made it the subject of the protracted competition known as the Great Game. The goal of this competition was at least as much to deny the area to imperial rivals as it was to control the people and other resources located there.[5] That round of the Great Game ended with the region largely subordinate to Russian control and later incorporated into the Soviet Union. Until the collapse of the Soviet Union in 1991, the People's Republic of China's dealings with Central Asia were a function of its relationship with Moscow. As a result, cross-border relations were severely limited for more than four decades. The region again became important to China in the 1990s, when it was eager to limit Moscow's ability to regain influence in its former republics, and after 2001, when it sought to constrain what it feared was an attempt by the United States to increase its presence and influence with the ultimate objective of surrounding and containing China. Central Asia acquired even greater importance for China in the twentieth century, when it began to import increasingly large amounts of hydrocarbons to fuel its growing economy and it became increasingly concerned about terrorism and separatism in Xinjiang.

## The Importance of Major Countries

All the most important relationships discussed in this book involve one and often two major powers in addition to China. India is an omnipresent factor in China's relations with South Asia; the Soviet Union played a more dominant role in Central Asia until 1991, and Russia has continued to be a major, albeit less dominant, player in the region since then.[6] The United States played a less direct role in the calculations of most regional states until the 1990s but now seems to be more worrisome to Beijing and more attractive to states in the region concerned about their growing economic dependence on China and uncertainty about Beijing's ultimate objectives. Other ways in which perceptions and behavior of major countries influence the calculations and policies of countries examined here include the impact of perceived uncertainty about what role the United States will play in the future of the region (Chapter 3) and the ability of particular countries to take advantage of missteps by one or more of the major powers (Chapter 11).

During much of the period examined here, China focused on India to the exclusion of other countries in South Asia. The exception is Pakistan, but a—if not the—principal reason for China's unusual interest in and relationship with Pakistan was its perceived utility in complicating India's strategic situation in ways that diminished the threat that India alone, or India and the Soviet Union, constituted for China.[7] Other countries in the region had deep ties to India and eschewed efforts to counterbalance Indian influence by developing strategic or economic relations with other major powers. Early in the Cold War, the United States aligned with Pakistan to contain the "Sino-Soviet threat," but as Chapter 6 makes clear, Pakistan viewed its relationship with the United States in purely instrumental terms; its primary focus was on India, and China seemed a more likely source of support against India than did the United States.[8] The chapter argues that China has understood and appreciated Pakistan's opportunistic approach to relations with the United States and that this understanding has contributed to an unusually high level of mutual trust in Sino-Pakistani relations. It remains to be seen, however, whether future Chinese policies toward Pakistan will be shaped more by loyalty and appreciation for Islamabad's maintenance of an arms-length relationship with Washington in the past than by reluctance to tie its own fate too closely to a country that has demonstrated perfidious behavior toward another major power.

Soviet intervention in Afghanistan in the 1970s, particularly after it invaded in 1979, led to unprecedented cooperation among China, Pakistan, and the United States. This cooperative arrangement had little impact on other states in the region and did not outlive the Soviet occupation.[9] Major power interaction again became a factor in the region in the late 1990s when US-India relations began to improve and China became concerned that a triumphant United States was eager to align with India against the only remaining Communist power.[10] A few years later, when Moscow began to assist the US-led intervention in Afghanistan after the attacks of September 11 and Washington began to use military bases in Central Asia, China became sufficiently concerned that it reconceived the Shanghai Five, which evolved into the Shanghai Cooperation Organisation (SCO). The announced goals were to reduce troops along common borders and increase security cooperation, particularly counterterrorism cooperation, but China clearly also sought to limit the influence of Moscow and Washington on its vulnerable western frontier.[11]

The smaller states in the region were not entirely passive or disinterested as the major powers executed the latest version of the Great Game, but they seem to have seen little opportunity to advance their own interests or constrain the bigger players. That situation changed as China became more engaged in the region's economies, the smaller states of South Asia acquired an alternative to dependence on India, and Central Asians obtained a new way to counterbalance dependence on Russia. In that important respect, China's increasing economic engagement in the region has changed the game in ways that are welcomed by the smaller states and, so far, acceptable to the other major powers.

The magnitude and variety of ways in which countries pay special attention to the actions and intentions of big powers, both inside and outside the region, are particularly important to the analyses in Chapter 2 (the importance of the Soviet Union and the United States to China), Chapter 3 (the importance of China and the United States to India), Chapter 6 (the importance of China and the United States to Pakistan), Chapter 9 (the importance of India and China to the smaller states of South Asia), Chapter 10 (the importance of Russia and China to the newly independent states of Central Asia), and Chapter 11 (Russia and China in Central Asia).

## The Importance of Changes in the International System and the Policies of Regional States

A number of changes in the international system during the last thirty-five years required or enabled China to adjust its policies toward states in South and/or Central Asia. The most important change was the end of the Cold War. The demise of the Soviet Union degraded what China's leaders had long considered the most serious threat to their country and transformed the United States from tacit ally into a largely unchecked potential adversary. It took a few years for the magnitude and consequences of this shock to the international system to be incorporated into the strategic calculus of China, the United States, and most other nations, including those in South and Central Asia. As it became clear that Russia was not a scaled-down version of the Soviet Union with fewer capabilities but similar objectives, India realized that it had lost its most important security partner. The newly independent Central Asian states explored—and discovered—how much they could or must change their economic, security, and other relationships with Russia, and China recalculated its security and developmental challenges and readjusted its policies to meet the perils and opportunities of the emerging global and regional orders.[12]

While the dust settled and leaders everywhere adjusted to the new situation, China made few changes to its assessment of the security situation or policies toward South and Central Asia. The apparent conclusion of its reassessment was to stick with the strategy that was beginning to produce substantial benefits for China and the legitimacy of the Communist Party. Other nations reached different conclusions about their own policies. The collapse of the Soviet Union, primarily because of its economic weakness and inability to keep pace with Western technological advances, eroded faith in the socialist models adopted by dozens of countries that became independent after World War II. One of those countries was India, which initiated reforms in the early 1990s that accelerated growth and opened the way to greater economic interchange with the United States and other market economies.

India and other countries in the region appear also to have been influenced by increasing evidence that China's decision to open its economy to foreign investment and to adapt to the rules and norms of what had been the free-world system but now constituted the only game in town. Taken together, changes in the economic and foreign policies of regional states and their increased interest in learning from and taking advantage of China's sustained economic growth created substantially more opportunities for China to engage in, and greater incentives for governments and people on both sides of the border to open, expand, and modernize, cross-border contacts.

A second major change in the international arena occurred after the September 11, 2001, terrorist attacks on the United States. Until, and notwithstanding, the US invasion of Iraq, South Asia became the principal locus of US-led international efforts to overthrow the Taliban regime in Afghanistan and to close down terrorist safe havens in that country and, later, in northern Pakistan. Tens of thousands of US troops flowed into the region, Moscow supported US use of military bases in Central Asia, and Chinese leaders became increasingly concerned about indigenous and foreign-supported terrorists and separatists in China's frontier regions. These developments caused Beijing to rethink and rework its approach to security in the region. On the issue of counterterrorism, Beijing discovered that it had more in common with New Delhi and Washington than it did with longtime ally Pakistan. Shared concerns about terrorism also provided the basis for cooperation between China and the states of Central Asia. Beijing effectively used this common interest to deepen its security ties with Central Asia and to justify formation of the SCO on grounds other than the Chinese desire to use the new organization to constrain Russia and limit US engagement in the region.

None of the most significant developments in the international system affecting China's engagement with the region were the direct result of actions by the People's Republic except the success of its drive for rapid and sustained economic growth, but all were important to the perceptions and possibilities of China and countries in South and Central Asia. Chapters that address these developments include Chapters 2 and 4–11.

## The Importance of China in Driving Economic Activity

China's economic engagement with the states of South and Central Asia remained very limited until the late 1990s and did not really take off until the twenty-first century. During the first decade and more of reform and opening, China concentrated on developing relationships with the countries—primarily those in the Organisation for Economic Co-operation and Development—that had the most to contribute to China's quest for modernity and were assumed to be eager to capitalize on opportunities to enter the "China market." During these years, China did not really need products available in South and Central Asia, and those countries had neither the desire nor the money to buy significant quantities of Chinese goods. Engagement was further constrained by geography, the paucity and poor quality of transport networks, and political impediments to trade and investment.

A number of developments came together in the late 1990s that substantially increased the potential for cross-border economic activity. These developments included cumulative Chinese economic gains that increased the demand for raw materials and the number of Chinese firms looking for export markets for their low-quality products. They also included changes in the economic policies of regional states and greater interest in taking advantage of China's economic success and willingness to invest in infrastructure. Additional factors included the desire of smaller states in the region to develop ties with China that would lessen their economic dependence on India or Russia and Beijing's realization that economic backwardness in its frontier provinces was contributing to the growing problems of alienation and political unrest.

The concatenation of these factors motivated Beijing to work more actively to expand cross-border ties and made states on the other side of the frontier more receptive to China's initiatives. It required greater interest and activism on both sides of the frontier, but the most important factor was China's money and determination to transform the frontier from a barrier into a bridge. Growth rates, prosperity, trade figures, and other statistics increased on both sides of the Chinese border and both governments and publics understood that it was money from China that had made the improvements possible. China's stock in the region went up, as did its influence. However, as dependence on China increased, so, too, did regional concern about the extent of dependence and possible downsides of the new relationship with the People's Republic. Chapters 7–10 and 12 discuss different aspects of China's catalytic effect on the region.

## The Importance of China's Rise to Balancing and Hedging in the Region

Changes in the international system and China's increasing capabilities and activism have made balancing and hedging behaviors in South and Central Asia more common and more complex than they were just a few decades ago. When the Central Asian republics were part of the Soviet Union, they had no capacity to forge coalitions among themselves or to partner with an outside power to counterbalance Moscow's ability to dictate their foreign relations and dominate their economies. If the Soviet Union had dissolved a decade earlier than it did, it is unlikely that the newly independent states would have turned to China for support because China was not yet in a position to serve as a security or economic counterweight to Russia. In any event, however, by the time the Cold War ended, China had both greater capacity and stronger incentives to engage with Central Asia in ways that had the effect—mostly by design—of providing an alternative to continued Russian dominance.

The situation in South Asia was similar but with one very important exception. India dominated the subcontinent, economically and militarily, and New Delhi had the backing of Moscow. Only Pakistan had the incentive and opportunity to align with outside powers in order to enhance security and avoid economic dependence on India. As Chapter 6 makes clear, Islamabad turned first to the United States but seems never to have had much confidence in that relationship. Moreover, Pakistan had an alternative after Sino-Indian relations deteriorated following the 1962 war and Beijing adopted a "the enemy of my enemy is my friend" strategy to complicate Indian security planning and counter what it perceived to be Soviet designs on the region by aligning with Islamabad. Aligning with Pakistan contributed to China's own security but did not expand opportunities for influence or engagement elsewhere in the region, both because China did not try to engage with others and because China's limited ability to offer economic alternatives and regional states' dependence on India were formidable impediments to greater Chinese engagement.

The concatenation of changes in the international system, adoption of policies designed to accelerate growth and modernization through greater engagement with the global economy in many regional states, and China's increased capacity and desire to engage with the states of South and

Central Asia changed prospects for and patterns of balancing. In Central Asia, China's initiative in establishing and shaping the SCO made that multilateral organization the major institutional mechanism to balance Russia's traditional advantages and to limit American and Indian inroads. China's ability to use the SCO to achieve its own geopolitical objectives is reinforced by leverage gained from its growing investments and economic engagement with regional states.

Recent years have witnessed the steady increase of Chinese trade with and investment in South and Central Asia. Its partners, particularly the smaller states in South Asia, welcome China's interest and engagement, both for the economic benefits and as a counterbalance to India. But none wishes to alienate the local power by appearing to align too closely or exclusively with China, especially as India's own rise creates new possibilities and alternatives to dependence on China. In important respects, all are hedging in ways that were not possible before China became more active in the region.

Hedging and counterbalancing occur in both the security and the economic arena and are noted in most of the chapters in this book.

## The Importance of Increasing Interdependence and Integration

China's increased engagement, especially its investments in infrastructure projects, is fostering interdependence and regional integration that far exceed what has been accomplished as a result of South Asian Association for Regional Cooperation and other regional groupings. Countries, peoples, and economies that had been isolated by geography, policy, and disinterest now interact more frequently and in more ways than ever before. China has provided the catalyst for this transformation.

China's engagement with the region is intended primarily to enhance its own security, economic performance, and stability in the frontier provinces. Fostering dependence on China is a part of the strategy pursued by Beijing; creating interdependencies among its partner states is at most a secondary objective. But improved infrastructure, increased prosperity, and easier travel and communication across borders are changing the region in ways likely to increase in both scope and momentum. Whether to capitalize on economies of scale, to take advantage of possibilities associated with multinational production and supply chains, or to respond to concerns about becoming too dependent on any single company or country, people and organizations in the region are accepting and seeking ever wider networks of relationships and becoming increasingly integrated into regional and global arrangements. As noted in Chapter 8, competition (and other forms of interaction) is shaped by the rules and norms of the existing global order.

Distributing dependence among multiple partners is part of the hedging behavior pursued by all nations in the region, and some of this behavior is motivated by dissatisfaction with or concern about Chinese actions and intentions. But the extent and types of integration occurring in South and Central Asia now did not happen until China acquired the capacity to serve as an economic catalyst and made the decision to address its frontier security and stability problems by building bridges instead of erecting barriers.

The catalytic effects of China's engagement and increasing interdependence facilitated and fueled by economic reform in South Asia are most apparent in Chapters 9 and 12 but also noted in Chapters 4 and 5.

## *The Shift from Security to Economics as the Principal Driver*

The chapters in this book describe a steady and substantial shift from perceptions and policies focused primarily on security (broadly defined) to forms of engagement motivated primarily by economic considerations. Security concerns drove, shaped, and limited interaction in the region for many decades and were particularly salient for China, India, and Pakistan. Indeed, it was largely their security concerns that limited economic and other forms of engagement involving all other states in South Asia. Taken together, the chapters in this book suggest that the shift occurred for a combination of reasons (e.g., Pakistan's acquisition of a nuclear deterrent, India's rise, and the growing stake of all countries in maintenance of a peaceful regional and global environment), the most important of which may be China's judgment that its own rise had reduced the danger of attack by India and that sustained economic growth, including in its frontier provinces, was necessary for internal stability and continued Communist Party rule.

As India and other regional states made policy changes necessary to attract foreign investment and gain access to foreign markets and learned to take advantage of China's greater prosperity and eagerness to expand economic ties, interaction led to interdependencies and greater integration. Security everywhere began to be defined more in economic than military terms, ambitious young people with technical skills had an increasing number of alternatives to careers in the military, and China's willingness to provide arms and other forms of military support appears to have increased the confidence of smaller nations that had been almost entirely dependent on India.

Even though most contributors note the shift from security toward development and economic growth and the increasingly close interconnections of security, economic strength, internal stability, and regime legitimacy, none argue that economic interdependence in the rules-based international order has completely displaced territorial disputes; issues of ethnic, cultural, and religious identity; concerns about history and justice; or other sources of rivalry and insecurity. Indeed, virtually all describe suspicion and distrust as continuing problems.

## Ambivalence About the Costs and Consequences of Interdependence

Beijing's policies to maintain high rates of economic growth and increase China's security and influence have spawned a large and growing mix of interests, attitudes, and concerns. Engagement with its neighbors in South and Central Asia has facilitated greater prosperity, integration, and interdependence, but it has also rekindled old fears and created new sources of unease. All the contributors to this volume have treated China and other countries as unitary actors, but all acknowledge the plurality of interests and attitudes that now characterize relationships. Interests, actors, and attitudes within each country are different at the national level than they are in different subnational regional jurisdictions.

The stakes and perceptions of national and subnational actors differ by sector, firm, ethnic group, and myriad other groupings. Some benefit more than others from engagement with China, and all have expectations, concerns, and aspirations keyed to the future of their relationship with China and Chinese entities. What happens at the state-to-state level—the level of analysis in this compendium—is increasingly the product of pressures and demands from constituents and stakeholders seeking protection or assistance from government policy makers. Some are more favorably disposed toward China, the Chinese government, Han Chinese, state-owned enterprises, and other relevant players than are others in each country. The same is true, mutatis mutandis, of attitudes within China, especially the frontier provinces that border on South and Central Asia.

Greater and growing dependence on China has fueled animosity and ambivalence as well as appreciation and admiration. As noted previously, suspicion and distrust are alive and well in the region and may actually be growing despite increasing interdependence. China's engagement with the region has unquestionably changed many things, but it has not yet caused old fears to die out or allayed all sources of disdain and distrust. The book on China's engagement with the region is still being written, and it is too soon to predict with confidence how it will evolve.

## Notes

1. See Robert D. Kaplan, *The Revenge of Geography* (New York: Random House, 2012).

2. For comparison of China's historical interactions with different regions, see John King Fairbank, ed., *The Chinese World Order: Traditional China's Foreign Relations* (Cambridge, MA: Harvard University Press, 1968).

3. See, for example, Gi-Wook Shin and Daniel Sneider, eds., *History Textbooks and the Wars in Asia: Divided Memories* (New York: Routledge, 2011).

4. See, for example, Peter Golden, *Central Asia in World History* (Oxford: Oxford University Press, 2011); and Christopher I. Beckwith, *Empires of the Silk Road* (Princeton, NJ: Princeton University Press, 2009).

5. See, for example, Peter Hopkirk, *The Great Game: The Struggle for Empire in Central Asia* (New York: Kodansha, 1992).

6. See, for example, Thomas Stephan Eder, *China-Russia Relations in Central Asia* (Wiesbaden, Germany: Springer, 2014).

7. See, for example, Ashok Kapur, *India and the South Asian Strategic Triangle* (New York: Routledge, 2011).

8. See, for example, Dennis Kux, *The United States and Pakistan, 1947–2000: Disenchanted Allies* (Baltimore: Johns Hopkins University Press, 2001).

9. See, for example, Panagiotis Dimitrakis, *The Secret War in Afghanistan* (New York: Palgrave MacMillan, 2013).

10. See, for example, John W. Garver, *The China-India-US Triangle: Strategic Relations in the Post–Cold War Era* (Seattle, WA: National Bureau of Asian Research, 2002).

11. Chien-peng Chung, "The Shanghai Cooperation Organization: China's Changing Influence in Central Asia," *China Quarterly* 180 (2004): 989–1009.

12. See, for example, Russell Ong, *China's Security Interests in the Post–Cold War Era* (New York: Routledge, 2002), especially chap. 2.

# Index

*Page numbers in italics indicate material in figures or tables.*

Acheson, Dean, 242

Afghanistan, generally: Central Asia gaining strategic importance, 174; ETIM separatists in, 134; Mujahadeen, 129, 159; old-age dependency ratio, *300*; planned ISAF withdrawal, 100, 256; Putin on US lingering in, 256; relationship with India, 194, *195*; relationship with Pakistan, 37, 47, 125, 129, 134; Russia and Baluchistan, 143n70; and SCO/"Shanghai Five," 44, 173–174, 176; Soviet invasion of, 37, 38, 129; US aid to resistance, 37–38

Afghanistan and China, relationship between: Brezhnev doctrine, 129; FDI from China, 286, *287*; fears of terrorism spillover, 154; perceptions about threat and development, *8, 9, 15*; possible pipeline with China, 198; providing reconstruction funding, 45; and India and Pakistan, 192–193; and United States and Pakistan, 311; support for Afghan resistance, 37–38, 129, 159; tourism, *289*; trade, 45, *155*, 155–156, 194, *195*, 276–278, *277, 278, 280*, 281–283, *282*; Wakhan corridor, 159, 163

Africa and China, 7, *8*, 135, 191, 197. *See also* BRICS nations

Agni V (India), 57

Akayev, Askar, 220–221

Aksai Chin, 142n45

alliance formation theories, 138n1

anarchy, 117, 124, 138n2, 141n41

Anderson, Benedict, 151

Anderson, Perry, 243

APTA (Asia Pacific Trade Agreement), 193–194, 196, 209

Arbatov, Aleksei, 255–256

arms racing, 62, 124. *See also* nuclear arms racing

Arunachal Pradesh, 77, 97, 99, 103, 142n45

ASEAN (Association of Southeast Asia Nations): ASEAN-5 group, 283; China FTA with, 181, 188n36, 283, 290; Indian support for, 78, 102; intra-industry trade, 199; Myanmar's membership in, 159; preferential tariffs on Chinese imports, *291*; proposed Code of Conduct, 78; Regional Forum meetings, 102; trade with China, *282, 291*; United States support for, 43

Asian Collective Security Plan (1969), 127

"Asia Rebalance" strategy/US pivot to Asia, 61–62, 78, 85, 104, 132, 157, 174
Auezov, Murat, 223, 226
Australia, 68n34, 104, 109, 292
Awami League, 127–128
Ayub Khan, Mohammad, 121–123, 126, 140n24
Aziz, Jahangir, 303n19

Baghdad Pact (1955), 118
balancing, 124, 315–316; China and India, 47, 99–100, 201, 204–209, 310; India's external and internal balancing, 57–58, 68n34; United States and China, 30, 34, 35, 39; United States and India, 79, 190, 201. *See also* "Asia Rebalance" strategy/ US pivot to Asia
Baluchistan province (Pakistan), 129, 134, 135–136, 143n70
Bandung meeting, 118–119, 124, 141n43
bandwagoning, 124
Bangladesh, generally: BCIM Economic Corridor, 81, 83, 85, 91n35, 157, 160; Bangladesh War (1971), 55; becoming more authoritarian, 199; gas and oil reserves, 161; old-age dependency ratio, *300*; relationship with India, 157, 194, *195*, 203; safety standards concerns, 211n19
Bangladesh and China, relationship between, 137; China assisting in power plants, 198; China blocking admission to UN, 201; China's outward FDI flows, *196*, 197, *288*; Chittagong deep sea port, 137, 191, 197; "friendship bridges," 198; military assistance, 99–100, *200*, 200–201; mutual defense statement, 202; perceptions about threat and development, *8–10*, *15*, 81, 192; possible pipeline, 198; river water from China, 161; supporting China SAARC membership, 108; tourism, *288*, *289*; trade, 155, 194–196, *195*, 276–278, *277*, *278*, *280*, 280–283, *282*; trade deficit, 203
Barnds, William J., 138n3
*bashlik* *loben* (wealthiest Chinese businessmen), 232
Bay of Bengal, 76, 137, 150, 159

Bayoumi, Tamim, 300
BCIM (Bangladesh-China-India-Myanmar) Economic Corridor, 81, 83, 85, 91n35, 157, 160
Behar, Alberto, 302–303n13
Belarus, 243
Berdymukhamedov, Gurbanguly, 178
Bhutan, generally, *300*; relationship with India, 194, 203
Bhutan and China, relationship between: lingering distrust and border disputes, 157, 160, 163; perceptions about threat and development, *8–10*, *15*, 193, 202–203; rail and road connections, 197; Tibetan refugees in Bhutan, 98–99; tourism, 158, 286, *288*, *289*; trade, 155, 158, 276–278, *277*, *278*, *280*, 281–283, *282*
Bhutto, Zulfikar Ali, 121, 128, 129
bin Laden, Osama, 131
Blake, Robert O., Jr., 183
Blank, Stephen, 162
Boao Forum, 136–137
Bogra, Mohammed Ali, 118–119
Brazil, 69, 82, 85, 105–107, 289
Brezhnev doctrine, 126–127, 129
BRICS nations, 69, 82, 85, 105–107, 289
Buddhists, 164–165, 205
Bush, George W., 104

Cambodia, 36–37, 197, 291
Carter, Jimmy, 33
CENTO, 31
Central Asia, generally, 9; color revolution (2005) in, 183; dissatisfaction with border resolution, 224–226; gaining importance because of oil, 173–174; goal of goodwill foreign policies, 182; historical borders of, 245; petty trade and shop tourism, 228–229; rationale for focus on, 4–6; resolving border disputes, 181–182, 218–221; role of cross-border minorities, 226–233; situated between two empires, 245–247; status and ability to govern, 252
Central Asia and China, relationship between, 21–22; aiding Xinjiang's economic development, 179–181, 261;

China driving economic growth,
313–314; China overtaking Russia as
main trading partner, 259; China vio-
lating demilitarization agreements, 234,
239n54; Chinese businessmen, 232–233;
diplomatic relations (1992), 172; energy,
177–179; geostrategic perspectives,
181–184; Han Chinese favored over
local laborers, 217; infrastructure investment, 259; long-term predictions on,
234–235; low marriage rates to Chinese,
233; minority groups living in China,
230–231; perceptions about threat and
development, *8–10*, 162, 306; pro- and
anti-Chinese factions, 217; security concerns, 175–177; trade, 172, 179–180; as
vassalization, 261, 271–272n78; Xinjiang
as strategic beachhead, 247
Central Asia and Russia, relationship between: China and Russia as strategic
partners in, 183–184; as counterweight
to China, 262; post-USSR situation,
216, 247, 250–262, 310; Russia claiming
zone of influence, 183, 243, 254–255;
Russian and Soviet annexations, 171–
172, 246; Russia's lack of purpose in,
255; views on US presence, 256
Chaadaev, Petr, 243
Chagan-Obo Valley, 220
Chen Bingde, 156
Chiang Kai-shek, 249, 266n29
China: alliances within developing world,
124; banks, 81, 206–207; becoming net
oil importer (1993), 173, 177; border
disputes, 56, 157, 160, 163, 263, 266n28;
"century of humiliation," 3, 248;
changing priorities (1992–2001), 38–42;
changing priorities (2001–present), 42–
46; China-centric analysis, 3, 151; Chinese labor in Chinese-funded projects,
212n27; Communist Party after Mao,
10–11; contribution to annual world
growth, 274; de-ideologization of, 153;
economic rebalancing from external to
internal demand, 299; excluded from
pan-Pacific naval exercises, 78; "Far
West" development programs, 221; FDI

flows from, *196*, 196–198, 278; "Five
Principles of Peaceful Co-existence,"
133; foreign direct investment in, 97;
GDP, 94, *275*, 301; generosity in border
disputes, 120, 139–140n19, 141n43; going abroad policy (1999), 42; grand
strategy objectives, 133; Great Leap
Forward, 33, 149, 152, 163; hydrocarbon
needs, 135–136; increasing oil imports
(2001), 174; on inevitability of war, 11,
30; infrastructure development in, 290;
Japanese invasion of, 151; largest exporter of electronics-communications,
textiles-clothing, 293; as manufacturing hub, 210–211n13; military budget
(2013), 94; as model of economic development, 198–200; modernization of, 5,
38; national security as highest priority,
5; no free-riding opportunities, 85; not
a traditional naval power, 31; not seeking regional hegemony, 262; old-age
dependency ratio, *300*; "one country,
many systems" federalism, 247; predictions regarding rise of, 59–60; promoting transnational transportation
network, 136; proposed "March West"
strategy, 174; purchasing power parity
of, 274, *276*; relying on hydroelectric
stations, 222; reorienting foreign policy,
34; and SCO, 44–45, 106–107; security
and development as twin pillars, 11–15;
Tibet, Taiwan, South China Sea as core
interests, 98; transition from empire to
nation-state, 242, 260; Turkmenistan-
Uzbekistan-Kazakhstan-China gas
pipeline, 178; uniquely Chinese security
path, 29–30; Wakhan corridor, 159, 163;
water-sharing mechanisms with neighbors, 160–161; in WTO, 69–70, 79,
276, 293. *See also* BRICS nations; Deng
Xiaoping; reform and opening policy;
SCO (Shanghai Cooperation Organization); "Shanghai Five"; Uighurs; *individual countries for relationship with China*
China-Eurasia Expo, 180
China threat theory, 76, 99, 101, 144–
145n90

Chittagong, 137, 160, 191, 197–198, 202

CIS (Commonwealth of Independent States), 219–221, 230, 232, 234

"civilizational" identity, Russia's, 243, 251–254

Clarke, Michael, 247, 271–272n78

"closure of the steppe," 246

coal, 75, 135, 196, 198, 202, 205

Cold War, end of, 9, 38–39, 46, 70, 312

"color revolutions," 183

constructivism, 116

"costly signaling," 117

cotton, 221, *279*, 292

CSTO (Collective Security Treaty Organization), 253, 255

Cultural Revolution (China), 33, 149, 152, 225

Dalai Lama, 31, 75, 98–99, 156, 163

Damanski/Zhenbao Island quasi-war, 218

Davis, Sara, 149

Deichmann, Uwe, 290

Deng Xiaoping: reform and opening policy, 11–12, 29–30, 148, 153, 227; responding to Carter administration, 33–34; response to overthrow of Khmer Rouge, 36–37; "southern tour" of, 97; war inevitable but not imminent, 11, 30

Depsang Plains incursion (2013), 99

Doha round, 69–70, 79

Dollar, David, 304n26

drugs: India as pharmaceuticals hub, 81, 97, 210–211n13, 293; transport and trafficking, 106, 155, 182–183, 257

Dunaway, Steven, 303n19

Dungans, 227–228, 232

East Asia: China and, 144–145n90, *285*, 289–290; East Asian Summit, 105–106, 115n52; expansion of trade within, 289–290; FDI from Japan in 1980s, 198; India and, 70, 76; Russia and, 253, 259; United States and, 43

East Turkestan separatists: and article V in China-Pakistan treaty, 134; China crossing borders to pursue, 183; laying claim to Xinjiang, 172; posited US double standard regarding, 183; proclaiming Islamic Republics (1933, 1944), 175, 249; recent attacks by, 177; "Shanghai Five" response to, 176; supported by Soviets (1944–1949), 249; using economic development to weaken, 180

economic growth and development of China, 14, 306, 313–314; changing value of Central Asia, 178, 216, 261; changing value of frontier regions, 150, 153; costs and consequences of interdependence, 318–319; demand for resources, 42; economic clout as always relative, 240; government legitimacy resting on, 10; as higher priority than security, 83–84; need for cross-border ties, 313–314; as opportunity for South Asia, 191–193; perceptions about threat and development, 6–10, *7–10*, 14, 21, 35–36; and power, 132; Russian response to, 253–254; security and stability through, 29–30, 56, 136–137, 261, 317–318; unrest threatening, 75

electronics-communications, 293, *296*

engineering, 160, 197, 210–211n13, 229, 231–233

ETIM (East Turkestan Islamic Movement), 134. *See also* East Turkestan separatists

Eurasian Union, 184, 251–256

European Union (EU), 7, 104, 108, 243–244, 253, 261

external balancing, 57–58, 68n34, 124

extremism, separatism, terrorism: Chinese Uighur training in Pakistan, 44; India's concerns about arms supplies to counter, 212n33; Islamic, 23, 42, 44; Naxalite, 74–75; as "three evil forces," 134, 176, 186n16; in XUAR, 44, 100, 134, 159, 172. *See also* East Turkestan separatists

"Far West" development programs, 221, 229

FDI (foreign direct investment), 291; from China, *196*, 196–197, 199, 208, 278, 286; to China, 97, 190; from India, 197, 199, 211n20; to India, 71, 97; from Japan, 198, *285*

fences, redrawing of, 250, 258, 263
Fernandes, George, 101
financial integration, *280–281*, 285–291, *287–289*
"Five Principles of Peaceful Co-existence," 85, 133–134
Forward Policy, 124, 142n45
free riding, 45, 85
free world, 30, 33–36, 38–39, 313
Friedberg, Aaron, 2
Fund for Peace, 54

G-20 organization, 69, 82, 105
Gandhi, Indira, 204
Gandhi, Rajiv, 204
Gansu province, 150, 167n5, 171
gas. *See* oil and gas
"geobody," 261
geopolitics, 6–8, *7, 8,* 258, 308–310
Gibbon, Edward, 240
Gill, Indermit, 290
global financial crisis, 71, 85, 107, 199, 291
globalization, 34, 95, 104, 199, 213n47
Gorbachev, Mikhail, 218
"Go West" initiatives, 154, 261
gravity model of trade, 281–286, *282, 285*
Great Britain, 154–155, 167n5, 242, 248
Great Game, 24, 167n5, 309, 311–312; Central Asia, 182, 251–252; China, 147, 149, 174; fluctuations of relative strength, 240; great power(s), 124; India, 70–75, 109; rise and fall of Rome, 240; Russia's "postimperium," 241, 242–245, 251–255, 258, 260, 265n8
Great Leap Forward, 33, 149, 152, 163
Gromyko, Andrei, 143n62
Guangxi province, 150, 155, 165
Guizhou province, 150, 165, 167n2
Gujarat state, 71, 74, 80–81
Gwadar, 45–46, 91, 134–137, 191, 197

Haider, Ziad, 135–136
Hambantota, 46, 137, 191, 197–198, 207, 214–215n61
Han Chinese: in Central Asia, 231–232, 242; cross-border suspicions toward, 162; friction with ethnic minorities within China, 164; Han dynasty, 154; labor practices favoring, 147–148, 217; migration flows of, 230–232; in Myanmar, 164; skilled migrants, 232; trading cross-border in Central Asia, 228; treatment of frontiers by, 309; Uighur traders displaced by, 227–228; in Xinjiang, 221, 242, 249
"handshake across the Himalayas," 136
Hanwu, 171
Harrell, Steven, 149
Harrison, Selig, 100
hedging strategies, 13, 75–76, 78, 315–316
Herman, John, 151–152
Herz, John, 141n41
Hill, Fiona, 265n14
Himalayas, 29, 31, 103, 124, 126, 136, 161
"Hindi-Chini bhai bhai," 124
historical memory, 3
Hoffman, Aarron F., 117
Hong Kong, 158, 197, 208, 247, 285
Hormuz, 135, 137
Hu Jintao, 83, 104, 133, 178
Hunza border negotiations, 139–140n19
hydrocarbons: access to, 135, 259; coal, 75, 135, 196, 198, 202, 205; consumption of, 101, 310; natural gas, 162, 178–179, 196. *See also* oil and gas

Ikenberry, G. John, 2, 144–145n90
IL-CEPA (India–Sri Lanka Comprehensive Economic Partnership Agreement), 214n57
Ili Kazakh autonomous prefecture, 231
Ili River/Valley, 221–223, 226, 249
*Imagined Communities* (Anderson), 151
IMEMO (Institute of World Economy and International Relations), 255
IMF (International Monetary Fund), 69, 79, 106, 214n58
"imperial exit," 270–271n72
"imperialist powers," 11–12
India, generally: access to Indian Ocean/Asia-Pacific, 61, 70–71, 75–76; accused of protectionism, 194; aircraft carriers, 56, 71–72, 77; Arunachal Pradesh, 77,

India, generally (*continued*)
97, 99, 103, 142n45; and Bangladesh,
157; becoming a nuclear power, 129;
building a "Blue Water Navy," 77;
constraints on rise of, 72–73; contributions to regional economy, 274; defense
modernization by, 56; Depsang Plains
incursion (2013), 99; economic reforms
and growth, 7, 40, 71, 75; effects of
globalization on, 95, 199; external balancing strategies, 57–58, 68n34; favorable geographic factors, 70–71; foreign
direct investment in, 97; GDP, 56,
94; government subsidies and deficit
spending, 73; great-power-status prospects, 70–75; imports from small South
Asian countries, 194–196, *195*; India-
Lanka Political Accord, 204; as information technology hub, 71; and Japan,
78, 79; labor and bankruptcy laws,
88n18; maintaining dominant-power
status, 191; military budget (2013), 94;
modernizing of military, 71; multiparty
system, 72–73; Mumbai attacks, 54, 55;
Naxalism, 74–75; no free-riding opportunities, 85; nonalignment, preference for, 32; old-age dependency ratio,
*300*; poor strategic thinking by, 53–54;
possible pipeline with China, 198; promoting free navigation in South China
Sea, 78; rebalancing from external to
internal demand, 299; religious fatal-
ism, 72; rigid labor laws, 74; as rising
power, 69, 70, 94, 108–109, 166; and
SCO/"Shanghai Five," 44, 107, 176;
social stability, 72; as source of outward
FDI, 197; and Soviet Union/Russia,
127, 312; and Sri Lanka, 202, 204, 205;
toy industry, 203; US-India-Japan-
Australia quadrilateral security, 104;
and Vietnam, 78, 101. *See also* BRICS
nations
India and China, relationship between, 17–
19; in 1950s, 85; Arunachal Pradesh as
"southern Tibet," 99; bilateral maritime
cooperation, 80; border "cartographic
imperialism," 124; border clashes, 56,
76, 78–79, 99, 102–103; border negotiations, 42, 84, 92n47, 93, 97, 102–103;
businesses operating in China, 81–82,
97; rising together, 80, 85–86, 93–95;
changing views of (2000s), 43; China as
counterbalance to India, 201, 204–209;
China controlling transborder water
flow, 75–76; China's ideational threat,
56; China's material threat, 55–56; and
China's UN membership, 105; China
supporting New Delhi Agreement,
128–129; China supporting Pakistan,
37, 42, 84, 101, 122–123, 126; China
supporting Simla Agreement, 128; Chinese companies in India, 95; clashes in
South China Sea, 102; common-ground
rhetoric, 79; competing or complementing in world trade, 40, 292–293;
competition over Kazakhstan, 101–102;
concern about 2009 US-China statement, 104; concerns about encouraging
separatists, 81; cooperation and competition over energy, 101–102; cooperation on international issues, 69–70;
Dalai Lama issue, 31, 98; development
trumping security, 83; EAS membership, 105–106; economic concerns, 190;
encirclement, 56; encouraging BCIM
participation, 81, 83, 85; encouraging
participation in regional groupings,
82–83; engagement as best strategy, 93;
"equal distance" policy, 79; external balancing strategies, 56–57, 68n34; failed
Indian diplomacy, 202; FDIs between,
286, *287*; Forward Policy, 124, 142n45;
friction over Tibet and Tibetan refugees, 98–99, 111–112n17, 112n18, 122–123;
Gwadar project, 45–46, 100, 134–137,
191, 197; "handshake across the Himalayas" speech, 136; hedging strategies,
75–76, 78; helping build "intelligent"
cities, 82; India-China-US strategic
triangle, 17, 60; during Indo-Pakistan
war (1971), 128; interaction in multilateral institutions, 105–108; internal
balancing strategies, 56, 68n34; investment imbalance, 97–98; joint energy

projects, 101–102; Kashmir issue, 84, 121, 125–126; Kerala as model society, 81; "letter T" issues, 75; limited interactions historically, 31; national security concerns, 96; need to stabilize bilateral relations, 78–79; nuclear issues, 43, 57, 65n19, 76; post–Cold War relations, 38, 40–41; predictions on China's rise, 59–60; rise of India as positive, 69–70; seeing China as number-one challenge, 54–56; shared-water issues, 89n26; Singh assurances to China, 104; Sino-Indian Maritime Security Dialogue, 84; Sino-Indian Strategic Cooperative Partnership, 84; Sino-Indian War (1962), 31, 99, 120, 124, 154; in South China Sea, 78, 101–102; stable relationship despite disagreements, 82–83; perceptions about threat and development, *8–10, 15*, 30, 54, 69–70, 93; tourism, *288, 289*; trade, 54, 59, 81–83, 95–98, 193–194, 276–283, *277–282*; in United Nations, 105; US most important partner for both, 104; working to avoid "anti-China" coalition, 42

India and Pakistan, relationship between: fears of failed or Talibanized state, 89n27; India's second-strike capability, 55; Indo-Pakistan War (1965), 121–125; Indo-Pakistan War (1971), 128–129; nuclear arms race, 40; Pakistan's threat to, 54–55; US support for Pakistan, 60; war over Kashmir (1965), 121–123

India and United States, relationship between: arms shipments (1962), 120–121, 140nn23–24; benefiting from US regional engagement, 57; defense and civil nuclear agreements, 103; friction points with United States, 32, 59; Bush visit to New Delhi, 104; improving relations, 7, 44, 104; India-China-US strategic triangle, 17; Indian Caucus in US Congress, 71; military aid cutoff, 32, 125; Pakistan issues, 32, 60, 120–121, 125; pressuring India to ostracize Iran, 59; pulling out of trilateral naval exercises, 79; spectrum of cooperation, 58–59; US as untrustworthy, 60–61, 140nn23–24; US cultural influence, 70; US global retreat concerns, 61–62; US-India Civil Nuclear Agreement (2006), 43, 71, 104, 131; US pressure regarding Iran, 59

Indian Ocean/Asia-Pacific region, 76–77; "China threat" camp in India, 101; Chinese presence in, 76–77, 109; India-China de-escalation in, 80, 82; Indian Ocean Rim Association, 150, 193; Indian presence in, 72, 76, 109, 191; India's influence/advantage in, 70–71, 77; Myanmar as China link to, 162; open access issue, 61; Pakistan, 125–126; ports in, 136–137, 160, 191, 197, 214–215n61; Soviet invasion of Afghanistan as a threat to, 129, 143n70; "string of pearls" strategy in, 207; US credibility gap in, 60–61

India–United States–China strategic triangle, 53–62, 104

Indo-Pakistan Wars, 121–125, 128–129

Indo-Soviet Treaty of Friendship and Peace (1971), 127

"Inner Asian Frontier," 245

Inner Mongolian Autonomous Region, 245

INS *Airawat*, 102

interdependence and integration, 316–319

Iran: and BRICS forum, 106; China's nuclear assistance to, 40–41; and ISAF withdrawal, 100; possible pipeline with China, 198; Russia and Baluchistan, 143n70; sanctions against, 115n47; and SCO/"Shanghai Five," 44, 176; trade with Central Asia, 229; US pressure on India to ostracize, 59

IR (international relations) theory: China's views on, 261–262; focus on major powers, 3; Russia's goals, 251–252, 255, 258–259; on Sino-Pakistan ties, 117; three-worlds theory, 35; treating China as generic rising power, 2; trust in, 117–118

Irtysh River, 221–226

ISAF (International Security Assistance Force), 45, 100, 134, 159

Islamist militants: and China, 15, 44, 175, 239n54; East Turkestan Islamic Movement, 134, 175; and India, 57, 74; and Pakistan, 23, 55, 63n5; and Russia, 256. *See also* East Turkestan separatists

isolation, 316; China's, 30, 120, 127, 159, 308–309; Myanmar's, 159; Russia's, 244, 265n14

Jammu region, 54

Jana Andolan-II (People's Movement II), 202

Japan: as an "Asian tiger," 29; and Australia, 68n34; and China, 35, 56, 79, 151–152, 175, 178; competing for Russian oil, 178; economic growth model, 29, 33; FDI to Asia, 198, 285; and India, 68n34, 78–79, 98, 104–105, 109; and Philippines, 68n34; as SAARC observer, 108; US-India-Japan-Australia quadrilateral security, 104; and Vietnam, 68n34

Jervis, Robert, 141n41

Jiang Zemin, 188n37, 218, 220

Ji Pengfei, 128

Johnson, Lyndon, 122

Jones, Bruce, 2

Kairylmans, 231

Kapchagay reservoir, 222–223

Kaplan, Robert, 308

Kara Irtysh-Karamay Canal, 222–223, 225

Karakoram Highway, 135

Karzi, Hamid, 43

Kashgar, 136, 175, 229, 262

Kashi special economic zone, 180

Kashmir region: Chinese investment in, 100; Chinese positions on, 84, 125–126; Operation Gibraltar (1965), 121; separatist movement in, 74; spin-off terrorism from, 44, 54–55; US positions on, 121

Kazakhstan, generally: canceling cross-border travel without visas, 230; China-India competition over, 101–102; cross-border river management with China, 221–224; Dungans in, 227–228,

232; legal and illegal migration, 230; migrants from China, 231–232; protectionist laws on cross-border trading, 227; Russian construction companies in, 232; and SCO/"Shanghai Five," 44. *See also* Central Asia, generally; SCO (Shanghai Cooperation Organization); "Shanghai Five"

Kazakhstan and China, relationship between: border issues, 219–220, 225, 263; China diverting water from rivers, 222–224; coercion to endorse "one China," 224; encouraging shop tourism, 229; ethnic Kazakhs in China, 231; gas exports to China, 178–179; perceptions about threat and development, *8–10*, *15*; supplying gas to China, 173–174, 178–179; water use, 221–224, 234

Kennedy, John F., 121–122, 140nn23–24

Kennedy, Paul, 240–241

Kerala Pradesh, 81, 91n42

Kerr, David, 247

Khan, Abdul Qadeer, 130, 143n74

Khmer Rouge, 36–37

Khrushchev, Nikita, 218, 249

Khulna project, 202

Khurshid, Salman, 80

Kissinger, Henry, 127, 143n62

Kokang Myanmar National Democratic Alliance Army, 164

Komer, Robert, 122, 125

Kongka Pass, 139–140n19

Kotkin, Stephen, 244, 252, 260

Kulma-Kalasu pass, 230

Kunming region, 81, 168n23, 213n45, 159, 165. *See also* Yunnan province

Kydd, Andrew H., 117

Kyrgyzstan, generally, 174; canceling visa-free cross-border travel, 230; Dungans in, 227–228, 232; interethnic riots (2010), 255; migration into and out of, 217, 230–232; and SCO/"Shanghai Five," 44, 173, 176; perceptions about threat and development, *8–10*, *15*; Tulip Revolution, 221; US base access in, 43, 174. *See also* Central Asia, generally

Kyrgyzstan and China, relationship between: border issues, 172–173, 218–221, 225, 234, 263; coercion to endorse "one China," 224; frictions with Chinese immigrants/traders, 217, 229–232, 262; visa-free travel/overstaying visas, 229–230; water use, 234; Xinjiang border, 180–181

labor: Central Asian migrants in Russia, 251, 257–258; China and India/South Asia compared, 292–293, 300; Chinese labor in Chinese-funded projects, 198, 207, 212n27, 217, 232; Chinese outsourcing for lower costs of, 196; Japan seeking low-cost labor, 285; labor laws in India, 72, 74, 75
Ladakh, 97, 103, 139–140n19
Lake Balkhash, 219–220, 222–223, 237n20, 249
Lake Zaysan, 222–223
Latin America, 7, 8
Lattimore, Owen, 245, 272n82
Lavrov, Sergei, 251
"league of democracies," 43
Lewis Turning Point, 300
Lhasa, 98, 156, 160, 198. *See also* Tibet
liberal internationalism, 2, 39
Libya, 40, 106
Lieven, Dominic, 260
Li Keqiang: attending China-Eurasia Expo (2011), 180; as "fifth-generation leader," 132; state visit to India (2013), 80, 84, 86, 93, 96, 136, 160
Li Mi, 163
linkages of regional economic powers, *280–281, 285–291, 287–289*
Li Peng, 133
Liu Shaoqi, 126, 142n54
Li Zhaoxing, 188n37
Lo, Bobo, 250, 265n14
*loben/ bashlik* (wealthiest Chinese businessmen), 232
Longju, 139–140n19
"Look East" policy, 78, 91n35, 101
Lousianin, Sergey, 189n41

LTTE (Liberation Tigers of Tamil Eelam), 100, 200–201, 204, 214n54

Maharashtra state, 71, 81
Mahendra (king), 213n37
Mahsum, Hasan, 134
Mair, Victor, 149
"Malacca Dilemma," 137
Malashenko, Aleksei V., 184, 256
Maldives: becoming more authoritarian, 199; and India, 109, 202; Marao port, 197; old-age dependency ratio, *300*; perceptions about threat and development, *8–10, 15*, 192; tourists to/from China, 286, *288, 289*; trade with China, 276–278, *277, 278, 280. See also* South Asia, generally
Mann, Michael, 240
Manners, Phil, 302–303n13
Mao Zedong: China losing ground under, 32–33; choosing between US and USSR, 13; clashes with Khrushchev, 218, 249–250; death of, 11; support for Pakistan under, 123; on "unequal treaties" with Russia/USSR, 218–219; and unique Chinese path, 29, 33; on war as both inevitable and imminent, 11, 30
"March West" proposal, 174
Maslov, Aleksei, 270n69
Mathai, Ranjan, 91n35
Matveeva, Anna, 268n51
McCain, John, 43
McMahon Line, 163
McNeill, William, 240, 270–271n72
Mearsheimer, John J., 2, 144–145n90
*mestorazvitie* (developmental space), 243
Middle East, 7, 118, 197
missiles, 77, 131
*mission civilisatrice*, Russia's, 244
Modi, Narendra, 80
Moldova, 243
Mongolia, 44, 120, 176, 245–246, 249, 266n29
"Move East" policy, 78
Mujahedeen, 129, 159
multilateralism, 105–108, 261–262
multipolarity, 41, 251, 258–259

Muni, S. D., 204

Musharraf, Pervez, 131

Myanmar, generally, 101, 159, 161, 163–164

Myanmar and China, relationship between, 84; BCIM Economic Corridor, 81; China's influence waning, 165; Chinese-built infrastructure, 159; growing bilateral trade, *155*, 155–157; Kuomintang retreat to Burma, 163; Myanmar as China's link to Indian Ocean, 162; Myanmar as energy supplier, 162; perceptions about threat and development, *8–10, 15*; possible pipeline, 198; public criticism of China, 157; rail and road connections, 197; resolving border issues, 120; shared isolation, 158–159

Naqvi, Syed Zamin, 130

Nasheed, Mohamed, 202

natural gas, 162, 178–179, 196. *See also* hydrocarbons

Nawaz Sharif, Mian, 136–137

Nazarbayev, Nursultan, 185n7, 219

Nehru, Jawaharlal, 105, 124, 140n23

Nelson, Benjamin, 302–303n13

Nepal, generally: old-age dependency ratio, *300*; relations with Tibet, 98–99, 151, 164; trade with India, 194, *195*

Nepal and China, relationship between, 84; border projects, 159; boundary agreement (1960), 163; China's SAARC membership, 108; direct air link, 156; land port on border, 137; military assistance, 99–100, *200*, 200–201; mutual defense statement, 201–202; rail and road connections, 197; perceptions about threat and development, *8–10, 15*, 192; tourism, 286, *288, 289*; trade, *155*, 155–156, 194–196, *195, 196*, 276–283, *277, 278, 280, 282*

"new Eastern Europe," 243

Nixon, Richard, 33, 127

"Nonalignment 2.0" (India), 77

North America, 7, 8, 284–285, 306

Northeast Asia, 7, 306, 308–309

North Korea, 40, 78, 106, 118

northwestern borders and frontier, 164, 175, 185n4, 216, 225, 249, 309–310. *See also* XUAR (Xinjiang Uighur Autonomous Region)

NTPC (National Thermal Power Corporation), 202

nuclear arms racing: in China, 11, 33, 40–41, 65n19, 76, 103, 126–129; Chinese aid to Iran, 41; Chinese aid to Pakistan, 19, 40–41, 100–101, 129–131, 135, 143n74; in India, 40, 43, 53–57, 59–60, 62, 71–72, 103–104; in Iran, 115n47; in Pakistan, 19, 54–55, 60, 63n5, 104, 126, 129–130, 317; Pakistan aid to North Korea, Iran, Libya, 40; in Soviet Union, 127; in United States, 43, 60, 62, 71; US aid to Pakistan, 131; US civil nuclear aid to India, 43, 71, 103–104, 131

Nye, Joseph, 2

Obama, Barack, 78, 85, 103

Ob River, 222

Ohnsorge, Franziska, 300

oil and gas: in Cauvery Basin sea, 198; China-Kazakhstan pipeline, 178; China's oil strategy, 187n22; Chinese companies in Bangladesh, Myanmar, Sri Lanka, 161–162, 178–179, 196; Chinese energy independence, 217; crude oil, 135–136; diesel oil and cooking fuel, 73; Gazprom, 259; Hambantota oil refinery, 207; imports/exports by China, 35, 136, 173–174, 177–179; Indian companies in Vietnam, 101–102; Junggar Basin oil fields, 222; natural gas, 162; pipelines bypassing Russia, 259; prices before and after September 11 attacks, 177–178; proposed Angarsk-Daqing pipeline, 178; Turkmenistan-Uzbekistan-Kazakhstan-China pipeline, 178

Okunev, Igor, 252

"One Belt, One Road" initiative, 147

"one China" policy, 201, 204, 224

Operation Gibraltar, 121

opium trade, 155

Opium Wars, 248
Oralmans, 231
Otsuki, Tsunehiro, 302–303n13
Outer Mongolia (Republic of Mongolia), 120, 245, 249, 266n29

Paine, S. C. M., 248
Pakistan, generally: Awami League war of secession, 127–128; ballpoint pen industry, 203; Chinese port of Gwadar project, 45–46, 91, 134–137, 191, 197; contributions to regional economy, 274; designated a fragile state, 54; East Pakistan crisis, 127–128; founders called "running dogs" by Stalin, 123; F-6 Aircraft Rebuild Factory, 129; Heavy Rebuild Factory, 129; and India, 84, 121–123; joining Baghdad Pact (1955), 118; joining SEATO (1954), 118; nuclear weapons, 63n5; old-age dependency ratio, 300; PML-N party, 136; and SCO, 44, 176; threat perceptions of, 124–125
Pakistan and China, relationship between, 19; air travel agreement (1963), 120; "all-weather" relationship, 100, 116–117; balancing against India's rise, 99–100, 310; Bandung talks to allay mistrust, 118–119; border agreement (1963), 119–120; China aid for energy crisis, 136; China aiding nuclear program, 41, 129–131, 135, 143n74; China financing development, 135–136; and China SAARC membership, 108; China's endorsement of Pakistani position on Kashmir, 126; China's neutrality on East Pakistan, 128; China's public praise for Pakistan, 134; China's vetoing of UN membership for Bangladesh, 128; China terrorism concerns, 154, 313; China-US-Pakistan issues, 127, 310–311; Chinese aid to Afghanistan through, 129; Chinese endorsement of position on Kashmir, 126; Chinese military assistance, 99, 126, 129, 131–132; Chinese public praise, 134; Chinese support in 1965 war, 122, 125–126; cooperating with aid to

Afghan resistance, 37; cultural contacts, 119; economic corridor plans, 136–137; FDI from China, 286, 287; free trade agreement (2006), 193, 277; history of mutual trust, 30–31, 117–124; Hunza border agreement (1963), 119–120, 139–140n19; increasing dependency, 37, 47; Indo-Pakistan war (1971), 128; ISAF troop withdrawal, 100; Kashmir issue, 84, 121, 125–126; mutual defense statement, 202; neutrality on East Pakistan, 128; New Delhi Agreement, 128–129; Operation Gibraltar (1965), 121; Pakistan aiding US-China rapprochement, 127; Pakistan approving of China's rise, 132–133; Pakistan's early recognition of PRC, 118; Pakistan ties to Uighurs, 44, 100; Pakistan tilting away from China, 42; perceptions about threat and development, 8–10, 15; port of Gwadar project, 45–46, 100; possible pipeline, 198; post–Cold War strategic value of, 38, 40–42, 306; predictions about, 50n48; promoting China in Muslim world, 142n49; rail and road connections, 197; strategic sympathy, 123–124; Simla Agreement, 128; terrorist attacks against Chinese in Pakistan, 134–135; tourism, 288, 289; trade, 276–278, 277, 278, 280, 281–283, 282; Treaty of Friendship, Cooperation, and Good-Neighborly Relations (2005), 133; trying to prevent failed state, 45
Pakistan and United States, relationship between: anti-American demonstrations, attacks, 121; fear of India driving alliance, 124; LBJ cancelling Ayub's proposed visit, 122–123; military aid cutoff during 1965 war, 125; military aid to India issue, 120–121; mutual security agreement (1954), 118; US Afghanistan drawdown, 47; US military assistance, 125, 131
Pamir, 219, 221
Panchshila, 124
Panetta, Leon, 79
Persian Gulf, 135, 137, 143n70, 191

pharmaceuticals. *See* drugs
Philippines, 56, 68n34, *291*. *See also*
    ASEAN (Association of Southeast Asia
    Nations)
"The Philosophy of Russian Foreign
    Policy" (Lavrov), 251
pipelines, 154, 161–164, 173, 178–179, 185n7,
    198, 259
pivot to Asia, 61–62, 78, 85, 104, 132, 157,
    174
Pol Pot, 36
ports, 45–46, 100, 134–137, 160, 191, 197,
    214–215n61
possibility spaces, 12, 24, 308
"postimperium" of Russia, 241, 242–245,
    253, 258, 260, 265n8
Prague Spring, 126
"prisoners of geography," 308
Purdue, Peter, 246
Putin, Vladimir, 252–254, 256

Qianlong (emperor), 151
Qing dynasty, 151, 175, 218, 246, 248–249,
    260, 266n28
Qinghai province, 150

railways, 100, 136–137, 154, 159–160, 162,
    197–198, 290
Rakhmon, Emomali, 225
Rana Plaza, 211n19
Reagan, Ronald, 38
realist internationalism, 2, 138n1
Reed, Bradley, 151
reform and opening policy, 4, 11; agri-
    cultural productivity (1980s), 199;
    encouraging small private companies,
    227, 301; finance and banking reforms,
    199; highest priority to United States,
    35; increased diplomatic interchange,
    38–39; regional interest in example of,
    191; reorientation toward southwest
    frontier, 148, 152–154; security through
    prosperity and modernization, 33; self-
    sufficient in natural resources initially,
    35; South Asia as a low priority during,
    35; supporting UN peacekeeping, 34;
    and three-worlds theory, 35

repatriation programs, 176, 226, 231
resources, natural, 35, 42, 45. *See also* hy-
    drocarbons; water
rising power, China as, 2–3, 153, 259, 192
rising power, India as, 69, 70, 94, 108–109,
    166
roads, 77, 100, 103, 135–137, 150, 158–159,
    *206*, 206–207, 290
Rosneft, 259, 270n69
Rubber-Rice Agreement (1952), 208,
    215n64
Russia, generally: altered geopolitical
    setting of, 243; attempts to procure
    warm-water harbors, 143n70; as BRICS
    member, 44, 105–107; "civilizational
    identity," 251–254; Eurasia goals as dis-
    tracting from European identity, 258;
    Eurasian Union vision, 251–252; goal of
    equality with China, 254; goal of mul-
    tipolarity, 251; goal to be link between
    Europe and Asia, 244, 253; importance
    of status, prestige, privilege, 252; and
    ISAF withdrawal, 100; as neither West
    nor East, 252, 265n14; and new Great
    Game with United States, 182; "post-
    imperium" of, 241, 242–245, 253, 258,
    260, 265n8; relative size of, compared
    to EU and China, 243–244; Romanovs
    extending empire to Central Asia, 246;
    "rump Russia," 243; "Russia First"
    strategy, 254, 257; and SCO/"Shanghai
    Five," 44, 173; Special Operations
    Command, 256–257; strategic inde-
    pendence of, 244–245; strategy toward
    Central Asia, 251; strategy toward East
    Asia, 253; as supplier of raw materials,
    260; and United States, 256, 311, 313;
    use of soft power, 253. *See also* BRICS
    nations; SCO (Shanghai Cooperation
    Organization); "Shanghai Five"; Soviet
    Union
Russia and Central Asia, relationship
    between, 22; economic risks of engage-
    ment, 257–258; impact of migration,
    257–258; public desire for disengage-
    ment, 254, 257; Soviet annexation,
    171–172

Russia and China, relationship between, 22; competition in Central Asia, 189n41, 248–249; differing perceptions of, 247–250; and Eurasian Union project, 184; Mao's remark to Khrushchev, 249–250; recent shift in balance of power, 241; Russia's *mission civilisatrice* toward Asia, 244

SAARC (South Asian Association for Regional Cooperation), 80, 107–108, 115n52, 150, 157–158, 192, 194, 200, 215n67
SAFTA (South Asia Free Trade Agreement), 194, 199–200
salinization, 223
SAPTA (SAARC Preferential Trade Arrangement), 194
Sardy-Cheldy district, 220
Sattar, Abdul, 120, 125
Sayed, Mushahid Hussain, 132–133
SCO (Shanghai Cooperation Organization), 311; China and Russian as partners in, 183, 253; China's motivation for supporting, 313; combatting "three evil forces," 176, 186n16; free economic zone talks, 181; India observer status in, 80, 106–107; joint military exercises, 176; members and observer states, 115n52, 176; "new regionalism," 261; Russia supporting Central Asian states in, 219. *See also* "Shanghai Five"
SEATO (Southeast Asia Treaty Organization), 31, 118–119
separatism. *See* extremism, separatism, terrorism
September 11 terrorist attacks, 173, 313
"Shanghai Five," 44–45, 46, 173, 176. *See also* SCO (Shanghai Cooperation Organization)
Sher Ali Khan, 127
Shi Huangdi, 167n2
"shop tourists," 228–229
shuttle trade, 226–227, 229
Sichuan province, 150–151, 155, 165, 167n2, 168n23
Silk Road, 154

Silk Road Economic Belt, 25, 175, 185, 254
Singapore, 95, 98, 105, 135, 285, 292. *See also* ASEAN (Association of Southeast Asia Nations)
Singh, Manmohan, 74, 83–84, 93, 104, 107
Single Economic Space, 253
Sinhalese, 205
Sino-Indian Maritime Security Dialogue, 84
Sino-Indian Strategic Cooperative Partnership, 84
Sino-Indian War (1962), 31, 99, 120
social constructivism, 116, 138n2
soft support, 203, 213n49
South Africa, 279–281. *See also* BRICS nations
South Asia, generally, 21–23, 273; contribution to annual world growth, 274; effect of geographical distance on trade, 283–285, *285*; exports of small South Asian countries, 194–196, *195*; high transport costs from poor infrastructure, 290; percentages of world/regional GDP, *275–276*, 276; purchasing power parity of, 274, *276*; rationale for focus on, 4–6; rebalancing from external to internal demand, 299; shares in world GDP, *275*; tariffs, *291*; and US campaign against Taliban, 313
South Asia and China, relationship between, 20; arms trade, *200*, 200–201; Bangkok Agreement, 193; as buffer against containment, encirclement, 46; capitalizing on China's prosperity, 191, 193; China as counterbalance against US and India, 190, 201; China as model of economic development, 198–200; China driving economic growth, 313–314; China offering transborder connectivity, 136; China's goals in, 29–30, 37–38, 45; competing or complementing in world trade, 291–292; concern about authoritarian world power, 190; differing views on China's rise, 190; FDI flows, *196*, 196–197, *287*; financial integration, 286–291, *287–289*; Himalayan barrier, 308–309; imports from small South Asian countries, 194–196,

South Asia and China, relationship
between (*continued*)
    *195*; India as factor in, 310; mutual
    defense statements, 201–202; during
    reform and opening period (1979), 7,
    30, 35–37; perceptions about threat and
    development, *7–10*, 30, 162, 306; tour-
    ism, 286, *288, 289*; trade, 194–196, *195*,
    203, 276, *277, 280*
South Caucasus, 243
South China Sea, 78, 98, 101–102
Southeast Asia, 7, 31, 118–119
South Korea (ROK), 33, 98, 108, 118, 283,
    285, 292
southwestern frontier: China's "charm
    offensives" to, 158; concerns about
    terrorism spillover across border, 154;
    cross-border sociocultural linkages,
    147–148, 163–165; economic growth,
    153, *165*; energy transmission and pipe-
    lines, 161–162; infrastructure building
    in, 150, 158–160; neglect alternating
    with intervention, 149–152; physical
    and cultural challenges of, 150; as "soft
    underbelly," 149–152; water-sharing
    mechanisms, 160–161
Soviet Union, generally: in Afghanistan,
    37–38, 129; backing "East Turkestan
    Republic," 175; Brezhnev doctrine, 129;
    collapse of (1991), 8–9, 38, 216; federal
    republics' right to secede, 246–247; Gro-
    myko on Pakistan, 143n62; and India,
    30, 127; Stalin on Pakistanis as "running
    dogs," 123; Vietnam alliance, 37
Soviet Union and China, relationship
    between: during Afghan invasion, 129;
    China's fear of preemptive attack, 127;
    China's fears of encirclement, 36–37;
    China's response to Afghan invasion,
    Brezhnev doctrine, 129; China's re-
    sponse to fall of Soviet Union, 216, 245;
    China's US balancing, 30, 34; end of
    Cold War (1989), 38, 39–40; militariza-
    tion of border, 247; perceptions about
    threat and development, 7–8, 36; Sino-
    Soviet cold war, 125–127, 247; visa-free
    border travel, 229–230

Sri Lanka, generally, 199, 203, *300*
Sri Lanka and China, relationship be-
    tween, 84, 137; China as balance to
    India, 204–209; Chinese investment
    and development, 46, 84, *196*, 198, *206*,
    207–209, *208, 287*; growing trade be-
    tween, 194; Hambantota deep-sea port,
    137, 191; limited technology transfer,
    212n27; Lotus Tower in Colombo, 207;
    military assistance and trade, 99–100,
    *200*, 200–201, 205; mutual defense
    statement, 202; Norachchalai Power
    Plant breakdowns, 212n27; Puttalam
    power plant, 205; share of imports, 194,
    *195*; perceptions about threat and devel-
    opment, *7–9, 15*, 192; tourism, *288, 289*;
    trade, 276–278, *277, 278, 280*
Sri Lanka and India, relationship between,
    202; delayed power plant project, 202,
    205; fishing disputes, 205; free trade
    agreement, 194; IL-CEPA, 214n57; In-
    dia as FDI source, 197; Indian share of
    imports declining, 194, *195*, 208–209
Stalin, Joseph, 13, 123, 249–250, 266n29
Strait of Hormuz, 137
strategic sympathy, 124
"string of pearls" strategy, 137, 197, 207
Sudan, 101
Suhrawardy, Hussain Shaheed, 119
"supply chain" development, 290–293
Suu Kyi, Aung San, 157
Swanstrom, Niklas, 262
Syria, 106
Syroezhkin, Konstantin, 225–226

Taiwan, 33, 95, 98, 103, 247, 285. *See also*
    "one China" policy
Tajikistan, generally: and ISAF withdrawal,
    100; and SCO, 44
Tajikistan and China, relationship between:
    border issues, 219, 221, 225, 229–230,
    263; coercion to endorse "one China,"
    224; legal and illegal migration, 230,
    233; perceptions about threat and devel-
    opment, *8–10, 15*; Tajiks in China, 231
Taliban, 43, 89n27, 134, 158, 182, 256, 313
Tamil Elam insurgency, 100, 204

Tang Meng, 152
Tan Tai Yong, 204
tariffs, 157, 194, 202, 290, *291*, *292*
Tashkorgan autonomous district, 231
terrorism. *See* extremism, separatism, terrorism
textiles, 197, 292–294, *297*
"three evil forces," 173, 176, 186n16
three-worlds theory, 35
Thucydides, 124
Tiananmen, 219
Tibet, 167n5; China 1965 intervention threat, 122–123; as China-India issue, 75, 84, 98–99, 111–112n17, 112n18, 154; as core interest, 98; government-in-exile in India, 75, 98; Great Britain in, 163, 167n5; growth and income in, 165; India response to Chinese military in, 90n32, 98, 102–103; Kuomintang refuge in, 163; in late nineteenth century, 151; Lhasa-Kathmandu air link, 156; national security concerns, 149; proposed water diversion, 89n26; railways in, 154, 160, 198; relations with Nepal, 151, 161, 164; seen as needing civilizing, 149; self-immolation of Buddhist monks, 98, 165; and southwest frontier boundaries, 167n2; strategic importance of, to China, 149, 151; travel to and through Nepal, 156, 159–160; treatment of minorities in, 98–99, 150, 204; as "water tank of the world," 160–161. *See also* Dalai Lama
tourism to and from China, 158, 228–229, 286, *288–289*
transnational transportation network, 136–137, 154, 158–160, 197, *206*, 206–207
treaties, 100, 127–128, 176, 249
Trincomalee region, 205, 207
*Trust and Mistrust in International Relations* (Kydd), 117
Tulip Revolution, 221
Turkestan, 246. *See also* ETIM (East Turkestan Islamic Movement)
Turkmenistan: gas exports to China, 178–179; restricting Chinese immigration, 230; shuttle trade with China, 229; perceptions about threat and development, *8–10*, *15*. *See also* Central Asia, generally

Uighurs, 44, 100, 159, 172, 227–228, 231
Ukraine, 243
United Nations: antipiracy mission, 77; China and, 34, 69, 126, 201; India and, 87, 102, 104, 105, 115n52, 123, 191; India-Pakistan ceasefire agreement (1965), 123; India's desire for Security Council seat, 87, 105, 191; requirements for SCO, 107; SC resolution 1172 on nuclear programs, 104, 115n47; on Sri Lanka Tamil minority issue, 214n54
United States, generally: and Afghanistan, 37–38; and Central Asia, 174; increasing naval forces in Asia-Pacific, 61; as long-term Asian power, 61; possible global retrenchment by, 60–61; during recession, 71; as SAARC observer, 108; unipolar status after Cold War, 41; US-India-Japan-Australia quadrilateral security, 104. *See also* "Asia Rebalance" strategy/US pivot to Asia; India–United States–China strategic triangle
United States and China, relationship between, 310–311; aid to Afghan resistance, 37; Carter administration, 33; central under reform and opening, 103; China hedging possibilities, 13; China's concerns about US encirclement, 43; China's concerns about US post–Cold War attitudes, 38–39; China's concerns about US unipolar status, 41; China's initial support for US attacks on Taliban, 43; China's modernization, 38, 39; China's rise, 144–145n90; defense and civil nuclear agreements, 103; joint statement (2009), 104; LBJ on China as "outlaw" state, 122; Nixon's overtures, 33, 127; opening diplomatic relations, 29–30; partnering against Soviet Union, 30, 34, 129; and SCO/"Shanghai Five," 44; US presence in Central Asia, 182–183; and US support for ASEAN, 43
United States and India, relationship between, 68n34, 78–79; as deepening

United States and India, relationship between (*continued*)
  after economic reforms, 40; Bush visit to New Delhi, 104; Indian congressional caucus, 71; military aid cutoff during 1965 war, 32, 125; seen as meant to check China's rise, 44; shipping arms without notifying Pakistan, 120–121; as strategic partnership, 61–62, 79; US-India Civil Nuclear Agreement (2006), 43, 71, 104, 131
United States and Pakistan, relationship between: intermittent US military aid, 39–40, 125–126, 131; LBJ cancelling Ayub's proposed visit, 122; mutual security agreement (1954), 118; Pakistan's nuclear weapons program, 130; Pakistan's objections to US military aid to India, 121; sanctions after 1998 nuclear tests, 40; US aid to Pakistan, 45
Urumqi, 136, 159, 177, 180, 229
US-India-Japan-Australia security dialogue, 104
USSR. *See* Russia, generally; Soviet Union, generally
Uzbekistan: and SCO, 44, 176; shuttle trade with China, 229; supplying gas to China, 178–179; perceptions about threat and development, *8–10, 15*; US base access in, 43, 174; Uzbeks in China, 231. *See also* Central Asia, generally
Uzengi-Kuush, 220, 225

Vajpayee, A. B., 57, 96
"vertical disaggregation," 290
Vietnam: Chinese attack on, 37; and India, 68n34, 78, 79, 101–102; Nixon's attempt to end war with, 127; overthrowing Khmer Rouge, 36–37; OVL oil blocks, 102; Pakistan interceding for, with China, 123; tariffs on Chinese imports, *291*; territorial disputes with China, 56, 101–102
Virgil, 240
Virmani, Arvind, 292
visa-free travel, 227, 229–230, 258

von Hörnigk, Philipp, 241, 263
von Ranke, Leopold, 240

Wakhan corridor, 159, 163
Wangchujk, Lyonpo Khandu, 158
Wang Guangya, 158
water, 89n26, 160–161, 222–224
Wendt, Alexander, 138n2
Wen Jiabao, 83, 133–134, 180
"white man's burden," Russian, 244
Wilson, John, 302–303n13
World Bank, 40, 69, 79, 106
World Tourism Organization, 158
WTO (World Trade Organization), 69–70, 79, 98, 105, 276, 293

Xi Jinping, 25, 86, 103, 132, 147, 175
Xiyu (Western Regions), 171, 175
XUAR (Xinjiang Uighur Autonomous Region): accelerated development policy for, 180, 221–222; base for training Mujahadeen in, 129; China conquest and reconquest of, 246, 260–261; as "China in Central Asia" and vice versa, 245; cross-border ecological concerns, 226; cross-border resale of Chinese goods, 227; historically part of Central Asia, 245; Muslim Uprising (1862–1878), 249; "regional national autonomy" under PRC, 247; Russian troops in (1871–1881), 249; special economic zones within, 180; as strategic beachhead into Central Asia, 247; trade with Central Asia, 179–180; Urumqi, 136, 159, 177, 180; violent suppression of riots in, 142n49. *See also* East Turkestan separatists; northwestern borders and frontier; Uighurs

Yahya Kahn, 127
Yellow River (*Huanghe*), 160
Yunnan province: and Beijing, 150; China-South Asia Exposition in, 168n23; drug trafficking into, 155; growth and income in, 165; Kunming as gateway to India, 213n45; Kunming-Ruili ex-

pressway, 159; trade with Myanmar, 156–157, 165; Yunnan-Guizhou plateau, 151, 167n2

Zhang Chunxian, 177
Zhang Qian, 171

Zhenbao Island/Damanski quasi-war, 218
Zhou Enlai, 118–120, 126–127, 139n15, 141n43
Zhuge Liang, 152
Zia-ul-Haq, Muhammad, 130